Classics in Psychiatry

This is a volume in the Arno Press collection

Classics in Psychiatry

Advisory Editor

Eric T. Carlson

Editorial Board

Erwin H. Ackerknecht
Gerald N. Grob
Denis Leigh
George Mora
Jacques M. Quen

INSANITY

AND ITS TREATMENT

BY

G. FIELDING BLANDFORD

ARNO PRESS

A New York Times Company

New York • 1976

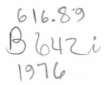

Editorial Supervision: EVE NELSON

———◆———

Reprint Edition 1976 by Arno Press Inc.

Reprinted from a copy in
  The University of Michigan Library

CLASSICS IN PSYCHIATRY
ISBN for complete set: 0-405-07410-7
See last pages of this volume for titles.

Manufactured in the United States of America

———◆———

Library of Congress Cataloging in Publication Data

Blandford, George Fielding, 1829-1911.
    Insanity and its treatment.

    (Classics in psychiatry)
    Reprint of the 1871 ed. published by H. C. Lea,
Philadelphia.
    1. Psychiatry--Early works to 1900. 2. Psychiatry--
Great Britain. 3. Mental health laws--Great Britain.
4. Mental health laws--United States. I. Title.
II. Series. [DNLM: WM B642i 1871a]
RC340.B57 1975   616.8'9   75-16684
ISBN 0-405-07416-6

INSANITY

AND ITS TREATMENT:

LECTURES

ON

THE TREATMENT, MEDICAL AND LEGAL, OF INSANE PATIENTS.

BY

G. FIELDING BLANDFORD, M.D. Oxon.,

FELLOW OF THE ROYAL COLLEGE OF PHYSICIANS IN LONDON;
LECTURER ON PSYCHOLOGICAL MEDICINE AT THE SCHOOL OF ST. GEORGE'S
HOSPITAL, LONDON.

WITH A SUMMARY

OF THE

LAWS IN FORCE IN THE UNITED STATES ON THE CONFINEMENT OF THE INSANE.

BY ISAAC RAY, M.D.

PHILADELPHIA:

HENRY C. LEA.

1871.

SHERMAN & CO., PRINTERS.

PREFACE.

THE following Lectures, in an abridged form, were delivered by me at the School of St. George's Hospital, and I now publish them, with the hope that they may serve to some extent as a handy book concerning Insanity, on which subject there exist in our language few works of the character of a text-book.

Written for students, they make no claim to be a complete treatise on Psychology; neither have all questions connected with Insanity been discussed in them—such as the management of asylums, the problem of disposing of the crowds of our chronic patients, or amending the present Lunacy law.

A difficulty which has ever attended the delivery of lectures on Insanity is not removed when they are printed for general use. It is the difficulty in speaking upon the subject with the precision and certainty demanded by those who are learning how to deal medically with a grave disorder. The lecturer on Medicine, when speaking of diseases of lung, heart, or kidney, can lay down the pathology in a way that to a psychologist is at present impossible. He can put his finger on the exact seat of the malady, can say what is going on amiss during life, and what will be discovered after death, and can speak with exactness of both the early and late symptoms. Far different is it when we have to teach the nature or treatment of that which we call insanity—to speak not of respiration, circulation, or digestion, but of mind, of feelings, and ideas, in an abnormal or distorted state.

Nevertheless, I am convinced that the only method by which

we shall attain an insight into the mysterious phenomena of unsound mind, is to keep ever before us the fact that disorder of the mind means disorder of the brain, and that the latter is an organ liable to disease and disturbance, like other organs of the body, to be investigated by the same methods, and subject to the same laws. In speaking of the pathology of insanity, I have endeavored to keep this in view.

For utterances too dogmatic, for iterations and recapitulations too numerous, and for the too frequent presence of the personal pronoun, the form and style of " lectures," which I have thought fit to preserve, must be my apology.

So, too, I have omitted references beyond a very few. To many authors, home and foreign, whose works I havé consulted, I am under obligations not easy to acknowledge. Especially I would mention the now numerous volumes of the " Journal of Mental Science," which constitute a mine of information on this special subject, having, I believe, no equal. And I am not a little indebted for advice, suggestions, and corrections to many friends, especially Drs. Broadbent, Dickinson, and Maudsley.

71 GROSVENOR STREET, LONDON, W.,
December, 1870.

CONTENTS.

INSANITY AND ITS TREATMENT.

LECTURE I.

Introductory—Impossibility of avoiding Insanity—Why the Study of Insanity is a Branch of Medicine—The Organ of Mind—The Nerve Centres and Cells—The Nerve Fibres—Their Distribution—The Blood Supply of the Brain—Nerve Function—Method of Study Two-fold.

GENTLEMEN,—If there be one branch of the great study of medicine which more than another deserves to be called an art and a mystery, it is the treatment and investigation of insanity. The treatment is an art, which, during the present century, has advanced in a degree not inferior to other arts, and in which by practice and example we may hope to attain skill, as in surgery or midwifery; but the disorder which we call insanity is a mystery not yet unravelled. Can we even define it?

> " To define true madness,
> What is't but to be nothing else than mad ?"

In truth, its inscrutable appearance without assignable cause in a man hitherto sane, and its no less inscrutable departure, are things which we must confess are not yet explicable by human knowledge. Nevertheless, it is a branch of our art which is constantly forcing itself upon our attention. There are diseases described in the lectures you here attend which throughout your lives may never come before you: you may never see a patient die of hydrophobia: you may be so blessed with a healthy locality that you may never have to treat Asiatic cholera or ague. And other ailments due to locality or to special occupations you may never witness. But fortunate indeed will you be, if you spend many years in practice without being called upon to treat or to pronounce an opinion upon, some case of unsoundness of mind. Your female patients after parturition will be attacked with insanity; their boys and girls as they come to the age of puberty will show symptoms of it; at the climacteric of life men and women will break down; and in old age insanity will merge into fatuity and dotage in the general decay of mind and body. From the cradle to the grave the mental no less than the bodily health of your patients must be your care. And not only will you have to treat them, you will have to send them away from home under legal restraint, to plead their irresponsibility in courts of law, if in their frenzy or folly they commit crime; and when they are dead, you will be called on to testify to their competency or incompetency to make the will they have left behind.

Impossibility of avoiding insanity.

Now, if your attention has been drawn to insanity chiefly by notices of the grave disputes that arise in courts of law both upon the subject in general and also upon the sanity or insanity of individuals, you may shrink from the prospect I have set forth, and may determine to have nothing to do with such cases. You may resolve, like others I have known, never to sign a certificate. You may possibly carry out your resolution in London, but in the country you can no more escape from this duty than from other branches of our profession, which here we may hand over to specialists; and an opinion you may have to give on the state of mind of any of your patients; therefore it behooves you to have some idea of what you may have to say on the subject, as well as of the treatment of the various kinds of insane patients. In my lectures I shall endeavor to direct your attention to both of these points, that you may be able to refer to them as notes for future guidance in your medical, and also your medico-legal capacity. About the mysterious psychological part of the question, I shall only say so much as will enable you to understand various doctrines and theories which have been put forth, and which may be propounded in opposition to your own by others, whether lawyers or doctors. You will be asked if you agree or disagree with the theory of Dr. A. concerning "moral insanity," or of Dr. B. as to "emotional insanity," or of Dr. C. as to "volitional insanity." You will be told that delusions are essential to constitute a man legally insane, that insane people are responsible if they know right from wrong. Some amount of information as to mind in general is therefore necessary: this I shall try to make as brief as possible, in which I may succeed; and as little obscure as I can, in which my success may be less.

We will suppose that you have for the first time walked through the wards and inspected the patients in a lunatic asylum, sufficiently populous to have given you the opportunity of seeing all or nearly all the phases of this malady. You have seen some whose appearance, acts and language showed at once that something was wrong with them, others whose manner betrayed nothing, but whose conversation immediately indicated that they were not like men in general: some, on the contrary, appeared rational both in conduct and conversation, while in a considerable number you noticed a negative, not a positive alienation, an absence of word and thought, of work or amusement, a mental blank. You have not, however, gained much insight into the one thing, insanity, which you came to look for. You have failed to recognize one disorder from which all are suffering; to see how it is that these, who one and all are secluded in this abode, differ from the rest of mankind on the other side of the wall. Why they are here, and how they are to be cured so as to re-enter the world, is what I wish to show.

But a great number never will be cured; they must be taken care of for the rest of their lives. The curability and incurability I shall point out, but into the details of the care and treatment of such incurable patients I shall not enter.

If you ask me in what particular the inmates of the asylum agree, I can only say that they are all persons of unsound mind. Some are congenital idiots; some are epileptic patients, whose minds, memory, and understanding have been destroyed by frequent fits; some have had paralytic strokes with a similar result; some are in the dotage of age; others are insane in the common meaning of the word, holding extraordinary opinions and doing outrageous acts, and incarcerated here because they cannot be taken care of in any other way, or because their chance of recovery is increased by the restraint and treatment they receive. They resemble one another only in this, that they are all of unsound mind, incapable of taking care of themselves or of managing their affairs. This you see is a mere legal or civil distinction, yet it is one we cannot overlook, for it is the link which binds them all together. On analyzing them, we find that in antecedents and history, in capacity, in peculiarities, in propensities, they are of infinite variety: no two are alike, yet all are confined here *nolentes volentes*, and are here upon the certificates of medical men. What then, you ask, is Why the meant by this legal term, unsoundness of mind? in study of in- what way does it become a branch of medical study sanity is a branch of and practice? by what application of the art and medicine. science of medicine is it to be removed?

The answer is, that unsoundness of mind is but another term for disorder of the human brain, or rather of that portion of nerve matter which has for its function that which we call mind and mental operation. For all that is contained within the cranium is not concerned with the operations of mind proper, but a portion only, so that the function of certain parts may be disordered, the mind remaining sound; and, conversely, the mind may be deranged and defective, while other nerve functions, as the senses, continue intact. The proper function of the mental portion of the brain is, moreover, not essential to existence, and patients may live in a state of unsound mind during the whole term of a natural life.

It is not within the province of my lectures to discuss the functions of the various parts of that which, as a whole, we call the brain. From your lecturer on physiology you will already have learned what is known about them, and will have heard that great doubt exists even now as to the duties which they discharge, and their relations one to another. I shall only mention such points with regard to them as are essential to my purpose; but it is to be remembered that there is within the cavity of the cranium a number of organs capable, more or less, of acting independently of each other, and more or less developed in different animals. These all agree, however, in certain particulars: all are compounded of nerve cells, having certain special properties, and connected with one another by means of nerve fibres, bundles of which conduct to other cell-groups or to the periphery. These groups of cells, which I shall call *nerve centres*, are supplied by bloodvessels, and on the supply depends mainly the proper performance of their special function. If this be inadequate or ill-regulated, or if the blood itself be impure, the function shows an equal disturbance. Here, then we have four things to consider, the nerve centres, the nerve fibres, the supply of blood, and the function or property of the centres. These can be studied to some extent by experiment, as well as observed in health and disease. In this manner much has been learned by various experimental physiologists which can be advantageously applied to the consideration of the physiology and pathology of the special centres of human mind, the two great hemispheres of the cerebrum.

The nerve centres are aggregates of nerve cells which are
The nerve centres and cells. imbedded in a substance or *stroma* called the "neuroglia," which in the brain appears to be a "trans-
parent, nucleated, homogeneous, non-fibrillated matrix, representing the fibrillated connective tissue of the
spinal cord."[1] Of this as yet little is known, but I believe
that it will be found to play an important part in the pathology, if not as an immediate agent, of mind.

These cells or vesicles consist of a very fine membrane,
containing granular matter of various colors. They differ
in shape, being round, pyriform, stellate, irregular, and also
in size, ranging in man from the $\frac{1}{12000}$th to the $\frac{1}{300}$th of an
inch in diameter. From cell to cell proceed the nerve fibres
connecting them with each other and with other parts. Mr.
Lockhart Clark has given us a description of the way in
which these cells are arranged in the human brain, which I
can do no less than describe verbatim. It was contributed
by him to the second edition of Dr. Maudsley's work on the
Physiology and Pathology of Mind. "In the human brain
most of the convolutions, when properly examined, may
be seen to consist of at least seven distinct and concen-
tric layers of nervous substance, which are alternately paler
and darker from the circumference to the centre. The lam-
inated structure is most strongly marked at the extremity of
the posterior lobe. In this situation all the nerve cells are
small but differ considerably in shape, and are much more
abundant in some layers than in others. In the superficial
layer, which is pale, they are round, oval, fusiform, and
angular, but not numerous. The second and darker layer is
densely crowded with cells of a similar kind, in company
with others that are pyriform and pyramidal, and lie with
their tapering ends either towards the surface or parallel
with it, in connection with fibres which run in corresponding

---

[1] Drs. Tuke and Rutherford on Morbid Appearances in the Brains of the Insane, "Edinburgh Medical Journal," Oct. 1869.

directions. The broader ends of the pyramidal cells give off two, three, four or more processes, which run partly towards the central white axis of the convolution, and in part horizontally along the plane of the layer, to be continuous, like those at the opposite ends of the cells, with nerve fibres running in different directions.

" The third layer is of a much paler color. It is crossed, however, at right angles by narrow and elongated groups of small cells and nuclei of the same general appearance as those of the preceding layer. These groups are separated from each other by bundles of fibres radiating towards the surface from the central white axis of the convolution, and together with them form a beautiful fan-like structure.

" The fourth layer also contains elongated groups of small cells and nuclei, radiating at right angles to its plane, but the groups are broader, more regular, and, together with the bundles of fibres between them, present a more distinctly fan-like arrangement.

" The fifth layer is again paler and somewhat white. It contains, however, cells and nuclei which have a general resemblance to those of the preceding layers, but they exhibit only a faintly radiating arrangement.

" The sixth and most internal layer is reddish gray. It not only abounds with cells like those already described, but contains others that are rather larger. It is only here and there that the cells are collected into elongated groups, which give the appearance of radiations. On its under side it gradually blends with the central white axis of the convolution, into which its cells are scattered for some distance.

" The seventh layer is this central white stem or axis of the convolution. On every side it gives off bundles of fibres, which diverge in all directions, and in a fan-like manner, towards the surface through the several gray layers. As they pass between the elongated and radiating groups of cells in the inner gray layers, some of them become continuous with the processes of the cells in the same section or plane, but others bend round and run horizontally, both in a transverse and longitudinal direction (in reference to the course of the entire convolution), and with various degrees of obliquity. While the bundles themselves are by this means reduced in size, their component fibres become finer in proportion as they traverse the layers towards the surface, in consequence, apparently, of branches which they give off to be connected with cells in their course. Those which reach the outer gray layer are reduced to the finest demensions, and form a close network, with which the nuclei and cells are in connection.

" Besides these fibres, which diverge from the central white axis of the convolution, another set, springing from the same source, converge, or rather curve inwards from opposite sides to form arches along some of the gray layers. These archiform fibres run in different planes—transversely, obliquely, and longitudinally—and appear to be partly continuous with those of the diverging set which bend round, as already stated, to follow a similar course. All these fibres establish an infinite number of communications in every direction between different parts of each convolution, between different convolutions, and between these and the central white substance.

" The other convolutions of the central hemispheres differ from those at the extremities of the posterior lobes, not only by the comparative faintness of their several layers, but also by the appearance of some of their cells. We have already seen that at the extremity of the posterior lobe the cells of *all* the layers are small, and of nearly uniform size, the inner layer only containing some that are a little larger. But on proceeding forward from this point, the convolutions are found to contain a number of cells of a much larger kind. A section, for instance, taken from a convolution at the vertex, contains a number of large, triangular, oval, and pyramidal cells, scattered at various intervals through the two inner bands of archiform fibres and the gray layer between them, in company with a multitude of smaller cells, which differ but little from those at the extremity of the posterior lobe. The pyramidal cells are very peculiar. Their bases are quadrangular, directed towards the central white substance, and each gives off four or more processes, which run partly towards the centre, to be continuous with fibres radiating from the central white axis, and partly parallel with the surface of the convolution, to be continuous with archiform fibres. The processes frequently subdivide into minute branches, which form part of the network between them. The opposite end of the cell tapers gradually into a straight process, which runs directly towards the surface of the convolution, and may be traced to a surprising distance, giving off minute branches in its course, and becoming lost, like the others, in the surrounding network. Many of these cells, as well as others of a triangular, oval, and pyriform shape, are as large as those in the anterior gray substance of the spinal cord.

" In other convolutions the vesicular structure is again somewhat modified. Thus, in the surface convolution of the great longitudinal fissure, on a level with the anterior extremity of the corpus callosum, and, therefore, corresponding to what is called the superior frontal convolution, all the three inner layers of gray substance are thronged with pyramidal, triangular, and oval cells of considerable size, and in much greater number than in the situation last mentioned. Between these, as usual, is a multitude of nuclei and smaller cells. The inner orbital convolution, situated on the outer side of the olfactory bulb, contains a vast multitude of pyriform, pyramidal, and triangular cells, arranged in very regular order, but none that are so large as many of those found in the convolutions of the vertex. Again in the *insula*, or island of Reil, which overlies the extra-ventricular portion of the corpus striatum, a great number of the cells are somewhat larger, and the general aspect of the tissue is rather different. A further variety is presented by the temporo-sphenoidal lobe, which covers the *insula*, and is continuous with it; for, while in the superficial and deep layers the cells are rather small, the middle layer is crowded with pyramidal and oval cells of considerable and rather uniform size. But not only in different convolutions does the structure assume to a greater or less extent a variety of modifications, but even different parts of the same convolution may vary with regard either to the arrangement or the relative size of their cells.

"Between the cells of the convolutions in man and those of the ape tribe I could not perceive any difference whatever; but they certainly differ in some respects from those of the larger mammalia—from those, for instance, of the ox, sheep, or cat."

The nerve fibres, or nerve tubes, as they are often called, The nerve which conduct to and from the nerve centres, also vary fibres. in size from the millionth to the $\frac{1}{1500}$th of an inch in diameter. They form the white or commissural substance of the nervous system, being gathered into fasciculi, comprising a large number of these fibres. Each fibre consists of a very delicate membrane, forming a tube, and containing a viscid, albuminous and fatty pulp. Inclosed in this tube is a minute fibre, or "axis cylinder," which is in truth the real nerve fibre, and which exists in places without its investing sheath. At the peripheral extremity it parts with the latter, and is divided and subdivided as it permeates and blends with the structure in which it is distributed, while at the other end it becomes continuous with the contents of the nerve cells, also parting with its sheath at this point. That the nerve fibre is protected from disturbance by the investing sheath and pulp there can be no doubt, and that the latter plays a part in the preservation of the healthy working of the whole system seems probable from the changes observable in it in certain diseases. You will not forget that a nerve fibre possesses a power of its own, even when severed from its connection with a nerve centre, and that this power, if exhausted by stimulation, may by rest be again recovered; and it apears to me likely that the nerve elements surrounding the fibre may contribute materially to the restoration of this power.

The white or commissural portion of the brain deserves attention no less than the gray matter or centres, because by it the latter are brought into relation one with another. You have probably heard elsewhere of the hemispheres of the brain, of their convolutions, and of their function, of the sensory ganglia and their function, and of the relations of the one to the other. You have heard of sensori-motor acts, and the independence of the sensory ganglia. You will see it stated that in the corpora striata and optic thalami end all the fibres coming from below, and that in consequence all external stimuli are transmitted indirectly through the sensory ganglia to the hemispheres, while in turn they are the starting-point of all motor impulses which come from the cerebrum. Flourens, Hertwig, Magendie, Longet, Schiff, and others, have removed the cerebral hemispheres in mammals, birds, and reptiles, and observed what could be done by creatures in this condition. A pigeon followed a lighted candle with a corresponding movement of the head, and sought out the light part of a darkened room. If a pistol was fired close to it, it raised its head, opened its eyes, stretched out its neck, and then relapsed into a state of sleep. But though such animals indicate that they possess the senses of seeing and hearing, they appear destitute of memory or judgment. They are not frightened at the cry of birds of prey. They cannot regulate their movements so as to avoid an obstacle, but unwittingly dash against it. They have not lost hearing or sight, but are deprived of ideation and intelligence. "The condition of such beings," says Dr. Carpenter,[1] "seems to resemble that of a man who is in a slumber sufficiently deep to lose all perception of objects, but who is conscious of sensations, as appears from the movements occasioned by light or by sounds, or from those which he executes to withdraw the body from an uneasy position." These experiments prove that the cerebral hemispheres are not necessary to the life of such creatures, nor to the existence of the senses; but interesting as they are, they teach us little of the anatomy or physiology of the brain of man. The functions of the various ganglia situated below the hemispheres of our own brain are not as yet made out with anything like certainty. But one important step will be gained when we accurately ascertain the commissural connections of the various ganglia below the hemispheres, and the various convolutions of the latter. Dr. Broadbent has communicated to the Royal Society an account of certain dissections made by him, which are of the greatest importance to those who are studying the functions of the various parts of the brain. Distribution of the fibres. He has found that the fibres ascending in the crus cerebri do not all pass to and terminate in the central ganglia, but that a portion passes by the latter, while others pass through them to the convolutions. In their passage through the ganglia, they are reinforced by numerous fibres, arising both in the corpus striatum and thalamus, but mainly in the latter. It would appear that many fibres of the crus end in the gray matter of the corpus striatum, but apparently not in the thalamus. Till this is definitely settled, no conclusions can be drawn as to the function of the thalamus and corpus striatum. It will also be necessary to determine whence come the fibres which do terminate in the corpus striatum. "In the distribution to the convolutions of the fibres which emerge from the cerebral mass, they are for the

---

[1] Human Physiology, 6th edition, p. 546.

most part intermingled, and pass to the same regions. Those of the crust and tegment (the two portions of the crus cerebri) are so mixed up as to be quite indistinguishable; in the fronto-parietal part of the hemisphere, those of the thalamus pass with and cannot be distinguished from those of the crus, while the fibres of the corpus striatum, though following an independent course, reach the same destination. Again, in the occipital lobe the fibres of the crus and ganglia, which here are not mingled together, run to the same convolutions, and in the temporo-sphenoidal lobe the thalamus and corpus striatum give fibres to the same parts. Anatomical structure does not, therefore, lead us to expect that there will be a distinct sensory and motor region of convolutions. It is very remarkable, again, that the fibres of the corpus callosum are distributed to the same parts of the surface gray matter as the fibres issuing from the centres. Assuming that the corpus callosum is not only the transverse commissure of the two hemispheres, but that the fibres in it connect correspond-ing parts (as can be demonstrated with regard to some parts of this commissure), this would imply that the points of the surface gray matter of the two hemispheres in which the central fibres ended were bilaterally associated.

" It has further been found, that throughout the hemisphere the distribution of the central and callosal fibres is to the margin of the respective lobes, *leaving extensive intermediate tracts of convolutions, which receive no fibres from either crus, central ganglia, or corpus callosum.* It is at once obvious that these superadded convolutions will be the convolutions most characteristic of the human brain, and will constitute the dif-ference between one brain and another. This is seen if we compare the brain of a monkey with that of man. The sen-sations transmitted upwards from the several sense centres must first impinge upon those parts of the surface gray mat-ter in which the fibres from the sensory tract or ganglia end; so again, wherever volitions may be originated, the downward

starting-point of the motor impulse must be in some convolutions connected by fibres with the motor ganglion or tract.
These convolutions, then, which receive central fibres, and
are bilaterally associated by the corpus callosum, will constitute perceptive centres, and centres for the emission of volitional or ideo-motor impulses. But the perception of sensations and the emission of motor impulses are psychical
operations of the simplest character, and are common to man
and the lower animals. The higher and more complex operations of combining and comparing perceptions, the formation and elaboration of ideas, are thus almost by way of ex-
clusion assigned to the superadded convolutions; and it can
scarcely be considered fanciful to see in the withdrawal of the
nerve cells engaged in these intellectual operations from immediate relation with the external world, and in the intricate
associations of different parts of the surface, conditions adapted
to the function attributed to them."[1]

I shall not wait to discuss the probable changes which take
place in the nerve tubes or nerve centres as they are stimulated into sensation, and as this results in motion. The most
abstruse questions of chemistry and physics are here involved,
questions which verge on the metaphysical, and, if discussed
at all, must be discussed at length. The cells of the nervous
system must be looked upon chemically as the most prone to
decomposition and recomposition, perhaps, of all the structures of our body. That these changes are set up in them
by the motion or change conducted thither by the nerve
fibres, and that decomposition results in other changes produced in the efferent fibres, and thus carried to other centres
of the muscular system, we may accept as a fact. But the
chemistry and the physics of the brain are not yet sufficiently
investigated for me to say anything about them. Much has
been written and said concerning the electrical condition of
nerve, but for this I must refer you to the writings of those

---

[1] Journal of Mental Science, April, 1870.

who have made it their study. Their opinions on the subject vary widely, and into an examination of them I cannot
enter here.

The next point we have to consider is the blood supply of
the brain; and this is of so great importance, that if we   The blood
could comprehend it beyond all manner of dispute,   supply of
the brain.
we should go far towards explaining most of the phenomena of brain function and disorder. One might, in truth,
write a volume in discussing the brain circulation, as has been
done ere now, and the most that I can do within the limits
of a lecture is to direct your attention to some of the most
striking facts connected with it.

The arterial system, whether in its trunks, branches, or
capillaries, is peculiar; not less so is the venous. The arteries supplying the entire encephalon are four in number,—
the two internal carotids and the two vertebrals coming from
the subclavian and uniting to form the single basilar. Now,
if you look at the arrangement of these arteries within the
cranium, you will see that the encephalon is not supplied
with blood, as the kidney, or the liver, or the spleen, by
means of a large artery entering the substance of the organ,
and subdividing into smaller ones; but, on the contrary, all
the larger vessels are arranged on the outside, and only their
fine prolongations enter it. And in the case of the cerebral
hemispheres, which are the parts with which we are chiefly
concerned, we find that the blood is conveyed to the gray
matter entirely from the outside, by means of very minute
vessels dipping into it from the branches ramifying in the pia
mater.

Most of these arteries have great facilities for rapid contraction and dilatation after they have once passed through
the bony canals by which they enter the cranium. The internal carotids pass through the cavernous sinus, and are protected from pressure by the blood there; and then, like the
vertebrals and basilar, they are surrounded by the subarach-

noid fluid at the base of the brain, and the vessels in the pia
mater have facilities for contraction and dilatation which
they could not have were they imbedded in the interior of
the organ.

I need not here describe the course of these arteries within
the cranium—how the two vertebral join to form the basilar,
and afterwards divide into the posterior cerebral; how these
are connected by means of the posterior-communicating with
the internal carotids, which are, themselves, connected by
the anterior-communicating, forming in this manner the
so-called circle of Willis. We are not to suppose that this
"circle" implies a circulation, or that under ordinary circumstances there is any admixture of the blood coming from these
various sources. The posterior-communicating arteries are
the merest twigs, and in the rapid and constant contraction
and dilatation of the cerebral vessels their function must ordinarily be *nil;* consequently we may practically affirm that
the whole posterior portion of the encephalon is supplied by
the vertebrals, viz., the posterior cerebral lobes, the back part
of the corpus callosum, the fornix, optic thalami, corpora
quadrigemina, pons, cerebellum, and medulla oblongata.

We find, then, the anterior brain supplied by the carotids,
viz., the anterior and middle lobes, the anterior and greater
portion of the corpus callosum, the corpora striata, the olfactory lobes, and the front part of the optic tract. That free
anastomosis does not exist between the vessels supplying
these parts and those of the vertebrals, and even between the
two carotid arteries, is proved by the results of many an operation upon the carotid. That compression of the carotids
in man produces stupor and collapse was known before the
time of Galen, and during this century it has been proposed
as a remedial measure. Tying the common carotid on one
side is generally followed by some amount of cerebral symptoms, and is occasionally the cause of paralysis and shrinking
of one hemisphere, showing that even the comparatively large

anterior-communicating artery is not sufficient in all cases to provide a due supply. You know, of course, that after deligation of an important vessel in other parts of the body, some time must elapse before the collateral circulation is established, and the patient is in danger till this happens. But there is greater danger to the brain than to structures less highly organized, and an interruption of brain function may occur when one or other of these arterial streams is checked, not stopped, by causes other than deligation.

Now the contraction and dilatation of arteries are under the control of what we call the vaso-motor system of nerves, that system which is now so greatly attracting the attention of physiologists, about which, however, there are so many doubts and difficulties. The trunks and branches within the cranium are largely supplied with vaso-motor nerves, which may be seen running along them so far as the pia-mater. In the gray cerebral substance, the smaller branches and capillaries are without nerves, and so it needs must be that the contraction and dilatation of these vessels must depend on that of others, and on causes external to the gray substance. It depends, in fact, upon the influence of the vaso-motor nerves, which influence is derived from the special nerve-centre whence they emanate. And tracing them back to this, we find that those which accompany the internal carotid and its branches are derived from the first great cervical ganglion of the sympathetic; those which belong to the vertebro-basilar system come from the second and third cervical ganglia: consequently the two systems of vessels are still further kept distinct by their nervous supply.

All these considerations assist us in our endeavors to form some ideas as to the functions of various parts of the encephalon. They confirm the probability of various vascular areas, as Dr. Hughlings Jackson suggests. They indicate how MM. Prevost and Cotard's experiments on animals produced their effects. These gentlemen injected extremely fine seeds into the carotids of animals, which, being carried into the brain substance, caused softening, showing that no anastomosis came to the rescue. They assist us, moreover, in understanding many of the phenomena of sleep, dreams, and somnambulism, and these it is incumbent on every student of insanity closely to watch and analyze.

Passing from the consideration of these various organs, the Nerve nerve centres, the connecting fibres, and the bloodvesfunction. sels which supply them with life, we have next to inquire into this life, into their uses and properties, into what is commonly called their function. We must ascertain if there be any functions common to all of them, or, where they differ, in what respect they differ, and what their relations are one to another. By such researches we shall be better able to understand how these functions may be disturbed and altered; in other words, what is the pathology of the nervous system.

If we go down to the lowest forms of life, we shall find that nerve force or function is in itself a specialization of something lower, which we must call vital force. We have no other name for it. We see animals leading lives and manifesting the phenomena of sensibility and motion, in whom we can discover no nervous system at all; and as we ascend the scale, at first the same organs appear to subserve many purposes, and only at last do we find special organs for special functions. Nay, it is even yet a question whether in man the sensory and motor nerves may not occasionally interchange functions, and motor nerves become sensory, and sensory, motor.[1]

The method by which we approach the study of nerve function is twofold. On the one hand, it may be Method of study two- contemplated as it is exhibited by all beings,—men, fold. children, lunatics, idiots, animals of every grade; on the other, we may examine ourselves. The former is called

---

[1] Carpenter's Physiology, 6th edition, p. 451.

the *objective*, the latter the *subjective* mode of inquiry. By the first is revealed to us the nature of the nerve functions of other men and animals, as derived from the operations thereof, from the movements, acts, and speech. By the other is to be studied our own feeling and our own consciousness, that knowledge of ourselves and what goes on within us, which to some has appeared the only true knowledge, and the only real subject of contemplation and study. Now, it is quite true that we can only judge of the feelings of others by inference; that which is really known to us is our own feeling, and nothing beyond; our own consciousness limits in a sense our *knowledge*. But it is clear that there is much beyond our consciousness which it is necessary to examine. There is the whole range of mental phenomena exhibited by others, whether normal or abnormal. This we must study objectively, as we see it exhibited. But we may also bring to our assistance that knowledge which we derive from the contemplation of our own feelings and existence, always keeping in mind, that although this helps us much in the examination of the minds and consciousness of others, such examination must ever be imperfect, and the wider the difference between ourselves and the individual we are studying, the less correctly shall we be able to analyze the feelings of the latter by the light of our own. Pre-eminently is this the case in the consideration of the insane mind. People cannot comprehend how an insane patient can do this, or say that, because they judge of his disordered *feelings* by their own. And if he does or says certain things as they would do or say them, they argue that his mind must be in all respects similar to their own.

By experiment and observation, by post-mortem examination and vivisection, we connect the movements and actions of other beings with the functions of the various organs of the nervous system, and we infer from such examinations that there are in ourselves also a brain and nerve organs, a fact of which consciousness reveals nothing. Examining experimentally the actions of other living creatures, we arrive at the conclusion that they consist of contractions of various muscles or groups of muscles brought about by nerves emanating from nerve centres, which centres are stimulated by impressions conveyed to them by other nerves coming from the periphery. Thus, it appears that every act is the result of a stimulation of a nerve centre, which in turn gives rise to a movement. The stimulus may act directly from without—as light, or sound, or touch; or it may be central and mental; it may be conscious, in which case some present feeling, either by itself or united to the experiences of the past, gives rise to conscious action; or it may be unconscious, as what we call automatic or reflex action: yet the law is the same, that from the conscious or unconscious stimulation of some nerve centre the act arises. The movement is all that we experimentally can observe and know; the feeling that accompanies the stimulation we can only conjecture; and although we can learn much from the information afforded us by other men, by comparison of our own feelings under similar circumstances, and by the evidences of pain or pleasure displayed by children and animals on the application of various stimuli, yet there comes a point when we can only surmise, and that doubtfully, concerning the presence or absence of feeling and consciousness in beings other than ourselves. Hence arise the different opinions of authors upon the presence of " mind " in certain animals. We can observe the progressive development of movements, and the increasing specialization of the organs, and the acts of the lower animals; but when we try to determine their feeling, or consciousness, or mind, we are driven to conjectures and arguments from analogy, without having any facts or foundations to rest our theories upon. One writer makes " mind" coextensive with nervous action, and sees " mind " in the movements of a headless frog; another sees in this

not "mind," but "consciousness;" another, "reflex action."
Now, it is plainly a mere affair of words to discuss the question whether such movements imply mind or consciousness.
And similarly with regard to animals low in the scale of
creation, one person says that those which have no cerebral
hemispheres have not mind, but mere sensation, their acts
being sensori-motor. Another attributes to them mind, seeing purpose and deliberation in their acts. On this point, I
would say that, doubtless, they have mind—a mind not
specialized, as in our own or that of higher beings, but one
suited to their life and surroundings, and endowed with a
capacity of feeling in accordance with the excitations of their
daily life. But to argue concerning all this from the analogy
of our own mind and consciousness, will only lead us further
and further from the truth, and blind us to that which we
can really see and determine objectively.

LECTURE II.

The Phenomena of Mind—The Growth of Mind—The Divisions of Mind—Ideas—Feelings or Emotions—Emotions Correspond to Ideas—Feelings vary according to the Condition of the Centres—Will—Conditions Necessary for the Right Operation of Mind—A Healthy Blood-flow—Food—A Normal Temperature—Light—Sleep.

In considering the objective or physiological aspect of mind, we speak of nerve centres and nerve fibres, of stimuli conveyed by the latter to the former, resulting in movements visible to the eye, but we must now consider such mental phenomena as feelings and ideas. In treatises on insanity, you will see, as I have already said, such expressions as "emotional" or "volitional" insanity. If you turn to works on the mind, you will see the latter divided into the intellect, the emotions, and the will; and therefore I am bound to speak of these subjects. But what I have to say will be as brief as possible, my object being to point out what questions are essential for you to examine previously to entering upon the study of insanity, and what, in fact, are the component parts of that which we call mind, and which may be at times disordered, if the conditions of its healthy working are not fulfilled.

The first remark that I shall make with regard to mind is, that it varies greatly at different periods of life; that we are not born with it, but that it is developed by slow degrees and by the aid of our external surroundings. Our study of it must be carried on not only in adults of fully developed and perfect mind; we must also observe all its imperfect manifestations and developments in children, idiots, and the savage dwellers of uncivilized lands, and compare these with minds diseased and disordered, and with the still less developed mental functions of the lower animals.

Let us take an infant and see what its brain functions are, and how they grow into the full intelligence of manhood. You have probably heard of the controversy as to innate ideas, a sense of duty born with us, and the like. But infants are not born with ideas and knowledge. They acquire ideas, but they are born with a brain, and the power of developing the function of it, and of acquiring knowledge. The brain they inherit, but their acquisitions must depend on its healthy working, and on their surronndings and opportunities of receiving ideas. We shall find no intelligence at first; an infant's nerve phenomena are those of bodily feel- The growth ing and sensation rather than of mind. It passes a of mind. considerable portion of its time in sleep: when hungry or cold, it wakes and cries; when fed and warm, it sleeps again. It sees nothing, in our sense of the word; the rays of light strike on its eye, and, according to the intensity of the luminosity, it receives an excitation, pleasurable or painful, of the organ of vision. So we find that when exposed to a very strong light, it cries, but in the dark it is often pacified by being brought in view of a lighted candle. Thus, although the infant cannot be said to have any true perception of objects, we infer from its movements that it experiences certain *feelings* of pleasure or pain from the excitation of its faculty of vision, and the changes produced in the vision-centres. As time goes on, it habitually sees certain things, some more agreeable than others, as its mother and nurse. Not only is the sight pleasant at the moment, but the object remains fixed in the memory, and a pleasant feeling is associated with it. The child *recollects* the mother, and the sight of her arrests its tears, even before the wished for nourishment is afforded. Here it experiences pleasure from seeing a well-known face,—a great advance from the time when it was pleased by a certain amount of light, the pleasure being, however, the stimulation of a portion of the brain through the eye.

Similarly, if we examine the sense of hearing, we find that at a very early age it can hardly be said to exist. The infant's slumbers are not disturbed by a noise that would wake adults. Yet, when awake, a violent, sudden or harsh sound will cause it discomfort; a soft, rhythmical, or musical one will please, especially if it come from some familiar person, as the singing of its mother or nurse. Then the sound becomes associated with the individual, and it testifies delight at the voice, even when the speaker is out of sight. When first it begins not merely to recognize sounds, but to recollect names, it associates the latter with certain concrete objects,— with a horse, a dog, or a cat; and as each of these objects when seen causes a feeling of pleasure or the reverse, so does the memory of it cause the same, when laid up in the mind under the name associated with it.

There can be no question that the great majority of objects which are laid up in the memory are taken into the mind by the avenues of the senses of sight and hearing; yet the experiences of taste, smell, and touch are registered in the same way, though they are not so multitudinous and varied. Those who are so unfortunate as to have been born without one or both of the former senses bring the latter three to their aid in a degree which others who have no such need of them can hardly appreciate. However they enter, whether by sight or hearing, taste, touch, or smell, all impressions are conveyed by the senses to the brain, and are there stored away and associated together, and so become food for thought and reflection, and thus we attain to a thinking mind. Till this comes to pass, the young infant is much in the condition of the animal whose hemispheres have been removed. It passes most of its time in sleep, cries when in pain, follows a light with its eyes, and executes such movements as sucking.

All these ideal feelings stored up in the child's memory have, as I have said, come to it from without, and have for the most part been associated with some feeling either of pleasure or pain at the time they were perceived. The excitation of vision representing the nurse is associated with the pleasurable sensation of appeased hunger, and so the two are connected afterwards, and the sight of the nurse gives pleasure, and also recalls the gratification of the hungry appetite. The association of such ideas is plain enough, and it must be that certain portions of the brain corresponding to these are also associated, and give rise to associated action.

A child a twelvemonth old shakes his head when I ask him to come to me : he must have learned by his eye to discriminate persons, and to know mine to be an unfamiliar face; also he must have learned that unfamiliar faces, *i. e.*, strangers, are productive of less gratification to him than are nurses and friends. So he dissents by shaking his head; but he does not cry as he would have done at an earlier age, or as he would now, were I to take him by force : he has learned that shaking his head indicates unwillingness, and averts the evil. Here is a variety of ideas arising out of sight and sound, which must have passed through a number of associated brain-centres, and, culminating in a deliberate act of volition, finally result in setting in motion the muscles that move the head. We see decided will, the outcome of a feeling of dislike or distrust, which the sight of a stranger has roused, but there is very little that deserves the name of intellect. Some degree of memory and association we see connected with the stimulation of the organs of sense; but the intellectual powers of a child of this age are below those of an intelligent dog.

If we contemplate the same child at the age of three, we see that he has made a vast stride. He has gone far beyond canine intelligence and canine powers. Supposing him to be one of fair average capacity, mental and bodily, we see in him in a certain stage all the capabilities of adult mind. He can convey to others his ideas in intelligible speech; he can commit to memory what he hears; he can reason and perceive the consequences of his acts, and can abstain from what he would fain do if permitted. He has, it may be, a determined will, earning for himself the character of being a "wilful" child. His intellect will have greatly developed. But what of his emotional phenomena? We find this portion of his organization more developed still. His whole day is devoted to enjoyment, to gratifying his bodily sense and appetite, to running about, eating, singing, shouting, and amusing his mind by pictures, sights, and play. As the infant passes its days in sleeping and feeding, in looking at the light, and kicking its limbs in the delight of muscular exertion, so does the three-year-old child live in the perpetual indulgence of his pleasures and his self-feeling. If we observe the manifestations of emotion, we shall see that he exhibits anger, fear, jealousy, hatred and love, wonder combined with pleasure or with pain which becomes fear, self-importance, and a desire to be first and to have precedence in all pleasant things. These all grow out of the mere feelings of pleasure or pain, which at first constituted the whole of the infant's emotional state.

In this microcosm of humanity, a strong and healthy child, you may study without fear of mistake the development of mind. You will find no better field elsewhere, and he who has learned what mind is from an analysis of his own internal consciousness, and has not studied it in the manner above mentioned, has only half learned his lesson.

In the works of modern writers upon mind, there is a general agreement among most of them to divide it into three, the intellect, the emotions, and the will; and these are described separately, and spoken of as having an independent function. Hence it has happened that physiological writers and inquirers, hearing from

The three divisions of mind.

metaphysicians that there are three divisions of mind, have thought it necessary to have three portions of the brain corresponding to the three parts of mind; and we shall hereafter find that classifications of insanity have been laid down in accordance with the threefold division; and it has been supposed that one such portion of the brain might become unsound, the other remaining sound. The separate existence of these faculties, however, is more apparent than real. That for which an independence has been claimed, more than for any, is the will. On this are supposed to hinge the questions of free will, necessity, responsibility, and the like; yet, after the examination of the acutest reasoners of all ages, what is there laid down concerning it on which men are agreed? Looking at these divisions from the phenomenalist point of view, and considering them as they appear in their developing stage in childhood, we may, I think, come to some practical conclusions without much difficulty.

I have already spoken of the storing up in the brain of the memories of impressions conveyed thither from the external world by the various senses,—sight, hearing, taste, or smell. We call these impressions, when they are thus stored up, ideas—ιδέαι, the images of the original impressions. The brain receives these by means of its machinery of cells and connecting fibres, and deals with them, associating them into groups, so that the idea of one thing calls up another, which is habitually associated with it. The idea of form calls up color; the sound of a trumpet calls up the form of one. And when we have thus filled our brain with ideas, we unconsciously compare them, discover the *simile inter dissimilia*, and the *dissimile inter similia;* we advance from the *simplex apprehensio* of the logicians, the mere reception of things, to *judicium* and *discursus*, the forming judgments, and proceeding from certain judgments to another founded upon them. For all this it is necessary that the organs involved be in sound working condition. The

Ideas.

child that sees collects ideas inaccessible to one that is blind;
the latter's store is so much the less, and ideas of certain
kinds, as of colors, are absolutely unknown to him; ideas of
objects he derives from touch, and this sense becomes greatly
developed from the increased use he makes of it, and the
communications of the various brain-cells in which these
stores are laid up must be perfect, so that they may all be
brought to bear upon the formation of a given judgment.
The man whose memory is good, who has all his knowledge
available, and can concentrate quickly the whole of it on a
single point, will form a sound judgment, and is popularly
said to have all his wits about him. The various operations
of the intellect, call them what we will, may be reduced to
those of retaining or remembering, discriminating or sorting,
and reproducing or creating new ideas or judgments out of
our previous stock.

For all this we must have *mens sana in corpore sano.*
Perfect intelligence, pure intellect, has been conceived as
existing without the drawback of corporeity, because we
cannot but feel that the latter constantly interferes with
the perfect use thereof. How this comes about, how man's
intelligence and sound mind are marred by his bodily imperfection, it is the chief object of these lectures to show.

We have seen that the child, besides showing signs of a
developing intellect, indicates that it possesses emotions and
will—that is, it lets it be known that it likes or dislikes persons and things, and executes various movements in accordance. This brings me to the consideration of what is meant
by emotion and will in children and in adults. They are
constantly spoken of as being divisions of the mind, together
with intellect. It will, however, be seen that they are something very different.

What we generally call emotion, as rage, terror, or joy, is
Feelings or the feeling of the higher brain, the pleasure or pain
emotions. of the mind, as ordinary pain or its opposite is of

the body. It is a physical condition or state depending on a certain excitation of a nerve centre or centres, varying in its character according to the centres excited; consequently, as the latter are developed in complexity and specialty up to the highest point of refined and educated adult life, so will the emotions be complex and special in their character. A feeling of pleasure or pain coexists, we may almost say, with life itself. The humblest animals, far below those in which we first find cerebral hemispheres, indicate by their movements that their well-being is promoted or retarded. The youngest infant testifies to pain. If we use the term "feeling" instead of "emotion," we shall better understand how much there is in common between the bodily and mental feelings, how they are exalted or depressed by similar causes. An infant cries if it experiences bodily pain, or the discomfort caused by cold or hunger. Its bodily well-being is arrested, and it testifies this by appropriate acts, which are in accordance with its nerve development at the time. If this development advances no further, and the child remains in the condition of the lowest idiot, it may go through life without indicating any higher feeling; but if it progresses normally, we find in a short time signs of mental feeling in addition to bodily. Besides crying, ceasing to cry, and going to sleep, which at first is almost all that we can observe in addition to the movements of the extremities, we notice that it smiles when it sees an accustomed face, and shows in a short time by vocal sounds its pleasure as well as its pain. In all this we see that an excitation of its centres is followed by appropriate movements, which may at first be called voluntary or involuntary, so closely do they follow the excitation. If, however, we try to discover why a child is pleased or displeased, we find that this depends either on the character of the excitation, or on its physical condition at the particular time. A strong light, too loud a noise, a nauseous taste, a prick of a pin, a wound or blow, produce pain at once; but, besides these, we constantly see that when the child is ill everything causes pain, and nothing brings pleasure. It cries even with those it loves best, and will not be comforted by its toys, or by any of those things that pleased it when in health. We judge of a child's health by its emotional state, by its being fretful and cross, or gay and hilarious. As it grows in mind and brain, and lays up a store of ideas of all kinds, passing from mere concrete objects to abstractions, from particulars to generalizations, we find that excitation produces feelings equally varying and advancing in complexity and specialty. Herein we shall see the difference between one child and another, as between one man and another. The educated child, the de-

Emotions correspond with the ideas.

scendant of a line of educated ancestors, becomes a highly specialized man, with feelings and emotions of a refined and complex nature. The savage child—the child, that is, of savages—becomes a savage man, and his ideas and feelings are, compared with those of civilized man, childlike throughout life. He is, like a child, easily moved to joy, terror, or rage; but he is incapable of comprehending abstract ideas, as truth, justice, honor, or of feeling the complex emotions that belong to such ideas. And as his mental manifestations are simple, so we find also that the convolutions of his brain are simple, alike in both hemispheres, and more resembling the brain of the apes than does the complicated and convoluted brain of an educated European. His brain is undeveloped, and his mind is incapable of development. Little by little in successive generations this brain may increase in complexity and specialization, but in the individual savage this cannot take place. And as one savage inherits the simple and imperfect brain of former savages, so we shall find that amongst the educated nations a child may inherit the imperfect brain of ancestors who have retrograded from the development of civilization, or who have, from disease, overwork, debauchery, or drink, become degenerate and fallen. Like the savage child, this one will be incapable of attaining the perfection of intellectual and emotional life. Either he is so stunted and blighted that he is an imbecile and an idiot from the beginning, or when he enters upon life he is unequal to contend with the chances of fortune, or his organization is so unstable that every ordinary illness disturbs his reason. And even if he does not fall into a sudden and marked state of insanity, he nevertheless is unlike other people. His notions are warped and eccentric; he is destitute of the sense of duty and of right possessed by others of his country and social status. He becomes a criminal, if not a lunatic, and hands on to his descendants, if he has any, the inheritance of criminality or insanity, swelling the ranks of the criminal or the lunatic class. Each of these is a degenerate and degraded section of the community, which might be reclaimed through several generations, if we could select the healthiest specimens, and leave the worst to die out, as in fact they often do, in a state of sterility.

In ordinary health, excitations of our nerve centres produce certain feelings, which, though often very complex, may yet be all resolved into pleasure or pain. The result of the excitation, if it be powerful, is action of some kind—verbal, facial, or bodily—or desire for action, which we may repress. In the child or the savage this repression is not exercised, and there is an immediate display of muscular action demonstrating the feeling experienced. More civilized men, from other ideas habitual to them, repress these signs if they are able. But this they cannot always do, and the pent-up storm of rage or grief finds vent in words or action.

To a centre in its ordinary state any stimulation may be at once pleasant or painful; or it may be at first pleasant, and may afterwards be so prolonged as to cause pain. Familiar instances of the latter occur to every one. The exercise in which we at first take keen delight becomes irksome and painful, if continued so as to produce great fatigue. We are said to "get tired" in time of almost

Feelings vary according to the condition of the centres. anything—of music, of conversation, of our amusements—and hence we see that the particular feeling aroused by such things depends on the condition of the centres at a given moment; and as the act follows the feeling, this also will be regulated by the condition, whatever it may be.

A dog let loose from its kennel, a horse turned out of its stable into a field, a young child fresh from its rest, feels the highest delight in exercising its limbs in jumping and running; its centres are full of energy almost spontaneously discharged in motion. If, on the contrary, either of them does not move at all, or crawls along languidly and dejectedly, we say that it is not well with it. Similarly, if accustomed pleasures fail to delight a man, and he is gloomy and melancholy without any cause, we know that something is amiss. He may have been subjected to stimulation of a very painful character, to some grief, or loss or pressing anxiety, which has exhausted him, has robbed him of sleep, and brought him to this condition. He may have encountered some event which has caused so sudden a shock that he may have fallen as in a fit, or which may have excited him to rage or terror, with corresponding action and consequent exhaustion. Even pleasurable emotion may become exhausting, if prolonged. Laughter may turn to sobbing, and men may faint from intense joy. On the well-being of the nerve centres will depend our recovery from the effects of these excitations. They must needs violently disturb the balance of the brain circulation, which is roused to supply the force expended. If the circulation fall and sleep return, all is reduced to its former level, and we are said "to get over it." But if not, a permanant disturbance may take place.

Here, then, we may lay down the component parts of that which, for our purpose, we describe as mind. We see that it is evolved out of feelings, under which name we group both the sensations derived from the excitation of our senses, and the emotions attending the excitation of ideas or past feelings laid up in memory, which being recalled to consciousness, are united to the feeling of the moment, from whatever source this may have arisen. This union of the past and present is effected by various processes of reasoning and judgment, and the carrying out the action consequent upon this emanates from what we call will, about which I must say a few words.

Will is not one of the primary divisions of mind. Our mind is composed of feelings present and past, that   Will. have been produced by the various stimulations brought to the nerve centres or cells by the conducting nerve fibres. Will is only a process of energizing, which these structures possess when in a healthy and normal state, —a process which intervenes between the stimulation of the centres and the motion which is the ultimate result. If will does not intervene, the act is said to be automatic; if will directs it, it is voluntary. And when we say that will directs, we mean that in our mind we form a deliberate judgment concerning something which we wish to carry out, and then regulate our movements so as to accomplish this end. Will is concerned with action of some sort, mental or bodily; it does not exist as a metaphysical entity. There is no such thing as will apart from something willed. And if we examine the acts, mental or bodily, which are the result of deliberate will, we shall find that a vast number of our actions are not comprised in this category, and that those which really deserve the name are the result of the whole collected knowledge of our mind. Being what we are, we cannot help acting as we do. Involuntarily we avoid that which is painful, and seek that which is pleasant. In sudden self-defence or danger, we do that which truly is called involuntary. Many things are done unconsciously by habit and custom, and if we court danger, or choose the painful rather than the pleasant, it is because the ideas and knowledge stored up in our brain teach us that it is better for some reason or other so to do. People differ in that which they choose to do, because of the difference in the general constitution and furnishing of their minds. One man can practice great self-denial which another cannot. He is enabled to do this, not because one part of his brain, inhabited by a function called his will, is larger than that of the other man, but because his whole mind is stored with feelings and experiences which counteract the impulse to gratify a present desire, a desire not resisted by a man less endowed. Our criminal law can only be enforced by supposing that all men are alike, even to the point of all being acquainted with every law that is made; but, practically, we make great differences and allowances for individuals according to their opportunities, their rearing, education, and past history. Were an educated gentleman to steal a watch, we should affix to the act a stigma very different from that which accompanies the theft committed by one who has been reared in vice and crime.

If we consider what can be done by dint of our will, we shall find that willing can do very little *per se*. We learn to walk, we learn to ride, to write, to dance. By long and laborious practice we acquire the power of executing such movements, and no effort of will can enable us to perform them till we have learned the method. When this is acquired, such things are done unconsciously. If we apply our will to mental operations, frequently we cannot fix our attention on one subject for ten minutes at a time, or do what we will we cannot exclude an idea from our thoughts. We cannot by our will recall a name or a circumstance; and when we are conscious of exercising a choice, and of deliberately resolving to do this or that, it is because our reason, judging by the aid of experience of the past, and the probabilities of the future, based on such experience, indicates that which we *must* choose. We say emphatically of a man, when we wish to assert that he did something freely and voluntarily, that he *deliberately* did the thing; *i. e.*, that he, after due reflection and consideration, proceeded to act. Therefore *volitional* insanity must imply an insane reason and judgment, not only an insane will, and is no more a separate and special form than are ideational and emotional insanity, which are supposed severally to represent an insane intellect and insane emotions. We can no more divorce intellect and emotions than we can divorce intellect and ideas from consciousness.

I discard the will, then, as a third component of mind, and retain only feelings and ideas, which in truth are not two, but one, as they arise from present stimulation, are stored away in memory, and in new combinations come again into consciousness upon fresh excitations. Under the term feeling we may range the bodily sensations of pain or pleasure, the sensations of the special senses, as the eye or ear, and the emotions which are but the feelings of the highest centres of the brain concerned with the intellectual, the æsthetic, or the religious. For the due operation of our feelings and resulting ideas, we require the healthy working of the nerve centres, with the system of nerve fibres, Conditions and adequate supply of blood, which I have described necessary for the right to you. When this goes on aright, our minds are operation of healthy; when anything interferes with the proper the mind. working, we have the evidence of it in an irregular or abnormal manifestation of mind-action. And before I come to the subject of insanity as generally understood, it may be as well to glance for a moment at a few of the conditions of the healthy working of brain and nerve.

We may sum up in a few words these several conditions. Given a healthy apparatus, free from defect, we require for its working a due amount of material in the shape of food, to be converted, through the agency of the digestive and circulatory system, into healthy blood, supplying the waste in the brain cells. This blood must be in all respects fit for its purpose, rich in oxygen and all necessary ingredients, and free from all impurities, as urea, bile, carbonic acid, or other poisons. Secondly, we require for the due discharge of mental action a certain amount of heat. Thirdly, we must at stated intervals have a period of rest and cessation, which in man is given by sleep. Failing any of these, mental action becomes disordered, and finally ceases.

The mere amount of blood circulating through the brain 1. A healthy must of necessity influence to a material degree its blood-flow. power of acting. Mechanically, I mean, the pressure of an undue quantity, or, conversely, the removal of the accustomed pressure, must affect the relations and the functions of such delicate structures as the nerve cells and nerve fibres. That pressure can be exerted upon the brain cells by increased blood supply is a fact which, I believe, may now be considered fully established, though formerly some held that this could not be the case. We may concede, however, that the amount of blood sent to the brain is, compared with that which may be injected into other organs, limited by the conditions of the arteries; nevertheless, it is certain that enough may be sent there to interfere with the healthy state, for after death we have traces of active hyperæmia plainly apparent. Another probable result of excessive hyperæmia and pressure is stasis of the blood in the vessels and capillaries: stasis both of the red corpuscles and the white, with blocking of the minute vessels, and consequent delirium or stupor. Upon this point I shall have more to say hereafter; but I wish only here to remind you of the writings of Mr. Lister on the phenomenon of stasis in inflammation, and of Dr. Charlton Bastian's paper, in which he describes this blocking as discovered by himself, in a case of erysipelas of the head with delirium, narrated in the "British Medical Journal" of January, 1869.

Into the varieties of food necessary or adequate to the proper discharge of brain function I shall not here enter. You will have heard of them elsewhere. It 2. Food. is a fact of observation that the dwellers in northern regions eat quantities of animal food and fat and grease of all kinds, which could only be consumed by those who live under such climatic conditions, while those who inhabit tropic lands may pass through an active life without eating anything save a vegetable diet. And this brings me to another head. For the due discharge of brain function it is necessary that the individual should live in a certain temperature, not 3. A normal too hot nor too cold. Life—the life, that is, of man tempera- ture. —can only exist in a certain temperature; and the first mode in which the invasion of cold is evidenced is in the effect produced upon the nervous system. An over- whelming desire to sleep comes over a man exposed for a long period to extreme cold; and, as you know, to sleep under such circumstances is fatal, unless some one is at hand to wake the sleeper. If this be the case, the sleep is benefi- cial, and recruits the exhausted powers, showing plainly that nervous exhaustion is the condition which the cold produces. In his most interesting book of Arctic travel, Dr. Kane relates how he and his companions were once nearly lost in the cold: "Our halts multiplied, and we fell half-sleeping on the snow. I could not prevent it. Strange to say, it refreshed us. I ventured upon the experiment myself, making Riley wake me at the end of three minutes, and I felt so much benefited by it that I timed the men in the same way. They sat on the runners of the sledge, fell asleep instantly, and were forced to wakefulness when their three minutes were out."[1]

The blood must be pure: it must contain no deleterious substance which may interfere with the healthy nutrition of the brain, or may actually poison it, and set up therein that

[1] Arctic Explorations, vol. i, p. 198.

inflammation and stasis which I have alluded to. It must not be vitiated by poison's introduced from without, as alcohol, opium, lead; neither ought it to contain those poisonous matters which, generated within the body, and in a healthy individual excreted thence, are occasionally retained, and give rise to symptoms of brain disorder, such as delirium, coma, or convulsions.

However we may explain the metamorphosis of other forms of motion or energy into mind, it is a fact of experience that an adequate supply of food is required for the wants of the nervous system, and that a failure of food results in a corresponding diminution of nerve-energy, and often in nervous disease. I shall have to return to this again and again, believing, as I do, that a plentiful supply of food is of all things the most efficacious in restoring exhausted nervous power, and in removing nervous disorder. If we read the accounts of shipwrecked sailors and others who have been compelled to live for some time upon a scanty supply of food, we see how weakness was the prominent symptom experienced, weakness rather than hunger, weakness not to be accounted for by the diminution of the muscular tissues, but rather by the want of nervous power. Not merely for the nourishment of the brain and other portions of the nervous system is the food required. It is demanded not only that the brain may live, but that it may duly discharge its function in a normal and healthy manner. The brain may live, and the owner may live for years in a state of the most abject fatuity.

The animals that have to pass the winter in countries where the cold is very severe, do so, many of them, in the state of hibernation. So little is expended in this condition of sleep, that often without food they exist for months, with all the functions of life reduced to a minimum, the amount of nervous energy required for these being derived from the blood, which is in turn renovated from the stores of their bodies, or by occasional meals from the supply of winter food laid up by some of them. But hibernation is not possible for us or for the more highly organized and developed animals, and cold deprives us of our nervous power even when we are supplied with adequate nourishment. Too great heat also incapacitates us from properly discharging our brain function, and causes that disorder called *coup de soleil*, which has its seat in the cerebral organs.

Not only is the warmth of the sun beneficial to the health and energy of the human mind, the light of it is also essential to its well-being. The protracted darkness 4. Light. of northern countries has been observed to bring about insanity, especially melancholia. Dr. Lauder Lindsay draws attention to this in a paper on " Insanity in Arctic Countries,"[1] to which I refer you. And Dr. Kane, from whose book I have just quoted, mentions the depressing effect of darkness, which affected, he says, even the dogs, though they were born within the Arctic circle. A disease which he considered clearly mental, affected them to such a degree that they were doctored and nursed like babies. They ate and slept well, and were strong, but an epileptic attack was followed by true lunacy. Of course, we cannot, in speaking of Arctic countries, eliminate the joint effect of cold, fatigue, and want of fresh food; but in other countries, in cities, dungeons, and elsewhere, the depression caused by prolonged darkness has been felt and noticed.

For the due discharge of its function, our brain requires rest, which rest it takes in sleep. Only in complete sleep does it thoroughly recruit itself, and lay up 5. Sleep. stores of energy to be expended in the waking hours. In sleep all work ceases save the processes of organic life, and these are reduced to the lowest point. There is no expenditure, but, on the contrary, there is constant renewal of nerve power. According to the exhaustion and previous waste of

---

[1] British and Foreign Medico-Chirurgical Review, January, 1870.

power will be the demand for sleep and the continuance of it. Men become so worn out that the strongest impressions, the loudest noises, or the most exciting news, cannot avert the sleep that comes over them; but the amount that will refresh them varies greatly in different individuals. Some require much sleep, some little; at times a brief snatch, even of a few minutes, will greatly recruit the wearied man. As you study insanity and observe insane patients, you will have to be constantly watching the phenomena of sleep and sleeplessness. You will see the consequences of the entire loss of sleep, of the partial loss. You will meet with some whose minds break down because their brain is constantly and habitually overworked by day, and not sufficiently renovated by sleep at night. Either their work pursues them into the night, and haunts their couch and disturbs their sleep by harassing thoughts and grave responsibilities, or they allow themselves an amount of sleep altogether out of proportion to that demanded by their daily task.

Such are the subjects to which I wish you to direct your attention before you enter on the study of the disorder termed Insanity, or unsoundness of mind. I have brought them under your notice roughly, not with the accuracy and perfect delineation of a photograph, but as men draw diagrams on a black-board, giving in broad outline just so much as will illustrate what they have to describe. You must bear in mind that you have to consider the nerve centres and the nerve fibres which connect them to each other and to other parts, the blood which furnishes them with life and energy, the bloodvessels that carry this to them and take it away, and the nervous system that regulates the supply; the nature of the resulting operations, whether of mind or motility, and the conditions under which they are carried on. Such are the data. When these organs all work harmoniously and healthily, sound mind is the result. When the mind is unsound, we must discover the defective spot in one or the other of these parts or processes.

LECTURE III.

The Pathology of Insanity—Characteristics of Commencing Insanity—
Varieties of Insanity—Insanity from Mental Shock—From long-con-
tinued Anxiety—Insanity in connection with the Sexual Organs—
Puerperal Insanity—Insanity of Masturbation—Insanity of Alcohol
—Various Forms—Insanity from other Poisons—From a Blow—
From Excessive Heat.

HAVING thus glanced at the phenomena of healthy mind,
we are in a position to study those of unhealthy or disordered
mind; having laid down the physiology, we proceed to the
pathology.

Now, by daily intercourse with sane people we know very
well what is meant when in ordinary phraseology Sound mind.
we speak of a man as being " right in his mind." It
is assumed that, being of full age, he has stored his brain
with a reasonable amount of knowledge and of facts of experience; that he can recall a fair proportion of what he has
seen and heard during the past years, and can act upon this
experience in an intelligent manner, giving good reasons for
so acting; that he can understand what is said to him upon
subjects within his comprehension and knowledge, and display judgment in what concerns him personally. Such is
what lawyers call a man "of sound mind, memory, and
understanding." Conversely, we say a man is " un- Unsoundness
sound of mind " when he forgets most of what hap- of mind.
pens to him; can form no judgment from what he has seen
or learned; when his acts are outrageous, and he can give
no good reasons for them; when his ideas concerning himself
are palpably false, i. e., delusions; or when he is quite unconscious of what he is doing.

According to the nature of the defect, we say that he is idiotic or imbecile, insane or delirious. These forms of unsoundness of mind may vary in degree, and no less in duration, lasting from hours to years. Yet, certain it is that they depend on alteration or defective action of those organs I spoke of in my first lecture, the nerve centres and conducting fibres, the bloodvessels, and the system by which the supply of blood is regulated. Unsoundness of mind may exist by itself, the bodily functions being apparently intact; it may be coupled with epilepsy, apoplexy, and other cerebral affections, or arise in the course of such diseases as measles, pneumonia, acute rheumatism, and fevers of all kinds, or may be traced to blood-poisons, to alcohol, haschisch, or opium. Whether we call it delirium, coma, wandering, or idiocy, mania, melancholia, or dementia, it depends on some pathological condition of the nerve centres, and implies a total or partial mental alteration or defect.

Having thus widened out the subject to the full, I must proceed to consider some of the details, for it is not within the scope of these lectures to examine *seriatim* every one of the conditions just enumerated. I pass over idiocy and congenital idiots, whose undeveloped organs and faculties are incapable of receiving the data of experience, and of forming out of them judgments. I leave to other teachers the condition of coma, which is rarely seen by those who observe the insane, except when it is the precursor of death. That to which I chiefly wish to direct your attention, and which is involved in the greatest obscurity, is the alteration which takes place in the mind of a man previously sane, and in a longer or shorter time may pass away, leaving him sane as before. The alteration may be so transient, and the restoration so complete, that it is impossible to believe the pathological change can be anything more than what is usually called "functional."

If you look carefully at a number of patients whose in-

sanity is just in its commencement, you will find Characteris-
certain characteristics in which they agree. I do tics of commencing in-
not mean that they will agree in their delusions, or sanity.
that they will perform the same acts, but certain physical
symptoms will be observable in all, which point to pathological disturbances of nerve function.

a. The first I shall mention is, that very few, if any, such
persons sleep in a normal or natural degree. Almost a. Want of
invariably, sleep will be in defect. This defect, this sleep.
sleeplessness, may be greater or less according to the severity
of the case, varying from entire loss lasting for days, and
threatening danger to life, to an amount which, though less
than usual, yet brings some renovation of strength to the
sufferer every twenty-four hours.

b. Another symptom not so universally present, which
may be overlooked by you, or denied by the patient, b. Pain, or
is pain and heat of head, frequently a flushed face, heat of head.
throbbing of the carotids, and suffused eyes.

c. Next, and this I think of the greatest importance, there
is almost always an alteration in the general emo- c. Alteration
tional condition of the individual. It has been said in emotional
state.
that in all insanity there is at first a period of depression, to be followed in mania by excitement. This I
doubt. I believe that excitement may be the first change
noticeable; but I think it certain that one or other, depression or excitement, a departure in one or other direction
from the normal emotional state, may be observed in most
patients at the commencement of an attack. Friends will
tell you that a man has become quiet and dull, or restless,
irritable, or excitable, and this in many instances long before any marked intellectual disturbance or delusions are
manifest. These are all symptoms which are the common
precursors of insanity, and I wish you particularly to recollect them, because they throw light on the nature of this
terrible malady, and by keeping them ever before your eyes

you may be able to avert the threatening evil; for we are reproached because we never attempt to deal with insanity till it has fully and unmistakably declared itself. There is no need to consider these symptoms separately; in speaking of one I shall touch on all.

If my views are correct, this depression or exaltation, this emotional alteration, points not to a disturbance of one portion of the brain, but to a pathological condition of the whole nervous system of the highest significance. You will find it called by some "emotional insanity," and will read that the emotional part of the mind may be disordered, the intellectual remaining sound, and delusions not being observable. This distinction cannot, I maintain, be upheld. Patients may, or may not, have delusions; they may have the same delusions, and yet be very different in their feelings concerning them; the delusions are the result of the emotional and general condition, not the cause, and this explains our finding almost identically the same delusions in so many patients; for the emotions are the result of alterations of the health and energy of the entire nerve centres, and accordingly the man is depressed or excited, angry, noisy, or hilarious.

This feeling of depression or gayety is apt to be overlooked, because it is such a common occurrence, but as we daily feel it ourselves, or witness it in others, we can understand that it is a physical condition depending upon the general bodily health. We never think of attributing it solely to mental causes. Without anxiety or care of any kind, a man may feel low; another even under a load of trouble feels cheerful and elastic. We talk of an "attack of the spleen," of being "jaundiced," of the liver being out of sorts, or the stomach, but we don't call our ailment "disorder of the brain," nor is this in many cases the part primarily affected. Quite possibly the digestive organs may be the seat of the mischief, and an alteration of diet or a dose of medicine may effect a

cure. Our fathers used to recognize this when they wrote of
"visceral sympathies." Little is known even now of the
relations of one organ to another, or of the sympathetic disturbances, so that we cannot always fix upon the peccant
part.

d. After the stage of emotional alteration has begun,
sooner or later in the majority of patients delu- d. Subse-
sions, or hallucinations, appear. In some we may quently,
not be able to discover any which merit the name. delusions.
Of such I shall speak hereafter; but, as I have said, in most
patients who are insane, and not imbecile or delirious, we
shall find delusions, false and erroneous notions about themselves and their relations to other people and things. A
part of the mind appears to be out of joint; it does not work
in harmony with the rest. Being perfectly clear on many
points, they assert what is utterly false or impossible concerning others, and all demonstration fails to point out that
they are mistaken. They are unable to compare their feelings with the facts of their own or others' experience; and
with these delusions there may be every variation of emotion,
from the profoundest gloom to the liveliest hilarity. Formerly insanity was divided according to the feeling displayed,
and for ages writers knew no classes but melancholia and
mania. As a reaction which might have been expected,
pathologists nowadays say that this is no division at all; that
it is but an accident if a man is melancholy or the reverse.
As usual, the truth is somewhere between; the melancholy
of a patient is a pathological condition different unquestionably from that of a man in gay and noisy mania, and requiring different treatment. But the whole pathology is not
summed up in either of these terms. Two women, from the
same cause, parturition, will become, the one maniacal, the
other melancholic. It is not sufficient here to set these down
as suffering from puerperal insanity. We must look for varieties in the conditions which may account for the varieties

in the phenomena exhibited. It has been proposed to classify insanity according to its causes. But it is entirely unscientific to describe the condition of a patient by simply naming an origin, possibly very remote, and to take no account of all the various steps by which the patient has advanced up to the time of our examination, or of the phenomena exhibited The form of at the latter period. Again, we shall find that in-
the insanity sanity is for the most part the outcome of a number
depends on
a number of of causes, not of one; and this, if true, would at
conditions.
once vitiate such a classification. That which is above everything needful is a consideration of the whole pathology of a patient at the time of the first manifestation of mental disorder. At this time we shall be best able to appreciate his exact condition, and to trace the course of the malady thence, mindful of the essential, and setting aside the non-essential phenomena thereof. In considering the pathology, we must also be studying the cause. The precise pathological condition may be hard to discern, yet the attempt must be made, and constant practice will enable us to do much.

If we consult the works of the chief writers upon the subject of insanity, we shall see that the varieties of the disorder are in almost every case determined by the mental symptoms; and so we find ever recurring the old divisions of mania, melancholia, and dementia. In describing the causes, we hear of other physical conditions, e. g., insanity brought about by epilepsy or syphilis, but the varieties or classes are usually not distinguished by pathological diversities, but by mental peculiarities only. One exception, however, I must mention. In 1863, Dr. Skae, of Edinburgh, read before the
Dr. Skae's Medico-Psychological Association a most suggestive
pathological paper on "A Rational and Practical Classification
classification.
of Insanity," which is printed in the "Journal of Mental Science." His scheme he puts forward not as complete, "but as one which may, by combined efforts, culminate

in a better, a more definite, and, at least, a more practical method than the one in present use." I look upon this system as so valuable, both on account of its own merits, and as the precursor of all that will certainly follow, that I cannot but transcribe it here. It is this:

Idiocy, } Intellectual.
Imbecility, } Moral.
Epileptic Mania.
Mania of Masturbation.
   "   Pubescence.
Satyriasis.
Nymphomania.
Hysterical Mania.
Amenorrhœal Mania.
Sexual Mania.
Mania of Pregnancy.
   "   Lactation.
   "   Childbearing.

Climacteric Mania.
Ovariomania (uteromania).
Senile Mania.
Phthisical Mania.
Metastatic   "
Traumatic   "
Sunstroke   "
Syphilitic   "
Delirium Tremens.
Dipsomania.
General Paralysis of the Insane.
Idiopathic Mania { Sthenic.
                   { Asthenic.

The merits of this division are so great, and its superiority over all preceding so manifest, that it requires little or no comment. Without being a classification based exclusively on etiology, it yet takes into consideration the pathological condition of the individual, and the origin of the disorder. One could have wished that Dr. Skae had gone one step further, and banished altogether the word *mania*, which he apparently uses as synonymous with insanity; but which, in common parlance, conveys the idea of a peculiar mental state. Idiopathic mania, sthenic and asthenic, conveys no pathological meaning, and is, if anything, misleading. Schroeder van der Kolk, it is true, divided all insanity into idiopathic and sympathetic, the former arising, as he supposed, in the brain, the latter being caused by sympathetic disturbance of the bodily organs; but such vague divisions have no practical value, pathological or therapeutical. As I shall hereafter point out, the insanity which has no apparent cause might almost invariably be termed hereditary, were it not that much more than this may as truly be called hereditary, the exciting cause only lighting up the transmitted and latent disease. Both Drs. Skae and Schroeder van der Kolk pass over too lightly the influence of hereditary taint. The pathological condition observable in a patient at the outbreak of insanity has its origin, in numberless cases, not in the individual, but in his ancestors, and no classification or pathological description can be exact which omits to take this great fact into account.

I will pass under review some classes or conditions which Varieties of are, as I conceive, pathological varieties, and you insanity. will be able to compare them with Dr. Skae's system, and will see how large a part is played by that hereditary insane temperament to which I have just alluded. I shall hereafter have something more to say on the subject of classification. At present, without professing to lay down all the classes of insanity, I will consider the pathology of certain groups of cases, which I believe differ from one another in a pathological point of view.

The first is disorder of the brain produced by a mental 1. Insanity shock, with sleeplessness, heat of head, depression, from mental or painful excitement, which may be accompanied shock. by confusion of thought or delusions. Sudden shock may be followed by a variety of grave consequences, by death if there be heart disease, by apoplectic effusion of blood, by epilepsy, by chorea in young persons, and by various forms of insanity, from acute mania to what is termed acute dementia.

Most men know what it is to have been kept awake for a considerable portion of the night by something which causes them anxiety or grief. There is a strong stimulation of the mind, causing continued thought, and followed by an excited brain circulation. Even the anticipation of pleasure may produce the same result. In the young this may more frequently be the disturber of sleep than care or sorrow, which comes to them seldom, and sits on them lightly. From one cause or other almost every one knows what it is to be rendered sleepless. Now, if we observe the succession of phenomena in persons of ordinary health, what do we find? The reception of a mental shock causes immediate activity of brain, rapid molecular change in the centres, and in consequence a determination of arterial blood to the head. Even muscular structures may be set in motion, and this involuntarily. Very likely there will be trembling, or sobbing, or crying. The sufferer may pace the room, or rock himself, or wring his hands. All such acts imply a continued change going on in the centres; and they also imply a want of controlling power. The weaker the individual, the more violent will be these manifestations. Take the first, trembling. This indicates a lack of force. If we hold out a weight with extended arm, a weight too heavy for our strength, our hand trembles more and more, till it falls exhausted. The muscles do not balance one another, and the emission of force is jerky and uneven; the organs are not co-ordinated. The same thing may be said of convulsions, which so frequently occur after hemorrhage or other exhausting causes. As the power of the centres becomes exhausted, it is manifested by the irregular and spasmodic action of the muscles, which are set free from one another, and act separately and uncontrolled. A common sequel of shock is chorea, which is another variety of this spasmodic action. The defect of power in this disorder is fully recognized, and it has been supposed that the sole cause of it is embolic closure of the arteries. Without examining the question, I may assume that there is defect of power, whether depending on exhaustion of the normal supply, or deficiency of the blood whence it is derived. I believe both conditions may be found.

In ordinary health sleep comes to the disturbed brain after a longer or shorter period, the sufferer wakes refreshed, and on the next day his mental disquiet wears a very different aspect. But in a man doomed to insanity the rapid molecular changes do not cease, sleep does not come, and soon there is evident emotional change, with confusion and want of co-ordination of ideas.

The form of the insanity will vary according to the condition of the whole nerve centres of the individual; in a young and vigorous subject it will most likely take the form of mania, with violent ebullitions of anger, and much muscular action; in the old or weakly, melancholia more commonly appears; while in one whose nerve power is for the time utterly prostrated, there will be some such variety as acute dementia, or *melancholia cum stupore*, where mind is a blank, and voluntary action altogether gone. That the patient presents this or that kind of mental disorder is, it is true, in one sense an accident. The exciting cause may produce in one man melancholia, in another mania; but I hold that the condition called melancholia is very different pathologically from that of mania. The first pathological condition, then, for your consideration and study is that of insanity caused by sudden mental shock, a rapid molecular change being set up in the brain, giving rise to accelerated circulation, heat, and want of sleep, with the phenomena of emotional disturbance and confusion of thought and idea, the symptoms varying according to the general constitutional energy of the individual. Here, to use an old expression, we may say that the circulation is disturbed by a *vis a fronte*, or, using another formula, *ubi stimulus, ibi fluxus*, we indicate that the changes which bring about the increased blood-flow have commenced in the organs of mind under the influence of undue stimulation from without.

I now come to a second pathological condition, where not

2. Insanity from long-continued anxiety or work.

a sudden mental shock, but a long-continued mental worry or anxiety, or long and laborious mental application and work, has overset the reason. We see the result of this very frequently in brain diseases other than insanity, in so-called softening and disorganization of structure, produced by years of overwork. Here the machine gradually wears out; but in another, whose brain function is more liable to disturbance, there may be at an earlier period signs of disorder rather than of decay. The carking cares of poverty, and the lack of means to support a family, the chronic torment of a bad husband or wife, or of prodigal sons or profligate daughters, constant harass and anxiety in businesses of a speculative character, or a perpetual craving ambition perpetually disappointed,—these and a thousand other miseries of human life are the things which upset reason and fill asylums. And what is the pathology here? We do not hear of a sudden mental shock causing an overwhelming emotional excitement, and bringing about almost at once sleeplessness and acute insanity. But we know that there must have been a constant stimulation of the brain, with increased emotion and increased expenditure going on for years. The brain circulation during all this time has been disturbed, and the nerve centres exposed to a greater demand and a greater amount of change than they are able to bear. Some men may endure this, may work early and late, and retain their faculties unharmed; but others, who are by nature more prone to change, who easily display emotional excitement, and do not easily subside into their normal calm, are one day excited beyond recovery, and insanity is manifested. Owing to the length of time that the stimulation has existed, and the consequent weakening and exhaustion which the whole of the machinery must have undergone, we find that this form of insanity does not usually subside rapidly, and too often see along with it signs of irremediable disorganization of the brain or the nutrient bloodvessels.

It follows that these patients are not very youthful, and as long-continued and exhausting anxiety is the main cause, we should expect melancholia to be the form the insanity will take, or monomania, with suspicion and ill temper, rather than violent sthenic mania.

Whereas one section of observers ascribes to "moral causes" the chief rôle in the causation of insanity; another, looking farther back, would deny to them any *status* in this regard, and would reduce all to physical causes and conditions. And with some reason; for in almost all the cases where insanity follows a mental trial, we shall detect in the physical constitution of the individual a predisposition, an instability of nerve constitution, which enables the mental cause to overthrow him. We must consider, not the events of the preceding month or year, but the history of the individual from his birth, and that of his parents before him. There are men who, with the misfortunes of a Job, or the anxieties of a Damocles, are nevertheless calm, equable, and active, ever ready to catch the turn of the tide, prepared for everything, good or bad; and, on the other hand, some fall down before the slightest buffet of fortune, and are said to be driven mad by grief, or loss, or worry. A man may have griefs and anxieties so severe as scarcely to fall short of disease; but the moral causes of the insanity of many are of so slight a nature, when looked at objectively, that it is at once clear that other causes and conditions must be sought. I have said already, and shall have to repeat it again and again, that insanity is the result of a number of events and conditions which go to make up one pathological state. To gather all these together is probably out of our power, for we should have to survey a series of phenomena of infinite extent, and far beyond our ken.

In a large number of cases we cannot help considering, in connection with the insanity, some condition of the

3. Insanity in connection with the sexual organs.

sexual organs, which, whether it be the cause or the concomitant of the mental symptoms, must at any rate be viewed as part of the pathological state of the patient. Women become insane during pregnancy, after parturition, during lactation; at the age when the catamenia first appear, and when they disappear. Excessive indulgence either in venery or masturbation are causes admitted by all, and there are other less defined varieties, known as satyriasis, nymphomania, and hysterical mania, of which the pathology is often obscure, and into which many various conditions enter. Also we may trace, or think we can trace, the brain disorder to such maladies as tumors of the womb or ovary, or to sudden suppression of the catamenial function. Here, then, is a large group necessarily somewhat allied, the pathology of which must be studied as a whole, partly by observation of cases, partly by the analogies of other pathological conditions of insanity, or other nervous disorders traceable to the same causes.

The sympathetic connection existing between the brain and the uterus is plainly seen by the most casual observer. Many women are completely prostrated while menstruating, and suffer intensely in the head. In many animals the analogous period of the rut produces mental phenomena which approach insanity as nearly as anything evinced by these lower minds can. The madness of March hares has passed into a proverb. The stag and the buck, in October, render unsafe the parks in which they dwell. In a woman whose brain is peculiarly unstable and prone to disturbance, it is no wonder if uterine irregularities cause corresponding mental symptoms.

If we consider the insanity that makes its appearance at the time of pubescence, what may be observed? _a._ Insanity First, that this period brings more dangers to girls of puberty. than to boys; that more girls between the ages of twelve and eighteen become insane than boys. This we should expect. The period of pubescence causes a greater functional change in a girl than in a boy, with an increased risk of functional disturbance. A boy grows into a man imperceptibly, as it were. His development is marked by a capacity of procreation; but this is something very different from the establishment of the menstrual function, which so often is attended by great general disturbance. We may assume that at this time every girl is in a condition peculiarly susceptible of nervous irritation; therefore, in one who inherits from her ancestors an unstable organization, two conditions exist very favorable for the production of mental disorder. These may be of themselves sufficient to originate it; but there may be superadded either a mental cause, as a fright or a loss, something startling, harassing, or afflicting, a dreary, companionless, and cheerless life, a physical disorder, as menorrhagia, or an illness of an acute character.

You will find that such a conjunction of causes does not always produce insanity in a girl or boy : it may produce chorea : instead of the highest mind-centres being affected, there is disturbance of the motor centres, resulting in that irregular and spasmodic extrication of force which is recognized in all the protean forms of chorea. So prone are the motor centres to be affected in early life, that even when the mind is upset, and genuine insanity is recognizable, it is most frequently accompanied by noisy and violent action. Irregular movements or cataleptic rigidity, with more or less of a choreic tendency, are constantly to be seen; in fact, the insanity is more often shown in violence and powerful demonstrations of emotional activity than in delusions and disorder of the general intellect. Here, then, is a pathological condition to be marked off from others—a nervous temperament undergoing the change which accompanies puberty, and unstable in consequence—upset, it may be, by some mental shock or debilitating illness, and characterized by disturbance of both mind and body, generally of a violent and spasmodic character.

Let us look at the obverse of this, at the insanity which is *b.* Insanity so frequently seen at what has been termed the climacteric of the cli- macteric period of life, at the time of the " change of life" in women, and at an analogous period, from the age of fifty to sixty years, in men. Here, as in early life, women break down more frequently, for the trial and the change is greater in them, and fraught with greater peril. But now we do not find noisy mania with great motility. Old age is approaching, when strength is but labor and sorrow, when the fading fires of life bring less supply to the centres, and so melancholia is the rule, mania the exception. It is to be noted that melancholia is exhibited at this period rather than in more advanced age, when dementia and decay mark a worn-out rather than a disordered brain. From the melancholy there is a way of escape, but the dementia will slowly and surely advance to absolute extinction of mental power.

Again, we may observe an assemblage of pathological conditions making up the unit of disease exhibited in the patient. He may have inherited an unstable nervous nature, so the first cause or condition is *hereditary taint*, and this may or may not have already shown itself in previous attacks. The next condition is *age*. He or she has come to a time of life when the bodily organization is undergoing a change, and when the nerve centres are apt to become irregular in action. There may be superadded some loss or anxiety, or some lowering disorder, the supply of nerve energy is diminished, and melancholia is the result in the majority of cases. Where it does not amount to melancholia, the disorder is generally monomania, with suspicion and dislike, equally indicating a lowered self-tone. Occasionally we see merely an alteration of character, or the commencement of an incurable habit of drinking, and a gradual approach of that which begins as moral insanity and ends as hopeless dementia.

Let us now consider the pathology of another group of cases where insanity shows itself during pregnancy *c. Puerperal* or after labor. When we see the thousands of women *insanity.* who go through these periods with perfect immunity from all such symptoms, it is clear that the pregnant or parturient condition is only one of a number of causes which must be sought and investigated. It must be connected with the insanity by means of a series of links which are often very hard to find. As I suppose not one woman in a thousand becomes insane after her confinement, we must search among the so-called predisposing causes for some reason of the mind-disorder in those who thus break down, and we must very closely investigate the physical symptoms at the time the mental first appear. Those of you who will attend cases of midwifery will see such symptoms at an earlier period than I do, and you may be able then to arrest them. In insanity, as in so many other diseases, prevention is better than cure, and it is to this that modern science must direct its efforts. The necessity for strict examination of the whole of the conditions at the first commencement of the mental symptoms is shown when we see that the latter appear at very various periods. They may be first noticed during labor, immediately after, within a week, within the month, in two months, six months—in fact, at almost any period within a twelvemonth. After this we should not attribute them to the confinement; at any rate it would be a much more remote cause. They may appear in or after a perfectly easy and natural labor, or after one very difficult, and attended, possibly, with great exhaustion or hemorrhage. They may come on during lactation, or in a woman who has not suckled at all, or has long ceased to do so. When they make their appearance soon after labor, their approach is usually rapid and accompanied by acute symptoms, pain in the head, and sleeplessness. Here we notice that there is an accelerated rate of brain metamorphosis, not depending, as in the cases mentioned at the beginning of this lecture, on mental causes, on shock or the like, but on purely physical conditions. Now, we may observe that the nearer the first development of symptoms is to the time of delivery, the more violent and acute they are. Those which come on in the course of a week or fortnight are almost always attended with violence, sleeplessness, and great excitement, amounting to mania, whether the tendency is suicidal or not. Before delivery, or at a longer subsequent interval, the form is commonly melancholia or quiet monomania. This is accounted for by such theories as excitement from exhaustion, from the exhausting effects of labor; but frequently insanity makes its appearance in cases where delivery has been rapid, no exhaustion has taken place, or when the exhausting effects must have passed away, some weeks or months having elapsed before any symptoms are seen. Other disorders occur at the time of parturition: there may be convulsions or paralysis, and not very unfrequently death occurs from embolism of the pulmonary artery. In all these cases we may infer that alterations in the brain have taken place, producing various manifestations of deficient nervous power. The normal molecular changes are arrested and perverted by the distant irritation, or the arterial current is diminished through constriction of the vessels, brought about by disturbance of the vaso-motor centres, propagated by "sympathy" from the womb or its dependent parts, as the mammary glands. We know how mental causes may affect the lacteal secretion, and therefore the converse may be expected, that the cerebral organs may be disturbed by sympathetic "irritation" propagated thence.

There are various disorders, known as nymphomania, satyriasis, hysterical mania, and the like, which also *d. Nymphomania.* point to a connection between the insanity and the sexual organs. That such a connection exists needs no demonstration; everyday experience shows it, but shows that these organs are affected from the head downwards quite as often as the reverse, *e. g.*, the sight or smell of the female excites the male and the male organs hitherto quiescent. And when we see violent sexual excitement in the insane, we must not always assume that the origin is in the sexual organs, for I am convinced that it may be propagated from the excited brain to them. Here we must search through the analogies of other diseases and the teachings of pathology in general, and not be led away by a nomenclature into a rash conclusion drawn from phenomena which but too readily present themselves. It is extremely common to find in recent cases of insanity, where the patient is debilitated and out of health, that the catamenia are altogether absent, and the cessation accordingly is returned as the "cause" of the insanity. When the patient is recovering, and bodily and mental health returning, the catamenia reappear, and are said to have "cured" the brain disorder. But the absence of the function is quite as likely to be the concomitant as the cause of the mental symptoms, and we may be drawn away from the true pathology by fixing our attention too much upon it. If we look at the general constitution and the past history of any one of these patients, what do we learn? That she has always been what is popularly called nervous or hysterical, prone to emotional display, to bursts of temper, to hysterical crying, exaggerated, it may be, at the menstrual period. Most likely other members of the family are nervous, possibly some are insane. Thus is the old story repeated,—hereditary predisposition to nervous disorder, a proneness to be upset by trifling occurrences, an unstable cerebral condition, greatly influenced by sympathetic disturbance of the sexual organs and functions, and reacting in turn upon and violently exciting them. At first all these disturbances are for the most part temporary, very variable, perhaps periodical; later, they may become fixed and incurable.

Insanity in patients who have indulged largely in sexual excess or masturbation does not necessarily come under the last head, though masturbation may be, and constantly is, practiced by nymphomaniacal and hysterical women. Insanity accompanied by masturbation is a

e. Insanity of masturbation.

different thing from insanity caused thereby—different in its oncoming, different in its course and character, and rendering different the prognosis to be made concerning it. Insanity caused by masturbation is, generally speaking, gradual in its approach, not attended with any sudden or acute symptoms, but manifested in unpleasant conceit and exalted self-feeling, with delusions in accordance; this gradually increases, nor is there any great hope of cure, for the brain seems to have undergone permanent damage from the constant irritation to which it has been exposed by the practice of the habit. Such a state of things altogether differs from the violent, but often transient, outbursts of hysterical or nymphomaniacal insanity, which are by no means incurable; and it points to a different pathological condition. In the one we have brain disturbance coming on suddenly, possibly from some sympathetic uterine or ovarian irritation, which causes great disorder of the cerebral circulation, and an acute attack of insanity, from which the patient may recover. In the other, first the brain is gradually altered and impaired by the unceasing demands made upon it, and the constant excitation caused by the act of masturbation. We may compare the latter, though less in degree, to frequently-renewed attacks of epilepsy or of alcoholic intoxication, which produce mental disorder by their constant recurrence through a series of years.

The insanity which masturbation produces is for the most part seen in young persons, but there is another form found in those of middle age, the result of sexual excess or masturbation, which is known under the name of general paralysis. I shall hereafter describe this at length. Suffice it to say, that I believe the chief cause is sexual excess, whether in married or single life. Like the insanity produced in the young by masturbation, it is characterized by intense self-exaltation, by ideas of grandeur and importance, and a feeling of the most perfect health and strength; and it would seem to be lighted up in the first instance by the constant irritation to which the brain is exposed by the frequent repetition of the sexual act. We see other effects of sexual excess every day in ordinary practice, such as lassitude, dyspepsia, giddiness, dimness of sight. These are the results of expenditure and exhaustion of nerve power; but here, if the cause is removed, the effect ceases, and the patient recovers. Once, however, the insanity called general paralysis is set going, there is at present no cure for it known. This, of course, points to a pathological condition entirely differing from that of any curable or transient form of insanity.

As in some mere nervous exhaustion and bodily disorder are produced by masturbation and sexual excess, while in others genuine insanity is the result, so other causes, as epilepsy and alcohol, give rise to insanity in some, to decay of mind and body in others. The original constitution and pathological condition of the individuals being different, the result is different, though the cause is the same. We find in practice that patients in various ways, and through various stages, arrive at legal undsoundness of mind. In the eye of the law they are all alike, all incapable of taking care of themselves or their affairs; but to the pathologist they present infinite diversities, and the points of difference will be multiplied more and more as our means of scientific research are extended.

Let us take the various pathological conditions produced 4. Insanity by alcohol: there can be no better illustration of of alcohol. what I have just said. First of all, a man may be drunk, paralyzed in speech and ideas by alcohol, furious with drink, or wholly insensible. Another may suffer from *delirium tremens*, even after he has ceased drinking, perhaps for days. Besides these, we may notice a third state: instead of delirium tremens, which runs its course in a week or so to recovery or death, an attack of ordinary insanity with delusions may come on in a person accustomed to drink.

From this he may recover after a considerable period. And, besides, the habitual drinker, man or woman, may lapse into dementia, into utter obliteration of memory and mental power, into premature old age, from which he never will emerge again. In each of these states there is for the time unsoundness of mind from drink, but how great is the difference in the pathology of them! In the man who is drunk we see the effect of the alcohol circulating in the *a.* Drunken-blood, and conveyed in it to the brain-cells and ness. fibres; in fact, to the whole nervous system; mind centres and motor centres, afferent and efferent fibres, are all affected, and their functions more and more impaired, till absolute insensibility and paralysis, nay death itself, ensue. Can we say which of our nerve organs are implicated in these various states? In intoxication, as I have said, all seem affected. There is a disordered cerebral circulation, after even a moderate amount of wine or spirits, shown in flushing of the face and excitement in talking and manner. Very soon the movements of the tongue and lips are affected. There is some loss of control. The words are somewhat clipped, are not enunciated in a measured and even manner. This may occur in some before there is any confusion or impairment of mind, and appears due to an affection of the motor centres or fibres, or of the commissures which co-ordinate and focus the movements. I hold that these phenomena are due to the presence of alcohol, and not to mere alteration in the blood supply of the part, because we notice them in some who are very drowsy after taking wine—and by drowsy I do not mean comatose from drink—while others who are noisy and talkative exhibit the same. The mental symptoms correspond to the motor. There is at first a want of co-ordination of thought, an inability to recall just what is wanted at the moment, and this after a very small amount of wine; and yet there may be an entire absence of excitement, or anything denoting any great difference in the cerebral circulation. The presence of the alcohol, then, in the blood is the main pathological fact in this condition. When this is eliminated, the man is well again; but if it be present in large quantity he will die, and the experiments of Dr. Anstie on animals show that the mode of death is paralysis. The good effects of a glass of wine are possibly due to an increased circulation, brought about by the influence exercised over the vaso-motor system. When a man is intensely sleepy after taking strong drink, it would seem that his brain is deadened to ordinary stimuli. Owing to impure blood, all changes therein cease, as in narcotization from chloroform, only violent shaking or shouting can then rouse him.

But in delirium tremens we have a widely different state *b. Delirium* of things. This is but little removed pathologi-
tremens. cally from the acute delirium of the insane, though it is shorter in duration. It is not the actual presence of alcohol which causes the symptoms, for none may have been taken for days, so that it is often asserted that the withdrawal of drink is the cause, and we are told that we must not fail to give the accustomed stimulus when treating the disease. The truth, however, seems to be that by constant drinking—and, I may add, by loss of food, which is almost always the concomitant—the nerve centres are reduced to so unstable a condition, that the slightest thing, an accident, or grief, or anxiety, or any mental shock, upsets the balance; and then ensues that indication of a lack of power exhibited by muscular tremor, together with that incessant talking, sleeplessness, and mental disturbance, with which you are so familiar, denoting rapid molecular decomposition in the brain centres. We may see nearly the same attack in patients brought to a like unstable condition by exhaustion or want of food. But we shall not in these see the peculiar muscular tremor, though there may be convulsive or cataleptic phenomena of other kinds.

In delirium tremens it is evident that there is a disturb-

ance of the brain to such an extent, that unless it subsides
the patient is liable to die of exhaustion of his nervous
power, which has no chance of renewal. Modern research
has not yet enabled us to lay down with precision the pathological state of the brain in this disorder. Though the want
of sleep, the exalted temperature, and rapid pulse, point to
an accelerated molecular change, yet many facts lead us to
suppose that delirium is the result of a defect of the normal
blood supply. And we are, in my opinion, driven to the
belief that a combination of these states exists in the violent
delirium called *delirium tremens*, as well as in the delirium of
acute mania; that the accelerated blood-flow which at first
is manifested in sleeplessness, excitement, and incoherence
of thought, may increase to a point when, instead of a rush
of blood, there is a stagnation, at any rate in certain portions, and then wild delirium at once sets in.

Not rarely does insanity, mania, or melancholia, make its
appearance in people who have for years led lives of ~c. Insanity~
intemperance. Here we meet with a somewhat dif- ~from drink.~
ferent pathological condition. There may never have been
an attack of delirium tremens. The patients either have
not taken enough, or they have escaped the accidents which
lead up to it, or their constitution does not expose them to
this particular form of disorder. So, instead of the busy
wakeful delirium and incoherent wandering, we find the
delusions and outrageous acts of ordinary insanity. Patients
recover from these attacks, return to intemperate habits,
break down again, and may recover again and again, but,
rarely giving up drinking, they for the most part die in confirmed insanity. A few consent to remain under some sort
of control or surveillance, and so escape. If we consider the
probable pathology, we must conclude that the repeated
states of intoxication, like constantly renewed anxiety or
incessant labor of brain, bring about in time an irregularity
of circulation and of function, a certain instability and de-

fect which do not amount to delirium, but may be manifested in delusion and violent and maniacal conduct, with irregular and imperfect sleep. Abstinence, however, and the quiet of a life under control, may enable the brain to recover its balance; but I have known two years elapse before the cure was effected.

There is one more pathological state connected with the *d.* Imbecility habitual use of alcohol. After years of habitual from drink. drinking, drinking which may hardly have amounted to intoxication, far less to delirium tremens, we may perceive the mind weakening, memory failing, and the dotage of premature old age coming on; and not unfrequently with this decrepitude of mental power, we notice some amount of bodily paralysis, which slowly advances at the same time. This is the manner in which women often show the effect of drink, and for them there is no hope. We may reasonably infer that, from the long-continued poisoning, irritation, or whatever we like to call it, the nerve centres and nerve cells and fibres are degenerate, and have lost their structural perfection and efficiency. These cases are very curious and interesting to watch. Quite suddenly, without illness, sleeplessness, or excitement, memory gives way. The patient talks quite rationally and calmly, but does not distinguish yesterday from last week, thinks friends long dead are alive, and when set right, makes the same mistake five minutes afterwards.

Here is commencing dementia, a pathological condition resulting from many antecedent events, of which drinking is one. I have known patients recover to a considerable extent, but in all there was left some amount of weakness, mental or bodily. They did not regain their former state as a man does after delirium tremens.

There are some substances besides alcohol which, by constant use, may bring about insanity. Notably, this 5. Insanity from other is the effect of bhang, or Indian hemp, which sends poisons. many patients to asylums in India, producing a form of excitable mania with delusions, from which they for the most part recover. You will not meet with these cases in our own country, but in certain parts of the East they are common. In Europe there is a preparation of *absinthium*, which is also said to produce mental symptoms, if largely taken. There is much controversy, however, concerning it, many asserting that the harm done by *absinthe* depends on the alcohol taken, and not on any peculiar properties of the herb. I am not aware that any but an alcoholic preparation is ever drunk, so that it is difficult to come to any decision on the subject. That opium produces curious phenomena and trains of ideas out of the control of the will, may, I think, be admitted by all. I cannot say, however, that in my experience it has been often found to produce insanity. The anomalous symptoms are due to the actual presence of opium, to a poisoning going on at the time; but if it is withdrawn, these vanish. The brain and nervous system are affected, as are those of a man breathing nitrous acid gas; but when the cause is removed, the effect ceases, and the pathological condition is not one which deserves the name of insanity, any more than that of a man who is drunk with alcohol, or delirious under the influence of chloroform or nitrous oxide. Practically, we do not find that opium eating or smoking swells the population of the lunatic asylums of this or other countries. There is an immense difference between the results of the continual use of opium and alcohol. Dr. Christison even thinks that opium-eating does not necessarily shorten life. Certain it is, that our two most noted opium-eaters, De Quincey and S. T. Coleridge, lived, the former to the age of seventy-four, the latter to that of sixty-one years.

Turn we now to a different pathological state, to that of a patient in whom insanity has appeared consequent 6. Insanity upon a blow on the head. So numerous are the cere- after a blow. bral symptoms which, at varying intervals, follow blows, that it can cause no surprise if among these we occasionally meet

with insanity. Imbecility, paralysis of limbs, a gradually
advancing decay of mental and bodily power, is perhaps a
more frequent sequel than insanity, strictly so called, yet this
is to be found. When after a blow a man or a woman develops insanity in the form of mania or melancholia, or gradually becomes altered in character, or subject to fixed delusions,
we may conclude that the injury the brain has undergone is
not of the coarse character described in works on surgery.
There is no traumatic inflammation of the brain-substance,
or the membranes, such as we are accustomed to see in the
post-mortem theatre of our hospitals. We have to deal with
a much more minute and molecular change—a change commencing, it may be, in the contusion of the gray matter
caused by a blow or fall, and producing an alteration in the
nourishment and growth of the part, in the blood supply, or
in the nerves presiding over it. That condition which I have
vaguely called instability of nerve function and force may be
in this manner set up, as it comes to others by inheritance;
and so it frequently happens that men who have received
blows on the head are driven to a state of frenzy or mania
by slight causes, which would produce little or no effect on
an uninjured and healthy brain, such as a very small amount
of drink, or trivial matters exciting anger or grief. From
such transient attacks patients recover, and return to their
normal state of equipoise, to be thrown off their balance again
by some other disturbing event. But when the change in
the mind is insidious and gradual, when acute symptoms are
absent, and either quiet and concealed delusions, or a mere
perversion and alteration of the whole man are alone to be
noticed, our prognosis must be extremely unfavorable, if we
hear a history of a blow or fall on the head.

There is yet another pathological condition brought about
by a cause external to the individual. This is the insanity
developed in people, chiefly men, who have been long exposed to the heat of the tropics, whether they have had an

actual sunstroke or not. Even here in exceptionally hot summers, such as that of 1868, not a few cases are directly attributable to this cause; and in my own ex- perience I have met with a large number of patients who, either in India, or on returning thence, have shown symptoms of insanity. Of course, when we say that heat causes insanity, we are speaking of patients who have been subjected to a degree of heat to which they are unaccustomed, and which by their race and constitution they are little fitted to endure. I am not now comparing the natives of tropical countries with those of colder regions. The former lead for the most part simple lives, and are temperate as regards the use of alcoholic drink. The dwellers in cold climates, as Sweden and Norway, are notoriously intemperate, and we have seen already how large a part this habit plays in the causation of insanity. Here, as in so many other conditions, we shall find that the man who is by inherited nature of an unstable nerve organization will succumb to the influences of climate, particularly if, in addition to these two causes, he combines the effect of intemperate habits, or of exhaustion produced by mental anxiety or bodily illness.

7. Insanity after exposure to heat.

LECTURE IV.

The Pathology of Insanity, continued—Senile Insanity—General Pa-
ralysis—Insanity in Acute Diseases—Recurrent Insanity—Idiopathic
Insanity—Insanity with Epilepsy—Insanity with Rheumatism—With
Syphilis—With other Neuroses—With Diseases of the Head, Liver,
Heart, Kidneys, Stomach—Insanity with Tuberculosis—With Pe-
ripheral Irritation—Do the Mental Symptoms correspond with the
Pathological variety ?—What is the Pathology of Insanity ?

THERE are patients who go through life as sane men, and
8. Senile break down and become insane when they have grown
insanity. old, not at the climacteric period, but when old age
has finally begun. Although we call this *senile dementia,* and set it down as dotage, second childhood, the commencement of a decay which is to spread over mind and
body, yet we may notice at the beginning many of the
symptoms of insanity. There may be at first mental alteration rather than alienation—that alteration of character,
habits, conduct, and affections, which, existing without delusions, has been called moral or emotional insanity. Or
delusions may exist with acute symptoms, violence, and
sleeplessness. We cannot but conclude here that the age,
and the decay or want of vigor in the various organs concerned in mind, guide us to the pathological state, and indicate that changes, both structural and functional, have commenced. When we see the numberless cases of old people
in which after death an atrophied condition of brain is found,
we can understand how the defect of circulation or of nutritive blood, which has led in some people to simple atrophy,
may cause in others more marked mental disturbance, resulting in positive insanity rather than in the negation of mind

termed *dementia*. That the one will merge into the other may reasonably be expected. We are not to hope for a cure of either, but as pathologists we may draw a distinction between senile insanity and senile dementia.

I may mention in this place, though I shall not now discuss it at length, that special form of insanity which is called *general*, or *progressive paralysis of the insane*, which I have already incidentally noticed in speaking of the insanity of masturbation. Here, beyond question, we have a disease well defined, recognizable, fatal to life, and running a rapid course, little influenced by care or treatment. The pathological conditions of this must needs be different from those of mental disorder lasting for the term of a life. There are various conditions which are quite peculiar to it. It is far more common in men than in women. It rarely, if ever, attacks people under the age of twenty or over sixty. Generally, we may say that it attacks men in the prime of life. Now, what is the causation of this disorder? I myself am strongly of opinion that in a large majority of cases sexual excess, either venery or masturbation, is the chief excitant of this fatal form of insanity. Then, what is the seat of it? We might surely expect that there would be no difficulty in determining the seat of a malady which destroys life in a year or two. But pathologists are not agreed on this point. One, at least, has tried to prove that the seat is in the spinal cord; and though this is not consistent with the mental symptoms and the affection of speech, yet if my theory of the origin being sexual excess is correct, we may expect to find that the spinal cord is involved, and even that disease of the latter precedes in some cases that of the brain. The peculiarity is that this form is progressive—that, even if we have remissions and apparent recoveries, the latter are not real, the damage already done is not thoroughly repaired, and after a brief interval the symptoms return in greater force, and advance gradually though surely to extinction of

9. General paralysis of the insane.

life. All these topics must be discussed at length hereafter. At present it suffices to place general paralysis apart as a special pathological variety, having affinities with the other forms of insanity, but distinct from them.

I know not whether I ought to speak of recurrent insanity as a pathological variety. All insanity is apt to recur, and to assume different forms at different times. But it sometimes happens that it recurs with such regularity as to constitute a marked and characteristic disorder, which for purposes of prognosis and treatment has to be considered apart. We may watch a man or a woman pass through an attack of, perhaps, acute mania. Gradually reason returns, the symptoms subside, and the patient goes on to convalescence without a single drawback; but just as we think that he may safely be freed from control, suddenly, perhaps in a few hours, the whole thing begins again, and he goes through the same stages, again to recover and again to relapse. This may go on for years, the intervals varying according to circumstances and surroundings; the attacks also differing in severity, but the disorder remaining uncured, and never losing its recurrent character, even when dementia has taken the place of a return to a state of sanity. These intervals vary from weeks to years. I formerly had under my care a man of more than eighty years, whose first attack happened when he was seventeen, and who, in the interval, had been put into confinement three-and-thirty times. I know another gentleman who breaks down every two years or thereabouts; but in many the attacks follow one another with so short an interval that they remain permanent inmates of asylums. Could we accurately define the condition of such patients, we should have solved the pathology of insanity. They seem to be the very *crux* of the whole matter, for we cannot, as a rule, assign any cause for the recurrence. The disorder once set up in the individual's constitution is prone to recur, and we must examine the whole question of the periodicity of disease, as well as the conditions of the first attack, before we can hope to throw any light on the subject. This much we may conclude, that the conditions which precede the first, are not necessary to subsequent attacks; that as epileptic seizures may continue after the ostensible cause of the first fit is removed, *e. g.*, worms, so the disorder once recurring may repeat itself, persistently remaining as a vice of the constitution of the individual, of which it now forms a portion. We know that there is a periodical rise and fall in almost all diseases— a time of day at which fever-patients are worse or better, a time of year at which other disorders recur—and we may compare with this the periodical season of sleep, of fecundation, of nutrition, and such like normal functions of the animal organism. These cases of recurrent insanity may present the phenomena of attacks of mania, alternating with recovery, or of melancholia, also alternating with recovery, but besides, mania may alternate with melancholia, constituting what the French call *folie circulaire*, or *folie à double forme*. The one may succeed the other immediately, or there may be between them a period of convalescence and sanity, such as is called by lawyers a "lucid interval." This has been described as a special form of insanity ; it is, however, but a variety of that which I have termed recurrent insanity, with an alternation in the emotional condition of the patient.

I now come to a class of cases which I do not myself hold to be a pathological variety, but which I mention Idiopathic because it is so arranged by some writers for whose insanity. opinion I have the utmost respect. This is the form which has been described as *idiopathic insanity*, whereby is meant that it cannot be brought under any one of the heads already mentioned, and no cause for it can be assigned. In the majority of the certificates brought with patients to asylums the cause of the insanity is returned as unknown, and frequently this may be the truth. In a great number of cases, however, we should more truly say that the patient is insane because his father, or mother, or grandfather, or grandmother was insane before him. Idiopathic insanity is that which makes its appearance in an individual without assignable cause, simply because by his inherited nature he has a tendency to become insane. But we must still ask the question, What is his pathological condition at the time the insanity is first manifested? In what does he differ from sane brothers and sisters, all offspring of the same parents? As the symptoms of this insanity differ in no respect from that which is brought about by other conditions, moral or physical, we can only say that the patient, through an inherited tendency to disturbance of his nerve centres, or through a disturbance engendered in them by an assemblage of conditions so obscure that we cannot demonstrate them, has arrived at the same state pathologically as others who through grief, or work, or parturition, or drink, have developed insanity. Whatever be the assemblage of conditions giving rise to an attack of mania or melancholia, it is probable that the pathological condition of the patients at the time is very nearly the same, and so we find that with little variety in the treatment a large majority of cases recover merely by being kept in rest and safety during a certain period of time; and we also find that patients recovered, though not in the same proportions, in former ages, when detention was all the benefit which they received, the treatment, when there was any, being of very questionable utility.

The remaining pathological conditions which I shall briefly review are all of them combinations of bodily diseases, such as may exist alone, and mental disturbance, giving rise to that which we call insanity. The latter may present itself in patients who are the victims of chronic diseases, as phthisis, syphilis, or rheumatism. It may coexist with disease of the heart, liver, or kidneys. It may accompany epilepsy, or come on quite suddenly in the course of acute disorders, measles, pneumonia, fevers, and the like. The consideration of all these conditions involves some most obscure and intricate questions of pathology; but I think that a careful examination of the phenomena throws some light on the nature of the disorder of the brain. In all these it is clear that we have a combination of conditions making up one pathological whole. As thousands of patients suffer from the above-mentioned diseases without any signs of insanity, we must look for other concomitant causes besides those I have mentioned.

The first class of such cases of which I shall speak is that of insanity occurring in the course or at the decline of acute disorders. And here, to shorten what I have to say, I may direct you to an interesting paper 10. Insanity in acute diseases. on the subject by Dr. Hermann Weber, in the 48th volume of the "Medico-Chirurgical Transactions." In this he gives the particulars of seven cases of measles, scarlatina, erysipelas, pneumonia, and typhoid fever, where, towards the decline of the disorder, maniacal delirium came on, with delusions of an anxious nature, and hallucinations of the senses, especially of hearing, but also of sight. The duration of the derangement was short, extending from less than eight to forty-eight hours. The outbreak was sudden, the time was in general the early morning. *Almost always the commencement was stated to have occurred immediately after waking.*

These cases are called by Dr. Weber the "delirium of collapse"—a name, however, which throws but little light on their pathology. The points to be borne in mind are the transitory nature of the attack, its sudden oncoming, especially on waking from sleep, and the partial nature of the delirium, this taking the form of delusions, and not being the general incoherent wandering of the ordinary delirium of fever. We may suppose that the combination of conditions is something of this kind. First, the patient is by inheritance "excitable;" his nerve-balance is easily upset. "Excitable," "naturally anxious and excitable," "over-conscientious," are terms applied by Dr. Weber to several of his patients. By the acute disorder and the accompanying fever, the temperature has been considerably raised, and the circulation necessarily disturbed. During the heightened temperature, Dr. Weber tells us, there was no delirium ; but the circulation and temperature fall, less blood is carried to the exhausted brain centres, sleep comes on when the brain circulation is even more reduced, and then on waking suddenly from a short sleep delusions more or less of a melancholic or anxious character manifest themselves ; food and opiates procure a long sleep, and the brain circulation having regained its normal condition, the delusions vanish. The sudden outbreak of insanity on waking from a short sleep is familiar to all who have the care of the insane. In acute mania, patients who sleep half an hour, or an hour, often wake in a furious paroxysm. Many a crime is committed by others subject to transient attacks of insanity, when they are just awakened from an insufficient sleep. Suddenly to wake even a sleeping dog is a thing which most look upon as attended with risk. It is a matter of common observation that melancholic patients, who especially manifest a lack of force, are almost invariably more dejected at first waking; and I have known a lady, who was in no sense insane, habitually depressed to an extreme degree when she first woke, the feeling passing away as the circulation was restored by exercise.

After these cases, I may proceed to the consideration of insanity caused by epilepsy. As we saw that there was a form of insanity, as well as imbecility and chronic dementia, brought about by alcohol, so after an epileptic attack, or series of attacks, we may have a transient outburst of delirium, or an invasion of insanity with delusions, lasting from days to weeks, and then passing off, and

11. Insanity with epilepsy.

leaving the patient sound in mind until a fresh seizure occurs. This is a condition quite distinct from the loss of memory and general dementia, which, if the fits are at all frequent, gradually encroaches upon the mind, and almost without exception terminates the career of every epileptic, even when there has been no insanity properly so called throughout the entire illness. Can we in any way account for an attack of delirium or of mania supervening in one person after epileptic attacks, while another comes out of them comparatively unscathed? Here we must suppose that the disturbance of the brain circulation implied by the epileptic seizure does not at once subside as it does in a patient who in an hour appears to be in all respects sane and unchanged; the reaction, if we may so term it, after the fit or fits, brings about a great disturbance of the circulation, and, according to the degree thereof, symptoms of insanity may appear, varying from a moderate mania to wild and unconscious delirium. The more numerous the attacks the more likely is mania to supervene. I have known a patient who, after three or four fits, woke sane; but if they were more numerous, if he had twelve or thirteen, he was for days in a state of mania, with many hallucinations and delusions—a state which was not cured at once by a sleep, but which gradually subsided like an attack of ordinary insanity, and was, in fact, in all respects the counterpart of it. The point to notice is that so many patients suffer from epileptic fits without undergoing this general disturbance; though their brain circulation is so disordered that we see first the fit, and then possibly a prolonged condition of comatose sleep, yet here the disturbance terminates, and the sufferer wakes sane.

The dementia attending upon chronic epilepsy is at any rate more easy to comprehend; but we must not too hastily set this down to structural change, for it is marvellous how some patients, long lost in speechless idiocy, recover intelligence and power, if by some chance, or some medicine, the fits are arrested. Exhaustion of force is clearly here to be noticed. The constant fits prevent this from ever accumulating in adequate quantity; but, if they cease, it again shows its presence in the centres. For I take it that in the convulsions the force of the entire cerebral system is poured out in muscular movement. When the attack is but slight, then consciousness is not lost at all, or only for a moment.

Passing from the combination of insanity and epilepsy, we come to another, insanity and rheumatism or gout. This is a commonly recognized complication, and we not unfrequently find stated in books, and observe in practice, that the symptoms of the one disorder vanish as those of the other appear, and *vice versa*. I myself have seen phenomena of very acute insanity disappear quite suddenly, to be followed by great pain and swelling of hands or feet. This has been called *metastatic* insanity, and it has been supposed that the seat of the inflammation, caused by a blood poison, is transferred from the brain or its membranes to the joints. We may, at any rate, remark that there is a marked analogy between the way that the acute symptoms of transient mania often entirely subside and vanish, and that in which we see the pain, heat, and redness of a joint disappear within a few hours, leaving nothing behind but some stiffness and tenderness as relics of what appeared most acute inflammation. It is not for me to tell you what is the exact pathology of acute rheumatism or of gout; the differences of opinion which still exist among observers of these common maladies may at any rate be some set-off against the doubts and difficulties that beset me in trying to lay down as facts the pathological conditions of insanity. But when we see how the connective tissue is attacked by these disorders, how acute are the symptoms, and how rapid and complete their disappearance, we may suspect that the connective tissue of the brain may occasionally participate;

12. Insanity with rheumatism or gout.

and as the vessels going to the gray substance are meshed
in this, it may well be that the brain circulation is in this
manner greatly disturbed.

The connection between rheumatism and insanity, rheumatism and chorea, and rheumatism and other head symptoms, has been dwelt upon by many physicians—Griesinger,
Trousseau, Sander, Hughlings Jackson—and a most interesting account of two cases, in which rheumatism, chorea, and
insanity coexisted, is given by Dr. Clouston in the "Journal
of Mental Science," July, 1870. Here the rheumatism was
the first symptom. In one case, a woman aged twenty-four,
the rheumatism existed for two months before the insanity.
It suddenly abated, and mental and choreic symptoms commenced. There was loss of power in all the limbs, the legs
were quite paralyzed, and reflex action destroyed. The mind
was in a state of stupor and depression. Recovery took place
in about three months. The second patient, a lad of nineteen, had already had chorea at the age of seven and thirteen. After an acute attack of rheumatism of two weeks,
choreic symptoms commenced, with strangeness of manner,
restlessness, and inattention. His mind then became greatly
confused, with hallucinations of vision, delusions, and occasionally refusal of food. Recovery took place in about three
months. Dr. Clouston remarks, that the symptoms were
very similar in both these cases; in both the rheumatism
was the commencement of the attack; in both there were
choreic symptoms, paralysis of motor power, a deadening of
the reflex action of the legs, similar mental phenomena,
high temperature, increased at night, and a tendency to improvement in all the symptoms coincident with the lowering
of the temperature, showing that the same lesion existed in
both. All this, he thinks, indicates " a serious but transitory
interference with the functions of the nerve cells and fibres
in the spinal cord, such as might be produced by slight rheu-

matic inflammation, and infiltration of the connective tissue of the cord causing pressure on the nerve elements."

Other cases which appear to constitute a pathological class

13. Insanity with syphilis. are those in connection with syphilis. Probably, as inquirers pursue their investigation of this form, we shall gain a clearer insight into the manner in which the constitutional poison affects the higher brain centres. There have been various observations published of late on disease caused remotely by syphilis, producing alterations in the walls of arteries, and other lesions. I have seen a woman whose insanity appeared to be unquestionably of syphilitic origin, and who had had symptoms of paralysis, such as ptosis, also looked upon as syphilitic, and treated as such. This woman was placed in an asylum, where she recovered perfectly. Here the pathological changes could not have advanced far, and may have consisted in alterations in the quality of the blood, or in the supplying vessels, of a nature which treatment removed. But such cases of recovery are not very common. Syphilitic insanity is usually spoken of as syphilitic dementia, which gradually progresses till life is extinguished in no long time. And the appearance found after death is described as syphiloma, or a gummy tumor found within the brain itself, or a diffuse fibrinous exudation between the membranes and the brain. The whole points to a condition I shall have to advert to again, in which the normal textures, the brain-cells, fibres, and vessels undergo a retrograde metamorphosis, and are invaded by, or converted into, lower forms of life, connective tissue, exudation corpuscles, or albuminous products hardly organized at all.

In speaking on the subject of hereditary transmission, I

14. Insanity with other neuroses. shall have occasion to point out to you that amongst the children of nervous or insane parents one may be hysterical, one hypochondriacal, a third a drunkard, a fourth epileptic, or a fifth insane. But you may also find two of these neuroses combined in one individual, or

alternating in him or her. Thus hypochondria may drift into insanity, and, as the insanity passes off, the symptoms of hypochondria will again become prominent. So with hysteria. Besides the hysterical mania so often witnessed, insanity, mania, or melancholia may take the place of the former hysterical attacks. And it has often been remarked, and I myself have several times met with instances, that neuralgia may be followed by insanity, the pain vanishing during the mental disturbance, and reappearing as the latter passed away. In one case, neuralgia of the spine, for which a gentleman was kept to the sofa for some months, was followed by deep melancholia. In another, very acute mania followed neuralgic pain, which a young lady had endured for a long period. Sir B. Brodie narrates similar cases in his work on " Local Nervous Affections." Now, that hysteria and hypochondria are mental affections is all but universally acknowledged, and we merely see an alteration in the symptoms of the neurosis, depending upon some altered condition of the patient, just as mania alternates with melancholia in the so-called *folie circulaire*. And in the transition of a neuralgia we may well believe that the neurotic affection is merely changed from one nerve centre to another. from the centres of sensation to those of mind. The prognosis, so far as the passing away of the first attack of insanity is concerned, is favorable in all these cases, but the whole state of the patient is one of evil omen; for it is clear that the nervous system is highly unstable, and not likely to be free from disorder of some kind or other, while, as years go by, the form of this will probably be more and more serious and incurable.

Insanity coexists not only with acute disorders, or such as epilepsy, syphilis, or rheumatism, but also with others, whether it be caused by them or not. We find it coexisting with diseases of the head, of the lungs, the heart, the liver, and kidneys. I must pass in review each of these organs, but this much may be said with reference to them all. In estimating the connection which exists between insanity and diseases of the above-mentioned organs, it is of no use to examine the statistics of post mortem examinations conducted in large lunatic asylums, unless we tabulate the results in a manner much more precise than that usually met with. The commonest source of fallacy is this. A large number of the patients who die in asylums have been insane for years; it is therefore impossible to say whether the disease of lungs, heart, or liver, found after death, was, or was not, a pathological condition coexisting with the commencement of the insanity. When we discover tubercles in the lungs of a patient who has for perhaps twenty years undergone confinement in an asylum, with all the concomitants and depression arising out of such a life, we may well believe that the lung disease is long subsequent to the insanity. When another patient has been for an equal time constantly subject to violent excitement, we need not be surprised to find his heart in an altered state.

Let us first take the head : if you examine the records of 15. Insanity the post-mortem examinations made in any large with diseases asylum, you will probably be struck with the ab- of the head. sence of disease in the brain sufficient to account for death: and if you compare them with the case-books, you will learn that patients die comatose after the exhaustion of acute mania, or sink from exhaustion without coma, or die of apnœa or syncope, but will comparatively seldom find the diseases of the brain met with in the post-mortem theatres of our general hospitals, such as tumor, abscess, hydatids, inflammation of an acute character of the brain or membranes, or tubercular meningitis. From the latter causes unsoundness of mind may undoubtedly spring, and legally we may have to deal with patients brought by one of them to this condition, but they chiefly produce feebleness of intellect, and wandering and dementia, or delirium or coma, such as you see in the wards here, and not insanity proper, such as I am more especially speaking of, which is treated in special asylums and institutions for the insane. Nevertheless, the presence of a tumor in any part within the cranial cavity may give rise to insanity, and in our autopsies of the insane we occasionally find such. We must conjecture that the derangement is caused by the sympathetic irritation of such foreign bodies rather than by their actual invasion of the parts concerned in mental operations. When the latter happens, we should expect dulness and imbecility, not insanity. We may also conjecture that in a patient in whom insanity is caused by a tumor, other pathological conditions exist favorable to the development; thus, of a woman who died at St. Luke's Hospital, in whose right cerebral hemisphere was found a tumor of the size of a pullet's egg, it is recorded that her sister was insane. In this case mania existed for two months, but before death there were noticed drowsiness, ptosis of the left eyelid, and loss of memory. In assigning a pathological value as " causes " of insanity to the various morbid products found after death, we must consider well whether they may not be the results of the excessive action which has gone on in the head. The various effusions, extravasations, and layers of exudation found among the cerebral membranes may be given as instances, with other appearances hereafter to be mentioned. Important questions may hinge upon our interpretation of these, as, for example, the duration of mental disease, estimated by post-mortem examination,—a point not unfrequently raised in the Court of Probate.

We may conclude that the ordinary forms of insanity, such as we term mania, monomania, or melancholia, are rarely caused by morbid growths within the head, or by acute inflammation of the brain or membranes; that where they are thus produced, there is usually a strong predisposition depending on other pathological conditions coexisting

in the individual; and this insanity may disappear for a time
and then recur, being lighted up anew by the irremovable
cause. We may learn from this what a functional disturbance insanity is, even when springing from an organized
cause, and how strong the tendency of the individual life
of the brain-cells is towards recovery, so long as it is not
seriously interfered with by conflicting morbid conditions.

In spite of the ancient theories of insanity being caused by
black bile, I believe the liver has little to do with the
pathological condition of a patient who has recently
become insane. In the general disorder of the system existing at such a time, the liver may participate, but it
is not the cause of all the mischief, as so many, especially the
friends, try to establish. The liver is the best abused organ
of the body; whatever be the matter, nine people out of ten
ascribe the blame to the liver, and cannot be convinced of
the contrary. Little is to be learned from post-mortem appearances; there is nothing more than may be observed in
the livers of those dying of ordinary diseases in a general
hospital. Congestion, a softened and friable state, enlargement rather than shrinking, are what we chiefly see.

16. Insanity with disease of the liver.

In the post-mortem theatre the hearts of insane patients
very frequently present morbid appearances, but we
are not to connect these with the outbreak of the insanity. Their nature indicates that they are the
result of the long-continued, violent, and the irregular action
of the organ during many years. That which we shall most
commonly find in chronic cases is that the right side is very
much thinner than usual, and probably dilated, and that the
left ventricle is thickened. In quite recent cases the whole
may be healthy, or possibly there is a softened, friable, greasy
condition without loss of substance. The valves are not diseased more frequently than usual, but the right auriculo-
ventricular opening is often very large. Dr. Sutherland
states, in his Croonian Lectures, that of forty-two patients

17. Insanity with disease of the heart.

examined at St. Luke's Hospital in the years 1853–56, the heart was healthy in eight cases only.

There is little to be said concerning the kidneys. In the pathology of commencing insanity they play a very unimportant part, and even after death they are not often found diseased. Acute renal disease with albuminuria and dropsy is decidedly rare amongst the insane.

18. Insanity with disease of the kidney.

Dyspepsia and functional derangement of the stomach are common, but are not to be looked upon as primary disorders, but rather as caused by the disturbance of the nervous system. Vomiting is not common even amongst patients who refuse their food from alleged dislike and want of appetite, and the whole of the phenomena of dyspepsia are to be studied most carefully from an objective point of view. We are not to be too much influenced by the patient's own subjective sensations : numberless are the delusions connected with the stomach and intestines.

19. Insanity with disease of stomach and bowels.

Similarly functional derangement of the bowels and the uterine organs may exist without actual disease. Obstinate constipation is a common symptom also to be referred to the nervous condition, and varying with it. Much has been made of an occasional displacement of the large intestine met with after death. The transverse colon descends and lies across the hypogastric region or in the pelvis. I think it possible that violent struggling and straining, especially under mechanical restraint, have something to do with this. We find tumors of the womb or ovaries, and are able to connect these with the insanity, and even with the delusions. I have already spoken of insanity in connection with the sexual organs, and have nothing further to add here.

I have left till last the question of the connection of insanity and tuberculosis, because authors differ on this. In the "Journal of Mental Science," April, 1863, Dr. Clouston has described a variety as *phthisical insanity*, characterized, as he says, by suspicion, irrita-

20. Insanity with tuberculosis.

bility, unsociableness, disinclination to exert the mind and body, and the absence of any acute symptoms. These cases of pure monomania of suspicion terminate, almost all, according to Dr. Clouston, in tuberculosis. But not only does Dr. Clouston describe this special form of phthisical insanity; he asserts, in addition, that tubercle is found in the bodies of those dying insane much more frequently than in the sane; that in the former it is to be found in 60 per cent., in the latter in about 25 per cent. We must recollect, however, that Dr. Clouston's statistics are based mainly on the records of the Royal Edinburgh Asylum, though he casually mentions the asylums of Prague, Vienna, and the Salpêtrière. When, however, we turn to the carefully recorded post-mortem examinations of Dr. Boyd, at the Somerset Asylum, we find that of 302 examinations conducted in the years 1862-67, only in 61 were tubercles found. I hold that statistics drawn from asylum life prove little as regards the connection between phthisis and insanity, unless it can be shown that tubercles existed previous to the admission, and coexisted with the commencement of the mental symptoms. The fact of tubercle existing in the body of a patient who has died after twenty years in an asylum is of little import. If it were possible, we ought to compare with such statistics those of insane patients who have never been in an asylum. From my own experience, I should say that there is no more tuberculosis among these than amongst the non-insane world. I have inquired at the Hospital for Consumption whether in that establishment any connection between insanity and tuberculosis is recognized, and I am assured by the senior physician, who is corroborated by the gentleman who has been the resident officer for twenty years, that no more, but probably a less number of cases of insanity occur there than in a general hospital. An insane patient is quite an exception in the wards of the Consumption Hospital, the only head symptoms being in connection with tubercular meningitis.

Dr. Cotton also says that it has been stated that families in which consumption is prevalent exhibit a strong tendency to insanity, but that his own experience is quite opposed to such a conclusion. He goes on to remark that phthisis and melancholia are seldom seen together; that consumptive patients are, as a rule, cheerful and hopeful; that in the very many absolutely hopeless cases of consumption he has seen, he has never suspected a tendency to suicide. Now, we see phthisis and insanity combined in asylums, but I am disposed to believe that there is no necessary connection between them, no connection other than may exist between insanity and any depressing or wasting disorder. Dr. Clouston, in his Report of the Cumberland Asylum, 1870, says: "The small number of patients that have died of consumption in the asylum up to this year, and the comparatively small number of cases of that special form of insanity which I have alluded to, attest, I think, the sufficiency of our dietary, the healthy situation of the asylum, and the attention paid to cleanliness and ventilation in it." From this it would seem that Dr. Clouston himself suspects that the phthisis may be due to asylum influences, and not necessarily connected with the insanity. Looking at the statistics of phthisical insanity, I find that most of the cases are returned as mania, and that melancholia is comparatively rare. Whatever be the disease in the lungs, the circulation in the brain appears to be vigorous, as we should expect from the high rate of the pulse. And we know that phthisical patients, beyond any others, retain their mental faculties unimpaired to the last.

When various pathological conditions favorable to the development of insanity coexist in an individual, there wants but some one weakening or depressing agent to bring about the result. And this may be effected by tuberculosis of the lung, or by some other disease, acute or chronic. I have just seen acute insanity produced or preceded in two men by disease of the bladder, in a woman by chronic vomiting. The pathology here is not difficult to comprehend; but we also read of mental disorder following the healing of eruptions, ulcers, discharges, and the like. I confess that I think the *post hoc* and *propter hoc* in these cases are often confounded.

Cases are on record where an attack of insanity has passed
21. Insanity with periph- eral irrita- tion.
off upon the expulsion of a tape-worm, upon the removal of a piece of glass from the sole of a boy's foot, or the cure of a displaced uterus. Here a central disturbance is caused by an irritation of a peripheral nerve akin to the reflex paralysis which often follows injuries of the periphery. Such cases warn us closely to examine into the condition of all patients brought under our observation, for by the discovery of such matters we may cure an insanity which otherwise might have become chronic.

Thus have I briefly mentioned certain assemblages of pathological conditions which may be found coexisting in insane patients, and which may warrant our calling the malady with which they are visited puerperal insanity, alcoholic insanity, and so on. I have indicated them in mere outline. At present we can do little more; but as observations accumulate, we shall be able to fill in this outline, and probably add to or subdivide these classes. That which is now so often called idiopathic insanity will, by the light of a clearer knowledge, be resolved into its true pathological colors, and we shall be better able to trace the connection between the conditions and causes of insanity and the mental manifestations which are the symptoms of it. And here I must advert for a moment to this classification of insanity. You will see that if these are varieties and divisions of insanity, they are not the varieties of which you have been accustomed to hear. I do not divide the disease into mania, melancholia, dementia. The latter terms express the mental symptoms;

the divisions I have given aim at the expression of the pathological condition of the patient. But some phy- Do the mental sicians have thought that with certain of these symptoms correspond with pathological conditions there is to be seen a pecu- the pathological variety? liar assemblage of mental symptoms characteristic of that variety of insanity. Dr. Maudsley tells us that masturbating insanity has its proper symptoms; Dr. Clouston thinks those of phthisical insanity are marked and peculiar, just as are those of the great majority of the cases of general paralysis or of climacteric insanity. These opinions may be quite true, but yet they explain little. The mental symptoms of a patient at any particular moment are the expression of the pathological state of his brain at the time, and, as I have already said (p. 61), the same patient may be one day maniacal and the next melancholic; or of two women insane after confinement, one may be melancholic, the other maniacal. But every person differs in mind from all others, though to some extent he resembles them, and he differs according to the physical organization of his system, his nervous, visceral, and muscular development. He may vary also at different times, vary in strength and endurance, in nervous as in muscular power, according as he is in or out of health. If we could find a dozen men exactly alike, the same cause of insanity would produce the same mental phenomena by producing the same pathological state of brain; but as men and women vary indefinitely, it appears to me a mere accident if the same cause produces the same symptoms. Masturbating insanity, as described by Dr. Maudsley, comes on in young men of about the age of twenty; therefore in their disorder they closely resemble one another. Climacteric insanity comes on in those who are beginning to decline in years and strength; hence the symptoms are alike, and are chiefly those of melancholia. But if we look at the enormous number of cases of melancholia which occur in patients not in their climacteric, and if we find symptoms similar to those of phthisical insanity, or masturbating insanity, in patients who are not phthisical and who do not masturbate, it is obvious that a like pathological condition has arisen, though from some other cause or assemblage of causes, just as we have the same symptoms arising from idiopathic or traumatic tetanus and from strychnia poison. I believe that mental symptoms are most valuable indications, and are not to be neglected; that melancholia or mania implies a state of the nervous centres which must be taken into account in our prognosis and treatment; but that this insane state may be brought about in the individual by many different pathological causes. We find every exalted delusion, such as is noticed among paralytics, in those who are not paralytic, and in paralytics we may see the deepest melancholia. We are told that when puerperal insanity commences in the first fortnight after confinement, it shows itself in puerperal mania; when later, in melancholia. Here the difference must be due to the different state of health of the patient at the two dates, not to anything special in the exciting cause of the disease.

If, after due consideration of the causes and symptoms of insanity, coupled with an accurate estimate of the health and strength of the patient at the time of the outbreak, we ask ourselves the question, what is the pathology of this disordered state of brain and mind manifestation, what can we answer? A weakly person may drift into a depressed condition, which we call melancholia, remain in it for months or years, and then gradually recover; a young and vigorous subject may be almost suddenly attacked by acute delirium, pass a week or longer in a state of raving mania wholly without sleep, then sleep, and recover perfectly in a month. Another experiences a shock or fright, falls into a condition of blank demented idiocy, and yet recovers. Another gradually becomes altered and eccentric, conceives some odd delusions and fancies, and

What is, then, the pathology of insanity?

remains so for the rest of his days. All these are insane, but how different is their insanity, and how different their bodily appearance, development, age, and strength! Can we suppose that the condition of them all is the same, or nearly the same?

I am inclined to say that in all these cases the brain is insufficiently fed; that the supply from which it is to derive its power of working is in defect; but this deficiency may, I think, depend upon various conditions. There may be an absolute defect of blood, an anæmia, or a blood too poor for its purpose, or poisoned by deleterious ingredients. The defect may be from too much blood, causing by its pressure a congestion or stasis, and arresting in this way the supply which should be conveyed to every cell. And the increased arterial circulation, ending in obstruction and stasis, may be due to diminished arterial tension, depending on disturbances of the vaso-motor system, arising in ways of which we can take no cognizance. We know that in almost all acute insanity sleep is absent, or at any rate greatly diminished; and we know that when such a medicine as hydrate of chloral produces sleep, it increases the arterial tension, for this is shown by the sphygmographic trace.

If arterial tension were to be so increased as to arrest the flow of blood, delirium or convulsions might occur, and it is supposed that this actually happens in epilepsy. We have seen how close is the connection between epilepsy and insanity, and how the one may take the place of the other. Chorea, too, has been thought to be due to embolic closure of the arteries, and there is much in common between chorea and insanity.

In short, from whichever side we look at the disease, whether we look at the sthenic or the asthenic forms, or consider it in the young or the old, in those previously well or in the victims of other diseases, there seems in all some reason for thinking either that the nutrition and metamorphosis of the brain are in parts impeded or rendered irregular, or that of the whole disordered or obstructed. Such disorder may be overcome quickly, and things may return at once to their normal state, or there may be absolute defect, and only by months of feeding and care will the anæmia be overcome, and the brain be again nourished and restored to its former level. The traces which we find of hyperæmia of the brain may indicate that there has been excessive arterial action, and the fierce excitement, the hilarity, the flushed face and quickened pulse, may all point to the same fact; but this hyperæmia, no less than an opposite state of anæmia, may denote a want of healthy conversion, a want of the normal renewal of the wasting nerve-element. As fever in an old demented patient will sometimes bring back, while it lasts, mental vigor and clear intelligence, the pulse being quickened and the blood-flow increased, so will it in a healthy subject cause delirium by the obstruction caused by the abnormal rush of blood in the cerebral vessels.

LECTURE V.

Morbid Appearances—In Acute Insanity—Meninges—Brain—Vessels —In Chronic Insanity—Vessels—Brain—Nerve Cells and Tubes— Connective Tissue Growths—The Insane Ear—Classification—Various Systems—Points to be observed.

VAGUE and uncertain as are our speculations upon the pathological conditions of insanity, they receive little if any help from the changes noticeable after death in the brains of the insane. That which I have to say, concerning the post-mortem appearances and the morbid products observed in such patients, is said with the utmost diffidence, because it amounts in truth to very little, and rests on the researches and labors of others, not on my own. I claim no credit for the discovery of the various lesions described. Concerning these phenomena observers differ, and differ widely; in fact, the method of observation of each one differs from that of others, and according to the method so is the result observed. Yet we may be well assured that a time will come, probably not long hence, when much more will be laid down as clearly ascertained fact than has been known hitherto. We wade through wearisome pages of examinations, conducted in the rough-and-ready method of bygone days, when nothing beyond a scalpel was called in to assist in the process—when brains were weighed with pound weights, sliced up, and flung away—when gray matter and white were the two divisions of which, and of which alone, notice was taken—when the coverings rather than the brain itself attracted attention. Before pathology could note morbid changes, it was necessary that minute anatomy should further advance. Now we are in a position to speak of changed tissues, knowing in a much higher degree the normal condition of those we examine.

But even now, after so much has been done, we are but at the threshold of this great field of research. I believe that any one who patiently and skilfully examines the brain of the insane, not of ten or twenty, but of many hundreds, will throw an entirely new light upon mind pathology and brain pathology. No brain has been satisfactorily examined that has only been looked at with the naked eye, and all the records of former autopsies made in this fashion are as so much waste paper. Morbid phenomena studied by the aid of the microscope reveal themselves as definite changes and lesions, instead of indefinite "softening," "hardening," "thickening," "discoloration," such as are enumerated by naked-eye observers. And no brain can be said to be properly examined that has not been examined throughout. Not every cell and nerve-tube need pass over the field of the microscope; but parts of every region and district are to be submitted to scrutiny—not only those obviously changed, but others also at a distance.

If we consult the records of the deaths of the insane, it will at once be seen that the proportion of those who die of recent and acute insanity is very small. The majority will be patients who have been insane for some years, fewer will be the cases for some months, and only here and there shall we discover one whose malady has lasted but a few weeks or days. In some the insanity may be said to be the cause of death, but many chronic patients die of other diseases—of bronchitis, phthisis, and so on. From what we find after death, we have to infer the morbid process which has gone on in life. The appearances found in the chronic insane are not those met with in recent and acute insanity. The former are the result of a disease which has slowly dragged itself along for years, the latter indicate the beginning of the disease; and from a comparison the one with the other, we are left to infer the nature thereof.

Now, scanty and imperfect as are the observations of morbid appearances found in acute and chronic cases Appearances of insanity, the tale they tell is consecutive and found in those dying of recertain, and is illustrated by the changes and dis- cent insanity. eases of other organs. I will mention first that which is observed, whether by the naked eye or by the aid of the microscope, in patients dying of acute and recent insanity, and then on reviewing the phenomena found in the brains of patients who have been insane for years, I think it will be found that the pathology of the one class tallies with that of the other.

A man becomes maniacal; his mania passes into violent delirium, and in the delirium he dies perhaps in a week: it is the most rapid mode of death in a state of insanity. There may have been no bodily complication, no assignable cause; the case may become what is called genuine "idiopathic" mania. We open the head, and expect to find sufficient to account for death. All the organs of the body be quite healthy, and yet that which is seen in the brain does not seem enough to kill a strong man so speedily. But in truth the appearances point to the great storm that has raged there during the last week or fortnight of life—a storm that has brought about death by its violence, though the traces may by some be summed up as great vascularity or congestion of the brain and its membranes.

To take the first naked-eye appearances, we find signs of violent disturbance manifested in the meninges, the The vehicles of the blood-supply of the brain itself. meninges. "Sinuses and veins of pia mater full of blood—considerable serous effusions in subarachnoid space." This was in a female who died of mania in fourteen days. "Pia mater much congested, arachnoid slightly opalescent." This also was in a female. Opacity of the arachnoid is common; you will find it often in patients not insane; but in the cases of which I am speaking it denotes excessive action tending to meningitis. So violent may it have been, that not unfrequently we find effusions of blood from the rupture of small vessels between the membranes. And much serous effusion is commonly found, which probably precedes death only a short time, and accompanies the coma in which so many of these patients sink. In others who have had previous attacks, or have been excitable, semi-insane, and constantly liable to disturbance of the cerebral circulation, we find great thickening and eburnation of the cranial bones, and extensive adhesion of the dura mater. These appearances point to a low inflammatory and degenerative change which has been going on for some time, and you will constantly see them in patients not insane. When we remove the pia mater, and this in a recent case can generally be accomplished without difficulty, we find the same traces of violent action. The brain is not uniform and healthy in tint. In places it is discolored from pink to purple, and is often softened. Its structures, cells, tubes, and connecting tissue are obviously altered and damaged by the hyperæmia which has existed. There has been great vascularity; on slicing it we see many bleeding puncta, and the vessels have manifestly been dilated.

As might be expected, there are to be found in the brains The brain. of the insane extravasation of all kinds and degrees, especially in those who have died after a brief period of violent excitement. Blood-cysts are found in the cavity of the arachnoid, and stains and spots of extravasated blood are seen on the surface of the convolutions and in the substance of the brain: capillary apoplexies, extravasated blood-corpuscles, and yellowish or reddened brain matter, are appearances well known to those who have examined such patients after death.

In the membranes we rarely find marks of active inflammation, but there may be great adhesion of the dura mater

to the bone, and adhesion of the pia mater to the convolutions, so that in removing it we tear away the brain substance.
And the arachnoid will often be milky and thickened, or
atrophied and perforated.

The bone is often enormously thickened, the diploe being
absorbed, the whole having undergone a retrograde metamorphosis.

In a thesis read before the University of Oxford in 1867,
I propounded the theory that the cause of delirium Blocking of
and death in acute and rapid cases of insanity, deli- the vessels.
rium tremens, and the like, is stasis of the capillary circulation, the result of pressure or inflammatory changes in the
blood. In a paper already referred to (page 52), published
in the "British Medical Journal" of January 23, 1869, Dr.
Charlton Bastian narrates certain post-mortem appearances
found by him in the brain of an intemperate man, who died
of erysipelas of the scalp, following a fall on the head, with
violent delirium. These, I think, strongly confirm the conjectures I put forth in 1867—conjectures based chiefly on
Mr. Lister's Experiments and Observations on Inflammation,
published in the Philosophical Transactions, 1859. To the
naked eye all parts of the brain showed a decidedly abnormal
amount of vascularity, and this was particularly evident on
the venous side of the circulation. The veins of the surface
of the lateral ventricles, and those of the choroid plexuses,
were all notably distended with dark blood, though there
was no obstruction in the venæ magnæ Galeni or in the
straight sinus. The lateral ventricles, however, contained
only a small quantity of pale serum. The "red points" were
very abundant wherever sections were made through the
white substance of the hemispheres. On microscopical examination of some minute vessels and capillaries taken from
the gray matter of the convolutions, every specimen looked
at showed minute embolic masses in various parts of the
course of the small arteries and capillaries, of a most unmis-

takable nature, though apparently of recent origin.   Distinct masses, of irregular shape and size, could be seen, made up of an agglomeration of white blood-corpuscles.   In some cases the masses were small, and formed by the union of three or four white corpuscles only; whilst in others large irregularly-shaped aggregations could be seen within some of the bigger vessels, which may have been made up by the mutual adhesion of two or three hundred of such corpuscles. The largest mass actually measured was $\frac{1}{100}$ in. long by $\frac{1}{250}$ in. broad.   In other parts large rounded bodies were seen, whose nature was not at first sight so obvious, though after a little careful examination I became convinced that these had, in all probability, been formed by the complete fusion of corpuscles into a single mass, which had afterwards under-gone more or less of a granular degeneration."

In commenting on this case, Dr. Bastian mentions others; one, a case of rheumatic fever, with delirium; another, of double pneumonia, progressing favorably, when maniacal delirium set in, lasted about thirty-six hours, and then gradu-ally subsided.   The latter was, in fact, an instance of mania arising in the course of an acute disease, akin to that already mentioned, which Dr. Weber has termed the "delirium of collapse."   Dr. Bastian was strongly impressed at the time with the probability that the delirium, in the latter case at least, was due to some accidental plugging of minute vessels of the brain by means of aggregated white blood-corpuscles, and to the consequent total disturbance in the incidence of blood-pressure, and in the conditions of nutritive supply in the convolutional gray matter of the brain.   "It was there-fore with a feeling of considerable interest that I proceeded to examine the brain in this case of erysipelas of the scalp, which had been associated during life with delirium and stupor."

From the actual appearances described by Dr. Bastian, and from the similarity of the symptoms in acute insanity, we may infer that the violent delirium which so often exists may arise from some such blocking of the vessels; and if death occurs, it may be the result either of this obstruction increasing till it causes coma or convulsions, or of exhaustion supervening upon the delirium. It is to be remembered that delirium occurring in the course of fevers, pneumonia, and like disorders, almost always passes off, and recovery takes place. Many transitory attacks are likewise seen in what is called hysterical or transitory mania. Whether the disorder in the brain circulation depends on some disturbance arising out of the vaso-motor system, such as spasm of the arteries, or on other causes producing temporary arrest of the blood-flow, it is clear that the evil soon passes away, and it is not likely, even if the patient were to die soon after, that we should discover post-mortem appearances sufficient to account for the mental symptoms. Where, however, delirium runs on to death after a week or upwards, such a condition as that described by Dr. Bastian may be found, and should certainly be looked for.

So far as I gather from published reports, the cervical ganglia of the sympathetic, which are closely connected with the brain circulation, have been examined but seldom in patients dying insane. I cannot tell you, therefore, whether morbid appearances are to be found there. It is possible that by disturbance carried thither from distant parts considerable effects might be produced without much trace being left, but at any rate I wish that they could be examined by some of our leading microscopists.

There seems to be a prevailing opinion abroad amongst pathologists that acute mental symptoms, especially delirium, are brought about by obstruction of the cerebral blood-flow; and even the chorea often noticed in connection with rheumatism has been thought to be caused by emboli carried to the nerve-centres from the heart. Obstruction of the circulation is probably the condition, and the greater the obstruc-

tion the more acute will be the delirium.   But I think it will
be found that this obstruction may arise from a number of
various causes.   It is clear that it is often temporary, and
must depend on something easily and quickly removed.   It
may be caused by some spasm of arteries, and may depend
on the vaso-motor system.   It may arise from some inflammation of the part, or of adjoining parts, as in Dr. Bastian's
case.   It may depend on such a poison as that of gout or
rheumatism, or it may be not an obstruction, but an anæmia
produced by a failure of the heart's action, or a poverty of
oxygen-carrying red corpuscles.   By due examination and
weighing of such matters, we may connect the causes of insanity with the actual pathological changes, and establish a
much closer connection between them than has hitherto existed.   Above all, there is needed an accurate observation of
the brain of those dying of acute insanity.   I have quoted
Dr. Bastian's remarks, as worthy of the greatest attention;
but it is to be remembered that the case he examined was
not one of ordinary insanity.   Moreover, we want the examination, not of two or three, but of many patients, and
more must be determined as to what are normal, and what
abnormal phenomena, amongst those revealed by the microscope.   We know little as yet concerning the changes which
occur in the blood and tissues at the time of death, or immediately after.

When we examine the brains of patients who have died
Examination after a long period of insanity, and seek for traces
of the chronic of their malady, our labors are better rewarded.
insane.
We find degeneration of all the structures which
join in the working of the brain, and an increase of the
lowest tissues, together with a growth of adventitious and
abnormal products, which supplant the healthy structure,
and subvert its function.   We find, in fact, the same evidences which testify to degeneration and decay of the other
organs of the body; and, so far as we can observe, these

changes appear to be the ultimate end and result of the acute disease which was first manifested in symptoms which exist in the early stages of almost every variety of insanity.

I have said that the appearances found in those who die of acute insanity point to a violent disturbance of the cerebral circulation. The changes we meet with in the chronic insane point to the results of this disturbance, to damage of the vessels, to extravasation of their contents, to a consequent interference with their life and function, and nutrition of the tissues they supply. Degeneration and atrophy have wasted the cells and tubes, while more lowly organized structures—bone, connective tissue, fatty and amyloid corpuscles—flourish and abound, as they ever do where the normal tissues and the normal nutrition are at fault.

What, then, are the changes observed in the bloodvessels? Various pathologists have directed their attention to these, and have recorded not a few deviations from the healthy state.

One which Dr. Sankey has described in the "Journal of Mental Science,"[1] is an hypertrophied·condition of the walls of the small arteries and capillaries. Struck by Dr. George Johnson's discovery of hypertrophy of the small renal arteries, Dr. Sankey examined those of twenty-five insane patients. Of eight cases of general paralysis, he found the hypertrophy in one only. Of seven cases of chronic dementia, all save one presented some amount; the one exception was the youngest patient, thirty-five years of age. Two cases of epilepsy, and one of acute mania, apparently presented no deviation from the normal condition. Of seven cases of chronic insanity, hypertrophy existed in four. Dr. Sankey is of opinion that this alteration indicates that the muscular coat of the arteries has had at one period an excessive amount of work to do.

Hypertrophy of the walls of the small arteries.

---

[1] January, 1869.

The cause of the excess of work may, of course, vary indefinitely. Dr. Sankey thinks that an impure state of the blood may frequently be at the bottom of it. However this may be, we know that violent cerebral excitement and action accompany the acute stage of insanity, and that hypertrophy may be the result; and, moreover, that in this way there may be great disturbance of the circulation and nutrition of the brain.

There is also another condition of the small arteries and Twisting of the arteries. capillaries not coexistent with hypertrophy, but on the contrary, found where the latter is not, yet apparently brought about by the same cause,—the violent action which leaves so many traces behind. An extreme varicosity of the capillaries is to be seen, a kinking or twisting together with dilatation, as if at some period so great a rush of blood had taken place that the vessel could not carry it on, but had become distorted, strained, and twisted in the attempt. This appearance Dr. Sankey has found in the subjects of general paralysis in which hypertrophy seldom exists, and he thinks that the vessel not interposing to check the blood-flow, owing possibly to deficient nervous power, does not become hypertrophied, but undergoes the other change which he has described.

Nor are these the only changes which the bloodvessels undergo. Attention has been directed lately to their sheaths, to the canals in which they run—the perivascular canals, as they are called—and also to certain holes existing in the brain tissue, which seem to have their origin in the vessels.

Upon the vessels a deposit of hyaline connective tissue has Sheaths of vessels. been seen, studded with nuclei and proliferated neurogliar cells, taking its origin either from the nuclei of the walls, or from the neuroglia beyond them. Dr. Lockhart Clarke points out that in healthy brains the capillaries and small arteries are surrounded by secondary sheaths, but the morbid sheaths are thicker, darker, and studded with hæmatoidin, or other deposits. It is common also to find the vessels in a state of fatty degeneration.

The perivascular canals in which the vessels run have been found in a very dilated condition in the insane, especially in those dying of general paralysis, the vessel lying as if adherent to one side. This perivascular covering is sometimes transparent, sometimes opaque, and presents variations and changes manifestly morbid.

Somewhat akin possibly to this dilatation of the perivascular canals, or a further stage of the process, are certain holes described by Dr. Lockhart Clarke, and found by him in the white substance of the convolutions and optic thalamus of a patient who died of general paralysis. "On making slices with a very sharp instrument through the convolutions, their central white substance presented numerous cavities, of a round, oval, fusiform, crescentic, or somewhat cylindrical shape, and varying from the size of a small pea or a barleycorn to that of a grain of sand, so that the surfaces in some sections strikingly resembled the cut surface of Gruyère cheese, while those of others had more resemblance to a slice of the crumb of bread. For the most part they were empty, had perfectly smooth walls, without any lining membrane, and seemed as if they had been sharply cut out of the tissue. A few, however, were found to contain what appeared to be the remains or débris of bloodvessels, mixed with a few granules of hæmatoidin. One or two were found to communicate with the surface of the convolutions through the natural fissures between them, and to contain a perfect bloodvessel, with its branches. On removing the bloodvessel, the walls of the broad but shallow cavity was seen to be perforated by a multitude of minute orifices, through which the finer branches of the vessel had passed. These latter circumstances, together with a comparison of the shape and course of some of the natural fissures transmitting bloodvessels from the surface, render it almost certain that at least the greater number of these cavities were perivascular spaces or canals, which originally contained bloodvessels, surrounded by their peculiar sheaths, and which subsequently became empty by the destruction and absorption of those vessels."[1]

Doubtless you are aware that Dr. Dickinson has discovered similar holes in the brain and spinal cord of diabetic patients. The preparations in his possession appear to throw great light on the mode in which these holes are produced, and illustrate not a little the pathology of insanity.

In more than one a bloodvessel is seen in a state of great congestion, so great that the blood-corpuscles have apparently transuded through the walls of the vessel, and invaded the tissue in which it is imbedded. If the patient does not die in this stage, the acute congestive stage of insanity, we may suppose that the exuded blood becomes absorbed, and then a hole, possibly with ragged edge, is left behind. This is the view Dr. Dickinson takes of the origin of these holes, and it seems very probable. Drs. Tuke and Rutherford[2] say that they observed holes in the white matter of the brain—holes differing, however, from those described by Dr. Lockhart Clarke, "inasmuch as they have no apparent connection with bloodvessels, and are manifestly due to a solution of the continuity of nerve-elements, as is evident from the ragged character of the walls." It is, however, possible, I think, that the latter appearance may be due to invasion and subsequent absorption of extravasated blood, and to absorption of the remains of the vessel itself.

The whole points to violent action producing hypertrophy of the walls, variocosity, congestion, extravasation, absorption, and destruction of nerve-tissue.

Another result is an interference with the nutrition of all parts. The vessels themselves are strained and twisted, and

---

[1] Journal of Mental Science, Jan., 1870.
[2] Edinburgh Medical Journal, Oct., 1869.

become fatty, or disappear by absorption, and degeneration of various kinds attacks the gray and white matter, the nerve-cells, and nerve-fibres.

The cells of the convolutions, and also of the corpora striata, and other nerve-centres of the mesocephalon, Nerve-cells. are often found in a state of *pigmentary* degeneration. The cell may contain a few pigment granules, or may be full of them, retaining its cell outline, or it may be completely broken up, the pigment granules remaining in heaps to mark the place of the original cells. And instead of the pigmentary there may be a *fatty* degeneration, the cells being filled with fat granules. There may be merely an aggregate of fat globules, with the outline and nucleus of nerve-cells, or half of the outline of the cell may be preserved, the other being replaced by a margin of fat globules. Nay, *calcification* of the cells has also been discovered, phosphate of lime occupying and rendering them opaque. And, in addition to these degenerative metamorphoses, we find the cells *atrophied*. Atrophy occurs from a variety of causes, from pressure of other growths, cysts, or extravasations. It arises from arrested nutrition, or from the decay of old age. Atrophy of the cells of the cortical substance is often met with in the chronic insane, as it is in those who have died from the more rapid ravages of general paralysis.

Atrophy may also be observed attacking the nerve-tubes; and Drs. Tuke and Rutherford tell us that in a case Nerve-tubes. of chronic dementia, complicated with chorea, the nerve-tubes of the anterior and posterior roots of the spinal nerves were found to have undergone a pigmentary degeneration similar to that noticed in the nerve-cells.

More attention has, perhaps, been paid to the changes in the connective tissue than to those of any other part Connective of the brain. A morbid increase has been described tissue. by several writers—Rokitansky, Rindfleisch, and others— and the gray degeneration or sclerosis of many authors appears to be due to a modification of this connective tissue. Referring to the valuable paper of Drs. Tuke and Rutherford, from which I have already quoted, I find the following description : " We have observed this lesion only in the white matter of the brains examined by us. As to the nature of the morbid change, our observations lead us to agree with Rokitansky in regarding it as primarily a modification of the connective tissue. In the spinal cord, medulla oblongata, and pons, it appears to us that the connective tissue or neuroglia is a nucleated, transparent, homogeneous, non-fibrillated matrix, representing the fibrillated connective tissue of the spinal cord. Owing to the extreme fineness of the nerve-tubes of the white matter of the brain, as compared with those of the spinal cord, an inquiry into the diseased conditions of the white matter of the former is much more difficult than in the case of the latter ; but a careful inspection of numerous finely-prepared sections, by means of a magnifying power of 800 diameters linear (Hartnack's immersion lens No. 10, eye-piece No. 3), has resulted in the demonstration that fibrillation and increase of the neurogliar matrix, together with proliferation of its nuclei, are the essential changes in gray degeneration, as Rokitansky has already pointed out. Sometimes proliferation of the nuclei precedes fibrillation of the matrix, at other times the converse holds good. Sometimes there is a marked proliferation in the nuclei of the capillary walls in the diseased tracts, but we have not been able to confirm Rindfleisch's observation that the diseased process invariably starts from these. Indeed, our specimens show that the morbid change just as often begins at a distance from, as in the immediate neighborhood of, the vessels. Regarding the fate of the nerve-tubes in the diseased tracts in the white matter of the brain, our observations, owing to the fineness of these elements, scarcely enable us to speak with confidence. They appear, however, to undergo atrophy, and this need scarcely be doubted, seeing that they certainly do so under similar conditions in the spinal cord." Dr. Rutherford also describes a lesion consisting of a patch where the nuclei of the neuroglia are proliferated and surrounded not with fibres, as in the gray degeneration or sclerosis, but with semi-transparent, finely granular material. He also describes another lesion, termed by him *miliary sclerosis*, which consists of semi-opaque whitish spots, resembling very small millet-seeds, and is almost confined to white nerve-matter. When far advanced, the spots are discernible with the naked eye, and consist of semi-opaque molecular material, lying amid a few exceedingly delicate colorless fibres. The cell-like masses probably originate in the nuclei of the neuroglia, not in the nuclei of the vascular walls. There is no increase of the connective tissue or neuroglia, which at once distinguishes it from the gray degeneration of Rokitansky or Rindfleisch.

Granulations of the lining membrane of the ventricles have been thought by M. Joire to be peculiar to general paralysis, which they are not. They have been observed in old-standing cases of mania and dementia, together with similar granulations of the pia mater of the parietal and occipital lobes and medulla oblongata. They are no doubt an aggregated and abnormal condition of the epithelial cells, and seem to contain a homogeneous substance, probably exuded lymph.[1] Amyloid and colloid corpuscles are to be found in almost all old cases of insanity. Controversy exists regarding their nature, but the majority consider them to be pathological products. These are of two sizes, the larger being found in both the gray and white matter of the brain; the smaller chiefly on the surface of the convolutions, medulla oblongata, and spinal cord.

There are to be seen occasionally in the brains of the insane, appearances denoting that there has been at some time or other an injury of the head, in the

Tumors, &c.

---

[1] Tuke and Rutherford, *loc. cit.*

shape of old extravasations, remains of blood-cysts, and the
like, which point to events which may have been the cause
of the insanity years before. And it is to be noted that such
patients may not have been always insane since the date of
the injury. They may have recovered, and again become
insane, again to recover. So great is the tendency to recovery on the part of nature, and so great the tendency to
recurrence on that of the disease, that alternations may take
place even when actual changes are to be found in the brain.
And the same remark applies to tumors and other growths
of similar nature. As some people live without symptoms
up to the day when they die of these, so others become
insane, and yet again recover, even when the tumor is still
present and growing. I need say little about such maladies
as abscess, tumor, or cysticercus, because, although they are
found in the insane, they are met with still more frequently
in those who die in the wards of general hospitals, displaying mental symptoms of every kind—delirium, imbecility,
coma, and paralysis—without insanity in the ordinary ac-
ceptation of the word.

There is one morbid appearance peculiar, I believe, to the
The insane insane, which may be mentioned here. It is called
ear.   the "insane ear," or *hæmatoma auris*, and is an
effusion of blood under the perichondrium, between it and
the cartilage, or, according to others, within the cartilage.
It may come on gradually, or even quite suddenly, in a night,
may attain a large size, and appear at the point of burst-
ing. I have known a slight oozing, but it seldom bursts.
Slowly and gradually it shrinks, and becomes absorbed,
leaving the ear withered and shrivelled. Of a man with
such a shrivelled ear, it may be safely predicated that at
some time he has had an attack of insanity. When it appears, the prognosis is said to be unfavorable, and it certainly
occurs most frequently in paralytic and chronic insanity.
Some have asserted that it is always the result of violence.

I cannot say if this be so, but in two cases it was certainly due to it. In one, the patient fell out of bed, striking the ear. In the other, it followed the holding of the head, necessitated by refusal of food and medicine, and consequent forcible feeding. It has been supposed that it arises in many instances from the mere weight of the head as it rests on the pillow.

CLASSIFICATIONS OF INSANITY.

Great differences of opinion have existed for many years as to the classification of insanity and insane patients, and various systems and principles have been laid down. The old writers divided the disorder into Mania and Melancholia: Arnold (1782) into Ideal and Notional insanity; Pinel makes four divisions, Mania, Melancholia, Dementia, and Idiocy; Esquirol adds another, Monomania. Guislain's classification runs thus: 1. *Phrenalgia*, or Melancholy; 2. *Phrenoplexia*, or Ecstasy; 3. *Hyperphrenia*, or Mania; 4. *Paraphrenia*, or Folly; 5. *Ideophrenia*, or Delirium; 6. *Aphrenia*, or Dementia. Dr. Conolly speaks of Mania, Melancholia, and Dementia; Dr. Prichard of Moral and Intellectual Insanity; Dr. Bucknill says that insanity may be Intellectual, Emotional, or Volitional; Dr. Noble's division gives Emotional, Notional, and Intelligential disorder. Dr. Daniel Tuke divides it according to the disturbance of — 1. The Intellect; 2. The Moral Sentiments; 3. The Propensities; and his division is as follows: Idiocy, Dementia, Delusional Insanity, Emotional Insanity, Mania. Then, again, M. Morel _{Morel.} rejects all these divisions as artificial, and based merely upon the symptoms of the disease, or on supposed divisions of the human mind, and he proposes to divide it strictly according to its ætiology into six groups: 1. Cases of Hereditary Transmission; 2. Toxic Insanity; 3. Those resulting from the transformation of other Neuroses; 4. Idiopathic Insanity; 5. Sympathetic Insanity; 6. Dementia. I will not stop to comment on the imperfections of this classification; suffice it to say, that it is not even what it professes to be, ætiological.

The latest writer, so far as I am aware, who divides insanity Maudsley. according to the mental symptoms, is Dr. Maudsley, whose classification is as follows:

I. Affective or Pathetic Insanity.
  1. Maniacal Perversion of the Affective life. Mania sine delirio.
  2. Melancholic depression without delusion. Simple Melancholia.
  3. Moral Alienation Proper. Approaching this, but not reaching the degree of positive insanity, is the Insane Temperament.

II. Ideational Insanity.
  1. General.
    a. Mania, } Acute.
    b. Melancholia, } Chronic.
  2. Partial.
    a. Monomania.
    b. Melancholia.
  3. Dementia, { Primary. Secondary.
  4. General Paralysis.
  5. Idiocy and Imbecility.

At the International Congress of Alienists, held in Paris The International Congress. in 1867, there was adopted a system of statistics prepared by a committee appointed for that purpose, and the following classification was put forward as denoting the typical forms of the disease:

I. *Simple Insanity,* embracing the different varieties of mania, melancholia, and monomania, circular insanity and mixed insanity, delusion of persecution, moral insanity, and the dementia following these different forms of insanity.

II. *Epileptic Insanity,* or insanity with epilepsy, whether the convulsive affection has preceded the insanity, and has seemed to have been the cause; or whether, on the contrary, it has appeared, during the course of the mental disease, only as a symptom or a complication.

III. *Paralytic Insanity.*—The commission regards the disease called general paralysis of the insane as a distinct morbid entity, and not at all as a complication, a termination of insanity. It proposes, then, to comprehend under the name of paralytic insane, all the insane who show in any degree whatever the characteristic symptoms of this disease.

IV. *Senile Dementia*, which we would define as the slow and progressive enfeeblement of the intellectual and moral faculties, consequent upon old age.

V. *Organic Dementia*, a term by which the commission means to designate a disease which is neither the dementia consequent upon insanity or epilepsy, nor paralytic dementia, nor senile dementia, but that which is consequent upon organic lesion of the brain, nearly always local, and which presents, as an almost constant symptom, hemiplegic occurrences more or less prolonged.

VI. *Idiocy*, characterized by the absence or arrest of development of the intellectual and moral faculties. Imbecility and weakness of mind constitute, hereof, two degrees or varieties.

VII. *Cretinism*, characterized by a lesion of the intellectual faculties, more or less analogous to that observed in idiocy, but with which is uniformly associated a characteristic vicious conformation of the body, an arrest of the development of the entirety of the organism. Outside of these typical forms there are such as—

1. Delirium tremens.
2. Delirium of acute diseases: traumatic delirium.
3. Simple epilepsy.

A committee of the Medico-Psychological Association, appointed, in 1869, for the purpose of taking into consideration certain questions relating to the uniform recording of cases of insanity, and the medical treatment of insanity, recommends that cases should be classified according to two methods—1. That depending on the bodily causes and natural history of the disease, as proposed by Dr. Skae; 2. That proposed by the International Congress of Alienists, as given above.

Committee of Medico-Psychological Association.

The following table is put forth by this committee as a specimen of the way in which cases may be arranged:

		PREDOMINANT FEATURES.									
		a	b	c	d	e	f	g	h	i	k
		Acute Delirium and Incoherence.	Simple Excitement.	Simple Depression.	Stupor.	Hypochondria.	Strong Suicidal Impulses.	Remittency or Intermittency.	Chorea.	Hallucinations.	Enfeeblement.
CURABLE.											
1. Insanity of Pregnancy,	Mania,										
2. " "	Melancholia,										
3. Insanity of Childbirth,	Mania,										
4. " "	Melancholia,										
5. Insanity of Lactation,	Mania,										
6. " "	Melancholia,										
7. Climacteric Insanity,	Mania,										
8. " "	Melancholia,										
9. Insanity from Uterine Disorder,	Mania,										
10. " "	Melancholia,										
11. Insanity from Tuberculosis,	Mania,										
12. " "	Melancholia,										
13. Insanity from Masturbation,	Mania,										
14. " "	Melancholia,										
15. Insanity from Alcoholism,	Mania,										
16. " "	Melancholia,										
17. Delirium Tremens,	Delirium Tremens,										
18. Post-febrile Insanity,	Mania,										
19. " "	Melancholia,										
20. Hysterical Insanity,	Mania,										
INCURABLE.											
1. General Paralysis,	Paralytic Insanity,										
2. Epileptic Insanity,	Epileptic,										
3. Senile Insanity,	Senile Dementia,										
4. Paralytic Insanity,	Organic Dementia,										

Dr. Skae's division I have already given. A modification of it has been proposed by Dr. Batty Tuke, of the Fife Asylum. He enumerates seven classes of insanity, and twenty-nine sub-classes.

Dr. B. Tuke.

Class I.—Insanity resulting from arrested or impaired development of the brain. } Idiocy, congenital and acquired.

Class II.—Idiophrenic Insanity. . .
- Sthenic and Asthenic Idiopathic Insanity.
- Phrenitic Insanity (Inflammatory).
- General Paresis.
- Paralysis with Insanity.
- Traumatic Insanity.
- Epileptic Insanity.

Class III.—Sympathetic Insanity. .
- Epileptic Insanity.
- Insanity of Masturbation.
- Insanity of Pubescence.
- Climacteric Insanity.
- Ovarian and Uterine Insanity.
- Insanity of Pregnancy.
- Puerperal Insanity.
- Post-Connubial Insanity.
- Hysterical Insanity.
- Enteric Insanity.

Class IV.—Anæmic Insanity. . . .
- Limopsoitos (from starvation).
- Post-febrile Insanity.
- Insanity of Lactation.

Class V.—Diathetic Insanity. . . .
- Insanity of Tuberculosis.
- Syphilitic Insanity.

Class VI.—Toxic Insanity. . . .
- Cretinism.
- Delirium Tremens.
- Insanity of Alcoholism.
- Insanity from Opium-eating.

Class VII.—Metastatic Insanity. .
- Rheumatic.
- Pellagrous.
- Metastatic Insanity, from healing of long-established issues.

Examining these various schemes of classification, we find them to be based on one or other of three principles. Either they are framed according to the mental peculiarities of the patient, his exaltation, his depression, his imbecility; or they point to a disorder of one or other of the portions into which the human mind is by some authors divided; or, the mental symptoms being put entirely aside, the malady is classified according to its pathological cause and its relations to the bodily organism. Objections are easily raised to any one of these plans. A patient, it is said, may be melancholic one week and maniacal the next; therefore melancholia and mania are not scientific divisions. Most true is it that a patient may have no delusions one week, but may have so far advanced as to have plenty in the week following; therefore it may be said that effective and ideational insanity are not true divisions. Then, if we take causes as our basis of classification, we may find two patients whose insanity springs from the same cause, yet they are in every shape and way the opposite one of another, requiring different treatment, differing as regards diagnosis and prognosis, the one hopelessly incurable, the other bidding fair to recover. Can we adopt such a basis as this? If not, what are we to look for to guide us in our attempt?

It appears to me, that if we classify not the so-called forms Points to be of insanity, but insane patients, we shall be re-observed. minded practically of certain points which otherwise we might overlook. We wish, of course, to ascertain for the purposes of our classification as many as possible of the conditions of the patients before us. If the conditions of any two were precisely alike, the insanity would be identical; but as no two people are alike, no two people's insanity is alike. If we have before us a dozen patients whom we are to classify, and we find that four of these are in an extreme state of depression, four are delirious and in a state of furious mania, while the remaining are gay and exalted, presenting the well-known symptoms of general paralysis, it is plain that there must be allied conditions existing in the members of each one of these groups which bring about the peculiar features of it, and which do not exist in the other groups. What these conditions are we cannot scientifically determine, but we may be sure that those which give rise to melancholy in a man of fifty are not the same as those which exist in a young man suffering from acute mania at twenty-five. Yet we may, according to some, group them together, and give to each the name of idiopathic insanity. I maintain that mania or melancholia denotes a group of conditions, most of which are unknown to us, though some may be ascertainable; that in our scientific classification the sum-total of these conditions, which is presented to us by the whole of the symptoms evinced by the patient, is not to be laid aside in favor of some one condition or cause, whether proximate or remote. As physicians engaged in the cure and treatment of insanity will never be able practically to lay aside the classification of mania and melancholia, will be forever compelled to treat melancholy as one thing and mania as another, so I believe that as pathologists they will comprehend under these general names a multitude of conditions which must be assumed, but cannot at present be demonstrated, but which year by year will be more and more differentiated and specialized, not by fixing our attention upon one, and one only, in each case, but by looking on every case as the result of an infinite number. One objection to the divisions of mania and melancholia is, that many patients cannot be ranged under either of these heads. They either hold a position midway between the two, so that they may be called by one maniacal, by another melancholic, or they cannot be said to be at all maniacal or at all melancholic, their insanity being denoted either by a total loss of mind, such as we call dementia, or by a mere assemblage of delusions, or even by one delusion without emotional display of any kind. For this state the term monomania has been invented, but it is applied also to other varieties of unsoundness of mind. Now, with regard to the above objection, I would say that such

The mental symptoms cannot be disregarded in acute cases.

patients are for the most part chronic and incurable, present-ing to us the results of former attacks and pathological states. As the damaged valves of the heart point to a long-past condition of endocardiac inflammation, so the fixed delusions or hallucinations of an incurable monomaniac point not to a present but to a past pathological state. Were we always called upon to examine and classify patients in the very earliest stage of their insanity, we might possibly classify them according to the pathological origin of their disorder; but after years of alienation we necessarily lose sight of the origin and original condition, and our attention is di-rected to the mental symptoms; and for the purposes of treatment and safe custody we cannot ignore these. We are obliged practically to classify our patients as melancholic or maniacal, paralytic or demented. To take the illustration already used, we recognize as most important the distinction between mitral and aortic disease, yet, pathologically, we might say that each may spring from rheumatic endocarditis, and therefore the division is an accident, and not scientific. But it is one thing to lay down the pathological varieties of insanity, as I have attempted in my third and fourth lectures; it is another to classify insane who may be set before us in all stages and periods of the disorder. If we can examine the individual at the outset of the disorder, and thoroughly ascertain his history, we may be able to lay down with con-siderable accuracy his pathological condition. He is not yet in a state which warrants the name of mania or of melan-cholia, still less of dementia; but his state is clearly aberra-tion of mind and disturbance of brain function, depending on some conditions or causes such as I have been describing to you. But as the disorder becomes more marked and sys-tematized, it will be found to assume one or other of certain forms, and to be accompanied by certain symptoms which have gained for it the name of mania, or melancholia, or acute dementia; and as the treatment and prognosis must

Nor in chronic.

vary according to the symptoms, I shall pass in review some specimens of these different patients, that I may be enabled to give you some practical advice as to what you are to do when called upon to treat them. To classify insanity perfectly, we ought to be able to connect the symptoms of exaltation or depression with the pathological history of the individual, but this at present we cannot do. We are obliged to make two classifications, to lay down abstractedly a pathological classification of insanity, such as I have endeavored to give, and on the other hand to describe according to the most prominent and important symptoms the various patients we have to protect and cure. Classifying not the disorder, but patients, I would reverse the order suggested by the committee of the Medico-Psychological Association, and note in the first place the mental symptoms observable at the time of inspection, and afterwards assign to these their pathological significance, if the history or the symptoms enable us to do so. As in all diseases, the immediate symptoms must direct the immediate treatment, though the pathology will also have an importance which it is hard to over-estimate.

LECTURE VI.

Causes of Insanity—Predisposing Causes or Tendencies—Hereditary Predisposition — Prognosis — Statistics — Age— Sex — Condition of Life—Is Insanity on the Increase?—Exciting Causes—1. Moral— How to be Avoided—2. Physical—Prevention of the Recurrence of Insanity.

IN my lecture on the Pathology of Insanity I pointed out that each case at its commencement ought to be examined as a whole, and all the various conditions considered, which, by preceding it, become the cause. These conditions are, some of them, extremely complex, some comparatively simple. They often require themselves to be resolved into simpler causes, and for this reason it is necessary that we should investigate them at greater length than has been already done; and first I must set before you certain states, which are often called predisposing causes of insanity, such as sex, age, degree of civilization, inherited taint, and the like. It is clear that these can only be called causes in the sense of their being concurrent conditions of the individual who for the time is insane. A man in one or other of these states has a greater tendency to become insane, if other circumstances also tend to produce insanity in him. The latter may be the result of a number of tendencies which may exist separately in others without producing anything of the kind, but which, concurring in him, are the cause of it; or these tendencies may remain for years unproductive of evil, till some external circumstance completes the series, and overthrows the stability of the mind. Speaking generally, we may examine the causes of insanity under

Predisposing causes or tendencies.

the heads of *tendencies*, or, to use a commoner term, *pre-disposing causes*, and *events*, more or less accidental to the individual, such as are generally called *moral and physical* causes. It is not my intention to examine these various causes with the idea of connecting them with the pathological state of the brain in insanity. I have already considered this, and have spoken of some from this point of view: I mention them now in order to make some suggestions of a practical nature.

The first *tendency* which demands your attention is hereditary transmission, for it is of all the most potent, and ought always to be kept in view by those aware of its existence, whether medical men, parents, or guardians. Here is a cause of insanity which cannot be got rid of, a part and parcel of the individual's constitution and being; consequently his surroundings must be adapted to it; and, so far as we can, we should avert such events as are likely to upset his mental balance. Much may be done in this way if friends will only look the threatening evil in the face, and not try to hide it away, in the vain hope that no one will ever know it.

The first remark to be made is, that children may inherit insanity from parents who are not insane; and this we can explain in two ways: *first*, although the parents may not have been insane, insanity may have existed in their parents and reappeared in the grandchildren, skipping a generation; *secondly*, though the parents may not have been insane, they may have been the subjects of neuroses, which in their progeny become insanity; they may have been chronic drunkards, epileptics, hypochondriacs, weak-minded, or have indicated their nervous condition by chorea, stammering, and the like. The reverse of this is also true: insane parents, either or both, may have a number of children, some insane, others idiots, others epileptics, deaf mutes, or nervous, and some perfectly sane and sound. Two laws of nature are concerned

in the production of these phenomena. One is, that peculiarities and abnormities are apt to recur in descendants for
many generations; the other, that there is always a tendency
to return to the type of health in beings which have sufficient
vitality to perpetuate their existence and carry on their race
for successive generations. We could not breed an insane
family, of which all the members should be insane for generations. We should have sterility and extinction, or a return
to a healthy type. Were this not so, the numbers of our
lunatics would be tenfold what they are. We may see one
child in a family insane, and the others sane. The one has
inherited more of the ancestral defect than the others, but in
the descendants of the latter the family taint may again reveal itself. All these points you will have to consider if
Advice as to   you are consulted as to the marriage of persons of
marriage.   whose families some member is insane. This question will come before you in various ways. You will be asked
whether you can sanction the marriage of a man or a woman
who has once been insane; also, whether you advise that of
a person whose father, mother, brother, sister, or more distant
relative, is or has been insane. You will be consulted on
both sides, on behalf of the individual, and also by him or
her who is about to enter into matrimonial relations with the
tainted family. Here professional confidence and ethics are
involved, and cases arise of no little difficulty. It is not easy
to lay down any rules for your guidance. This much I may
say, that if any one has already had an attack of insanity,
there is always good reason for thinking that he or she will
have another sooner or later; consequently, whoever is about
to marry such a man or woman, ought, beyond all question,
to be informed of the preceding, and the chances of subsequent attacks. You will find, however, that such matters
are kept profound secrets; and not once or twice, but over
and over again, complaints have been made to me that they
not only were not made known to the intended, but that the

most flagrant falsehoods were told when the direct question was asked.   There is also another consideration,—the prospects of the children.   Where a woman has been insane, her insanity is so likely to recur during pregnancy, or after parturition, or even during the first excitement of nuptial intercourse, that I never could bring myself to consent to the marriage of such a one ; in addition, her children would run a great risk of being insane, nervous, epileptic, or idiots. A man is not exposed to so many causes of insanity as a woman, but his children are also liable to be affected with the inherited taint.   Of course, if the woman is past child-bearing, there is far less objection to her contracting marriage.   Then it is for the husband only to say whether he chooses to encounter the risk of marrying one who has already shown symptoms of the disorder.

If we have to consider the marriage of persons who have never themselves shown any signs of derangement, but whose parents, or brothers, or sisters, have been, or are, insane, we have a much more complicated problem to solve. Much must here depend on the number of individuals in a family who have been, or are, insane.   I have known a family in which, out of nine sons and daughters, six have shown unmistakable signs of mental disturbance : marriage with any one of these children should certainly be avoided. But we may see other families in which perhaps one member is insane and the rest perfectly sound.   In this case we can only argue in view of the particular individual.   I know brothers of insane men and women who are, in my opinion, as little likely to become insane as any of my acquaintance, but the transmitted taint may crop out in some of their children, even if the majority escape.   I would not go the length of forbidding every one to marry who had an insane relative, for the number thus barred would be immense ; but it must be considered that there is a certain element of risk, and this at any rate should be clearly set before the person who is thinking of entering into the union. And the risk is greater where either of the parents has been insane than where brothers or sisters have; also, it is greater for girls than for men, for obvious reasons; also, it is greater for a brother who has an insane brother, than for one who has an insane sister; and conversely, an insane sister increases the risk of a girl more than an insane brother. It is, I believe, a fact borne out by statistics, that daughters inherit insanity from an insane mother in greater proportion than sons, and in the same ratio sons inherit it from an insane father. The risk, therefore, to a daughter or son would be determined to some extent by the sex of an insane parent. I said that peculiarities are apt to return in descendants through many generations. The chance, however, of their appearing in any one individual, is lessened in proportion to his distance from the diseased ancestor. Insanity is most frequently derived from parents, but it may come from grandparents, great-grandparents, or progenitors even more remote. When it comes from grandparents, it is called *atavic*, and is Atavism. said to have skipped a generation. This is nothing but an instance of a defect reappearing at a longer interval than the first generation, and is only a variety of the general law. For we often find that although some one or more of the children may escape, yet others will show signs of insanity or other neuroses. If the descendants of these healthy children are affected, we may call it atavism, but the disorder cannot be truly said to have missed a generation if uncles and aunts were affected. I do not believe that we ever find a number of children of insane parents all entirely exempt from insanity or allied disorders, which afterwards are manifested in the grandchildren, the intermediate generation being completely unscathed. The fact is, that we have very imperfect data on which to base our laws of heredity. The paupers who come to our county asylums know little of the history of their family beyond their nearest of kin; the well-

to-do portion of the community deny the existence of hereditary insanity in their families in a way which must be heard
to be believed; and as nothing is called insanity but that
which necessitates incarceration in an asylum, and as other
neuroses are disregarded altogether, it is clear that our information is valueless. You may, possibly, some day be able to
follow the fortunes of a family in which insanity is manifested for two or three generations. A carefully recorded
history of such a one would be of the highest value.

I have said that among the descendants of insane patients
there is the tendency to revert to the healthy type, Hereditary
this being effected by the introduction of vigorous insanity
germs from other stocks, while a certain portion, not in two ways.
healthy enough for this, descends by gradual stages to sterility, idiocy, and extinction. Hence two things: first, we
are not likely to have to look back very many generations
to find the source of the inherited disease; secondly, it follows that people must be continually contracting that which
becomes in their descendants hereditary insanity—for hereditary insanity is not an entity to be acquired and transmitted
per se. It must itself have had a cause and a beginning, and
this we shall have to seek among the pathological causes and
conditions of nervous disorders.

If we have the opportunity of knowing and observing all
the children in a family tainted with insanity, it will not be
difficult to point out, even at an early age, those individuals
in which it is most likely to be developed. Children may
show signs of a nervous temperament almost from birth.
Convulsive attacks, night horrors, a tendency to spasmodic
ailments, chorea, or epilepsy, mark out those who inherit,
beyond others, the hereditary weakness. These we should
specially guard: their future and their external surroundings
must be regulated so as to preserve them from too great responsibilities, too continuous labor, too sudden changes of
fortune. We must, so far as is possible, create their circum-

stances, and not leave them to be the creatures of circumstance entirely beyond their control.   Although we cannot
guarantee any one against becoming insane, we can point to
those most threatened, and it may be necessary for such, if
they be women, to pass through life without encountering
the perils of childbearing.

But, besides this, there is another practical point in connection with the question of hereditary insanity.
Prognosis.   When we are called to an insane patient, and are
told that there is insanity in the family, how will the information affect our prognosis?   Many persons think that a
patient has no chance of recovery if the disorder is inherited.
Is this so?   I have found in my own experience that those
affected by inherited insanity recover, at any rate in the first
attack, quite as often as others.   Being unstable by nature
and constitution, they are thrown off their balance by something that is often trifling and removable, and often there
may be no assignable cause.   So by dint of seclusion and
quiet they regain their former equilibrium, probably to again
break down at some future time.   Such people, as you may
conceive, recover more surely than those who have brought
on insanity by years of alcoholism, or syphilis, or sexual
excess.   And possibly for the same reasons the death-rate is
less in them, at any rate in the first attack.   There is unquestionably a tendency to subsequent recurrence of the
malady, but this exists in all who have been insane, whatever may have been the cause.

Statistics on the subject are valueless.   One author attributes 10 per cent. of cases to this cause, another no
Statistics.   less than 90.   This arises from lack of information
on the part of some friends, and the wilful concealment of
others, and also because some statisticians seek for insanity
only, taking no account of other neuroses, such as epilepsy
or paralysis.   If we make the attempt, we shall soon find
how difficult it is to get an accurate account of the health of

the father and mother, and grandfather and grandmother of any one patient.

As insanity may be engendered of nervous disorders of other kinds in the parents, or as the parents' insanity may appear as the child's chorea, so may insanity of one kind in the parent reappear as insanity of another kind in the children; in fact, the latter may represent every variety of the disorder. As I have already said, the particular character of it, the mania or the melancholia, depends on the constitutional strength or weakness of the individual at the time of the outbreak, and the same person may be at the one time maniacal, at another melancholic. It is true that we frequently see the same form in successive generations, *e. g.*, suicidal melancholia or hereditary drunkenness, but this can only be looked upon as a coincidence, if we consider the vast number of cases where the form is different, and where various children are variously affected.

The tendency to become insane is greater or less according to the age of the individual, and the character of the insanity is also determined to a considerable extent _{Age.} by this. We find insanity, it is true, at all ages, but in the first decade of life it is rare. In the second it is more frequent; the mind developing, the child is growing into the man or the woman, and is acquiring knowledge, and is "looking before and after." But the next decade produces even more cases, and the period between twenty-five and forty years is that in which the number attains its maximum; this we recognize as the time of highest development, the prime of vigor, the height and climax of all hope and forward-looking, the time when strength is strained to the utmost in the battle of life. After this, in each successive decade, the number declines, just as in youth it rose.

According to the time of life, variations in the nature of the insanity are observable. In childhood, we find it displayed in violence of temper and act, in irregular and paroxysmal attacks, often of a convulsive character, alternating with cataleptoid states, recalling to our minds the choreic and convulsive condition of other children. The mental symptoms are not those of the fully-developed mind—delusions, but perverted feelings, hatred of relatives, wanton and indecent behavior, cruelty and destructiveness, and hallucinations of the senses—such as we often witness in the dreams and nightmares of the young. After puberty, we may find more of the ordinary insanity of adult life; but this will be generally attended with violence and mania rather than by depression. Of fifty-seven boys and girls admitted during five years into St. Luke's Hospital, all of whom were below the age of twenty, only eight were melancholic. Between the ages of twenty and forty we meet with violent and acute mania and acute delirium. This is especially the period at which we should expect these forms of insanity. Later in life, in the time of waning strength and declining vigor, both bodily and mental, we find melancholia prevail. Fear and religious despondency constantly accompany the weakened nervous condition of the old, while later still we see the mental faculties giving way, and dementia and vacuity, rather than insanity, come over the sufferer as he sinks into second childishness and mere oblivion.

These are, speaking generally, the forms we meet with at each epoch of life, but exceptions to them are not unfrequent. We may find melancholia in youth and early manhood; we may meet with acute delirium in patients past their climacteric. And when we do, the prognosis is bad; in the latter case especially. I have found melancholia in the young far more difficult to eradicate than mania. It is generally prolonged, even if recovery takes place at last. Melancholia after parturition is often extremely obstinate, and yields with difficulty to remedies.

What has the sex of the patient to do with the chance of insanity showing itself? Do more men or women become insane? Here authors differ, and statistics mislead. The records of various countries would seem to show that in some more males become insane, in others more fe- Sex. males. Into the figures and tables, and the many fallacies to be eliminated, I will not enter. In countries where the males predominate in the asylums, it is said that this is due to the fact that females are more easily managed at home, and therefore not sent so often to the asylum. On the other hand, the preponderance of females in our own asylums is explained by the lesser mortality among them, whereby they live a long time, swelling the lists of those in confinement. My own opinion is, that we have no accurate statistics on this point, for only those relating to new cases are of value. The comparative numbers of patients under confinement' at a given time must necessarily be influenced by a variety of circumstances. In the Report of the year 1868, the Commissioners give, as the number of the inhabitants of asylums and hospitals in England, 3363 private male patients, and 2489 private female; while of paupers there were 12,371 males, and 14,990 females. I explain this discrepancy in this way: more males become insane than females, but die in much larger proportion, consequently the number of pauper females goes on increasing from the accumulation of chronic cases. In the well-to-do classes, however, so many females are kept at home that the male population of asylums predominates. The deaths during the same year, 1868, in asylums and hospitals, were 1876 males and 1489 females; and this is probably about the usual proportion in which the sexes die while insane.

Probably the difference in the number of the two sexes who become insane is not very material, but I think the males must be the larger body; otherwise, considering the mortality, they would fall below the number of the females further than they do. It might be thought that females are more likely to become insane, inasmuch as they are manifestly more prone to many nervous disorders,—to chorea, hysteria, and allied neuroses. Yet, for all this, they are much less prone to serious brain disease. Men are the chief sufferers from apoplexy, hemiplegia, softening, and the like; and among the insane we find general paralysis attacking at least ten men for one woman, and among women of the higher classes it is quite unknown. It is this fatal form which swells the mortality of the male insane; and it has been said that, if we except the deaths from general paralysis, more women die than men. But I turn to the statistics of St. Luke's Hospital, where only curable cases are admitted, and where no paralytics are kept to die: out of 7311 males and 10,778 females admitted, 808 males died, and only 573 females, i. e., double the proportion of males.

Among the so-called predisposing causes of insanity are _{Condition} ranked the condition of life of the patient, and the _{of life.} degree of civilization. Are civilized nations more prone to insanity than barbarous? Are the poor more affected by it than the rich? The single than the married? Here is a field for much speculation, profitable, however, to the philanthropist and the philosopher, rather than to the practical physician; for it is obvious that when we discuss the chances of a poor man or a rich man becoming insane, we take into consideration the whole surroundings of the individual and his ancestors, and include in our survey circumstances that are entirely beyond the reach of the physician. It is equivalent to inquiring whether education or its absence tends towards insanity, or good food or scanty, or hard work or little work, or head-work or hand-work. Though of little practical value, inasmuch as there must ever be poor and rich, yet the question is interesting, and when rightly considered and compared with carefully scrutinized statistics, it is valuable in its bearings on the general history of our country.

And first with regard to civilization: of this we may say at once, almost from *a priori* consideration, that it tends to the production of insanity. The life of civilized man is a highly specialized and complex life; the variations of its surroundings are endless, and it requires to be adjusted to these unceasingly. And as is the life so must be the brain : the brain of the savage is a simple structure compared with our own, as the whole organism of one of the lower animals is simple, compared with the complex human system. To say that our specialized and complex brain is more apt to be disordered than that of lower men, is no more than saying that a compound piece of mechanism is more likely to get out of order than a simple one. Nevertheless, it is also true that much of the insanity of civilization might be prevented. It grows out of the evils and vices of civilization, just as fevers and such like disorders are engendered by the crowding of populations. Although it must always be that the hardworking brain of civilized man is more prone to disorder than that of the childlike savage of the wilderness, yet it is to be hoped that the preventible sources of insanity may be by degrees diminished, just as sanitary knowledge and laws will reduce the mortality from fevers, scarlatina, small-pox, and the like.

If we compare civilized with uncivilized countries by means of the statistics of insanity, we shall labor in vain. We have enough to do rightly to examine the statistics of our own country. There are not half-a-dozen other countries in the world, civilized or uncivilized, whose statistics are comparable with our own. In the year 1844, there were in the asylums of England and Wales 11,272 lunatics, and in workhouses and private dwellings, 9339. In 1858, there were in asylums 22,184; in workhouses, &c., 13,163. In 1868, in asylums 32,605; in workhouses, &c., 17,513. That is, the registered lunatics of England and Wales, who in 1844 numbered 20,611, in 1868 reach the total of 50,118. These figures include the whole lunatic population, private and pauper; but if we look at the statistics of the private patients only, we find that in 1858 these numbered 4612, and in 1868, 5244, being an increase of only 632, while the total of the lunatics of 1868 exceeds that of 1858 by 14,771.

We are told, however, that insanity is not on the increase, Is insanity on that these larger numbers are the result of the the increase? sending to asylums patients, especially paupers, who formerly were kept at home, and of more stringent legislation as regards private patients, also of the prolonged life of those who are cared for in the comfortable asylums of England. The last is probably the most valid reason; as for the first, pauper lunatics cannot be kept at home long; a few idiots and naturals may run about a village; as they used to do, so do they now. But in 1844 pauper lunatics were sent to workhouses, if not to asylums, and so were registered. If, however, we examine, not the numbers of patients remaining in asylums, but the numbers of those admitted in each year, we find that the increase is not so startling, that the average annual increase of admissions in the nine years, 1858–1867, was only three per cent. That lunacy is not on the increase among the upper classes is, I think, quite proved by these statistics; for with the present very stringent administration of the law, the increase of 632 private patients is extremely small, considering the increase of population. It is doubtful, however, whether the increase of the number of pauper lunatics can be looked upon as normal, and in proportion to the population. My own opinion is that among the lower classes of our countrymen insanity is on the increase: let us see if we can discover any sources of the disease existing among them, to which the richer portion of the community is less exposed. One thing we may at once observe: there is a degree of drunkenness among the lower classes of this country which is not to be found in the higher. Those who read the accounts of the habits and customs of the richer classes at the close of the last and the beginning of the present century must be aware that the gentlemen of our own day are, as regards temperance, entirely different from our grandfathers, with whom intemperance was the rule rather than the exception. It cannot but be that amongst these classes the children of our own times must benefit largely in all that concerns their nervous condition by this change in their parents' life. But it is to be feared that our lower orders are in no degree reformed in the matter of drink. Notwithstanding the exertions of temperance societies, the amount of drunkenness still prevalent is enormous, and is almost confined to the lower orders—the working men—below the shopkeeper class. Making all allowance for the highly-colored pictures drawn by the advocates of total abstinence, it is probable that intemperance is on the increase rather than decreasing. Hence, I believe, springs the ever-renewed insanity of our lower classes. For as insanity has a tendency to die out like other diseases—to cause the extinction of a race, or itself to be overcome by the greater vigor of some of the stock—it is clear that the enormous insane population of our country must owe its insanity to ever-present causes,—it cannot all have been inherited from our great-grandfathers. And if we could accurately ascertain the statistics of insanity in other countries, civilized, semi-civilized, or barbarous, I think it is probable that we should find insanity in proportion to the use of intoxicating liquors or substances. Secondly, poverty itself bears a part in the causation of insanity. The poorest counties in England contribute the largest numbers to their respective asylums. According to the returns, Dr. Thurnam tells us Wiltshire stands in the unenviable position of having a greater proportion of insane paupers than any other county of England and Wales. Those most nearly approaching it are Gloucester, Oxford, Berks, and Dorset—all agricultural counties. According to the poor-law returns, Wiltshire has a larger proportion of pauperism than any other county—viz., 1 in 12; the next in order being Dorset, Oxford, Gloucester, Berks, and Hereford.

The fact that in Ireland, with a decreasing population, we find an increase in the numbers of the insane, may aid us somewhat in discussing the causes of insanity. Here we have no keen encounter for success in the battle of life, no overwhelming business, or speculation, or accumulation of wealth; all is on the decline: poverty, ignorance, and fanaticism, and withal drink, are the chief causes to which we must ascribe the increase of insanity. That the poor must be more prone to become insane than the rich, is consistent with the pathology of the disorder. Insufficient food is an acknowledged source of defect in the nerve-power, and with this there must be the concomitant anxiety, the care for to-morrow, the spectacle of the family stinted of the necessaries of life, and want of early medical advice and treatment. Poverty of this kind must weigh heavily on the mind. When we say that the poor are more disposed to insanity, we virtually mean the poor in any class of life. There may be well-to-do people in all ranks of life, who, although they would not be classed among the rich, do not suffer from poverty. Amongst these well-to-do folks of the artisan class the great causes of insanity are, first, the want of education, which leads to the second, drink. Whether either the one or the other of these can be diminished by legislation is one of the questions of the age. If we could lessen drunkenness, we might close some of our asylums; till we do this we shall have to enlarge them.

I have thus glanced at some of what are called the pre-Exciting disposing causes of insanity, which are in truth the
causes.   conditions of certain classes of the community, and can only in a sense be considered causes. But there are others, special to the individual, which are called *exciting causes*, and whether preventible or not, frequently bring about the particular attack of insanity. Of many of these I have already spoken in discussing the pathology of the disorder, but some few words still remain to be said.

In speaking of one section of these exciting causes—namely, the *moral* or *psychical*—I divided them into those which operated suddenly, causing a great shock or *Moral causes.* fright, and those which produced insanity by anxiety or worry spread over many years. Of these, the former, I think, is more frequently the active agent in the causation of insanity. A sudden calamity, loss of a dearly-loved relative or friend, reverse of fortune, political catastrophe, or a shock or fright proceeding from some awful spectacle or violent quarrel, or near approach to death—these are the things which unhinge the mind, throw it from its balance, and may render even a tolerably strong-minded person incapable of taking care of himself for a time. The causes that operate, not suddenly, but slowly, may produce insanity, or other brain disease, the result of over-fatigue and work. The brain becomes worn out, and "softening" and such like conditions are the result.

The pathological causation of insanity I have not here to consider. When I speak of the causes, it is with the view of examining into such matters as may be prevented, or taken away from those who are insane or threatened with insanity. For it is certain that psychical causes preponderate in the production of insanity, because the persons who most frequently become insane are they who are strongly predisposed thereto, and are easily thrown off their balance by mental influences. Those who àre perfectly free from all predisposition and taint do not become insane from losses, worry, or work. They suffer, and are strong; they buffet vigorously the waves of adverse fortune, and when the malevolent tide again ebbs, they are none the worse for the contest. But it behooves us to counsel and advise those, or the friends of those, who by hereditary taint or previous attacks *How to be* of insanity are predisposed and liable to its invasion, *avoided.* to avoid to the utmost all that is likely to cause uncertainty, harass, or reverses in their daily life. There is much, of course, that no one can foresee, avoid, or escape. Health of self or family is a matter of uncertainty. Accidents may happen to wife or children, shocking sights may occur, but, nevertheless, in the choice of employment, and method and rule of life, much may be done to avoid that which is to some a fertile cause of insanity. Supposing we have to deal with a young man, whose parents, or brothers, or sisters have been insane, or who at an early age has shown that he is himself not free from the family taint—and insanity in the young is, as I have said, almost invariably due to hereditary influences —we should advise that such a one should be put to some occupation or calling not attended by any great harass or responsibility, one of which the duties and work are of a routine character, affording a fair opportunity of holiday and recreation. He should not follow the profession of a lawyer or a doctor, for in them he will find hard and constant work, heavy responsibility, and the necessity of appearing in public; and his work and anxieties will follow him to his fireside and hours of sleep. In the church he will or may be assailed by religious doubts, by a sense of duties insufficiently discharged, and by all that tends to religious melancholy. In the army he will be exposed to the temptations of an idle life, and the vicissitudes of climate. No post is so suited to these individuals as that of a government office. The hours are light, the responsibility is not formidable, the holidays are long, and if the emolument is not large, it is at any rate certain, and certainty is above everything desirable. For the latter reason the property of such persons should not consist of doubtful or speculative investments, which may expose them to great anxiety or possible ruin; but they should be induced, even at a loss of income, to place their capital in solid and sure securities. Many anxieties and worries which are every day occurring, might certainly be avoided by a little prudence and forethought.

It is no doubt of immense service to many such men that they should be happily married at an early age. The ten-

dency to eccentricity and a solitary life is thereby counteracted, as well as other habits or vices. But everything will
depend upon their finding wives who will be truly helpmeets
to them. Doctors can only speak in the most general terms
on such a subject; but it is right that parents and guardians
should put a stop so far as they can to the growing attach-
ments of a couple in no way fitted for each other. The wife
of such a man should be healthy, one who will not cause
him constant anxiety, broken nights, or the expense attendant upon bad health, who will not breed sickly children to
fade and die, or to grow up a perpetual misery to their parents; and, above all, she should not be a relation.

If the object of our solicitude is a girl, what can we do to
keep her from harm? The first question is, shall she marry?
Here I would say that no girl who has ever shown any
symptoms of actual insanity ought ever to marry at all.
Insanity is not the less likely to return because the attack
has been transitory. If it has come on at an early age without assignable cause, it is because it is inherited, and it is
very likely to reappear during pregnancy or after childbirth.

But if there have been no symptoms in the girl herself,
but she comes of parents, one or both of whom have been
insane, or if she has brothers or sisters insane, what are we
to say? We must be guided by what we know and see of
her, by her *physique*, her history, especially the history of
her infancy, the absence or presence of "fits," of "nervous-
ness," "hysteria," habitual sleeplessness, or irritability, especially at the catamenial time. If a girl who is predisposed
to insanity does marry, it is important that she should not
marry a poor man, whose life will be a constant struggle for
existence; nor a sickly man, whom she must always nurse;
nor one whom she must follow to tropic climates; nor one
who is violent, irritable, or jealous. If she is obliged to do
something for her livelihood, and does not marry, her work
should, if possible, be free from heavy responsibility. It is

obvious that we shall have very little to do with the arranging of all this. If we express our opinion, we often say our say, and say it in vain. And yet it is well to turn such subjects over in our minds, and to be ready with an opinion upon them. What I have said applies to the rich rather than the poor: it is about the rich and not the poor that we shall be consulted.

The physical causes of insanity are in many cases beyond Physical prevention. We can only deal with them as they causes. arise. They may be the sequel of other disorders, or accidents, or may be due to the time of life.

Insanity, the result of alcohol, opium, or haschisch, is no doubt preventable; but we have to deal with acquired habits in the majority of instances when brought into contact with persons who take these substances. When we have the opportunity of supervising the management of those predisposed to insanity, it is important to check at the outset that which may grow to be a habit hard to be abandoned. First and foremost they must be watched while children, lest they give themselves up to masturbation, for they will carry it to excess, and will be the least likely to abandon it, if it be once confirmed—a truth which applies equally to girls and boys. Early habits of drinking also are frequently contracted by weak-minded people, both males and females; and we constantly find that habitual drunkards, as well as dipso-maniacs, are the offspring of insane or epileptic parents. We must be careful lest we encourage a love of drink in "nervous" people, especially women, by an incautious administration of stimulants for the cure of hysterical, hypochondriacal, or neuralgic symptoms.

That which I believe to be the most common cause of general paralysis of the insane, viz., sexual excess, is a matter over which we have very little control. The disease does not commence in boyhood, rarely before the age of twenty-five. It occurs as often amongst married men as amongst single, and frequently until it shows its presence there is nothing to call for warning. Such warnings are rarely heeded, but it may be in our power to give them to many, both husbands and wives, for general paralysis is not the only ill that springs from unrestrained sexual intercourse.

In considering the causes of insanity, we shall have to bear in mind not only the prevention of insanity in a patient who has never been insane, but also the prevention of its recurrence in one who has had an attack. *Prevention of the return of insanity.* Here our difficulties will be in some respects greater, in others less. The same cause of worry or grief may not occur again, or may be removed or counteracted; the same bodily illness, as fever or measles, may not recur. Attention to the health, to diet and regimen, may remove some causes—syphilis may be eradicated, drink avoided. But, on the other hand, we have the fact to contend with, that insanity has really existed in the individual, and beyond all question has a tendency to recur either upon a very slight cause, or without any assignable cause whatever. This it is which makes it so hazardous a thing to marry a man or woman who has ever shown any symptoms of the disorder. When a patient leaves an asylum, we are generally asked what is to be done? what is to be guarded against? and our answers are for the most part very general: avoid hard work, all that calls for great emotional exhaustion, avoid disappointment. This may seem foolish counsel, but those who cannot bear disappointment should not encounter it. How many do we see aspiring to that to which they can never attain, trying for appointments and the prizes of life which are utterly out of their reach! Quiet and contentment are the qualities which favor health of mind, but it is not for us to give these to the restless spirit of a patient saturated with insanity.

Men and women become insane, because it is in their nature and constitution to develop insanity, and when we hear that this or that has caused their insanity, it is often their restless and half-crazy brain that has made mountains out of molehills, and given an objective existence to troubles and vexations which exist in their minds subjectively, and have no outward reality whatever.

LECTURE VII.

The Symptoms of Insanity—The False Beliefs of the Insane—Defini-
tions of Terms—Delusions—Their Rise—Varieties—Hallucinations
—Their Seat—Hallucinations of Sight—Hearing—Smell—Taste—
Touch.

HAVING hitherto spoken to you of the disease termed insanity, and the pathological condition of an insane man, I
now proceed to consider the symptoms, the things which
insane people do and say, by which we judge them to be of
unsound mind. Many acts and many ideas at once reveal
the state of the mind, though there may be no fixed line of
demarcation between acts or ideas, sane and insane.

If we take, first, the beliefs of insane persons, we shall
have to examine the meaning of certain words met with in
treatises on the subject. These are *delusions, illusions,* and
hallucinations—words used by different authors in various
senses, with some of which, at any rate, you must be
acquainted.

A *delusion* is a false belief in some fact which, generally
speaking, personally concerns the patient, of the Definition of
falsity of which he cannot be persuaded, either by Delusion.
his own knowledge and experience, by the evidence of his
senses, or by the demonstrations and declarations of others.
A man thinks his head is made of brass, that he has a fire
in his inside, that he is a beggar or a prince; and no amount
of proof convinces him of the contrary.

Hallucinations are false perceptions of the senses, the eye,
the ear, the nose, and so on. The hallucinated patient
thinks that he sees in the blackest darkness, or Definition of Hal-
hears a voice through any number of thick walls, lucination.

whereas his seeing or hearing is entirely subjective, taking place altogether within his own head without any excitation conveyed to his organs from the outer world—when, in fact, he would hear and see the same were he deaf or blind.

An *illusion* is also a false perception of the senses, or rather Definition of a mistaken perception. There is something to see Illusion. and something to hear; but that which the patient thinks he sees is not the real thing, but something else. He sees a chariot in the sky, when every other person sees a cloud; he hears a voice, when others hear the noise of a carriage or a distant footfall.

Such are, I believe, the commonly received meanings of these words, but such interpretations are necessarily arbitrary. And by some the word *illusion* is used as synonymous with *delusion*. Prichard, in his well-known work, nowhere speaks of *delusions*, but uses *illusion* instead.

There are various questions which arise in connection with these fancies of the insane—*e. g*, how do delusions and hallucinations arise? what is the relation between delusions and hallucinations? what is their significance in the diagnosis and prognosis of insanity?

We know too little of the physiology of the brain to be able to put our finger on the seat of an hallucination; we can only approach the study thereof by comparing analogous phenomena in healthy people, or in people not insane, and by contrasting the delusions and hallucinations of one insane person with those of another.

Hallucinations bear to delusions the same relation that the Relation of simple perception of objects does to judgment and hallucina- reasoning founded on the perception, and both haltions to delu- lucinations and delusions illustrate the growth of sions. ideas and intellect in the mind. For, as I have said already, sensations, the stimulation of the organs of sense and the resulting feelings, and also the feelings experienced by the organism generally, whether of pleasure or pain, are the origin and material out of which ideas and intellect are developed. These simple sensations, as they are linked together by memory, grow into complex ideas and complex feelings— feelings which we term emotions—but at the root of all are the bodily sensations caused originally in the majority of instances by stimulations coming from without, at any rate from without the cerebrum.

It would appear that delusions and hallucinations are false interpretations of morbid feelings and sensations Rise of occurring in various parts of the system, the falsity delusions. of which the disordered brain is not able to appreciate. In the case of delusions this is not difficult to trace. And thus we can explain how it is that the delusion of the insane man almost always refers to himself. Many sane persons believe in absurdities of all kinds—in charms, in witches, in ghosts, spirit-rapping, and the like—yet they may hold such beliefs without ever having seen or been concerned with any of these things. They entertain a mere abstract belief in them. But the delusions of the insane man have reference to himself, just as in dreams we are always present and see and hear what is going on : we do not dream abstract notions or facts which wholly concern others, in which we do not in some way participate.

Delusions are not the first indications of a change in the mental condition of the patient. This fact is important as regards both the pathology and also the legal diagnosis of insanity. The changed feeling may express itself in depressed manner, in unusual excitement, anger, restlessness, or in acts of an extraordinary or outrageous nature, without being translated at any time into what we know as delusions; and these when noticed have been usually preceded by a period of alteration, which may or not have attracted attention.

There is, as I have already said, an acute stage at the commencement of every case of insanity, though you may not see the patient during its continuance. But as insanity implies a deviation from the normal mental condition of the individual, so it connotes a physical disturbance of the brain-function, with impaired sleep, possibly pain, heat of head, flushed or pale face, suffusion of eyes, throbbing of carotids, and such like symptoms of cerebral disorder. This is the period of emotional alteration visible to others, of which the patient himself may or may not be conscious.

In the majority of instances this change is one which makes the patient feel or think that something is amiss with him, as in truth there is. His consciousness, however, of something being wrong with his head or his system generally, will vary much. He may be quite aware of it, and may seek advice and assistance like any other patient. He is more likely to be unconscious of his real condition, and to attribute the feeling he experiences to external causes. According to the feeling, its degree and intensity, will be the nature of the cause to which it is ascribed, and the means taken to get rid of it.

The defective condition of brain operates in two ways. First, the lack of nervous energy brings about the feeling of there being something wrong, and this may vary immensely in degree; secondly, the disorder in the various portions of the brain reduces it to such a state that the patient is unable to see the absurdity or impossibility of the explanations which he gives.

A man or woman feeling great depression of spirits pro-Gloomy ceeds to account for it according to his or her views. delusions. One thinks beggary the greatest evil that can befall him, and straightway fancies himself ruined, his wife and children starving, and the officers at the door to hale him to prison. So imperfect is the action of his entire brain, that he fails to assure himself from actual inspection of his accounts that everything is going on as usual. Another looks not at the things of this life, but at those of the future. His soul is lost, he is in the power of the Evil One, he is Satan himself, or Antichrist—there is no hope for him. And inasmuch as the feeling experienced is strange, unaccountable, mysterious, patients fly to the mysterious for the cause thereof. It is due to mesmerism, to electricity, to secret and loathsome disease hidden in the flesh and bones, destroying heart, stomach, and bowels, though not to be discerned outwardly. The ignorant man will think it due to witchcraft or the devil. According to his stores of knowledge, his education, and experience, each will invent a cause for that peculiar condition of which he is aware, but which he cannot rightly explain. Having no ideas connected with this feeling, he expresses it in those habitually associated with a feeling of deep gloom, anxiety, or displeasure. Feeling himself peculiar and changed, and another man, he thinks that all men are looking at him, pointing at him, deriding him. The cabmen and omnibusmen beckon to and mock him; the passers-by avoid him. And in the same way all the newspapers write about him; all the mysterious advertisements refer to him. If he cannot fix his annoyances on any one he knows, he thinks bands of unknown conspirators are plotting against him, and that these can, by occult and supernatural means, affect him, even when far distant. Then, as he feels discomfort in this or that part of his body, he says his head is of brass, or he is galvanized, or his inside burnt with fire. With all or some of these delusions he may vary greatly in his emotional display, being profoundly dejected and in a state of melancholia, or being irritated or angry, and inclined to act on the offensive, when we call his affection mania. And yet he may be equally melancholic and equally maniacal without his ideas being perverted into delusions, though they will be tinged with his prevailing feeling. Similarly, his delusions will range from possibilities, or even probabilities that require some examination before they can be pronounced delusions, up to the wildest absurdities and the most incoherent nonsense that a madman can utter. The latter are indications of a much greater brain-disturbance, a greater disconnecting of the relations of the various portions of the brain, and impairment of the brain-force and brain-circulation; but the prognosis is not always on this account more unfavorable. They bear the same relation to the possible delusions that the dreams and nightmares of the fever patient do to the natural dreams of the healthy sleeper.

There is a proneness on the part of most people to seek and assign a cause for all ailments, and for everything which is new, abnormal, or of which the origin is not plainly visible. Every one can tell us exactly where he caught his catarrh, what caused his diarrhœa, or what makes him "bilious." And people are still fond of flying to the mysterious, and of looking for their "causes" among things they do not understand. Take, for example, the common notions about the weather, the influence of the moon, of comets, and the like; and the superstitious and vulgar errors concerning all manner of diseases, from which quacks of every kind reap their fortunes. The only difference is that the delusions of the insane man, as I have said, have reference to himself alone, inasmuch as they are invented to account for a feeling of which he only is conscious. The proneness to account for it in this supernatural way is not peculiar to the insane, but is common to all, especially to those of uneducated or weak and unreflecting mind. Similarly, in dreams, cold feet make us imagine that we are walking on ice; an uneasy posture causes us to think we are in chains; or the general *malaise* of dyspepsia or a heavy supper calls up a succession of horrible fancies and vivid nightmares. We look on the brain of the dreamer as awake and acting in portions only; when it is all awake the dream is at an end; but in the case of some dreams which are extremely vivid, many moments may elapse before the whole force of the brain and the whole of its related parts can be so brought to

Cause assigned for the altered feeling.

bear upon the subject as to convince us that it is a dream and not a reality. The brain of the insane man fails in this power of perceiving the whole case.

So far we have considered those feelings of ill-being which express themselves in ideas of misfortune, accompanied Exalted by melancholy or anger; but there are patients mani- delusions. festing not only in idea and delusion, but in countenance, manner, and action, a feeling of well being, a conviction that the change is all for the better, that they are stronger, healthier, richer, happier than ever they were in their lives; and these symptoms in many cases, though not in all, are coincident with the presence of fatal brain disease, which will go on steadily and rapidly to death. All this is difficult to explain; nay, explain it precisely we cannot; we can only conjecture that the effect of this disease, which manifests itself in bodily paralysis as well as mental, is to blunt the sensibility of the brain, so that everything causes pleasure instead of pain to the half-roused centres: an asylum appears a palace, and a dinner of roast mutton a banquet of rich and *recherché* fare.

In all patients alike there is the same inability to see that the thing is a delusion. They see it when they recover—see it without the demonstration which failed to convince them while insane. Nothing, I think, can be more certain than this, that during the insane state the brain cannot act as a whole, cannot by means of one part correct the ideas which arise in another. These ideas are the concomitants of strange and altered feelings which have a real existence; and until the latter pass away, they are not to be removed by demonstration or argument. When the feeling subsides— the feeling of depression, or the excitement and elation which causes the grand and exalted fancies of some—the ideas in the majority of cases vanish also, especially if no long time has elapsed. The patient is said to have lost his delusions, and their gradual disappearance or occasional reappearance coincides markedly with the restoration of the general health and strength, of sleep, digestion, uterine or other functions. But it sometimes happens that the delusions remain after the feelings have gone, and we behold in the patient a confirmed monomaniac. The ideas which were at first the explanation to the patient of his altered sensations are stored up as facts of experience in a damaged brain, which never recovers from the injury it has received, and never resumes its entire working power; remaining permanently unable by means of one part to correct the false notions of another, it retains forever the dream that arose in its half-waking period.

The delusions most frequently met with amongst the insane may be arranged in comparatively a small number of classes. All, as I have said, are connected with self—the selfhood of the patient: all are supposed to indicate some change that has taken place with regard to himself. This change must be one for the better or the worse; a change affecting his worldly or his spiritual interests, his bodily condition or his surroundings; a change which has already happened, is happening, or is about to happen at some future time. The extravagance of the ideas will depend on the amount of brain-disorder, and we may often see this marked out by the delusions, as it rises to its climax, and then falls again to where it began.

The delusions presented by a patient who thinks that things are amiss with him, may be connected, as I have said, with his worldly or his spiritual interests. In the extreme melancholic condition which accompanies excessive depression and prostration of nerve-force, there will probably be delusions on both these points. The patient is ruined and a beggar, and he has also committed the unpardonable sin, and is doomed to eternal perdition, or he may fancy one of these things without the other. What do we learn from these de-

Delusions most commonly found.

Delusions characterized by despondency.

lusions? How do they affect the diagnosis and prognosis? We learn from them that the patient's condition is one of melancholia, and they ought to warn us, that in all probability he is, or will be, suicidal. Thinking that he is doomed, and that life is insupportable, incapable of reflection, and impelled by the ever-present horror of his position, he tries to shuffle off his mortal coil, and unless extreme precaution is used, he will certainly succeed. As regards diagnosis, the most valuable lesson taught by these delusions is, that the patient, being suicidal, will very likely try and escape, either that he may be free to commit suicide, or that he may wander over the face of the land to escape the evils that encompass him at home. The delusions may have reference to the past or the future; he may be in a state of profound remorse for imaginary crimes, or may shrink in terror from tortures and torments which are to come upon him unjustly hereafter; but practically there is little difference in the condition of these two varieties; frequently we find either kind of delusion in the same individual; either may impel a man to suicide, or to running away from the scene of his past sins or expected torments.

As for the prognosis, it is not very unfavorable in such cases, provided that the bodily condition is not too much reduced by disease or starvation: patients recover from melancholia in large numbers, and after long periods of time; in fact, if they do not succumb to the disorder and die at an early date, we may have great hopes of restoring them to their family and the enjoyment of life.

Prognosis.

Some may labor under a delusion that very much is amiss with them; yet their feelings may be not those of depression and melancholy, but rather of alarm, and restless anxiety, or anger and fury. So far as the delusions are concerned, it is evident that it is optional whether we call such persons melancholic or maniacal; but the general deportment and feeling of many of them is far from

Delusions characterized by anger or fear.

being melancholic, and is unquestionably maniacal; while a certain number may be ranged with equal propriety under either one or the other of the two classes.

Their delusions resemble, to some extent, those of the melancholic class. They imagine that some evil is going to happen to them. They do not, however, think they have deserved it, but that they are unjustly treated—that wicked men are conspiring to ruin them or their family, to blast their character, or put them to death. Here suicide will be rarer: more frequently we shall find attempts to escape, or avert by some means or other the impending catastrophe. Consequently you will understand that the diagnosis of such a patient involves the belief that he may be very dangerous to those about him. In order to escape he may set the house on fire, may try to obtain the keys from the attendants by force or bloodshed; may conceive the notion that those around him, especially strangers, are about to do him some evil, and murder them in supposed self-defence. A vast number of the homicides perpetrated by lunatics are done in fear and panic, especially those committed by patients suddenly waking out of sleep. Murders are committed by those who imagine that their victim has accused them of foul and unnatural crimes, and who suffer from hallucinations in which they actually hear a voice repeating these slanderous words. Or a man imagines that his food is poisoned, his clothes poisoned, the furniture and room tainted or filthy; he will say that his food contains blood or human flesh: and all these fancies make him refuse to eat, and very violent and dangerous without being melancholic.

The prognosis in such cases is not to be determined by the delusions alone, but must depend on the time they Prognosis. have existed, and on other circumstances which cannot be discussed here. Generally speaking, however, where such delusions as the foregoing have existed for a twelvemonth, and all the symptoms of acute disorder have subsided, the prognosis is bad, and the patient is likely to remain through life a dangerous homicidal lunatic.

A number of delusions are presented by those who fancy that the change they feel within them is all for the better. In their bodily or spiritual state, or worldly position and fortune, they are much better off than before. All these are said roughly to be suffering from mania with elation; but among them are included those afflicted with the most fatal of all the forms of insanity,—general paralysis. When a man between thirty and fifty-five years of age is full of delusions that he is of great strength, rank, and wealth, we may suspect that his malady is general paralysis, and test him by the rules I shall lay down in a future lecture. But frequently the same delusions appear in men and women who are not paralytic. They think they have, or are going to make, a great increase of income, that they are going into Parliament, are about to rise to the highest place in their profession, whatever that may be. All their speculations, however, venturesome or absurd, are to turn out very profitable, or they have invented, and are about to patent, new contrivances, which will be sources of endless wealth.

Delusions characterized by exaltation and gayety.

If the diagnosis in such cases leads us to conclude that the patient is suffering from general paralysis, the prognosis is summed up in one word,—the end is death; but we must not conclude too hastily from such delusions that paralysis is present: if it be not, patients often recover from this elated mania, always provided that the duration of the case is not so great as to make recovery hopeless. In fact, when there is no paralysis, no hallucination, and when the attack is recent, the prognosis is favorable. Neither are they suicidal or dangerous; suicidal they never are except by accident; they have too good an opinion of themselves and their position. They may be dangerous when thwarted, but it will be merely to escape from those who wish to confine

Prognosis.

them and curb their dignities and projects. They do more harm to property than to their own lives or those of others, and in their elated condition will squander a fortune in a few days or involve themselves in endless liabilities. And where recovery does not take place they often spend their existence very happily under a restraint which does not check their fancies, while it provides for their safety.

I now come to the subject of hallucinations which are met Hallucina- with daily amongst the insane, but, unlike delu-tions. sions, are found also in people who it must be conceded are sane. Difficult as it is to try to explain with anything like exactness the origin of delusions, it is still more difficult to account for hallucinations. We derive some assistance, however, from the sane and insane persons who can give an account of the rise and nature of these false perceptions of the senses; and I may say, I believe, without Do hallucina- fear of contradiction, that although hallucinations tions denote do not of themselves prove a patient to be insane, insanity? yet they accompany and indicate a disordered condition of brain. They come and go as the brain health and force fail or improve, and point to a defective state of brain circulation and organization no less than delusions. The difference is, that being mere perceptions — auditory and visual sensations—they are not necessarily compounded into judgments, and may exist and be recognized as hallucinations by the rest of the brain; whereas a delusion implies a judgment formed out of more than one perception or sensation—a proposition which necessarily consists of more than one term, the falsity of which the remaining portion of the brain is not able to understand. In other words, an hallucination implies a certain disturbance of brain causing the false sensation: if the hallucination is acted upon, if something is done because of it, a proposition or judgment is implied, and the patient may then be said to act because of the unsound condition of his brain and mind.

Hallucinations are closely allied to, nay, are, the same thing as frightful visions and nightmares which occur in children and adults, but do not come in perfect health, and point to some disturbance which ought to arrest the attention of a medical man. Writers on children's diseases have specially noticed these night-terrors, and all who have seen them will agree that a child thus affected is out of health. They often are witnessed in children when ill of acute disorders; in fact, hallucinations constitute the chief phenomena of the delirium of the young.

Whether the origin of an hallucination is primarily in the stomach, the periphery, or the organs of sense themselves, is immaterial. It is the idea-portion of the cerebrum that really is disordered, and that must be righted to dispel the false perception. The patient may be blind or _{Seat of hallu-} deaf, but the hallucination of sight or hearing may _{cinations.} be equally vivid and equally persistent. Hallucinations are in many cases so closely allied to delusions, and follow so nearly the general feeling of the patient—the melancholic and maniacal man hearing words which correspond to his gloomy thoughts, the elated having his own peculiar visions and voices—that it is difficult to say what is delusion and what hallucination; but in the case of sane and insane people, the sight or sound does not always appear to have any ascertainable origin or connections, any more than certain of our dreams. A lady of my acquaintance, when out of health, always saw a cat sitting on a particular stair. She was not averse to cats, nor afraid of the spectral cat, but it was to her an index of the state of her health; tonics and wine removed it, to return when next she fell to a weak state. We think to so great an extent, by means of sights and sounds, we picture so much in our thoughts and hear so much, it is no wonder that in a disturbed condition of brain our picturing and self-hearing go awry. That we can see when we shut our eyes, or hum an air in our heads without the least sound or motion of the larynx, we all know.

Possibly hallucinations may be explained somewhat as follows: We know that external sounds and sights

Explanation of hallucinations. come to us from without through the medium of an external ear or eye: that they are perceived by an internal organ of hearing or sight, and are then transmitted to the higher brain-centres, and laid up in memory as ideas, reproducible in consciousness without the agency of the organs. Thus, a person who is blind, either from disease of the external organ or the internal sensory ganglia, may yet see with the mind's eye, and reproduce in memory the appearances of objects which he has stored away. Now, we may suppose that in the case of an hallucination the internal organ is excited, not from without, as ordinarily happens, but downwards from the idea-portion of the brain. Accustomed, however, as he is, to connect all the sensations experienced with the external organ and the external world, the patient fails to perceive, sometimes at any rate, that the excitation is from within, and is firmly impressed with a belief that the sight which his organ of seeing really sees, and the voice he really hears, come from without, and not from within. The *idea* strikes his sensory ganglion so forcibly, that the shadow becomes a reality, which perchance may not be removable by demonstration or argument.

We may say a good deal about hallucinations with reference to diagnosis and prognosis, but it will be well to examine the hallucinations of the various senses.

The hallucinations which arise in the state of greatest exhaustion are those of sight; consequently, in acute

Hallucinations of sight. cases of insanity, as in acute disorders of the sane, we find these more frequently than any other kind. They arise and vanish with the acute stage; in chronic cases we find them less often than hallucinations of hearing.

Hallucinations of sight may be simply flashes of light,

shadows, colors, or fires, or they may be objects; sometimes they commence as the former, and merge by degrees into the latter. You are familiar with the hallucinations found in that disease of exhaustion which we term delirium tremens. In it by far the larger number are hallucinations of sight, visions of birds, animals, or snakes, in the room or on the bed. So, in fevers and other acute diseases, the wanderings and fears of the patient relate to what he sees rather than to what he hears, till at last he picks the imaginary flies from off the bedclothes in that stage which only precedes by a little the time when sight altogether fails, and he declares the room to be dark, though the sun is shining, or candles are burning in it.

Hallucinations of sight amongst the insane are frequently visions of the supernatural, especially in non-acute cases; patients see angels or visions of the Deity in some form or other, or spirits floating in the air in the shape of birds; they may see the forms of departed friends or heroes, or of the absent; they may also see fiends, spectres, or the devil. But, on examination of my notes of a great many cases, I find that the hallucinations of sight which most strictly deserved the name were observed far more frequently in acute than in chronic cases—in cases where there was at the time great cerebral disturbance with violent emotional display, heat of head, and want of sleep. Epilepsy in the insane is constantly followed by hallucinations both of sight and of the other senses.

Certain phenomena, termed by some hallucinations, ought rather to be looked upon as delusions: conspicuous among these are the mistakes of identity so common amongst the insane. A patient declares a stranger to be a relation or friend, or declares a near relation is not the person but somebody else—says her husband is not her husband, but a stranger, yet, possibly, asks after all at home—says the men in attendance are women, or the women men, or calls the medical attendant by the name of some former friend. Very curious are many of these assertions; but when they are made by patients who are free from all acute symptoms and can talk calmly on most points, we must look upon them as delusions of idea, and not as hallucinations, or even illusions of sight. They partake of the general change of feeling existing in the individual, which is projected outwards, and extended to all he sees. He thinks his wife and children are changed, just as he thinks himself changed into a most miserable or a most exalted person. The mistake is in his idea-region, and not in his organs of sight. Griesinger says:[1] "The seat of hallucination of sight must be the internal expansion of the optic nerves. Anatomical observations have yet to be made on this point; in dissections, the thalamal surfaces, the corpora quadrigemina and their neighborhood, also the centrum ovale, should be carefully examined." It is to be feared, however, that these phenomena are due frequently to disturbances of the entire brain-function of a very general kind, which are not likely to be traceable after death. In acute diseases, no one, so far as I am aware, has ever thought of looking, after death, for changes which would account for the particular phenomena of the delirium or hallucinations.

As hallucinations of sight occur in the acute rather than in the chronic stages of insanity, they do not warrant an unfavorable prognosis, inasmuch as there is more hope of recovery during the acute than during the chronic period. The prognosis of the case will depend, not upon these, but upon other symptoms, and the diagnosis will, by the same rule, be attended with no difficulty. In chronic cases I have generally found that where hallucinations of sight existed, others, especially of hearing, existed also. Of all the hallucinations caused by such substances as haschisch, opium, and the like, those of sight are the majority.

Prognosis.

---

[1] Sydenham Soc. Trans., p. 98.

Hallucinations of sight often occur in the dark, in which patients see not merely flashes of light, such as might be attributed to irritation of the optic apparatus, but actual objects—men or animals. This proves that the idea-region of the brain is the seat of the mischief, which is corroborated by the fact that blind persons are subject to hallucinations as well as those who can see. Curiously enough, many patients can dispel these hallucinations by closing the eyelids or covering the eyes. This is easily explained by the association of ideas. Being habitually unable to see anything with the eyelids closed, they do not see these phantoms of their diseased imagination.

In non-acute insanity, hallucinations of hearing are the most common and the most formidable. They are difficult to eradicate, and while they exist they render him who hears them the most dangerous of patients. In chronic cases, or in those in which insanity has revealed itself gradually and insidiously with few acute symptoms, hallucinations of hearing form at least two-thirds of all that we meet with. And when a patient of this class tells us that he or she hears "voices," not mere sounds, whistlings, humming, or the like, but words and sentences, we augur unfavorably of the case; our prognosis is gloomy, and our diagnosis is that such a one requires close watching and restraint. I have known patients lose the fancy of mere sounds. One gentleman used to hear "blowpipes" whistling down his chimney, and whistling at him in the street, and these by degrees vanished, but his mental health was never fully restored. He leads in solitude the life of a hypochondriac, and when he is a little more nervous than usual, he hears singing in his ears, and shows incipient symptoms of his former hallucinations. Patients hear voices either of those they know, or of unknown persons, natural or supernatural. As no one is to be seen, they generally imagine that the speaker is in the next room or house, or in a cupboard or

Hallucinations of hearing.

chimney. Of course, if it be a supernatural voice, it may come from the air inside or outside the house. One lady was so annoyed by voices coming through the wall that she purchased the adjoining house to compel them to cease. I need not say she did not so get rid of them. Many patients' whole lives are regulated by the commands they receive from "the voices." They eat, drink, walk, and sleep according to the commands they hear, and if compelled to act contrary to them, they tell us that they will suffer for such disobedience. They obey implicitly, holding the voice responsible, and so will commit frightful crimes without looking upon themselves as guilty or responsible. And as many patients will not reveal what the voices say, it follows that the whole class is eminently dangerous and uncertain. It often happens that there is great difficulty in extracting from a patient the confession that he hears voices, or that which the voices say. He appears afraid to tell, and seems bound down by some kind of compact not to do so. He thinks it a point of honor to conceal what passes, and it is only by our overhearing him answering in imaginary conversation that we ascertain the fact.

We may sometimes detect hallucinations of hearing in patients who have never revealed them, by noticing while we talk to them that they from time to time are inattentive, and appear to be listening to some one else. On being pressed, they will probably confess that they hear some one speaking. There is often the closest connection between the delusions of a patient and that which he hears. The latter is, in fact, the delusion done into audible words. Thus, a patient who hears a voice accusing him of various crimes, unnatural lust, and the like, entertains these delusions at all times. But there is great variety in what the voices say, and sometimes it appears to have no connection with other well-known delusions to which the individual is subject.

In some patients these hallucinations seem to deserve the

name of illusions, for though they take the form of voices and intelligible words, they are not heard in perfect stillness, but only when there is a noise going on ; which noise, whatever it may be—footsteps, the rattling of a door or window, or the wind—is converted into "voices." On the other hand, it is often difficult to distinguish between such hallucinations and mere delusions, to say whether the patient imagines that he is falsely slandered and accused, or hears voices repeating the words. And yet our prognosis may be materially affected by the one or other of these symptoms.

We know very little of the pathology of hallucinations of hearing. Empirically, we find that they are most Prognosis. difficult of removal, and that patients affected by them are amongst the most incurable of all lunatics ; but we have no knowledge of the pathological lesion which enables us to account for this. Neither can we say why they predominate in the non-acute forms of insanity, whilst in the acute hallucinations of sight are far more common. These are questions still open to examination.

Hallucinations of smell belong to the acute states of insanity rather than to the chronic ; and when the pa- Hallucinations of smell. tients get better, they vanish. Some will tell us that they smell fetid and noisome exhalations, the scent of the dead, or of vaults and catacombs, or say that their food or drink smells offensively, and for this reason refuse it. More frequently, however, they assert that an offensive odor proceeds from their own ·bodies, rendering them horrible to all about them, and contaminating the chairs, sofas, or beds they rest upon. This was the case with a gentleman, the subject of melancholia, who would only sit on a caned chair, because he thought that he polluted a stuffed one. A young lady always presented me with her smelling-bottle, because of the odor she believed to exhale from her, which must be disagreeable to me as I stood and talked to her. Both these patients recovered from somewhat acute attacks of melancholia.

Hallucinations of taste are so interwoven with disordered sensations, depending on the state of the tongue or alimentary canal, and with delusions concerning the food, that it is difficult to lay down anything with precision on this head. The patients who say that baby's flesh, human blood, human excrement, arsenic, or other poison, is put in their food, do not fancy they taste these substances. The idea is a delusion, not an hallucination. From my own experience, I am inclined to believe that true hallucinations of taste are uncommon, that they rarely exist alone, and that, depending on a disordered state of digestion, they generally are transient.

A number of curious phenomena may be grouped under the title of hallucinations of the skin and muscles. It is not uncommon to find a patient who calmly tells us that he feels himself touched on various parts of his body by little raps or shocks. A young gentleman felt these long after every other symptom of insanity had disappeared. They latterly gave him little concern, though at first he attributed them to supernatural causes. He had no other hallucinations. Others feel electric shocks, but these are often the subjects of delusions rather than of hallucinations. Some feel snakes in their inside. One lady had a dog in her head, and complained of the sensations it caused. This I look upon rather as a delusion. Some patients declare that they have felt persons have sexual connection with them. These are onanists, or patients with morbid sexual desires. Others constantly declare themselves to be with child, and say they feel it moving, or labor approaching. These are all delusions. Disordered muscular sensations, the feeling of being bound and incapable of moving, may be akin to that experienced in nightmare, when we are pursued by a lion and cannot run away, or are falling from a precipice.

Hallucinations of taste.

Other hallucinations.

Patients may experience hallucinations sometimes or always. One gentleman told me he could always hear the voices if he listened for them. Some only hear voices when there is a noise of some kind in or out of the room. In all who are subject to hallucinations, we find them most frequent and most distressing when the bodily strength is lowest. They point to an exhausted nervous state, even more than do delusions, especially the hallucinations of sight, which generally exist in acute diseases of exhaustion, as fever and delirium tremens, or can be produced by such poisons as haschisch, stramonium, or belladonna.

LECTURE VIII.

The Acts of the Insane—Stripping Naked—Indecent Exposure—Fantastic Dress—Eating and Drinking—Habitual Drunkenness—Suicide—Self-mutilation—Talking to Self—Squandering Property—Homicide, for various Reasons—Pyromania—Erotomania—Kleptomania.

By the discovery of false beliefs or delusions, we are led to the conclusion that patients are insane. Let us now consider insane *acts ;* for by these, no less than by delusions, we may be guided to the same opinion. As we find insane persons who have no delusions, so we see others whose unsoundness of mind is not displayed in acts, or, at any rate, in such of them as are observable by us ; for we should learn a great deal more of many patients if we could watch them without their knowledge. Without discussing in this place the diagnosis of insanity, and its recognition in those who commit insane acts without delusions, or have delusions without displaying anything insane in act or conduct, I wish to review the chief acts which arise from the insanity, and are the best evidence of it. As insane beliefs range themselves under certain heads, so we shall find that similar acts are perpetrated by many insane people, emanating without doubt from a corresponding mental condition. As the discovery of certain delusions leads us to inquire whether the individual has done, or attempted to do, certain things, so the acts help us to discover the delusions. Many acts which, taken by themselves, would not prove insanity, are, when explained or justified according to the insane ideas of the individual, valuable evidence of his state of mind, and often afford a clue which otherwise would be wanting.

We may roughly class insane acts under two heads,—those which affect the person or property of the patient, Two classes of acts. and those which affect the person or property of others. Under the first head, we shall consider such acts as stripping off all clothes, indecent exposure, fantastic 1. Those which relate to the pa- tient. dress, self-mutilation, starvation, suicide, dipso- mania, squandering of property; while under the second we find homicide, arson, rape, and acts of violence or mischief of innumerable kinds. Every one of these may become a subject of investigation in a court of law, and it is as well to examine them by themselves, just as we examine and consider delusions and hallucinations.

Stripping stark naked is not unfrequent amongst the in- sane. And in this condition they will run out of Stripping off clothes. their room, or the house, regardless of decency. Put- ting aside all the cases where patients have got rid of their clothes in a struggle, we shall find that they strip themselves either from a desire to destroy everything within reach, or from a wish to get rid of the feeling of heat or restraint engendered by clothing. In the latter case they may re- move without destroying it; this they may also do thinking it filthy or poisoned, or may ruin it from pure mischief and wrong-doing.

In acute insanity, acute delirium, acute mania, and melan- cholia, it is common to find patients stripping off their clothes, and tearing them to pieces to get them off. The feeling, whether of restraint or of heat of skin, is one due to the physical condition, and they accomplish their end without assigning any cause whatever. Such patients are beyond the reach of argument or expostulation. The symptom, like the disorder, is of a temporary nature, and must be met with measures best suited to the case, by fastening blankets round the patient, or by placing on him a suit of strong material laced up the back, which he can neither tear nor remove. It is essential that many of these persons should be kept warm, as also those affected with general paralysis, who are given to stripping themselves if left alone at night.

Chronic maniacs who are noisy, mischievous, and destructive, but perfectly conscious, destroy their clothes from pure wantonness, just as they smash furniture and windows, or befoul their beds and rooms. Blankets or strong suits are of little use for them, as they are quick and ingenious enough to pick these to pieces by dint of nails and teeth, and, if left alone, each morning discloses a scene of rags and pieces, the result of a diligent night's work. These patients are good illustrations of the nonsense talked about the knowledge of right and wrong being a test of sanity. They know as well as any one that what they do is wrong, and they delight in doing it, because it is wrong. I have never found any expedient of use but the presence of an attendant, or two, if necessary. When the patient finds that he is not allowed to destroy, he gives up, and in time loses the habit and desire.

In a case where the clothes are stripped off or destroyed in conformity with certain delusions, such delusions will commonly be assigned as the reason. These must be met like any others, and will pass away as the patient improves. They generally belong to an acute stage, and are found in connection with hallucinations of smell, or sensations of the cutaneous surface.

As a matter of diagnosis little need be said in connection with this subject; the insanity of such patients will be patent in many other ways; at the same time, sane people do not strip themselves naked except for justifiable reasons, and such stripping may be adduced as evidence of insanity along with the other symptoms which are sure to be observable.

The same cannot be said of the next topic I shall mention, Indecent exposure. indecent exposure of the person. This is constantly practiced by sane people, as the records of our criminal courts prove. It is done by the insane both in the acute and chronic state. It is a not unfrequent symptom in the early stages of general paralysis; it is often done by patients, men and women, who are passing from the stage of chronic mania to that most hopeless condition, chronic dementia. We are not to infer insanity from such an act unless there be other corroborating symptoms; but when these leave no doubt in our minds that the patient is insane, our prognosis of the case, whether it be acute or chronic, will be unfavorable. I am speaking, of course, of a deliberate act of indecent exposure, not of the accidental exposure which occurs when an excited patient strips himself or herself entirely.

Open and shameless masturbation is a common occurrence in patients both in the acute and chronic state.

We shall constantly see something bizarre or extravagant in a patient's dress and general appearance, which, Fantastic if it does not of itself prove insanity, may at any dress. rate reveal the delusions which prompted it. The hair, the condition of face and hands, the clothes, articles attached to the dress as ornaments, the state of the nether garments, shoes, and stockings, may all betray singularity, and corresponding singularity of ideas. One might fill a volume with anecdotes of the extraordinary appearances presented by patients under the influence of delusions. There are few who dress just as they ought, if they have the opportunity of giving the rein to their fancy. The man of exalted ideas wears a crown or coronet of paper or straw; orders and bits of ribbon adorn his button-hole; he winds shawls, rugs, or sofa-covers round him for robes. The melancholy man thinks it is not worth while to wash his face or body, or brush his hair; unwashed and unkempt, in ragged or untidy clothes, he mourns his destiny. The apartment in which a patient habitually dwells frequently presents appearances which correspond to his personal dress and demeanor, and may vary from the height of eccentric tidiness to the extreme of filth. Constantly, if it be one which the patient has tenanted for some time, we shall find signs of singularity of conduct and idea. Many choose to keep all their provisions and do all their own cooking in their living-room, from fear of poison; others sleep in strange fashion; others keep numberless animals. In every case where we notice oddity of appearance in an individual or his surroundings, we are to bear the facts in mind, and question the patient as to their meaning; but we are not in every case to infer insanity, for eccentricity may exist to a great extent without insanity, and is often displayed in outward adornments. If, however, we are called to a person who has never been eccentric in demeanor or dress, and who suddenly decks himself in strange and unwonted garb, we may do more than suspect insanity.

The degree of dirt compatible with sanity is a question which will vary according to the experience of the observer. Those who are familiar with the beggars of the south of Spain or Italy, will think this test very uncertain; but here, too, the same rule is applicable. If an educated and hitherto respectable gentleman appears in a state of deplorable filth, we may well question his sanity.

Our prognosis will not be much influenced by such appearances, but further information will be required. If the case is recent, the oddity of the appearance is of little moment; if chronic, some very slight token may point to a delusion which may have existed for years, and is not likely to be removed.

A patient's eating and drinking may arrest our attention. Eating and He may eat voraciously, or very little, or absolutely drinking. nothing. He may eat only such things as eggs, from fear of poison; or only the food cooked by himself; or he may require others to taste everything before he partakes of it. He may eat filth of all kinds: in fact, there is nothing too nasty to be carried to the mouth by the insane in all stages of the disease. Such acts are evidence of unsoundness of mind, generally of dementia or idiocy. Absolute abstinence from food would also warrant our coming to the conclusion that the individual was unable to take care of himself. Between these extremes, singularities of diet and mode of eating, like eccentric personal appearance, point our way to the detection of insanity, but are frequently not in themselves and by themselves evidence thereof. Cases are on record where patients have swallowed such articles as lancets or a pair of compasses, and have habitually eaten nails, coals, rags, tobacco-pipes, &c.; but we know, from the post-mortem examinations of our general hospitals, that these depraved and perverted tastes are not peculiar to the insane, but are indulged in similar ways by sane persons. The eating of hair by girls, and the chewing of slate-pencil, are by no means uncommon—and I have heard young ladies descant on the pleasures of the latter.

It may be as well to mention in this place that craving for alcoholic drink, which has been called by some a monomania, under such titles as dipsomania, oino- mania, methyskomania, and by others is merged in the class of *moral insanity*. Perhaps for the practitioner and the medico-jurist, this is the most perplexing of all varieties of unsoundness of mind, if—and this is a moot point—it is of itself unsoundness of mind. I have already, in my third lecture, said something concerning the pathology of alcoholism. I have here to inquire whether drinking to the extent of what is called dipsomania, is an insane act. There can be no question that there are hundreds of habitual drunkards who are in no sense insane. The very fact that a certain proportion of them abandon the habit, reform, and for the rest of their lives live temperately, shows that they are not suffering from chronic insanity. To them inebriate asylums are a boon, not because they are insane, but because they require assistance to enable them to break through a bad habit, like an inveterate smoker, snuff-taker, opium-eater, gambler, or masturbator. There is, again, a number of insane people who drink, whose insanity is shown not merely

[side note: Habitual drunkenness.]

by their drinking, but by their whole history and acts, or by the presence of other neuroses, as epilepsy. And there are patients who, by long-continued drinking, have brought about disease of brain; but habitual drinking, by itself, is not to be considered evidence of insanity, if the drinker, when sober, presents no other indication. Dipsomania is no more a special variety or monomania, than pyromania, erotomania, or kleptomania.

We may notice in the next place the acts of self-mutila-
Suicidal acts. tion and self-destruction so often committed by the insane. If we walk round the wards even of a small asylum, we shall rarely fail to find some one or more patients who have tried, with more or less success, to do damage to themselves. They may be laboring under suicidal melancholia, or other forms, as that which is called suicidal monomania or suicidal impulse. Critics and writers on the subject vary greatly in opinion, some thinking that all who commit suicide are insane, others that delusion must be ascertained before we can pronounce any suicidal or homicidal patient to be of unsound mind. I have coupled suicidal and homicidal patients, for the condition of the one is often closely allied, or even identical, with that of the other class. The same patient often commits both homicide and suicide, or at one time is homicidal, at another suicidal; and so, in reducing to a number of heads the patients who are homicidal, we find that we can range in almost identically the same divisions those who are suicidal. It is of the latter that I shall first speak.

That sane people commit suicide is a fact that must be apparent to every one who exercises common sense in looking upon the subject. The hundreds of poor creatures who are rescued from the Thames, or brought to our general hospitals half poisoned, or with throats half cut, are not insane in any medical sense of the word. Putting these aside, let us look at the insane who are suicidal.

I. First, we have the melancholic patient, who has been noticed by his friends to be a little low-spirited but nothing more. They have not heard of any delusions; he has not done or said anything that could warrant their calling him insane. He has only appeared changed in spirits and capacity of enjoying himself, and this they have thought it better not to notice; so he blows his brains out, or jumps from the top of the house, and then they are extremely anxious that he should be called *insane*, and not *felo de se*. This is pure suicidal melancholia, insane *tædium vitæ*, where, without any marked or overwhelming delusions, the whole feeling of the individual makes him look on life as not worth the keeping. He is perplexed and annoyed with everything and every-body:

" Weary, stale, flat, and unprofitable,
    Seem to him all the uses of this world."

And so he ends them. We see the insanity of the man in that he is entirely changed from what he was; there is no cause for his melancholy, but perhaps there is cause for his insanity, his suicidal melancholia.

II. The malady may still be fitly called suicidal melan-cholia; but the desire to commit suicide may be directly prompted by delusions, *e. g.*, that he is going to be horribly tortured; or he hears a voice commanding him to kill him-self; or he thinks that by this he shall gain heaven; or he is ruined, and shame and poverty are staring him in the face; or he sees visions of the departed beckoning him to come to them. This form is easy of diagnosis, and the prognosis is favorable if the general health be not much broken. Of this I shall have to speak when I come to the subject of melan-cholia.

III. In almost any case of acute insanity—in delirium tremens, in epileptic mania—suicide may be committed in fear, in a paroxysm of rage, or in a general outburst of de-structiveness; or in attempting to escape a man may jump from housetop or window without any definite idea of self-destruction. In all cases of acute insanity, acute delirium, acute mania, and the like, this must be borne in mind, and opportunities of self-harm removed from a patient. Many at this time are subject to paroxysms of ungovernable fury, and will then try and hurt themselves as well as others; they will dash their heads against a wall, bite their arms, or even do more serious mischief if they have the chance. We cannot say that they are suffering from suicidal melancholia or suicidal mania. Suicide is like breaking the windows, or tearing in pieces their clothes or furniture—a mode in which their vehement destructiveness finds vent. Of the insanity of such persons there is, of course, no doubt, and the prognosis is not affected by the fact that suicide has been attempted.

IV. Besides these, we find true suicidal mania and suicidal impulse. Patients both in an acute and unmistakable state of insanity, and in one that is hardly recognizable as being insanity except in this one feature, have a violent desire and longing to commit suicide. According to their capacity of self-control, they may make the attempt all day long, so as to require an attendant to be constantly within reach; or may keep it to themselves for days, weeks, or months, till they see a fitting opportunity of satisfying the desire. Although in a state of marked insanity, their delusions may have no connection with suicide, and their feelings and demeanor may be the reverse of melancholic. The most suicidal patient I ever saw was a friend who was perfectly free from everything like low spirits, and whose delusions, of which to me he made no secret, had no reference whatever to any of those things which usually prompt patients to suicide. One might have conversed for hours with this gentleman, and given an opinion that he was a patient not likely to be suicidal, yet he would do himself harm in every way he could—swallow scalding beef-tea, try to strangle himself over a five-barred gate; in short, in some way or other hurt himself.

He went on in this way for some two years, the suicidal impulses occurring in paroxysms every two or three months, and then died epileptic.

Suicidal impulse occurs in children, who, when they commit this act, do so usually not from delusions or from settled melancholy, but from pure motiveless impulse. There is an uncontrollable desire to gratify the morbid idea which is present in the mind, as in dipsomania there is the desire to gratify the physical craving of drink, regardless of all consequences. Just as in the case of a patient suffering from some foolish and absurd delusion, the rest of the brain is not sufficiently at work to correct the falsity thereof; so here it is not sufficiently at work to correct, by ideas of duty, prudence, and self-love, the feeling and idea which urge to self-destruction. Probably, in many cases both of murder and suicide, the insane man or woman experiences in an insane degree a feeling of anticipated pleasure or curiosity akin to that felt by the spectators of the horrors of the amphitheatre or auto-da-fè of past times, and of the bull-fights of our own days—a morbid delight, nay, a keen enjoyment of a ghastly spectacle.

Besides those who try in every way to put an end to themselves—who will refuse food for this purpose, and Self-mutilation. lose no opportunity of doing to themselves bodily harm, however trivial—there are patients who, for definite reasons, will damage or mutilate some one or other part of their bodies. Some, following the literal precept, will pluck out their eye or cut off their hand. I have a lady under my care now whose right eye was destroyed under these circumstances. Frequently the organs of generation—the penis, or the testicles, or the whole—are cut off, because they are supposed to have " offended," to have incited the patient to wicked lusts, or to have been the means of gratifying them through masturbation. Patients will set themselves on fire, place their hands in the candle or the coals, to inflict upon them the torments of hell, and will display a fortitude or an indifference to pain in so doing that is truly marvellous. All such acts are done from delusion, not from mere impulse, as the acts of suicide. Whether it be from one or other motive, such patients demand constant and unceasing vigilance on the part of those about them. They are safe nowhere save in an asylum, and even there they are the source of endless anxiety. Being for the most part in full possession of their faculties, they never let an opportunity escape of secreting a knife, a nail, a piece of broken glass, or a bit of cord. They will do themselves a mischief under the bedclothes with an attendant sitting by their side, and not indicate it by a muscle of their countenance; and when all weapons are taken away, they will gouge out their eye, or pull down the rectum with their fingers.

Besides desperate injuries inflicted on themselves by patients, either through strong delusion or expressly from suicidal motive, many daily do themselves smaller mischiefs without any motive at all. This one picks his face or hands till he covers them with sore places, from restless fidgetiness; another bites his nails down to the quick; another plucks out hair after hair from his head till he is nearly bald. Such tricks, less perhaps in magnitude, are common among nervous people who are not insane. Most nervous persons have some trick or twitching, and, like the insane, twist and fidget their dress, or pick and scratch their hands, face, head, or limbs: the extent to which they do it at any given time is often a valuable criterion of their nervous condition.

There is another common habit of the insane which must be noticed, that is, talking to themselves. Many people who Talking to are sane talk to themselves: they automatically conself. vert into audible words those they are combining in thought, so that this talking to self is not to be reckoned as a sign of insanity. But it is often done by the insane in a way and in a tone that is strongly symptomatic of the disorder; and frequently, if we listen, we find that they are holding conversations with imaginary beings, and answering imaginary voices. And by so listening valuable information may be gained as to what is passing in the patient's mind—information which he will not give us when questioned.

Hitherto I have spoken of what is done by a patient, so far as it relates to his own person. But he may also *Squandering property.* squander, destroy, or give away his property, and measures will be necessary to protect this no less than himself. But the man who squanders or destroys his property is not the same as he who harms himself. The latter is commonly a melancholic, who thinks he has no property, or, in the overwhelming fear and anxiety that possesses him, neglects it entirely. The man who squanders it is he who in his exalted notions thinks himself a millionaire; or, imagining he can find a source of endless wealth, beggars himself to discover his *El Dorado*, or who makes presents to every one he meets, and orders silk dresses or jewelry to be sent to all he knows. In every asylum we see such patients. They spend their days in writing letters to every shop whose advertisements they see in the *Times*, and ordering goods to the extent of hundreds or thousands of pounds. And before they are put under legal control such orders are often given, and great trouble is experienced in getting them annulled. Then there is the senseless squandering of money by the imbecile class, who have not brains enough to know its value. We may see the same thing done by patients in the first stage of senile or other dementia. This, together with debauchery and indecent conduct, is often the earliest symptom of the decay of mind.

I now proceed to consider insane acts committed upon the person or property of others. In this category we *2. Acts done towards others.* shall have to examine the so-called homicidal monomania; pyromania, or arson; erotomania, or rapé;

and kleptomania, or pilfering. And first of homicide, the
gravest question of all, as an excuse for which it has
been said that the homicidal monomania has been
invented. Here, as in the case of suicides, some writers and
physicians hold that the crime may be committed from moral
obliquity equivalent to insanity, which they term "moral
insanity;" others say that murders are committed from sudden
insane impulse; while many, especially lawyers, require that
delusions shall be found before they admit that the perpe-
trator is insane, and even then do not allow that in all cases
the insanity is a bar to punishment. This is not the place
for the consideration of moral or impulsive insanity. I shall
confine myself at present to the homicidal act, as it is committed by this or that patient, assuming that impulsive insanity has at any rate a recognized existence.

Homicide.

I. Homicide may be perpetrated without any impulse or
delusion by a patient enraged at being restrained,
simply to free himself from detention. Many of
the attacks to which attendants are subject are of this nature.

From a wish to escape.

II. It is frequently done under delusions of various kinds.
The patient thinks that he is himself about to be
tortured, murdured, or led to prison, and he slays
the man who is his fancied enemy. He will kill his wife or
children to save them from worse ills which he thinks are to
befall them. He fancies that he has a Divine mission to
murder some one, or hears a voice urging him on, or the
voice of some one he knows insulting him—and this will
probably be the voice he hears oftenest, his attendant's or
doctor's. These delusions vary indefinitely; but where the
crime is committed from such a motive, it is generally confessed, and the insanity is manifest. It is not possible in
every case to connect the delusions of a patient with the act
of murder, yet we are not on that account to assume, as do
the lawyers, that there is no connection between them.
Whence delusions spring, and whither they lead an insane

From delu-sion.

man, is what no one can tell. To attempt to trace a madman's ideas from their source to their outcome in act is at all
times an unprofitable task.

III. Murder is committed by an idiot, imbecile, or demented patient, from wanton mischief, or folly, from _From idiotic
ignorance of the act and its consequence, or from or wanton
mischief._
mere imitativeness. An idiot may kill a child because he has seen a fowl or a sheep killed.

In all the preceding classes the unsoundness of mind of
the homicide is patent. There is no question of diagnosis.
Lawyers may quibble about the responsibility, but medical
men will detect the insanity, which is not left to be inferred
from the homicidal act alone.

There are also acts of homicide committed by persons
whose soundness of mind was never called into question
before the murder, and these may be arranged in three
classes.

IV. Homicide is not unfrequently committed by epileptics.
Epilepsy is not the equivalent of insanity. Many _In epileptic
persons suffer from epileptic fits for years, yet mix furor._
in society and discharge the duties of sane and responsible
people. But it has been asserted, and not without good
grounds, that the mental condition of an epileptic is not
thoroughly sound. "All authors are agreed," says Baillarger,[1] "in admitting the fact that epilepsy, before leading
to complete insanity, produces very important modifications
in the intellectual and moral condition of certain patients.
These sufferers become susceptible, very irritable, and the
slightest motives often induce them to commit acts of violence;
all their passions acquire extreme energy." An act of murder may be committed by an epileptic in the furious mania
with hallucinations and delusions which follows a fit or succession of fits. It may also be done in the period which pre-

---

[1] Ann. Medico-Psych., Avril, 1861.

cedes a fit, a period during which, especially, some patients show strangeness of mind and manner. And the convulsion may be exploded, as it were, in the act of violence, the fit not occurring as it otherwise would have done. Murder may also be committed by patients rendered weak-minded by fits. In 1869, Bisgrove, an epileptic, was tried and found guilty of murder, but afterwards removed to the Broadmoor Asylum. He saw a man lying asleep in a field; he did not know him, but took a big stone that was lying near, dashed out his brains, then lay down by his victim's side and went to sleep. From epileptics, generally, we may expect acts of sudden and unaccountable violence, whether they occur in close connection with fits or take the place of them.

V. Murder may be committed during a paroxysm of insanity, brief, but furious, which, from its duration, In acute we may call transitory mania. Here, while it lasts, transitory the insanity will be recognizable; but as it rapidly mania. passes off, and possibly has never occurred before, the difficulty will be to discover any traces of unsoundness of mind a few days after the event. Such attacks are really for the time paroxysms of acute mania. The patient afterwards may not be conscious of what he has done, and by his expressions at the time may or may not indicate the feeling or delusion that prompts him. Frequently mania occurs in patients suddenly waking out of sleep, and is of the character of a nightmare, probably a continuation of some horrible dream. The act is often committed in a state of panic rather than rage, and the committal may thoroughly bring the patient to his waking senses, and to the contemplation of what he has done.

VI. Lastly, homicide, like suicide, may be committed from Impulsive "homicidal impulse." We are told that a man is homicide. impelled to commit murder by a craving impulse, like the craving thirst for drink. It is in cases of homicide that this variety, impulsive or instinctive insanity, is chiefly alleged and criticized; and, merely mentioning here that homicide may be committed in this fashion, I postpone the discussion of this insanity to a subsequent period.

Besides the homicidal monomania, we hear of others, as *erotomania, kleptomania, pyromania.* Having already Pyromania. said that I do not consider homicidal monomania to be a specific disease, I still less acknowledge that the acts which these terms indicate proceed from special disorders. They are committed by insane patients of various kinds, but the insanity is not likely to be confined to one of these acts, but is sure to be noticeable in other ways, if it exist at all. To take the last mentioned, *pyromania,* we might as well erect into a special form the window-breaking mania. Patients set fire to the house out of an insane impulse to destroy, as they break windows or anything else. They will do the same thing, in order to escape in the confusion. This has happened several times within my knowledge. They may do it from suicidal motive, or from commands received from hallucinatory voices. But a sufficient examination of such patients and their history will reveal insanity other than the mania for incendiarism.

Neither is erotomania a special form of insanity; there are numberless patients who in their mental disorder Erotomania. present marked erotic symptoms. The majority of young women in states of acute mania do this, and will assail the physician with words or embraces if he is not on his guard while visiting them; but all this is a result of their insanity: it does not constitute it. Those who have exalted erotomania into a special monomania, say that it is not the same thing as nymphomania or satyriasis; that the disorder is not in the reproductive organs, but in the head, and that it is an error of the understanding, an affection of the imagination, in which amatory delusions rule.[1] If this be so, *a*

---

[1] Esquirol, Malad. Ment. ii, p. 32.

fortiori we may deny that it is a special variety of insanity; it is a form of disordered intellect, accompanied by delusions. I have known girls conceive an insane love, not for men, but for other girls, and fancy themselves influenced by them, and in their power; and I presume this would come under Esquirol's *erotomania;* but in one case these preliminary fancies culminated in an attack of acute mania, and there was nothing about the case which removed it into any special category. In the acute stage, it might have been called *nymphomania* rather than *erotomania.* We may be justified in describing forms of insanity in which either the origin is in the sexual organs, or there is marked disturbance of the latter. Such a division would be in accordance with pathology; but a class distinguished by intellectual disturbance, in which love is the chief feature, is not really separable on this account from other forms of insanity where there is disorder of intellect, with or without delusion.

I now come to *kleptomania,* another of these forms of insanity from so-called perverted emotion or impulse.

Kleptomania.

And of this I would say, as of the foregoing, that it cannot be exalted into a class. Lunatics, undoubtedly, steal both in and out of asylums. When their lunacy is beyond a question, little is thought of their stealing; but when it is not so easy to detect, then the stealing is set up as proof of insanity, if the thief is in a social position to make us astonished at the act.

When we hear of a theft committed by a person supposed to be insane, but not clearly proved to be so, we may suspect one or other of several things.

1. If the thief be a man between twenty-five and fifty-five, we may suspect him to be in a very early stage of general paralysis, in which acts of foolish and unprofitable theft are not unfrequently committed. Here, of course, we should look for the early symptoms of general paralysis, an incipient stutter, loss of memory, by which sometimes the so-called

thefts may be explained, the occurrence of epileptiform attacks, a general condition of exaltation, and ideas of being able to afford anything.

2. We may meet with that form of insanity called *moral*, when the patient is either on the high road to general intellectual insanity, or, stopping short of delusions, shows his malady in insane acts which he justifies, in general alteration of character, and intellectual defect.

3. The individual may be congenitally idiotic, or imbecile, or may become demented gradually, after reaching adult age, from brain disorder. This introduces us to a class of half-witted boys and girls, who go sometimes to jail, sometimes to an asylum, according to their good or bad fortune, friends, and circumstances. To lay down the exact amount of responsibility of each of these is no easy task; but one thing is certain, each case must be examined and considered by itself, in view of the general mental capacity, bodily disorders, and history. We shall gain no assistance from constituting out of these weak-minded people one special class of thieves. Whether their propensity is thieving, drinking, squandering their money, or frequenting the company of the lowest of the low, they must all be judged by their capacity of intellect, and not by their acts alone.

4. With regard to acts of theft committed by well-to-do women in a pregnant state from supposed longings, I confess I should look upon any such with the greatest suspicion, unless there was other corroborative evidence of insanity. Stealing in shops is not very uncommon amongst ladies, if we are to believe what we hear. The impulse to appropriate an article, if it appears that it can be done with safety and secrecy, is one that is not seldom felt by many ill-regulated minds, and to erect this into insanity would be fraught with the greatest danger to society. Acts of violence are common amongst the insane; acts of secret and systematic theft are, in my experience, much less frequent, and other evidence of insanity should always be looked for.

LECTURE IX.

IN this and the following lectures it is my intention to describe clinically certain patients who may come under your notice in ordinary practice. I shall portray their symptoms, and, so far as is possible, indicate the treatment. I shall also endeavor to connect the symptoms with the pathological varieties of the disease previously enumerated. Concerning some, however, you will be consulted, not so much with a view to cure or treatment, as to elicit your opinion upon the question of their sanity or insanity. Of these I shall speak later; but first I propose to enter upon a description of those forms of insanity which urgently demand medical treatment, and which interest us as practical physicians and pathologists. As a rule, there is no difficulty in perceiving that the patients are of unsound mind; the question is, are they curable, and how are they to be cured?

In what order am I to treat of these? After examining the pathological phenomena presented in the full development of the disorder, I think that there are two forms which may be placed, one at either end of the scale, and that between these all the rest may be ranged.

The patients I put at one end of my list are those suffering from acute delirium—acute delirious mania—which runs a rapid course to death or amelioration in a week or fortnight. Here we see, for the time, entire sleeplessness, incessant action of brain and body, with

The two extremes of insanity.

the evolution of great heat, speedy emaciation, a quick pulse, tongue coated and soon becoming brown, symptoms pointing to an excessive decomposition of every tissue, and a general excess of brain action, which, if it does not cease within a certain time, leads to death by exhaustion without apparent morbid change. No other kind of insanity is so rapidly fatal, or calls so imperatively for medical treatment.

Acute delirium.

At the other end of the list of cases I place patients suffering from what has been called "acute dementia." The name has been cavilled at, but it really describes the disorder, if we use the word acute in the sense of "recent," and "non-chronic." In such a patient we see almost the opposite of the former. There is not excess but defect of action and oxidation. The skin is cold, the hands and feet in hot weather are blue with cold, the patient sits motionless, lost, answers no questions, does not appear to understand them, looks idiotic, sometimes almost comatose; the pulse is very weak and slow, the tongue pale and moist, food is taken passively, and sleep is not absent. Such a case often resembles one of chronic dementia, the result of long-standing insanity, old age, or brain disease, and without a history we shall find it difficult to form an accurate diagnosis. However, I am not going to describe it in this place. As the very opposite of acute delirium I place it at the end of the scale, and between the excess of cerebral action and this extreme defect we may range all the varieties of disorder, and try to ascertain, both for the purposes of pathology and treatment, how far their departure in one or other of these directions corresponds to the mental symptoms exhibited. We shall, unquestionably, meet with cases that some would call melancholic, while others will think they ought rather to be termed maniacal; cases that one person will call acute delirium, another acute mania. There will be

Acute primary dementia.

such on the border-land of all diseases,—cases of rheumatism
that can hardly be called acute ; cases which one may term
rheumatism, another gout; others which one calls typhus,
another typhoid. Yet, speaking generally, we employ the
names acute rheumatism, gout, typhus, and typhoid, not to
describe a disease, but to denote a number of symptoms which
usually coexist in the individual said to be suffering from it.
In the same way we may use such terms as mania, melancholia, and dementia. These names do not, as some object,
merely denote varieties of mental symptoms and delusions:
acute dementia is pathologically a different disorder from
acute delirium, occurring at a different age and running a
different course. It is a malady of youth, while acute delirium attacks patients in the prime of life, and melancholia
is most common in those whose vigor is on the wane. Each
variety may be due apparently to a similar cause, as a fright
or mental shock. Each may be idiopathic, that is, it may
come on without assignable cause, owing to the inherited
predisposition combined with some constitutional disturbance,
but when developed they are different diseases, requiring different treatment.

I shall not, however, commence by a description of either
of these extreme forms, but shall put before you the earliest
indications of mental disorder, and trace their progress and
development in various directions. In the exanthemata, in
fevers and allied diseases, they are premonitory symptoms
threatening approaching mischief, but not clearly indicating
what it is to be, so that we say the patient is "sickening"
for something, but cannot definitely say what; similarly,
many signs of mental disorder make us apprehensive of
coming insanity, but we cannot always say with certainty
what form the malady will assume. Speaking generally, the
more rapid the onset, the more acute are the symptoms, and
the shorter the attack : that which gradually and insidiously
comes on, gives us, it is true, a better chance of arresting its

progress short of actual acute disorder, but this, if reached, will probably be of considerable duration.

It often happens that a patient is conscious of there being something amiss with him for a very considerable time before he says anything about it, or any of his friends notice it. Frequently friends, and relatives *Early symptoms of insanity.* also, if they be not near relatives, are afraid of mentioning what they observe, even to the patient himself. This period of *alteration* precedes many forms of insanity, and I shall have again to allude to it. It is of the greatest consequence that treatment should be at once adopted, but often a long time elapses before the doctor hears of it—time which would have been most valuable in trying means of relief. Patients are sent to asylums whose insanity is stated to be of a week or a fortnight's duration, but who have been thought odd by servants or others perhaps for months. Many complain at first of confusion and dulness of head, of disinclination or inability to do their day's work; often they suffer headache; almost always they sleep badly; periods of depression alternate with periods of excitement. If there be less and less sleep the advance will be rapid, the depression more marked, the excitement more irrational; and now fancies, at first transient and recognized to be fancies, afterwards permanent and unmoved by the arguments and demonstrations of friends, vex and torment the patient, and drive him to acts of insanity.

Of this premonitory stage, what is the prognosis and treatment? Here the aid of the physician is sorely needed. What aid can we afford?

If we see the patient quite early, we may find, not excessive rapidity of pulse, but possibly slowness. Very likely it will not be more than fifty or sixty. We shall very probably hear of headache, or pains in the vertex *Treatment.* or back of the head, together with constipation. I am now assuming that the sufferer is in that condition that he can inform us or his friends of what he feels; but not every patient in this state will see a doctor. If a woman, there is in all likelihood some irregularity in the catamenial function. You inquire the cause of all this. There may be one, plain and palpable, as overwork, mental anxiety, a bodily illness, or pregnancy, lactation, or parturition. The cause may be removable or irremovable. And very probably you are informed of something which is not really the cause, though it is put forward as such by the friends; you will have to inquire further before you come to a conclusion on this point. The cause may have already passed away—as parturition: you only have to deal with the resulting condition. If it be lactation, you can end it; but if the patient be pregnant, you will have to nurse her through the period of gestation and parturition, or will have to consider the question of inducing premature labor. Yet when the cause is removed, we do not always at once arrest the disorder: the mischief is lighted up in the brain, and must run its course. Frequently, however, we may have the good fortune to restore the balance.

The two things to be kept in view may be called, in concise terms, moral and medical treatment. We must inquire into, and, if need be, correct, the patient's external surroundings, and must, by diet and medicine, try to restore his physical health. In many cases, perhaps in most, it will be Change of advisable to send him away from home—to produce an entire change of ideas and objects—to remove by this means painful subjects of thought constantly presented by the sight of home, or wife, or children, subjects already, it may be, distorted by fancies, and incapable of being regarded in their true aspect. Then comes the question, where is he to go, who is to accompany him? Here difficulties arising out of the patient's circumstances, pecuniary means, *impedimenta* of all kinds, may prevent us doing exactly what we wish. One thing is certain,—he should not go alone. Morbid fancies come thick and fast to a man who has no one with whom to interchange ideas. I lately saw a gentleman who had a transient attack of mania, and recovered quickly in his own home. Six months after he went away by himself on a sketching tour, and though he was quite well at starting, his old fancies all came back to him in his solitude in about ten days, and he fled back to his friends to have them dispelled; and happpily this was done. Who is to be the companion? Is the wife to go with the husband, the husband with the wife? Who is to go with single people? As to this there is no rule. The companion must be a person of sense and tact, and devoid of fear. Of this you must judge as best you can. If no one can be found ·fit for the post, the patient had better stay where he is. Where is he to go? Not abroad: a trip to the Continent is all very well at the end of an illness, to give the finishing stroke to the cure; but at the beginning, when we are uncertain what is about to happen, a patient should not go out of reach of assistance and immediate restraint and treatment. The place to which invalid Londoners and many others are chiefly sent is the seaside, but I do not find that sea air is beneficial to those threatened with insanity. I have seen so many get rapidly worse after a few days' sojourn at Brighton, that I cannot help coming to the conclusion that there is something about the seaside which tends to convert the preliminary stage of confusion and depression into wild excitement; and for this reason I prefer to send patients for change to an inland place. What can we do in addition to avert the evil that threatens our patient's reason? First, Food. with regard to diet: assuming that the incipient symptoms of insanity are those of deficient nerve-force, I inquire closely into the eating and drinking of the patient, and constantly find that, whatever may be the proportions of the latter, the former is in defect. Mental trouble or bodily ailment, fears of dyspepsia, anxieties about liver and constipation, have caused the amount eaten in the day to fall below the normal standard, often to a very considerable extent. Thus, for lack of nourishment the brain becomes more and more exhausted, just at the time that it ought to have an extra supply. Regularity in meals, by which I mean the eating an adequate quantity at regular intervals, and not allowing a very long period, even at night, to elapse without food, often does much good; for we constantly find that before any mental symptoms have been observed, the patient's friends have noticed that he has grown thinner. Malt liquor, wine, and the morning beverage, rum and milk, may be given as you see fit; but I attach more importance to the administration of good and wholesome food in this stage than to stimulants, which in many produce heat and pain of head, or undue excitement.

If sleep be insufficient and irregular—and you will rarely find it otherwise—are you to give medicine of any kind? At this time I think and trust that we shall derive valuable assistance from the hydrate of chloral. I have known more than one threatened attack of insanity warded off by its administration in the premonitory stage of sleeplessness, and I would make trial of it in preference to opium in any form. For the latter, as you well know, not only procures no sleep for some people, but absolutely prevents it, and by raising the bodily temperature causes the very symptoms we are endeavoring to dispel. At a later period it is often of the greatest service, but at the commencement it is hazardous to try it, and chloral is not attended with the same disadvantages, and in a mild attack is far more sure in its action. Should this fail, you may try bromide of potassium, or extract of henbane, or tincture of digitalis; but assuredly chloral should be given first, in doses of twenty-five or thirty grains. Tonics may be required,—iron, quinine, arsenic, or strychnia. There is nothing special to be said concerning these, which must be left to your discretion and judgment. Patients at this time are not capable of great fatigue, mental or bodily. If sent into the country, very hard exercise—as boating or very long walks—must be interdicted. I have known it produce suddenly a very acute attack. Neither must they be exposed to great heat of sun. Amusement they require, not work, and this must be regulated by the companion, without whom, as I have said, they are not to be trusted, and who is to have supreme authority in everything. In some such fashion many a threatened attack of insanity may be cut short or warded off.

Instead of subsiding, these symptoms may be the precursors of the severe and obstinate insanity which *The symptoms may become more serious.* requires to be treated under the restraint of an asylum or a quasi-asylum. Whether coming on suddenly, or gradually developing during weeks or months, it may reach those stages which in everyday parlance are called mania, melancholia, acute mania, acute melancholia, acute dementia, or general paralysis; for at the very beginning even the latter may present the same indications as other forms of derangement. Now, whatever be the cause, and whatever pathologically may be the variety of the insanity, we shall find practically that it may be ranged under one of these classes; though, as I said, cases do occur which seem to be on the border-land, rather than to fall completely within one of them. Yet typical cases of melancholia—of acute, noisy, conscious mania—of acute delirium—of general paralysis,—are so well marked, that if accurately described they cannot fail to be recognized, and they serve as a basis from which to consider the less defined and more doubtful cases. But we must recollect that the attack is determined, whatever its origin, by the constitutional peculiarities of the individual, so that he may suffer at one time from melancholia, at another from mania, at another from acute mania, according to the greater or less lack of nerve-force, or the greater or less irritability of his nerve-centres.

The insanity which gradually develops after a long period

of incubation is at first marked by depression: afterwards the
depression may pass away, and excitement of a fearful, angry,
or even hilarious character may take its place; or the depression may increase until it becomes silent and settled melancholia or panic-stricken frenzy.

I propose, in the first place, to speak of the forms of in-
Insanity with sanity attended by marked depression, such as are
depression. generically termed melancholia. They form a well-
defined group, distinguishable in many respects from other
varieties, requiring different treatment, and attended with
different results. The melancholy character is appparent
throughout, whether the patient is only slightly and temporarily depressed, or is raving in excited terror, and trying
with might and main to escape from the horrors of impending
torment.

The simplest form of melancholia is that feeling of depression which assails most men at some time of their lives, and
is generally attributed to dyspepsia. or the liver, or relaxing
climate, or may be caused by difficulties and disasters. Some
men feel it frequently; in some it lasts for a few hours only,
in others for days; some may require treatment in order to
disperse it, in others it passes away of itself. I have already
glanced at this in its simple and premonitory stage, and have
suggested what ought to be done by way of treatment. I am
now about to consider those cases which have not been cured
by the treatment already spoken of—change of scene, the
companionship of a friend, fresh air, and good diet. I assume
that the depression has become undoubted insanity, leading
to ideas and acts of an insane character, and requiring special
interference and constant medical care. What are the most
prominent symptoms of the disorder?

The patient is in a state of general depression. An utter
Delusions. lack of energy is exhibited in all his ideas, feelings,
and acts. Not only has he many insane delusions,
but he takes a desponding view of everything that happens

around him, and connects his own position and fancied misery or wickedness with all the disasters that he reads of in the papers, or hears in his own circle. The most distant events, earthquakes abroad, shipwrecks at sea, battles and murders, all depend on his evil fortune, or have happened for the express purpose of making his lot more wretched than before. He would give himself up to the police for the committal of all the murders he reads of, or would flee away, and hurry from place to place to escape those who are accusing him of crimes that never have been committed. Or he has committed sins so black, so unpardonable, that he dreads not human, but divine justice: his soul is lost beyond chance of redemption; he is without hope in the world. Again, he is beggared in fortune, his wife and children are going to the workhouse, he is to be arrested for debt. Then his health is in as sad a state as his affairs. He is eaten up with syphilis, his inside is all gone: he has in him a burning fire consuming his vitals, and reducing his excreta to cinders; he has the leprosy of the Old Testament: a loathsome smell emanates from his body, and contaminates every chair or sofa on which he sits. No amount of argument, no demonstration, however plain and undeniable, shakes his conviction or banishes his fears. These are to be removed by medical treatment, not by any method of moral persuasion.

If we examine his appearance and bodily condition, what do we find? His aspect is dejected, dull, and heavy, or woebegone to an extreme degree. He sits or stands in one place for hours, or constantly tries to wander away. He is, in all probability, much thinner than usual. He sleeps badly, and eats little; the tongue is foul, coated, and creamy, the bowels obstinately constipated, the breath offensive, the pulse slow and weak.

Now, among which of our pathological varieties are we to look for these melancholic patients? Chiefly we Climacteric find them among those who are passing into the melancholia.

decline of life, whose insanity has been termed " climacteric." We do indeed see melancholia in patients of all ages, and see it accompanying all causes and conditions; but it is the exception to find it in the young, the rule to find it in those whose vigor is beginning to fail, whether at forty, fifty, or sixty years of age. Of 338 cases of melancholia admitted into St. Luke's Hospital, only 9 patients were below the age of twenty. Occasionally it occurs after parturition in women who have been much weakened by their confinements. The insanity which appears some weeks after confinement generally takes this form, and often rises to a very acute state, with sleeplessness and obstinate refusal of food. The weaker the patient the more urgent are the symptoms, and the greater the need for active and immediate treatment. There is nothing of the sthenic character which marks the wild excitement of mania. It is not usually found in phthisical patients who are commonly excited and maniacal, but we sometimes see it thus associated. It is an old belief that it is connected with the abdominal organs, as the liver; or, according to Schroeder van der Kolk, the colon; but there seems reason to doubt this. The disorder of the liver and the loaded state of the colon are as likely to depend on the general derangement of the nervous system as to be the cause of the mental disorder. The question is not set at rest by their vanishing together. The *propter hoc* in such cases is very hard to come at.

Whatever be the cause of the insanity, whether we call it idiopathic or sympathetic, phthisical or sexual, or even paralytic, the melancholia is the effect and indication of the condition of the sufferer at a particular time. He is generally depressed, his slow and feeble circulation imparts little force to his brain-centres, and the supply there is always in defect. Not only is it in defect—for this appears to be the condition of almost every phase of insanity—but there is little action going on. The metamorphosis is not rapid; there is no im-

mediate danger to life, emaciation does not occur rapidly as
in acute mania. The patient is not absolutely sleepless,
though he may sleep little. This depressed state may last
for years and then pass away; and, so soon as the feeling is
gone, all the delusions and fancies bred of it vanish too. We
are far from understanding the exact pathology of that state
which gives rise to melancholic feeling. I have known it to
exist in a gentleman who ate heartily, who was stout in body
and florid in face, who was free from all bodily disease. In
him it appeared without assignable cause, and in process of
time it vanished; and all that we can say of such a case is,
that by some concurrence of conditions beyond our recognition, the nerve-power of this man's brain was insufficiently
produced.

We find patients whose melancholic delusions are attended
with so much excitement that they may rather be called
maniacal. This only indicates that their condition, though
one of depression and defect, is at the same time one of
greater disturbance of the brain and more rapid metamorphosis; and, as we shall see, when it attains a certain height,
it becomes as formidable and dangerous a disorder as any
other acute form of insanity.

But here I wish to point out the treatment of an ordinary
case of melancholia, attended with great depression Treatment of
and melancholic delusions, disinclination to take melancholia.
food, little sleep, and obstinate constipation.

The first thing you are to remember is, that every patient
of this kind is to be looked upon as suicidal. Never Suicide to be
mind whether he has, or has not as yet, made at- apprehended.
tempts, or shown signs of such a disposition. He may have
had no opportunity, or he may have never yet felt the particular idea or impulse. But this is the description of patient who jumps out of window, or into the river. Nay,
he may commit suicide in even an earlier stage, before his
friends have noticed anything like delusion, when "they only

thought him a little low," and were afraid to take any measures for his safety, "for fear of worrying him." Hundreds and hundreds of inquests are held upon patients of this kind, who, by the commonest care, might have been successfully treated and cured.

Where is the treatment of such a patient to be carried out? An asylum is not absolutely indispensable, if the patient's means will afford him what he requires elsewhere. If a poor man, there is nothing for it but to send him to an asylum. For he must not be left for a moment where he can do himself harm, or make his escape. He requires the companionship of some person his equal in education, as well as of attendants; must be removed from home to a house, airy, light, and quiet; and should have facilities for taking exercise without going into crowded thoroughfares. All this implies some considerable expense. If, as I say, his means suffice, such a plan often works a cure more rapidly, in my opinion, than the asylum, with its depressing influences, and lack of sane companions; but if funds are scanty, the latter is a necessity, for the other plan is impracticable unless carried out completely in all its details.

Having removed your patient into a suitable abode, and having arranged that he shall never be left alone
Medicines.
for a moment, what are you to do by way of treatment? Your object is to restore the defect of brain by means of food and sleep, and you will find that in many cases a most satisfactory result follows the treatment, and this in no long time. I have seen some very bad cases recover perfectly in two months, and recover in a manner which was clearly due to the medical treatment, and not to mere change of scene and surroundings; for this had been already tried, and tried in vain.

Besides the mental symptoms, there are three things specially to be attended to,—the want of sleep, the tendency to refuse food, and the constipation.

Chloral will produce sleep in these cases, as in others; but is better suited to the excited than the depressed forms of insanity. It is a sleep-compelling agent; beyond that its effect seems of little import. It does not appear to have such a *healing* influence as opium where the latter is beneficial. In violent and excited cases of acute melancholia, chloral can be given with benefit; but in subacute melancholia, the preparations of opium are of great service, whether given by the mouth or by subcutaneous injection. I have very rarely been obliged to discontinue them, and have almost invariably found the patient mend after their administration. The preparation which has, according to my experience, succeeded best is the *liquor morphiæ bimeconatis,* for it does not cause sickness or constipation, which too frequently follow the administration of the acetate or hydrochlorate of morphia. As the patient is already inclined to refuse food, often on the plea of nausea or loss of appetite, and as his bowels already are obstinately constipated, it is important that we do not increase this state of things by our remedies. Dover's powder, in some cases, or solid opium, or Battley's solution, we may give, and give freely, in full doses at night, and in smaller doses two or three times a day. It is of little use to give at night by the mouth less than the equivalent of half a grain of morphia.

We now come to the food question. We read that patients refuse their food because of dyspepsia, and that the latter is indicated by the foul, coated tongue, fetid breath, and loaded bowels. I am obliged to say that I think all the symptoms of dyspepsia are the result, and not the cause, of the depressed nervous condition; that the tongue is covered with old dead epithelium, which, for the same reason, is not thrown off; that the fetid breath is caused by this, or is due to actual starvation; and that the loaded bowels must also be ascribed to the want of general power. And I say this with some confidence, having treated a very

Food.

considerable number of these cases, and having removed all
the symptoms by means which were in no degree directed to
cure dyspepsia. This is the kind of diet which I have frequently given for the purpose. Before getting out of bed
in the morning, rum and milk, or egg and sherry; breakfast
of meat, eggs, and *café au lait*, or cocoa; beef-tea, with a
glass of port, at eleven o'clock; and a good dinner or lunch
at two, with a couple of glasses of sherry; at four, some more
beef-tea, or an equivalent; at seven, dinner or supper, with
stout and port wine; and at bed-time, stout or ale, with the
chloral or morphia. This allowance I have given to patients
who were said to be suffering from aggravated dyspepsia;
who, I was told, had suffered from it all their lives; who
had never been able to take malt liquor, or eat more than
the smallest quantity at a time; who, in fact, had constantly
been living on about half the quantity requisite for their
support, and through chronic starvation, had come to this
depressed condition. I need hardly tell you that the patients
and their friends were aghast at the quantity ordered to be
taken; but improvement has taken place immediately, the
tongue cleaned, the constipation given way, and the depression diminished; and I have known patients themselves
become so convinced of the necessity of this augmented diet,
that after recovery they have continued to take about twice
as much as before the illness. How dependent these melancholic patients are upon food has often been proved. Some,
when nearly well, if they were out for their walk or drive
longer than usual, or from any other cause postponed their
meal, felt at once a return of the depression and delusions,
which vanished again after the reception of food.

I am speaking now of patients who would refuse their
food if left to themselves, or protest against it, but who take
it when told to do so, or allow themselves to be fed without
downright resistance. Wherever you can, give solid food;
do not be content with beef-tea and stimulants, which are

supposed to be the sole diet suited to invalids. The best proof that dyspepsia has nothing to do with these patients' condition is, that even with this enormously increased diet, I never knew any reject it from the stomach, except one lady, who did it wilfully; when made to take another supply, she kept it down. You may vary the diet to any extent, for every kind of good, plain, nourishing food may be given —poultry, game, fish—not merely mutton and beef. But even turtle-soup and champagne are not to take the place of solid food, which is a far better sedative than mere liquids.

The constipation will often be remedied by the stimulus of the increased amount of food; but when the patient is first subjected to treatment, the colon is often clogged by hardened masses of fæces, which nothing but enemata will remove. You may use for this the *enema terebinthinæ* of the Pharmacopœia, with or without castor-oil, and the operation will probably have to be repeated more than once After-wards you may promote regular action of the bowels by giving a daily dinner-pill of the watery extract of aloes, or by a daily teaspoonful of castor-oil, or some such laxative. Active purgation only makes matters worse, and should be avoided. I have also found great benefit from giving such patients bran-bread. This has been called a cure for melan-cholia, and it certainly brings about a regular action of the bowels in persons who for years have never been relieved except after medicine.

Melancholic patients are almost invariably better towards evening, and worse on first rising in the morning, owing, in my opinion, to the long abstinence from food. When a patient habitually wakes after three or four hours, and cannot go to sleep again, some food, as a sandwich, glass of sherry, or some of his matutinal rum and milk, will often bring sleep back to him. If this fail, he may take a small dose of chloral.

These people all suffer much from cold, are generally worse in the winter, often lingering through the spring, and waiting for hot weather to thoroughly restore them. They will derive benefit from the hot-air or Turkish bath, if they can have it regularly, and in all respects they require warmth. Their rooms should be sunny, and their clothing sufficient.

Of course, in such cases moral treatment is not to be lost sight of; and although no precise rules can be laid down on this subject, yet the recovery of a patient may be greatly aided by the judicious care of those about him. Every one must be struck by the intense self-feeling of the melancholy man. His egotism exceeds even that of the paralytic or maniac. He thinks that everything is centred in him, that he has done the greatest sins, or is to endure the greatest torments. His superlative misery is a theme on which he loves to descant as much as the paralytic loves to describe his wealth and greatness. His depression is great, but he magnifies it in the recital of his woes. Therefore it is necessary to lead him away from his self-contemplation, and to awaken in him an interest in others; and it is curious and interesting to see the gradual improvement in this respect. By degrees he will listen to news told to him, or to what is mentioned in his presence. He will furtively look at letters or the newspapers, and in this way, little by little, return to his normal state. Many a patient has been suddenly cured of melancholy by some event which called for immediate action. Thus, a lady's only son was seized with a dangerous illness, and she was obliged to go and nurse him. In her work and anxiety she forgot her own melancholy, and when he recovered she too was well. Melancholy is banished in this way when the patient is on the road to recovery; but at the commencement of an attack, before the strength is restored, we are not to expect such a sudden termination.

What is the prognosis in these cases of subacute melancholia? Generally very good. In my experience almost every case of this kind, if it does not run on to acute and excited panic-stricken frenzy, with desperate

Moral treatment.

Prognosis.

determination to resist food, and total want of sleep, progresses to a favorable termination in a longer or shorter time, whether in or out of an asylum. Of former patients now at large and well, more have suffered from melancholia than from any other form of insanity, and some of these were inmates of asylums for long periods. In the second volume of the St. George's Hospital Reports, I have given an account of three patients who recovered after long treatment in asylums. One was a gentleman who thought he had committed the unpardonable sin—nay, that he was himself the devil. He also thought himself ruined and afflicted with leprosy, but did not refuse food. He went on in this way for seven years, till at last affairs necessitated action on his part, and he woke up out of his melancholy, and has since keenly enjoyed life and its pleasures. Another was a lady of fifty-six years of age, who had all the worst symptoms of melancholia, refused food, did not converse, but paced her room, ejaculating " My God, my God," and picked and rubbed her hands in terror and panic till they were sore. After five years she began to mend, gradually improved, and in six months was discharged quite well. Another was a gentleman, aged thirty-one, who had been in an unhealthy tropical climate. He had all the symptoms of melancholy, was suicidal, tried to avoid food, would not converse, but muttered to himself, and thought he was going to be put to death for murder and forgery. He too recovered perfectly, after being in this state for five years.

I believe that depression is the only form of insanity in which we may expect recovery after such a period as seven years, and we may perceive in such recovery an indication of the pathological state of the patients. It would appear that during the whole of the period the general nerve-energy is in a state of defect, the result of which is, first, the feeling of intense melancholy; secondly, ideas and fancies—in other words, delusions—growing out of the feeling. All the ideas,

in fact, are tinctured by the prevailing gloom. But if the
nerve-force is restored, if the physical condition of the brain
is raised again to its normal level, all such delusions vanish,
the abnormal feeling passes away, and the mind resumes its
proper work unimpaired by what it has gone through.

In dealing with cases of this kind, it is important, for
many reasons, that we should keep before us the possibility
of recovery after a long period. For our opinion will be
asked by those who, having the disposition of property, may
regulate their wills by what they hear of the chances of the
patient's recovery. I always advise that even an inquisition
in lunacy should in these cases be deferred as long as possible,
to give time and opportunity to see what the probable duration of the disorder will be. But a commission in lunacy
can be superseded, and the patient restored to the management of his affairs. A will, however, is another matter; the
testator may die, and soon after the lunatic may recover
from his melancholy to find himself disinherited.

If the patient gets worse, and his melancholy increases, it
will take one of two directions. Either he will sink into
profound dejection, and, speechless and motionless, will sit
all day, lost to everything around him, and apparently regardless of what is said or done; or he will become more
and more panic stricken, till in a wild frenzy of excitement
that may almost be called mania, he tries to rush away he
knows not whither, or struggles against the efforts of those
around him, all of whom are in his eyes about to torture or
drag him to prison or destruction. The first of these forms
Melancolie   is termed by the French *melancholie avec stupeur,*
avec stupeur. and is described as a special variety of insanity.
It has also been confounded with another form, of which I
shall have to speak hereafter, viz., acute dementia. If, however, we consider well this *melancholie avec stupeur,* we shall
see that it is· merely an advanced stage of that dull silent
depression, which is the ordinary type of melancholic in-

sanity. Of its treatment little need be said. Such patients are generally manageable and passive in the hands of those about them. They must be fed, but do not violently resist. They require to be led about for exercise, to be washed and dressed. Though they sit motionless for hours, they are not to be trusted alone, for they may eagerly avail themselves of an opportunity to commit suicide. They demand even more food and stimulants than those who suffer from the milder forms of depression, and must be kept as warm as possible, for their motionless condition does little to circulate the blood stagnating in their vessels.

Writers have speculated upon what is passing in the mind in this state of stupor, on the absence of will, on the hallucinations and illusions that torment the patient. Our information must necessarily be derived from the patient himself after recovery, and it must needs be that such testimony is very fallacious. In fact, it is just as trustworthy as an account of the whole psychological state of a man in sleep derived from what he himself recollects of his dreams. There is, however, a very close resemblance between the dreaming condition and profound melancholy. That which is going on around the patient is observed through the medium of the depressed feeling, and is altogether unreal and illusional. All people are changed, and places, and things; and, pathologically, the states of the dreamer and the melancholic are probably nearly akin; for in dreams it would appear that the brain is only partially at work, that the whole of the idea organs are not in a state of activity, but only a few, therefore there is no correction, but all seems real. Similarly the nerve-power in melancholia is so low that the entire idea-faculty of the brain cannot be employed. The depressed condition influences the ideas that are at work, and these are not corrected by the entire brain as they would be in health. The sensations experienced from affections of the skin or viscera are converted into flames, tortures, snakes, and so forth, just as in dreams cold feet make us think we are walking on ice, or dyspepsia originates ideas of legions of devils. These melancholic patients, though they present the appearance of stupor, sleep very little, and require chloral or morphia as much as the last mentioned class.

LECTURE X.

I HAVE been speaking hitherto of patients suffering from what may be called subacute melancholia, who require constant watching, but who are not violent, do not resist feeding, and are, in fact, sufficiently tractable to be kept till cured in an ordinary house, if there be means adequate to their necessities. Such generally recover, but I am now going to speak of some who do not stop in a quiet stage of melan- Acute melancholy, but go on from it to an acute condition, of cholia. which the prognosis is the very reverse of favorable.

This form of acute melancholia demands as much as any the care of an asylum. It is hardly possible to keep Symptoms. a patient in safety in any ordinary house, or to treat him with any but the large staff of officers which an asylum supplies. He is not in a state of mere depression or mild melancholy, nor in silent stupor, but he is panic-stricken. In violent frenzy and terror he paces the room, dashes at the doors or windows, eager to escape from the doom that awaits him, from the police who are on his track. He will not sit on a chair or lie still on his bed, but is incessantly running about, exclaiming that he is going to be burnt or tortured, that the room is on fire, the floor undermined, and everything ruined and lost. He is suicidal in an extreme degree, and may try not only to put an end to himself, but also to harm himself in every way he can, to gouge out his eyes, cram things down his throat, swallow nails or bits of glass, or break

his legs or arms in the furniture.   Though he will not attack
others like a dangerous paralytic, he nevertheless resists with
the utmost violence all that is done for him.   He will take
no food, will wear no clothes, will not be washed, neither will
he remain in bed.   This is a condition very different from
that last described.   It implies a much lower degree of nerve-
force, and a much more serious disorder of brain, and the
hopes to be entertained of cure are but small, if these patients
remain in this state beyond a very few days, for they are
generally broken in health before they reach it.   Often they
are advanced in life, or enfeebled by other diseases, and melancholia is in them the commencement of dying, the later
stages bringing not unfrequently gangrene of the lungs, or a
condition closely resembling scurvy, indicating a gradual termination of the vitality of the whole bodily frame.

Such patients refuse food, not with a passive resistance like
Refusal of the former, who allow themselves to be fed with a
food. spoon, but with all their might, ejecting it from their
mouths, even after we have managed to place it there.   They
drive us to the adoption of forcible alimentation, about which
I must say something.   We are not to wait long before we
have recourse to this.   They sink rapidly if not fed, and the
more they are weakened by lack of food, the more are all
their symptoms exaggerated.   It is of no use to let them go
for a day with a mouthful or two, neither can we afford to
let them wait till they are hungry, or are in the humor to eat.
The case is too serious, and too much is lost by abstinence,
even for twenty-four hours.   In the case of some insane persons there is no occasion for hurry.   When they are tolerably
strong and vigorous, and when the refusal of food is due to
mere opposition or whim, we may wait, and frequently the
humor will change, and they may be coaxed into taking food.
But coaxing does little with the terror-stricken melancholic.
Nevertheless, it must be tried.   It is an old suggestion that
the persuasiveness of the opposite sex may prevail upon pa-

tients to eat, that female friends and nurses should try to overcome the fears and reluctance of men, and males that of the women. In some forms of insanity this plan unquestionably is of service, but here I fear we shall find it of little use. The sufferer is determined not to eat, and will sink rather than do so; in fact, the refusal is generally from a suicidal motive. Now comes the question, How are we to feed such a one? Various authors advocate various plans of feeding, either through the nose, or through the mouth, with or without a tube passed down the œsophagus. Of these, Forcible feeding. I would say that no one is suited to all cases, that each has its merits and demerits; but that if I were compelled to choose one, and one only, I would select that of the ordinary stomach-tube passed into the œsophagus through the mouth. Many advocate feeding by a spoon through the mouth, the patient being held on his back by attendants, and his mouth forced open for the purpose. The objection to this plan, in my opinion, is the length of time it takes. We are dealing with people who are extremely weak and prostrated, but who, nevertheless, resist violently; and if the struggle is prolonged for half an hour, the patient loses as much through fatigue as he gains by the food; yet when the struggle is not great, when food can be got down easily by this method, and when he swallows readily the food once placed in his mouth, there is no necessity for the stomach-pump, and he may be fed four or five times in the twenty-four hours. I feel bound to describe to you the various methods, that you may be prepared to adopt one or other as circumstances or opportunity indicate. Feeding may be accomplished by the mouth without the introduction of any tube. This plan is set out By means of a by Dr. S. W. D. Williams, of the Sussex Asylum, spoon. in a paper in the "Journal of Mental Science," October, 1864, and this is his plan of procedure:

" With the aid of three attendants the patient is placed on his back on a mattress on the floor, and covered by bedclothes, being, as a *sine qua non*, in his nightdress as far as the armpits, the arms being free. The head rests on a well-filled bolster, an attendant kneels on each side of the bedclothes covering the patient, and thus easily but effectually secures the body. One hand is placed on the patient's wrist, and the other presses down the shoulder. By these means he is perfectly restrained in the least irksome way to both patient and attendant, and, which is of primary importance, but few if any bruises need be inflicted. Hold a person in any other part of his body, or by any other means, and he surely becomes covered, after a few operations, by a mass of bruises, which often leads to unpleasant recriminations and fancies on the part of friends and relatives, and tends to foster the prevailing ideas current among the many as to the management of institutions for the insane—ideas which it behooves every conscientious alienist physician to persistently endeavor to dissipate, if he would wish to hold any claims to philanthropy. The operator kneels at the patient's head, and if the patient is very restive, may steady his head with his knees; but this is seldom necessary. A third attendant takes his place at the operator's left elbow. It should be here ascertained that the patient's throat is quite free externally from any clothing. The next operation is to get the spoon into the patient's mouth : this, if the patient be a woman, is generally easily done by getting her to talk, and slipping it in when the mouth is opened to speak ; this device failing, however, persistent but moderate pressure with the spoon against the teeth, aided, if necessary, by inserting a finger between the upper and lower gums behind the last molar, will soon effect our object. Of course, in putting a finger into the mouth, one must look out for being bitten ; but if the spoon be firmly pressed against the teeth so as to slide between them immediately the masseters are relaxed, such an accident cannot readily occur. The best spoons to use are the small iron ones, to be found in most of our large asylums, with the handle straightened. This should be placed far enough into the mouth to command the tongue, care being taken not to excite the reflex action of the fauces. It should then be restrained by the thumb and index finger of the left hand, the palm and remaining fingers firmly grasping the chin and preventing any to-and-fro or lateral motion of the head. The third attendant now passes his right hand under the operator's engaged arm, and firmly closes the nostrils, leaving his other arm free for any emergency that may arise. The operator can now with his right hand pour the food into the patient's mouth, and, provided the spoon well commands the tongue, deglutition is easily and perforce obtained, even in the most obstinate cases; but the patients are really by this means so completely mastered that the majority of them drink the food down easily, and often the spoon is not required at all, but the nostrils being closed, the lips may be separated and the food poured into the mouth without opening the teeth. Indeed, for the first three weeks of last January, I fed a young lady in this way four times a day, although she was obstinately bent on refusing food. The most convenient instrument for containing the food is a gutta-percha bottle or ball holding about half a pint, and having for a stopper a bone tube like the extremity of an enema tube. This bottle can easily be commanded in the hand, and the bone tube having been inserted into the hollow of the spoon as it is held between the teeth, after a little practice, by squeezing the bottle the quantity of fluid to be injected can be judged to a nicety, and the tube removed after each injection. Not more than half an ounce should be injected into the mouth at once, one good respiration being allowed between each mouthful. After an expiration there is a short pause before the next inspiration, and if this moment of rest be chosen for filling the mouth, there is but little likelihood of the larynx being irritated by particles getting into it and delaying the operation by causing a fit of coughing. By a careful compliance with these rules, and a little practice, any one may administer, in all ordinary cases at least, a pint of liquid in from ten to fifteen minutes, without a possibility of any danger or harm accruing, which cannot be said of the various other modes in vogue."

This is, in other words, the ordinary attendants' mode of feeding a patient: place the patient on his back, support his head, hold it between the knees, force open the mouth and keep it open, usually with a "forcing-stick," pour in a mouthful of liquid, and hold the nose till it is swallowed. It is a very simple plan, which succeeds well, as Dr. Williams says, "in all ordinary cases," especially where the patient is by it "completely mastered," and takes the food quietly when placed in his mouth, but it fails in extraordinary cases. If we meet with a very powerful patient, two attendants will never keep him quiet, and in the struggle his arms, to say nothing of body and legs, will present the mass of bruises Dr. Williams so rightly deprecates. Then, as the mouth is held open all the time, the patient can eject by an expiration some, at any rate, of the fluid, and if he holds his breath as long as he can at each mouthful, the administration of a pint of liquid will occupy much more than fifteen minutes. The food being only placed in the fauces to be swallowed as respiration demands, some of it does always go the wrong way, and great is the coughing and choking produced thereby. Frequently more is wasted than taken in this way; nevertheless, it is well suited for many cases, and may always be tried before resorting to more instrumental means. Some use a funnel inserted behind the teeth; others a glass bottle with a valve controlled by a spring, on which the operator places his thumb, and by which he can let flow as much or as little as he likes. A bottle of this kind made by Coxeter, called Dr. Paley's feeding apparatus, has a flat metal mouthpiece which keeps down the tongue, and through which the fluid escapes. It is a most excellent contrivance, and by it many patients may be fed frequently and satisfactorily.

Much the same plan has been recommended by Dr. Moxey, in the "Lancet," March, 1869, the only difference being that, instead of putting the food into the fauces through the mouth, he pours it through a funnel placed in one of the nares.

In the fourth volume of the "Journal of Mental Science," is an interesting paper by Dr. Harrington Tuke, By the nasal who reviews the various methods of feeding, and tube. gives the preference to an œsophageal tube introduced through the nose and reaching the stomach. Dr. Tuke speaks strongly against the plan of forcibly feeding by a spoon or funnel. "It is not only the violence that must accompany the administration of food in this manner that inclines me strongly to deprecate this mode of treatment, but I believe that it must sometimes be an exceedingly painful operation. The sensation of something going the wrong way is familiar to us all, and it appears to me that pouring soup into the pharynx of a screaming and violently resisting patient is very apt to induce spasm of the glottis, or even cause the passage of some of the fluid into the lungs. I do not think that an exhausted patient could safely be submitted to such treatment." Another equally strong objection is urged by Dr. Tuke against this plan. "It involves the medical attendant in a sort of personal contest with his patient, which must engender feelings of hostility most detrimental to the exercise of moral influence. The medical attendant, living on terms of intimacy with his patients, should never descend to the position of a rough nurse. Feeding with a tube *secundum artem* is a painless surgical operation, which, if rapidly and skilfully done, will not give rise to the same feelings of degradation as I should imagine 'funnel' feeding must occasion."

Dr. Tuke has a great dread of the ordinary stomach-pump

tube, and prefers a small tube introduced into the stomach through the nose, if the patient will not open the mouth. "The instruments I use for injecting food into the stomach are œsophageal tubes about seventeen inches in length, made of elastic gum like an ordinary catheter, and of various diameters from the size of No. 3 to a No. 6 urethral catheter. One of these, if the patient will open his mouth, I pass down into the pharynx. If there is resistance, and the mouth is obstinately closed, I send the tube best adapted to the size of the nostril, without any stylet, but well oiled, along the floor of the nasal passage, and so into the cavity of the stomach."

Various objections may be urged against this method, some of which Dr. Tuke admits and comments on. First, the catheter strikes against the cervical vertebræ, and there remains fixed: to obviate this difficulty various ingenious but complicated contrivances have been invented by the French, with which I will not now trouble you. "The remedy," says Dr. Tuke, "is simple. Let the instrument be previously bent so as to give it a tendency to turn downwards; and, at the moment it approaches the posterior nares, let the head of the patient be thrown back, so as to diminish the sharpness of the angle it must describe. It is obvious that the operation should not be performed when the patient is in the supine position.

"The next problem, that of avoiding the entrance of the larynx or the opening of the fauces, is solved by bringing the patient's head forwards and downwards, which will send the point of the tube against the posterior wall of the pharynx; but to a practiced manipulator this will not be necessary, and this part of the operation will be as easily performed as the *tour de main* with which a good surgeon sends the sound below the arch of the pubes into the bladder. The tube having thus far proceeded comes within the grasp of the constrictor muscles, and now glides down the œsophagus almost without aid from the operator.

"The next objection is the likelihood of the catheter entering the larynx, and the danger of the lungs thus receiving the fluid intended for the stomach. This danger is common to tubes introduced either through the mouth or the nostril; perhaps in the latter case the smallness of the tube may render the accident more probable. A simple rule will prevent this mischance producing any serious result. The operator must never attach his injecting apparatus to the catheter, before at least fourteen inches of the tube have been passed. If no violence has been used this will sufficiently indicate that its point has entered the cavity of the stomach."

I confess I think this argument fallacious. A tube might pass fourteen inches down the trachea, bronchus, and bronchial ramifications, if we reckon these inches from the exterior of the nose; and it is not easy to bend the head of a resisting patient backwards and forwards at our pleasure. It is also a disadvantage not to be able to feed a patient in the supine position.

I have never seen any plan of feeding violent and refractory patients which equalled that of Dr. Henry Stevens, late Medical Superintendent of St. Luke's Hospital. Having had considerable experience of this method, I will here describe it, because by it many of the objections usually urged against the stomach-pump are removed. *By the stomach-pump.*

Where a patient can be fed without extraordinary difficulty or exhaustion by Dr. Williams's method, I adopt it, and the sight of the stomach-pump apparatus laid out on a table at hand often produces a moral effect, and facilitates the operation, which is conducted by attendants in my presence. If they cannot easily succeed, I use the stomach-pump after the following fashion :

In the first place, the patient is to be rendered incapable of sudden movements. Dr. Tuke says, " I have known one of the most expert surgeons in London pierce the thoracic aorta in consequence of the accidental movement of a patient while the tube of an ordinary stomach-pump was being passed down the œsophagus." Recollect that no grasping on the part of a number of attendants can hold a very powerful patient motionless, because they are not all the time acting together. The patient is to be placed in a wooden arm-chair, and his body, arms, and legs, are to be swathed in sheets drawn through the arms and legs of the chair so as to render him immovable. By this means all sudden movements and consequent accidents are prevented ; he cannot struggle, therefore there is no exhaustion, and bruising is prevented far more effectually than by Dr. Williams's method. When the patient is thus fastened, half of Dr. Tuke's objections disappear. If the teeth were firmly closed, they were slowly and gradually opened by Dr. Stevens by a silver-plated wedge, which expanded by means of a screw ; thus without the slightest violence or chance of breaking a tooth, the teeth were separated sufficiently to insert the hard-wood gag, which was held by an attendant standing behind the patient. All chance of passing a tube into the glottis is obviated by using one of a size that will not enter it. Nothing is gained by using a very small tube; as we do not use the smallest-sized catheter to pass along an unstrictured urethra, so we need not use a very fine tube to pass down the œsophagus, through which a coiner bolts his bad half-crowns with perfect impunity. The tube, then, should be at least of a size that will not enter the larynx; it must be flexible to the end, and must not have the stiff wooden extremity which generally terminates the tubes in the ordinary stomach-pump cases. Passing it through the hole in the gag, we direct it, not straight at the vertebræ, but to the right, having previously oiled it. No force what-

ever is to be used. In all probability the patient will hold
it with his tongue, preventing its descent; we are not to
force it, but simply hold it steadily; in a few seconds he is
obliged to take breath, he relaxes his hold, and the tube
slides within the action of the muscles by which it is swallowed, and so passes into the stomach. No haste is to be
used in pushing it down or drawing it back. We then affix
our injecting apparatus, which may be an ordinary brass
pump or an India-rubber bottle. If the tube is not too small,
the food need not be mere liquid drink, but may consist of a
mess of finely-pounded meat and beef-tea thickened with
potato or flour: it is important that there be an adequate
quantity of farinaceous material. Such things as brandy,
wine, eggs, and medicines may be added at discretion, and
the medicines may be mixed with the food in or out of the
sight of the patient, according as we think fit. Frequently,
when he finds that we can administer all we wish him to
take, he gives in, and takes his food. The preparations for
feeding often produce the same effect; but I have found that
patients do not experience any great pain or inconvenience
from this method, and sometimes will refuse their food merely
to give trouble. Such persons often dislike being fed by the
spoon method far more than by the stomach-pump, as it is a
longer process. One patient would eat all the rest of his
meals if I would give him his breakfast with the stomach-
pump; otherwise he would take nothing all day. This he
continued for a month. Another gentleman who had had
considerable experience of feeding in various ways, fell to
discussing the subject with the attendants one day after I
had fed him, and stoutly maintained that the stomach-pump,
used as described, was the least unpleasant of any. Only excessive violence can lead to such accidents as piercing the
aorta. Even teeth can be got open without breaking, by tact
and patience; and all danger of going the wrong way is at an
end if the tube be of the proper size. Doubtless, some will

talk about mechanical restraint, and so forth: to these I would say, compare a patient struggling for fifteen to thirty minutes in the hands of three or four attendants, with one fastened with sheets in a chair for five minutes. Let both be seen before judgment is passed.

It may occasionally happen that we are obliged to feed by force a patient who is not suffering from acute melancholia, but from some other variety of insanity—one who refuses food from sheer opposition, or because he thinks it poisoned. In such cases one or two operations generally work a cure; but in acute melancholia we feed because the patient's life is jeopardized by want of food; and, in spite of our feeding, such a one may sink, for this acutely melancholy state is often only the last stage of a melancholy which has been gradually reducing the strength of the individual for months, and which for want of vigorous treatment in the early stages has gone on to a point when cure is impossible. Nevertheless, we must not let a patient die of starvation, and as a long and exhausting struggle is not to be thought of, we must feed with the stomach-pump twice a day, or oftener.

Chloral will bring sleep to these patients as to others, and we may give it in full doses at night, and in less doses in the morning, to allay the restless panic and frenzied agitation. The sufferer may after a small dose sleep half an hour or an hour, and then be quiet for some time, allowing himself to be fed with less resistance. In this way his strength may be husbanded and supported. And, besides chloral, morphia is valuable here, and no mode of administration is so serviceable as the subcutaneous injections, for the patients
Drugs.
will no more take medicine than food, and in the struggle to give it by the mouth much may be wasted, and we may not know exactly how much has been taken. Chloral, too, though it cannot be administered subcutaneously, may be given by the rectum. Never give pills; patients will hold them in their mouths till your back is turned, and then

spit them out; you can never be certain that they are or are not swallowed. The morphia may be mixed with the food, but this is not nearly so satisfactory a method as the subcutaneous injection. Other medicines are not worth the struggle of getting them down. In so great debility, such drugs as bromide of potassium, tartar emetic, hydrocyanic acid, and digitalis, are, in my judgment, out of the question. The warm-bath may promote sleep, and great warmth of rooms and clothing will be necessary. Such persons are not to be allowed to lie on the floor of an ordinary room all night, which they are very prone to do. There is a tendency in all to fatal pneumonia and gangrene of lung, and rather than run any risk of exposure, I would employ mechanical restraint, and fasten them in bed. Suicide is their one end and aim; and, at the suggestion of the Commissioners in Lunacy themselves, I have employed mechanical restraint at night for such reasons as I have stated.

In addition to the ordinary warm bath, the hot-air or Turkish bath may be tried in these cases of acute melancholia, if opportunity enables us to do so. I myself have not been able to apply this mode of treatment to any except those who could be sent out of the asylum; but in some of our larger asylums it is systematically. adopted, with proper rooms for carrying it out.

The prognosis in this extreme form is, as I have already said, unfavorable. It occurs chiefly in persons de- Prognosis. bilitated by age, disease, or childbirth. And the obstinate refusal of food, and the struggles with which its administration is attended, add greatly to the danger of the disorder and to the difficulty of dealing with it. This form of melancholia is rapid compared with the other. Very rarely can we give sufficient food, if the refusal is persistent. Hence many of these patients gradually sink. If the disorder becomes chronic, and the bodily health improves, recovery may take place as in other forms of melancholia.

Our power of prognosis will, of course, be greatly aided in these acute cases by the thermometer and the sphygmograph. The chances of life or death will be indicated with tolerable certainty by the temperature and the character of the pulse. But I need not say that it is difficult in the extreme to take observations of such a kind in the case of patients who resist all that is done to them. Our fingers must be our guides, and by them we may learn the heightened temperature and rapid pulse which are of such evil omen in acute melancholia and acute delirium.

After speaking of these melancholy patients, I may fitly
Acute primary describe a class which has been by some confounded
dementia. with them. The form of disorder has received various names, and has been brought under one or other of the varieties of insanity according to the views of different writers. It was described by Esquirol, and called by him "acute dementia," and this name is more often applied to it than any other. Pinel confounded it with a kind of idiocy, and named it "stupidité." M. Baillarger pronounced it to be a variety of melancholia, and, owing to the torpor and inactivity of the patients, called it "*melancolie avec stupeur;*" and this name is still given to it by many—wrongly, however, for *melancolie avec stupeur* is a very different disorder. Dr. Monro has proposed to apply to it the term "cataleptoid" insanity, and this word not inaptly expresses the lost automatic condition so often witnessed in those suffering from it. They are not, however, lost in woe, like those buried in profound melancholia, in *melancolie avec stupeur*. Rather are they lost in vacuity; they look utterly idiotic and silly, like the chronic demented people seen in asylums and workhouses. Hence the name "acute dementia," "acute" being used in contradistinction to chronic, meaning a curable disorder lasting comparatively a short time. The term has been objected to, because it is said that we cannot call such a passive disorder "acute," and because the minds of such patients are

not really demented.   However, I will try to describe to you the disease, to which you may affix what name you like, provided you clearly understand the symptoms.   Dementia it is while it lasts, and perhaps we can give it no better name than " primary dementia," thus marking it off from the secondary chronic dementia which follows other forms of insanity or organic disease of the brain.   The patients are all young, from fifteen to twenty-five years of age.   When we hear of a man or woman of fifty being thus affected, we may presume that the malady is *melancolie avec stupeur*, or something of the kind.   It is not primary dementia.   A young man, then, or a young woman, after some shock or fright, some appalling sight or intelligence, is frightened

Symptoms.
" out of his senses."   He is horror-stricken, paralyzed in mind, not merely deranged, not depressed or excited, but deprived of feeling and intellect; his movements, if there be any, are automatic, but frequently he is motionless, standing or sitting, staring at vacancy for hours and days.   As I have said, this may come on suddenly after a fright, or it may be developed more gradually after some slight cause, so slight that it has been unnoticed or forgotten by the friends. In the case of one young man, it was a fall from a scaffold without injury beyond the fright and shake.   Such are always persons of weak nerves, boys and girls who have outgrown their strength, and whose nervous condition is still further weakened by delicate bodily health.   They do not converse; their answers are those of an idiot or demented patient. More frequently they give no reply.   They are not always motionless; often they are in incessant motion.   One girl used to snap her jaws together for days at a time, and then changed to wagging her head from side to side.   This action was truly automatic, for no effort of will could have kept up muscular motion for so long a time.   They do not stop when spoken to, but if we give them a shake, they may perchance direct their attention to us for a moment, and then begin

again. They do not always remain the same. After being for hours in a complete cataleptic or trance-like state, so as to make those about think they are in a fit or comatose, they will commence to laugh, chatter, or grimace in a silly and idiotic fashion. There is apparently a complete mental blank, and sometimes after recovery we find that nothing is recollected. Sometimes they recollect all that has passed, though at the time they had no power or control over their actions. They may, however, resist violently when fed, dressed, or moved, resisting like the chronic demented without any reason, except that their quiet or automatic action is interfered with.

The physical condition is peculiar. The circulation is so feeble that in the hottest weather hands and feet are blue with cold. In winter they are covered with chilblains, and there is great difficulty in keeping these from becoming sore. The heart's action and pulse are proportionately weak. Such patients do not lose flesh as those in acute mania or melancholia, but are flabby and pale. They do not eat, but can generally be fed without difficulty. They are wet and dirty, or do not pass water unless at long intervals, neither will the bowels of some act without enemata. Sleep may be irregular, but it is seldom absent, and frequently the amount is normal.

You will have to distinguish this form of insanity from Diagnosis and *melancholia cum stupore*, and from chronic dementia. prognosis. Now, the patients affected with *melancholia cum stupore* are seldom young. They have been melancholy from the commencement of the attack, are suicidal, rapidly emaciate, refuse food obstinately, and sleep little. In all of which they differ from those whose malady is primary dementia. The latter in the beginning are maniacal rather than melancholic, and rarely suicidal; and when they get better, and can tell us something about themselves, we see that depression is not the leading characteristic of their state, but that it is mainly extreme weakness of mind, consequent for the most part upon mental shock, or bodily debility, or both combined. How can we distinguish it from chronic dementia? In other words, how can we say whether the patient will recover or not? I confess that this is not easy. I have seen patients of whom I had hopes who have remained permanently in a demented condition. Everything will depend on the history. The appearance of the sufferer may be identical in primary and secondary dementia. You are shown a young man or a girl in a state of fatuous imbecility, grinning idiotically, lost, and dirty. Nothing can appear less promising. But if you are told that this condition came on almost suddenly, especially if it followed a mental fright or shock, which seems to have been the origin of it, and if you observe the physical symptoms I have mentioned, indicating great weakness of the system and circulation, you may pronounce hopefully as to the result. But if the patient has gradually and imperceptibly drifted into this imbecile condition without assigned cause, then you may set it down that the cause is hereditary taint in the first place, and masturbation in the second, and that though improvement may take place, recovery is impossible.

What is the treatment of these patients, and where is it to be carried out? I do not think an asylum absolutely necessary. In many the mental shock they *Treatment.* have undergone would be intensified by such removal. If they are passive and tractable, they may be treated in a family, or even at home. And as they improve, change of scene will be of infinite service. They require nutrition and stimulation—nutrition by means of abundance of food, and stimulation by wine and stout, and also such a stimulant as a shower-bath. In these cases especially, I believe shower-baths to be useful, a short sharp shower, and then plenty of friction to restore and promote the circulation. Above all, they require warmth: warmth which to us would be excessive heat will not do more than warm them, and you will find that many of them will continue in the same state through the winter, and wake up and recover when the hot summer comes. Tonics we may give, especially steel and small stimulating doses of morphia. Menstruation is sure to be absent, but we need not direct any special efforts towards it. As the general strength returns, it comes again, and meddling in this direction does more harm than good. We shall soon see, when a patient is subjected to treatment of this kind, whether there is an awakening of attention, and a return of mental strength. If there be, if we are conscious of an improvement, we need not despair, even if it be slow.

I said in my last lecture that patients attacked with primary dementia might be ranged at one end of the scale of the insane, for here we see the minimum of cerebral action and metamorphosis, the negative side of mind disorder, manifested in silly idiotic vacuity rather than in depression, excitement, or delusions. The bodily phenomena correspond: the circulation is lowered, the surface is cold, there is but little change going on, there is no waste, nothing but automatic movements or torpid inactivity. In my next lecture I shall present to you certain patients who are the very reverse of all this, whose insanity is shown in furious delirium, with incessant violence and entire sleeplessness, with so great waste and exhaustion that life may come to an end in a few days, or if recovery take place, the sufferer may be found to have lost flesh to a great extent, even in a very short period. This form I shall term acute delirious mania, and this may be fitly placed at the other end of the scale.

LECTURE XI.

Acute Delirious Mania—Diagnosis of Transitory Mania—How to Arrest it—Treatment of Prolonged Acute Delirium—Food—Nursing—Medicines—Baths—Purgatives—Prognosis—Diagnosis.

INSTEAD of a patient feeling something wrong for weeks or months, or the same thing being noticed for as long Acute a period by those around him, very acute symptoms delirium. of mania may arise in a few days or even hours. The premonitory stage of an attack of acute delirium, or acute mania, may be extremely brief; in fact, a patient may awake out of sleep, and at once become delirious. The more sudden the invasion, the shorter will be the duration of the attack in the majority of instances, but to all such rules there are many exceptions. Sudden outbursts of delirious mania frequently have their origin in a mental cause, as the death of a friend, a suddenly announced misfortune, a violent quarrel, a disappointment or cross in love. Any such circumstance occurring to a person of weak nerve, hysterical, and by nature predisposed to mental disturbance, may bring about very acute delirium in a few hours.

The same thing may proceed from a cause clearly physical. It may arise in the course or during the decline of acute disease, as pneumonia, measles, or fever. It may come on in a patient who is phthisical, or has acute rheumatism, or who has undergone too great fatigue, as a very long walk. It may succeed a paroxysm of epilepsy, or take the place of one. It may come on quite suddenly after childbirth, exposure to the sun, or indulgence in drink.

Now, we cannot say in every case whether an acute de-
May be lirium will last a few hours or days, or whether it will
transient. run the ordinary course of an attack of delirious
mania, and require special care and treatment for weeks or
months. But it is all-important that we should arrive at
some conclusion before we move a patient to an asylum. The
prognosis in such a case is of the greatest consequence, and
at the same time extremely difficult.

Some information may be derived, first, from a consideration of the character and constitution and past history of the
individual; secondly, from the cause of the attack; thirdly,
from the symptoms observed.

Some patients there are whose organization is so unstable,
who are so prone to violent disturbance of the nervous system,
that attacks of delirium may in them supervene upon an
occurrence comparatively trifling. It is reasonable to hope
that such an attack will be transient. If the individual has
been hitherto unknown to us, we must discover, so far as is
possible, what his or her temperament and character ordinarily are; above all, whether there have been previous
attacks of a similar nature, and whether they were of long or
short duration. If the attack has been gradually developing
during a week or longer, without any assignable cause, it is
not likely that it will suddenly terminate. Observation of
the patient will teach us something. If amidst the paroxysms
of delirium there are intervals of calm, during which the patient is rational, we hope that the attack will be brief; also
if there are intervals of sleep. If there is no sleep for three
or four days, except perhaps short snatches of half an hour,
and if during the whole of this time the patient is becoming
more and more maniacal and delirious, we conclude that an
attack of acute mania has begun, through which he must be
nursed, and which cannot now be arrested. We shall also
be aided by observing the physical condition, noticing if there
be symptoms of hysterical delirium, copious voiding of pale

urine, indications of amatory feeling, pretended inability to speak, and other peculiarities denoting that even with apparently very violent delirium there is complete appreciation of all that is going on, and considerable exercise of volition in what is done. We constantly see cases which would be described by one as mere hysterics, by another as an attack of transitory delirious mania, and it is not easy to distinguish one from the other.

What can we do to bring this condition to a conclusion? It is necessary above all things to determine whether How to the attack is going to be transient or prolonged before arrest it. we remove the sufferer to an asylum, for the terror inspired by the removal would be very likely to convert one of the short attacks into a prolonged and obstinate mania; and if this were not the result, we should yet regret that we had placed a person in such a position for an insanity of so passing a character. Three or four days will set our doubts at rest, and then if the patient cannot be managed out of an asylum, to an asylum he must go.

There are doubtless many patients who, if treated at home by friends and among friends, would rapidly recover, but who, when removed by force and placed among strangers, experience a much more prolonged and severe attack. Yet such a step is often unavoidable. Suppose that a man becomes acutely maniacal in a seaside lodging: he cannot remain there three or four days till it is decided whether his disorder will suddenly terminate or not. He would require to be violently restrained, most probably by strangers, and he might not be safe in such an abode : removal becomes imperative, and we can advise nothing else under the circumstances. But, as I have said, when it is possible to wait and watch the case, let it be done.

In the year 1869, I saw two most acute cases of delirious mania commencing in seaside lodgings. One was that of a gentleman aged thirty-one. He had had two previous attacks of mania within a twelvemonth. The first occurred in his own home. He was then full of fancies, which at times he recognized as delusions; but once or twice he woke in the night in a paroxysm of terror, accompanied by great excitement, and violently attacked a friend and his brother, who were his nurses. This great excitement, however, passed off in an hour or two, and in a few days he was well. The second attack merely consisted of a number of the old delusions, which reappeared and disappeared again after change of scene and visits to friends. The third, as I have said, commenced at the seaside, after premonitory symptoms of sleeplessness and religious delusions of about a week's duration. He was inclined to run away; his wife called in the police to her assistance, and he then broke out into violent delirium, was brought to London, and at once taken to an asylum, where I found him. He perpetually heard voices, talked of religious subjects, refused food, had paroxysms of violent fury, in which he attacked all about him, and intervals of rationality, in which he washed and bathed himself, and ate a hearty meal. He was treated with drachm doses of bromide of potassium. The first night he slept three hours, the second two, and the third four, and after that he slept naturally, and by the end of a week he was perfectly himself, and resumed his usual work and occupation in the asylum, where he stayed a fortnight longer. In six months he had another attack, which also began at the seaside. In this he was even more violent and desperately suicidal. He was now treated with chloral, which quickly subdued the sleeplessness and delirium. He has not, however, fully recovered, and it is a question whether he ever will. There is insanity in his family. He is one of the many examples met with of patients who hear voices. Whether these are chronic or acute cases, the prognosis is in all unfavorable. Here, though the patient seemed perfectly to recover, the symptoms returned every six months; and, as might be expected, they now threaten chronic insanity, and probably an early termination of life.

The other was a young lady of twenty-one, in whose family, as in that of the gentleman, insanity existed. She was not removed from the sea for a fortnight, her violence making it impossible. She experienced a most acute attack of delirious mania, recollecting nothing afterwards of what occurred. The contrast in these two cases was evident to one watching them. In the girl's the attack had been coming on for months: there was no sleep beyond the briefest snatches for a week, and there were no intervals of quiet or rationality. Her tongue, her odor, indicated from the first the serious nature of the disorder; but of this prolonged mania I shall speak hereafter. It ran a course of violence lasting nearly a month, and then came great weakness and prostration, and gradual but perfect recovery.

What treatment are we to adopt when this acute mania first breaks out? We cannot say for certain whether we can cut it short; but we hope to do so.

We have at this time a remedy in the hydrate of chloral, of more value than anything that ever was given be- Chloral. fore its discovery. Opium in anything like a sthenic case generally made matters worse. Bromide of potassium was of greater value, but it did not surely produce sleep. Hyoscyamus, digitalis, cannabis Indica, were uncertain remedies, on which we could not depend. But many of these cases are cut short and cured, like delirium tremens, if we can procure one long and sound sleep, and I believe that chloral will generally be found to cause sleep of a longer or shorter duration. If the patient is strong and the excitement waxing vehement, give a drachm. I have seen a very violent maniac sent to sleep by such a dose, and wake clear of everything like delirium, though he still had delusions. Chloral does not cure insanity: it is given nightly to the chronic insane; they sleep, but are not cured. In them the disorder of the brain is fixed and incurable; but in the early stages of acute insanity, after one sleep the sufferer often wakes restored, and this sleep we can bring about by chloral in a way we never could formerly.

By the side of this drug it seems scarcely worth while to mention the modes of attaining sleep which were once adopted. But I may say that I have seen the violent mania of an approaching attack subside more than once after a brisk purgative. Whatever be the action of this, whether we are to call it, in the language of a bygone age, a derivative, a revulsive, or a counter-irritant, its effect is often marked and evident, and the patient recovers.

There is another remedy sometimes tried, viz., packing in a wet sheet. A sheet dipped in water, hot or cold, according to circumstances, and wrung out, is laid on a mattress protected by a Mackintosh sheet and a blanket, and the patient, placed on this, is wrapped so as to include arms, legs, and in fact, the whole body with the exception of the head. The blanket is then tucked over him, and other blankets laid over all. Dr. Lockhart Robertson, the great advocate of the cold-water wet sheet, recommends that when the patient has been in the sheet for an hour or an hour and a half, he should be taken out, rubbed thoroughly with a dripping cold sheet, and replaced in another wet sheet and blankets, and that after each change of sheet two pails of cold water should be poured over him. He says that in some cases of recent mania he has pursued this system throughout the day, or three or four times in the day, or less frequently. We must be careful, however, how we employ it, for like the prolonged warm bath, the prolonged shower bath, and other desperate methods of cutting short mania, it is not unattended with risk. I believe, however, that merely packing up in a sheet wrung out of hot water gives us without danger the chief advantages of the system. It is a powerful sudorific, and promotes sleep by reducing to the minimum the power of motion.   There can be no question that when the latter is taken away, patients will often fall asleep.   This is one of the chief arguments used by the advocates of restraint, and I have no doubt that in their experience they saw this effect produced.   Now, the wet sheet, as a medical appliance, has advantages over the strait-waistcoat.   It will, I presume, be denied by those who use the wet sheet that its chief good arises from its being a form of mechanical restraint; but that it is the latter, for good or evil, there needs no argument to prove.

If a patient sleeps three hours at a time within twenty-four of the commencement of the delirious outbreak, and awakes calmer, and sleeps again in the next twenty-four hours—and if his attacks of violence are paroxysmal, with comparatively lucid intervals, his mind not getting more and more lost and confused,—we may hope that the malady will soon terminate in long and healthy sleep, after. which he may awake comparatively well, like one awakening from the sleep which terminates delirium tremens.   But if the snatches of sleep become shorter, the patient waking in a paroxysm of rage and terror—if the delusions grow wilder and more senseless, and he takes less notice of those about him, violently resisting all that is done for him,—we may make up our minds that he has entered upon an attack of acute delirious mania which cannot be cut short, but through which he must be nursed for days or weeks. Prolonged attack.

I need not take up your time by a lengthy description of the disorder, for in truth it is hardly possible to mistake it for any other.   The name "acute delirious mania" sufficiently describes it.   I shall have a few words to say on the diagnosis and distinction between it and some other forms of delirium; but however alike these may be for a time, the history and progress sufficiently distinguish them from this form of insanity.

I have already spoken of the premonitory symptoms of

acute delirium. The oncoming of a transitory attack is usually more rapid than that of one more prolonged. In the latter case the change may have been noticed for a long or a short time, from a week to three or four months, presenting the ordinary features of mental derangement, such as in one may terminate in melancholia, in another in mania, while in a third it may be fixed in a quiet monomania. Generally speaking, after a brief period of *alteration*, some casual opposition, heat of weather, or accidental circumstance, lights up the violent stage, while gradually-lessening sleep precipitates the attack. When any such symptoms are apparent, it is right to bear in mind that the night is the time when the acute stage is most likely to commence. This is important, because a patient is apt to be less guarded at this hour than at any other. Wives are alone with their husbands, out of reach, it may be, of all male assistance; or a man may be in a room at the top of the house by himself, possibly locked in. Friends are afraid to place attendants with a person in this condition, for fear of irritating him, and will often keep them out of sight till mischief is done. The most violent stage is not usually at the commencement of the malady, though a patient may be violent for a short time, paroxysmally. As I have said, this may terminate in sleep, or he will go on getting worse and worse, more full of delusions, more unconscious, and utterly sleepless, till all hope of speedy termination is past.

We have thus arrived at a stage when the patient, man or woman, cannot any longer be treated in an ordinary bedroom, or nursed by relatives and ordinary nurses. Whether he must be removed to an asylum will depend on his means, on his house and the inmates of it, or of adjoining houses. An asylum is not absolutely necessary to his recovery. He does not require amusement, or occupation, or grounds and garden. He is going to be actually ill for a fortnight or longer, and to be confined to one room

Disposal of patient.

for that time. Upon the room much will depend, but little on its locality. He cannot be nursed by near relatives; it is therefore essential that very skilful people shall be about him, in whom full confidence can be placed.

The room, in or out of an asylum, should be large enough to be airy and cool; the windows must be out of reach, or protected, yet capable of being opened, and also of being darkened, and the darkened state must be kept up during the height of the attack. The patient will not lie quietly on a bedstead, and attempts to compel him to do so will end in many bruises, if not in broken ribs. So the bed must be made up on the floor, a considerable surface of which may be covered with mattresses. Few patients will allow any clothes to remain on—they will strip them off and tear them in pieces. They must not, however, go naked; a strong suit, consisting of jacket and trousers, or petticoat, fastened together in one piece, and laced up the back, may be securely fastened on them, and underneath it may be placed the requisite body linen; or a patient may have a blanket fastened round his neck and shoulders so as to form a kind of poncho. If this be well fastened round his arms, they will not be very available for mischief, and yet there will be no irksome restraint. He can also be easily held without the infliction of a single bruise. The scantiest furniture should be left in the room—utensils will be little needed, for such patients are almost invariably wet and dirty — and for drinking, a horn-cup is better than glass or china. Near relatives must keep out of sight, for their presence will not be tranquillizing, but the reverse, to the bewildered mind; yet the occasional glimpse of some one he knows—an old servant, friend, or doctor—may reassure and make him think that the strange faces he sees are not those of enemies, persecutors, or fiends. Many are aware of what is going on, far more than is suspected; though they make no sign, they take in all that passes, and no better advice can be given to those in charge than to be careful that they say nothing in presence of a patient that he is not to hear. If we in his presence order medicine to be mixed with food, we may run the risk of its being refused, even if he is apparently in the most unconscious delirium.

The old writers used to describe in glowing terms the violence and ravings of these maniacs; and in the days of chains, manacles, stone floors, and straw, doubtless their appearance was terrible. But they are not the really dangerous lunatics, and their violence is for the most part temporary and paroxysmal, though they may pass hours and even days, in singing, shouting, and perpetual motion. There is not much to say about the mental symptoms: commonly the speech is an incoherent jumble of sentences, or the constant repetition of a word or phrase, beginning in a low tone and rising in a *crescendo* till the room rings with their piercing cry. They can in many cases be hardly said to have any delusions— at least these are not to be made out in their confused jargon, but the prevailing feeling is markedly shown in their expression, tone, and gestures. This may be fear, in which they will call on some familiar name for assistance, will scream "fire!" or "murder!" and in every way indicate the terror they are in. Or they may be filled with religious dread, and refuse food, remain incessantly on their knees, and see the horrors of hell before them. This is, in my opinion, a very unfavorable symptom, and this variety is closely akin to, if not identical with, the worst form of acute melancholia. They may be furiously angry, and attack those in charge, applying opprobrious names in accordance with their ideas; or they may be gay and hilarious, laughing and shouting with glee and mischief.

I believe our prognosis may be materially affected by a careful consideration of the emotional state. On the one hand we find the panic-stricken, on the other the hilarious. When I see a patient laugh and frolic, however noisy and outrageous his or her delirium, I augur favorably concerning the termination. I believe that the gayety indicates a reserve of force which does not exist in the other; we may often observe during the disorder that the spirits of the patient will rise or fall as he loses strength or regains it from food, or a period of quiet or sleep.

What are the bodily symptoms? Entire absence of sleep for days together. One young lady, in the heat of the summer of 1868, only slept one hour in eight Sleep. days. She then slept five hours, and began to mend. The time at which sleep first comes varies much, and the time also varies during which patients can go without sleep without fatal exhaustion occurring. Women can go much longer than men, and unless debilitated by some such cause as parturition, generally battle through an attack of mania: we have not the same need for alarm as in the case of the other sex. Young women from twenty to thirty years of age are often the subjects of this disorder, and almost always get well—at any rate in the first attack. Patients will exist a long time without becoming exhausted by want of sleep if they are well kept up with food, and are kept from wearing themselves out with incessant motion and fatiguing exertion.

The tongue of a patient in this condition is generally furred and coated with a thick sticky layer of dead epithe- Tongue. lium, and in proportion to the heat, feverishness, and shouting of the patient, this will become brown and dry, and the teeth will be covered with sordes. As exhaustion, and that condition we call typhoid, come on, all this will of course become worse. In some cases, however, particularly in women, the tongue keeps wonderfully clean and moist, even if the attack be a long one, and this is a good sign. Taken in conjunction with the pulse, the state of the tongue is a valuable indication. A very quick pulse is a bad symptom. During the paroxysms of violent struggling Pulse. and incessant motion the pulse may become very rapid, and then fall again in an interval of comparative quiet to a normal rate. Such a condition of things is hopeful. If, however, the acceleration continues, and, with the temperature, is kept up at a high rate, then the case is likely to do badly. Taken generally, the pulse of patients who recover is in frequency below that which we should expect when we see their great muscular efforts and profuse perspiration. The latter is very offensive, and in females we often perceive an overpowering odor of sexual excitement.

The water is generally scanty and high-colored, and may be contrasted with that of patients who are suffering from transitory or hysterical attacks, when it is often copious and pale. The bowels rarely act without medicine, and very powerful aperients may be required: the stools are usually dark and very offensive. Both urine and fæces are passed about the room or bed-clothes, and the latter may be daubed about the patient's person or surroundings.

The appetite is very capricious, but as a rule these patients do not refuse their food. At the commencement of the attack they may labor under the delusion that it is poisoned, but as the state of excitement increases they seem to forget this, and will take a large amount, if it is given to them judiciously.

What is the treatment and what the prognosis of these cases of acute delirious mania? Our object is to nurse a patient through the violent and sleepless stage, and to support his strength, so that he shall not die of exhaustion during it. It is exhaustion that kills: we do not find by post-mortem examination any lesion of the brain or other organ sufficient to cause death. It would seem as if the disorder is one which has a natural tendency to subside after a longer or shorter time, if only he can hold out till this time arrives; and so we see that the young and the strong pull through, while those debilitated from any cause succumb. Everything, then, depends on the amount of support we can introduce by dint of feeding, and the extent to

Treatment.

which we can prevent a patient from exhausting himself by violent struggles and want of sleep. When he is quiet—when he does not take much out of himself—our anxiety is comparatively small, even if sleep is long in coming. Now, with regard to food: skilful attendants will coax a patient into taking a large quantity, and we can hardly give too much. Messes of minced meat with potato and greens diluted with beef-tea, bread and milk, rum and milk, arrowroot, and so on, may be got down. Never give mere liquids so long as you can get down solids. As the malady progresses the tongue and mouth may become so dry and foul that nothing but liquids can be swallowed; but reserving our beef-tea and brandy, let us give plenty of solid food while we can. I never knew a patient in this state vomit his food, or suffer from diarrhœa. He will require plenty of drink _{Food.} also, especially if the weather be hot; and we may give cooling mixtures, as lemonade, in any quantity. If the patient is young and vigorous he will want no stimulants—that is, brandy and wine—at any rate at the commencement of the attack. These, like opium, will only increase the excitement. We may, however, give bottled ale or stout, a glass at a time. The waste of tissue in this disorder is enormous, and patients rapidly lose flesh, and we learn hence the necessity for an increased quantity of food. It is quite possible by patience and tact to get down a liberal allowance: without actual forcing, they will permit themselves to be fed, and a female nurse will often be of great service in this respect among male patients. In the same way a female will often take food from the doctor's hands rather than from the nurse's.

Good attendants will not only feed a patient—they will also nurse him. A man or woman in this condition is to be looked upon essentially as a sick person, and not as a mere violent and noisy lunatic to be allowed to run about, or to be shut in a padded room and occasionally looked at and fed. Such a patient should not be allowed to be on his legs

the whole of his time till he falls on the floor exhausted. At
Rest. times he can be made to lie quiet enough by the side
or in the lap of an attendant, especially if the latter
fans his face or applies cold cloths to his head, for his violence is, as I have said, paroxysmal, with frequent remissions, and he can either be allowed to walk about at his
quiet times, being held on his back during a paroxysm till
this subsides, or he can be allowed during the violent stage
to go at large, being made to rest during the intermediate
period. In this we must be guided by his strength, the
degree to which he exhausts himself by his fury, and by the
staff of attendants we have at hand. A man kept in the
recumbent posture is far more likely to drop off to sleep than
one who is perpetually pacing the room.

There remain for consideration the various methods by
which we are to procure or promote sleep. For a sleep of
some hours' duration will be the turning-point of the illness,
and this we look for anxiously till it arrives. Probably,
nowadays, chloral will be the remedy first thought of, and
none is more likely to succeed. Before its discovery those
who had most experience were disposed to lay aside all drugs,
as doing, upon the whole, more harm than good, and to trust
rather to baths and such appliances to bring about sleep.
But chloral has come to our aid, and by full doses repeated,
I have hopes that we may procure sufficient sleep at
any rate to save life, even if the disease is not cut short
thereby. I have never seen a drachm dose given without
being followed by some sleep, and that is more than I can
say of any of the drugs formerly advocated for this terrible
malady. It may occur to some that we ought to try opium
or its preparations. I have said something of this already,
and have only to add that in prolonged delirious mania I
believe opium never does good, and may do great harm.
Opium not to be given. We shall see the effects of narcotic poisoning if it be
pushed, but none that are beneficial. This applies

equally to opium given by the mouth and by subcutaneous injection. The latter, as it is more certain and effectual in producing good results, is also more deadly when it acts as a narcotic poison. After the administration of a dose of morphia by the subcutaneous method, the patient will not improbably at once fall asleep, and we congratulate ourselves that our long-wished-for object is attained. But after half an hour or so the sleep suddenly terminates, and the mania and excitement are worse than before. Here you may possibly think that had the dose been larger, instead of half an hour's sleep, you would have obtained one of longer duration, and you may administer more, but with a like result. Large doses of morphia not merely fail to procure refreshing sleep: they poison the patient, and produce, if not the symptoms of actual narcotic poisoning, at any rate that typhoid condition which indicates prostration and approaching collapse. I believe there is no drug, the use of which more often becomes abuse, than that of opium in the treatment of insanity. Among the ancients the disorder was treated invariably by hellebore; by our fathers by bleeding and tartar emetic; now, till lately, by opium. Do not be led away by the fatal facility with which you can administer it by subcutaneous injection. Inject it in the case of a melancholic patient, if you like, but here, in this furious delirium, you must abstain from the administration of opium in all its forms.

We may, however, promote the access of sleep by other means. And, first, I must speak of baths, which are largely used here, and still more abroad, as sedatives in cases of excited mania. The baths recommended for this Baths. purpose are always, so far as I know, hot: even mustard is to be added, according to some, to promote the determination of blood to the surface. This is the *rationale* of the treatment: cold is to be applied to the head by cloths and ice-bags while the patient is in the bath, and so the blood is to be "derived" thence.

The French employ these baths for very long periods. M. Brierre de Boismont recommends that a patient should be kept in one for ten, fifteen, or eighteen hours; but there must be considerable risk in so doing, and I should be sorry to recommend it. Unless the bath can be given effectually, it had better not be attempted. Merely holding a man in hot water for a few minutes, kicking and plunging, is not likely to quiet his mania, or to lower his circulation down to sleeping-point. To be of any use, it should be given for half an hour at least, with cold to the head. It should not be too hot: one at 90° or 92° is more likely to be cooling than one at 98°, and is less likely to cause syncope. After such a bath a patient may go to sleep. I have never seen a cold bath given; but I should like to see the effect of placing a patient in a tepid bath, and allowing him to remain there till the water cooled. I cannot help thinking that a great general cooling of the body would thereby be produced without any shock, and that by the skin much would be absorbed to allay the fever and thirst, and replace what is lost by the profuse perspiration.

Shower-baths are wholly inadmissible here; to produce a sedative effect they would require to be given for a considerable length of time, and would be productive of very great danger.

Concerning purgatives: if we see the patient at the commencement of the outbreak, we may give a brisk purgative with the hope of arresting it. Later we cannot arrest it by any means, and we do not wish to lower his strength by strong purgation. If it is necessary to interfere at all, we may give a few grains of calomel, because they are easy to administer, or a dose of castor oil, if we can get it down. The latter is perhaps more likely to act than anything else. We must beware of giving pill after pill, or dose after dose, because those taken previously have not acted;

Purgatives.

for when the stage of reaction sets in, we may have violent action from their combined effects.

Are we to bleed in this acute delirium? A few years ago such patients were invariably and largely bled. Nowadays general bleeding in insanity is in this country entirely abolished. Local bleeding by leeches or cupping is to some extent advocated and practiced, but of it I myself, having had no experience, can say nothing. There would be considerable difficulty in accomplishing it in most cases, and, in my opinion, it is not needed, for the only patients whom we should think of bleeding are the young and strong, and these almost invariably get well without it. The cases which succumb to this disorder are those in which we should never think of abstracting blood.

I have lately seen two girls to whose nape and spine blistering fluid had been applied. They passed many days in furious mania, and the sore places became dreadful wounds, depriving them of both sleep and rest, and, being followed by a crop of boils and pustules, retarded greatly their recovery. I advise you to abstain altogether from blisters, and from everything which is likely to make a wound and to excite suppuration, which is very prone to occur. Surgery under such circumstances is most difficult and unsatisfactory, and nothing should be done which is likely to call for surgical interference or dressing.

What is the prognosis? In my own experience I have not found this a hopeless disease, though it is most formidable to treat. A well-known French authority, Prognosis. M. Marcè, says that of these patients (*delire aigue*) scarcely one in three or four recovers. I should say about one in three or four dies. I have found that young unmarried women, who frequently are the subjects of this disorder, and of hereditary insanity, generally recover; that the women who die are those weakened by childbearing or phthisis, or advanced in age; that young men seldom die in the first attack; that the men who die are those who have had repeated attacks, or are advanced in life, or weakened by such causes as phthisis, hemorrhage, or want of food. The disease, as a rule, occurs in the young, in patients between the ages of twenty and thirty. Modifications and varieties of it occurring in older persons are more akin to delirium tremens, or the transitory delirium of wasting and acute diseases. But this is not the true acute delirious *mania* of which I have just been speaking.

The terminations are almost invariably recovery or death. If the delirium continues, and no sleep comes, the patient becomes weaker and weaker, the pulse more uniformly rapid, the mind more unconscious, not recognizing at all those in the room. The tongue is brown and dry, profuse sweating bedews the forehead, emaciation rapidly advances; and when at last the sufferer becomes quiet, and lies on his bed without attempting to rise, instead of sleep we see coma and collapse supervening, and an exhaustion which rest does not remove. When coma sets in, it generally increases quickly; there are evident signs of serous effusion taking place within the cranium, and death soon follows. When the termination is in recovery, sleep is the first harbinger of it. Sleep comes, perhaps at first for two or three hours, but on awaking there is manifestly an improvement, evidence that this short sleep has had an effect. Then probably in no long time we get other sleeps, then a long one of six or seven hours, and then we may consider the crisis past; and although there may be a very maniacal condition lasting perhaps for weeks, there will not be again the same absence of sleep, the same danger to life. The time occupied in recovery varies indefinitely. A patient may be perfectly well in a month from the commencement of a very acute attack with a long period of sleepless delirium. On the other hand, he may remain for weeks or months in a condition of nervous prostration and dementia, and then slowly recover. We find here and there a patient who never recovers, but remains permanently in a state of chronic mania or chronic dementia; but such instances are, I think, rare, and even those whose families are saturated with insanity, and who have an attack of acute delirium without other apparent cause, get well in a most satisfactory manner, at any rate in the first attack. There is one variety, however, which is the most formidable of all to treat, and which does not in general recover, but terminates fatally. This is a class of patients who, with all the violence, sleeplessness, and delirium of genuine acute delirious mania, obstinately persist in refusing food, as obstinately as others afflicted with acute melancholia. They do not make the passive resistance of the melancholy; they waste in their violent condition far faster, and require much food, yet none can be got down, except by force. As the utmost we can give in this way is inadequate to their need, and as it always implies a struggle, whatever method of feeding we adopt, they generally sink rapidly and die. Among them we do not find the gay and lively; but, on the contrary, they are filled for the most part with religious and other horrors. In fact, the malady merits the name of acute melancholia rather than acute mania.

I need say but a very few words concerning the diagnosis of this disorder. Those most likely to be confounded with it are various forms of delirium. 1. I have known a gentleman sent to an asylum as suffering from acute mania who was raving drunk. He had been drinking for days, but he had no delirium tremens; he was simply mad drunk, and so soon as he had slept off the liquor he was well, and could not be detained. Here a grave mistake was made, and it should be a rule with you never to sign a certificate for a patient who is at the time under the influence of drink. 2. A man may be in a condition of delirium tremens. If it can be helped, we do not send such patients to asylums, knowing that the attack will be brief. You will observe the tremor,

Diagnosis.

the busy restless fumbling, and the terrified aspect which is
not generally seen in maniacs. Even without a history you
can hardly mistake the two, and delirium tremens occurs in
men advanced in years much more frequently than acute
mania.   The delusions and hallucinations also are very different.   Maniacs seldom see snakes or rats, which so often
torment the drunkards.   3. The delirious fever patient is a
very different being to the maniac.   There is no difficulty in
keeping him in bed, though he be noisy and incoherent.   His
aspect is quite different, and of course his malady was not at
its commencement mental.   4. Still less need I mention patients suffering from acute disease of the brain, meningitis,
&c.   We have other symptoms to guide us,—rigors, squint-
ing, vomiting, coma, convulsions, a totally different pulse,
and complaints of excessive pain, which last is rarely complained of in mania.

LECTURE XII.

THE next form of insanity of which I have to speak to you
is very different. It is called by many acute mania,
as is also the last described. You may, if you like, Acute mania.
call it "acute mania without delirium," as the other is
"acute mania with delirium;" but it is a very different disorder. Whereas the former is a disease running a rapid
course to recovery or death in a week or two, this may last
for months without much danger to life. The patients are
little less violent or noisy, but they know what they are
about—their violence has in it far more of design; and sleep
is not absent as in acute delirium. This mania may come
on like the latter, almost suddenly, or with premonitory
symptoms of some duration. In two cases lately treated,
the disorder was stated to have lasted in one for three days,
in the other for a month. These persons are mischievous in
an extreme degree, wet and dirty, not from uncon-
sciousness, but to give trouble, abusive, filthy in Symptoms.
language and habits—presenting, in short, all the worst
features of the insane. Having their wits about them, they
know very well how they can annoy, and are extremely
ingenious in provoking the attendants, and complaining of
them afterwards. They may be, and often are, full of delusions, or their insanity may consist chiefly of outrageous

conduct and language. They are perfectly unmanageable out of an asylum: acute delirium can be treated in a suitable room in any house, and the sufferer may recover, as so many do who are said to have had "brain fever;" but I do not think that many of these noisy maniacs could be treated with a view to recovery in a private house. To keep them there at all would probably entail very rough handling.

What is the mental, and what the bodily state of these people? They may talk quite coherently for some time, or for a few minutes only, rambling off in incoherent nonsense, or may commence singing or shouting, or will abuse us violently, with full consciousness of who we are. Their mental state varies from a power of keeping up a conversation and concealing the insanity, so as almost to baffle us in signing a certificate, to a degree of wild incoherence which might be taken for delirium; and their acts and deeds vary also, but at the height of the disorder they almost all destroy clothes, furniture, sheets, and windows. They are abusive and inclined to fight, and rack their vocabulary for opprobrious and obscene terms. Often they are given to self-abuse, which they will practice with open and shameless audacity; at other times they expose their person to cause annoyance and disgust.

The bodily health is generally tolerably good, and suffers less than we might expect from the severity of the disorder. They seldom die of it unless their health is much broken at the commencement. It comes on, however, occasionally in persons whose strength has been much impaired, and then if they do not recover shortly, they may gradually wear themselves out and sink. This was the case with an officer who had suffered severely from wounds and exposure in India. He never recovered, but sank after being many months in confinement. He was in an extreme state of emaciation when it began.

Such patients are not all young, like the majority of those

who suffer from acute delirium. Many are men of forty
years and upwards, yet, as I say, few die. They generally
eat heartily, nay, voraciously, if allowed, and although in
time they get thinner, do not waste rapidly. Sleep is deficient. They pass a good night, sleeping six or seven hours,
and then go for days with perhaps only one or two hours'
sleep, making night hideous with shouting, laughing, and
singing, and disturbing all within hearing. They seem to
acquire an ability for doing without sleep, which may last
for a couple of months. The tongue is not particularly foul
or coated, and may after a short time become quite clean,
while the bowels will act without much trouble. In short,
the bodily health is not a matter of grave anxiety : our chief
object is to calm their unquiet mind. Now, although medicinal means are not to be neglected, much may be
effected by moral treatment, moral control, and dis- Treatment.
cipline. Not by stripes and chains, as was recommended
by Cullen and others, but by a system of moral rewards and
punishments, their violence is to be checked, and a wish for
a return to civilized life to be roused. Here no rule can be
laid down which is applicable to every case, or even to a
majority; but your own common sense will probably suggest
to you how a patient is to be encouraged, how repressed.
There are many things which he will delight in, and look
for, as tobacco, snuff, or·wine; various indulgences, as walks
or games. These may be granted for good behavior, and
withheld for bad. These noisy maniacs are very like children in many respects; their turbulent behavior, and mischief committed often for mere bravado, their dirtiness and
untidiness, and the utter senselessness and folly of their proceedings, remind one constantly of wilful and naughty children, and they are often capable of being influenced by
analogous processes. We must devise something which shall
help them to restrain themselves—something which they will
attain to if they behave properly—something which they

will lose if they continue in violence and mischief. I once had under my care a most outrageous patient, the terror of attendants and the pest of the asylum, who committed great damage and destruction to property. He went on in this way for four months. I then placed two men with him constantly, so as to give him no opportunity for mischief, and entirely stopped his tobacco, of which he was greatly enamoured. This had a marvellous effect, and in a month's time he was discharged, and continued well for some years. Some patients who tear their clothes to pieces will abstain if they have a new suit given to them, or a suit of a different kind or color; others will require the constant surveillance of attendants till the habit is broken through. For, like pulling out the hair, or picking the face or fingers, tearing-up is often a habit and employment for the hands, which must be kept from it, and, if possible, employed in something else. Nothing is of so much service in these cases as prolonged exercise in the open air. Let the patient be in the open air as much as possible, and let him be well walked between two attendants; his exuberance of spirits will be checked, and he will sleep all the better. As the last mentioned patients were to be considered sick, and kept in one room and nursed, so these are to be looked upon as in fair bodily health, are not to be kept in bed or in one room, but, on the contrary, are to have as much exercise as we can give them, unless it be contraindicated by some diseased condition.

Are medicines of use here? In many cases we shall find Medicines. them of great use, but may probably have to make trial of more than one before we cure our patient. Chloral will procure sleep with certainty if the dose be large enough. Some have said that this sleep is useless; that, procured by this means, it does not shorten the attack. Experience of the drug is as yet limited; but I cannot but think that six or seven hours' sleep even of this kind, repeated

night after night, must be in the end beneficial, and must
tend to shorten, not to prolong, the disorder. I lately saw
a patient suffering from acute mania with consciousness, who
had had a similar attack several years previously, in which
he had passed some six days and nights without sleep. He
now slept every night for three or four hours, after fifty
grains of chloral. By day he was noisy, violent, and dirty,
exhibiting the disease by well-marked and characteristic
symptoms. Yet the acute stage, on the latter occasion, lasted
no longer than on the former. Sometimes in the less sthenic
cases opium is of service, and procures sleep at night; we
cannot always say beforehand whether its effect will be beneficial, but here we can try it: it is not a matter on which
hangs life or death. If it is of no use, we may give digitalis,
bromide of potassium, extract of henbane, cannabis Indica,
or a combination of them, e. g., the bromide and cannabis.
We may administer the morphia by subcutaneous injection,
if there is a difficulty in getting medicines swallowed. Comparing this mode of administration with the ordinary plan,
I have found but little difference in the effect produced by
the drug; but a less quantity of the salt is required if it be
subcutaneously injected. Two other drugs I may mention: one,
which was formerly used almost universally in the treatment
of insanity, is the potassio-tartrate of antimony—*antimonium
tartaratum*, as it is now called; the other is hydrocyanic acid.
The former has been largely given for years in many asylums, and frequently acts beneficially, quieting the patients
I have described, and also chronic maniacs. Here it pro-
duces no nausea in small doses ($\frac{1}{3}$ or $\frac{1}{2}$ gr.), neither does it
cause any aversion to food. One young lady to whom I gave
it took food better than before. It might be given subcutaneously, but of this plan I have no experience. Its small
bulk, solubility, and the absence of taste and color, enable it
to be mixed with facility in any kind of drink.

The other, hydrocyanic acid, is, like digitalis, an old

remedy revived. Dr. Burrows, in his "Commentaries," tells us that Dr. Balmanno, of the Glasgow Asylum, used to give from 15 to 30 drops of a diluted solution of it, preparatory to giving narcotics, but that he himself had found no good results. In papers in the "Medical Times and Gazette," March, 1863, Dr. Kenneth McLeod, of the Durham Lunatic Asylum, strongly recommends its use as a calmant in cases of acute mania and melancholia, in doses of from ℥ij to ℥vj, to be given by the mouth or subcutaneously, and repeated every quarter of an hour till an effect is produced. I think this quite worth a trial in these cases; but if the dose, say of ℥v, which Dr. McLeod recommends, is to be repeated every quarter of an hour, it must be done under your own supervision.

What is the prognosis of the disorder? As in most forms of acute insanity, it is favorable, if there be no complications of other disease. Our opinion as to recovery will be founded on the consideration of the following facts: 1. How long has the attack lasted? This, of course, is a matter of some importance, for if the disorder is becoming chronic, our hopes will be less; but these patients often continue their violent conduct for a long time, and yet at last recover. I have known one recover after having been in an asylum nearly two years, and it was his fourth attack. 2. The character of the mania. If great noise and turbulent excitement are the predominant features, with no very marked delusions, or with delusions ever changing, and not fixed and immovable, we may have hope. If the delusions do not vary, if they have reference to the unseen and supernatural, above all, if the patient hears voices, the cure is very doubtful. 3. The age of the patients. Many of these are not very youthful, as I have said; the younger they are, however, the more chance they have of recovering; and, as a rule, I believe men recover more frequently from this form of insanity than women. 4. If the patient at the commence-

Prognosis.

ment of the disorder is greatly debilitated, or if there is other disease, the violence and want of sleep still further reduce his strength, and interfere with the chance of recovery, and if there be much difficulty in getting him to take food, his prospects are still more gloomy. And this brings me to another portion of my subject, viz., the terminations of the disorder. First, the patient may recover, and that after a very considerable time. And it is not to be Terminations. forgotten, that if medicines and the moral control of one asylum and one set of attendants have failed, great good may be effected by removal to another, to entirely new hands and surroundings. It is often the only thing left for us to try; but no less often is it a remedy of marvellous effect. I shall have to recur to this again; but I mention it here, as in these cases the good that is done is frequently very apparent. Secondly, the patient may sink and die, gradually worn out by the disorder, or by intercurrent disease. Thirdly, he may lapse into a chronic condition of mania or dementia; or, what is more favorable, he may quiet down into melancholia. From this he may recover, or after a period of depression may again become excited and maniacal, his disorder becoming the *folie circulaire* of the French.

There are, however, many patients whose insanity cannot be called melancholy of any kind, neither is it acute delirium or acute mania. It is something short of the latter, and, in ordinary parlance, it is called *mania*. Depression is not a marked feature, except, perhaps, at the outset. There is at times angry excitement, complaints of being detained, of delusions not being listened to, and requests not being complied with. Such patients are capricious in temper, sometimes friendly, sometimes hostile, dangerous according to their delusions, seldom suicidal, prompt to escape, threatening vengeance and an appeal to a jury. They require tact and patience, are not to be subjugated by intellects inferior to their own, and are as a class to be cured by moral rather than medicinal measures.

We feel no anxiety about the life of these maniacs. When the disorder is recent, and the acute symptoms at their height, sleep may be defective, their eating may be irregular, and they may threaten to refuse food. But they seldom do; hunger asserts its claim, and they satisfy it. And a dose of chloral, repeated for a few nights, generally produces sound sleep. We may notice other bodily ailments requiring medical attention, or a general debility, to be met by tonics and generous diet; but many have little the matter with the bodily health, and seclusion from home and the world, change of occupation and amusement, and regularity of life, work a cure with but little assistance from the Pharmacopœia. Frequently they refuse to take medicines, and none being specially necessary, none are forced upon them. If you search the case-books of any large asylum, you will see that a not inconsiderable proportion of the patients recovered are of this class. Probably they would be termed by certain writers cases of idiopathic mania, in persons who upon some moral or mental disquiet, or even without assignable cause, suddenly or gradually show signs of non-acute insanity, and when properly cared for, get well again without any very special treatment beyond seclusion and restraint. The majority of these inherit the disorder. They, too, are the people so often allowed to run loose, without care or treatment, till chance of cure is gone. The symptoms are not urgent, the patient is rational and well-conducted in many ways: it seems a shame to call him a madman, and deprive him of liberty, and so months and years are allowed to elapse, till the friends become tired of his vagaries or expenditure, and he is then brought to an asylum, where it is expected that he will immediately be cured, because they have always heard that it was the proper place for him. Possibly at the commencement the cure might have been effected; but it is certain that chronic mania, or monomania, as it is often called, cannot be cured when it is of two or three years' standing.

I am supposing that all these patients labor under delusions or hallucinations. When we speak of chronic mania this is implied. And the recent and curable mania which I am describing is equally characterized by these fancies. In a subsequent lecture I shall bring before your notice people whose insanity is not marked by delusions, but by insane acts and conduct. Now, however, you will bear in mind that in these patients delusions are a marked feature, and the prognosis will be determined in some degree by the characters and continuance of them. Of this subject I have already spoken, and have endeavored to point out how the prognosis is influenced by delusions or hallucinations of one kind or another.

If we try to connect the symptoms with the pathological conditions mentioned in my third and fourth lectures, how are the treatment and chance of cure affected thereby? There is an insanity of pubescence, of pregnancy, after childbirth, at the climacteric, an insanity connected with masturbation or sexual irritability, a sympathetic or reflex insanity, an insanity depending on alcohol. How does the diagnosis of one or other of these affect our prognosis or treatment? *Treatment of various insane patients.*

The insanity of pubescence is marked by violence, excitement, maniacal conduct, rarely by depression or melancholic features. Delusions there may be, and *Insanity of puberty.* hallucinations, but not of a formidable or persistent nature. The majority of cases would be called by some "sthenic" rather than "asthenic." Sleep, though defective, is not altogether absent, and may be brought about by exercise in the open air, and by chloral, or bromide of potassium, rather than by opium. Stimulants are not needed, and produce excitement and a prolongation of the symptoms. In girls, we shall find that the catamenial function is generally disordered, the menses scanty or profuse. In the latter case, local treatment is preferable to anything given by the mouth, and pessaries, containing tannin or matico, may be applied *per vaginam.* In the former, iron and aloetic preparations are often of service. The majority of these patients get well, at any rate in the first attack; but as they almost all inherit the malady—which inheritance is, in truth, the cause of it—its recurrence is to be looked for at some period or other of their lives.

After this, I may fitly speak of the insanity of masturba-
Insanity of tion, reminding you that patients whose insanity
masturbators. is caused by masturbation are generally by inheritance prone to mental disturbance. That masturbation by itself is not a frequent cause of insanity, is a fact of which all must be aware: were it so, in all our schools insanity would be an every-day occurrence. In some persons, already predisposed, it may light up the disorder, and may coexist with it in others without being the cause. The latter may, and do, get well, and when well may relinquish the habit. But the habitual masturbator, whose insanity has been gradually developing perhaps for years, is incurable. Thin and sickly-looking, he seems ever on the verge of consumption, and, though he may eat voraciously, his appearance is always a discredit to those who have to care for him. You have doubtless heard of various methods of preventing or curing this habit—of clitoridectomy, which is certainly inefficacious, the clitoris not being the only sensitive portion of the genital organs—of the application of ice to a female—of blistering the prepuce of a male—of the administration of antaphrodisiacs, of which bromide of potassium is supposed to be the most efficacious—and of various mechanical cages and contrivances for preventing the contact of the patient's fingers. After considerable experience, I am sure that it is next to impossible to prevent it in a very determined person. Slight

confinement of the hands of a quiet or demented patient in what is called a pinafore or muffler, may suffice; but many women will boast that they can effect their object by the friction of their thighs, or the application of the heel. And a man whose hands are confined may do the same by friction against the bedding. Blistering the prepuce can rarely be maintained for a sufficient time; and when the sore is healed, the man returns to his practice. I have certainly found bromide of potassium produce some effect; and one woman confessed that it took away the power of accomplishment. But bromide perseveringly given for weeks and months will make many patients wretchedly thin and weak, and it is by this effect that it appears to act. We are obliged to discontinue it, and with the strength the habit returns. Nothing but close personal watching will really stop it. A patient's clothes may be so constructed that he cannot by day carry it on in the presence of others; and at night, some slight confinement of the hands, and rigorous surveillance, may greatly check it. It will also be necessary to see that it is not practiced at the closet, whither such patients frequently resort on pretence of a legitimate desire. In many instances, while a prospect of cure exists, it is worth while to exercise every precaution, and to try if a total suspension may not only eradicate the habit, but also restore the mind. An examination of the linen will afford us information of the continuance or discontinuance of it in males: in females it is often difficult to arrive at a just conclusion, for questions upon the subject are better avoided. We gain little information, for by all but the most hopeless it is sure to be denied. We are not to suppose that every patient suffering from acute insanity who may be detected in this is therefore incurable. I have known many recover, even after a considerable period, who were guilty of such acts. But of their insanity masturbation was not the cause, but only the concomitant, and when reason returned, this, like any other insane and dirty habit, was abandoned. Yet I have heard a most unfavorable prognosis pronounced, which was founded solely on the fact that such acts were perpetrated. In acute delirium occurring in young women, we may find it in the large majority of cases: it existed to an extreme degree in two lately under my care, yet both recovered rapidly and perfectly.

Turning to another form, viz., climacteric insanity, we see Climacteric insanity. a number of patients whose malady and condition is truly asthenic, whose disorder is evidenced for the most part by deep depression, who are suffering, in short, from melancholia. The treatment I have sufficiently indicated in my ninth and tenth lectures.

Puerperal mania is a disorder often described in works Puerperal insanity. upon midwifery, as well as in those upon mental disorders; but the term very inadequately describes the condition of the women who from this cause become insane; for they may show signs of aberration before childbirth, and both before and after it the symptoms may be those not of mania but of melancholia. Dr. T. Batty Tuke, in an examination of 155 cases admitted into the Royal Edinburgh Asylum, tells us that 28 were of the insanity of pregnancy, and that the symptoms in these are, as a rule, of the melancholic type, the suicidal tendency being very marked. "The prognosis in this form of disease is generally favorable; nineteen cases recovered within six months; and of itself it is not fatal." My own experience confirms this. Such women are suicidal, refuse their food, and require to be treated in all respects like other melancholic patients. With care and good feeding they usually recover. The question will arise, ought labor to be induced prematurely? Looking at the favorable results of cases which have gone their full time, I should say that, except for very special reasons, such a proceeding is not necessary.

Dr. Batty Tuke examined the records of 73 cases of puerperal insanity, in all save two of which, symptoms appeared within one month of confinement.   Where they commenced in the first sixteen days the form of insanity was acute mania; later it was melancholia.

Bearing out my own observations as to the general treatment of the two types, Dr. Tuke tells us that in the melancholic women the administration of large doses of morphia was attended with the very best results, while he feels certain that where mania has established itself, sedatives in large doses will not be found successful in the majority of cases. In the very commencement of puerperal insanity, I know that the greatest good has followed the administration of chloral, and that an impending attack has been cut short; but at this critical period I should apprehend as much evil as good from a dose of morphia.   As the period after childbirth is lengthened, the maniacal symptoms decrease, and those of melancholia become more prominent.   Of 54 cases called by Dr. Tuke "insanity of lactation," 10 were examples of acute mania, 39 of melancholia, and 5 of dementia.   "The acute mania, as a rule, in this form of insanity, is severe, but evanescent; it rarely lasts more than ten days or a fortnight, and is generally attended with hallucinations of the different senses, and delusions, as in puerperal mania, of mistaken identity.   In almost all cases of insanity of lactation which have come under my notice during the last two years, exophthalmia and bruit de diable have been marked symptoms."

I think these cases plainly indicate, what I have so strongly insisted on, that the mental symptoms depend on the general pathological strength and condition of the patient at the moment of the outbreak, and not upon the nature of the exciting cause.

Of the remaining pathological varieties of insanity, some are incurable, and require little notice here.   That which follows a blow on the head, and gradually and in-   Insanity after sidiously makes its appearance, is a form from   a blow. which recovery rarely takes place.   Treatment can do little, for as a rule such patients are not subjected to treatment till the disorder is chronic. Many persons, however, who have received blows on the head, though not chronic lunatics, suffer from attacks of temporary insanity, if subjected to any exciting controversy or irritation, or if they partake even of a moderate amount of strong drink. Precautionary measures and advice may be of benefit, and may ward off more serious evil. We frequently meet with patients of this class who are in an incipient state of insanity—in what is termed moral insanity—and are very difficult to deal with legally till they arrive at a stage when hopes of cure are small. With this form another—viz., insanity following sunstroke—has been coupled by Dr. F. Skae.* It is, however, a mere conjecture to suppose that the pathological state produced by a blow is identical with that produced by *coup de soleil*. In this country Insanity after we find but few examples of the latter. In my ex-coup de soleil. perience the insanity does not come on gradually as in patients who have had a blow, but quickly develops, runs the course of acute mania with acute hyperæmia of the brain, and terminates in death or recovery in a comparatively short time. I have seen many persons who went through such attacks in India, were invalided home, and arrived in England quite well. Some had subsequent attacks, the mania recurring as it might have done in any one who had suffered from an attack of acute insanity. The prognosis here is very much more favorable than in cases where the disorder follows a blow. It is worth while, however, to note that writers, and amongst them Drs. Bucknill and Robertson, have recorded the fact that a blow on the head has produced sanity in a patient previously of unsound mind.

You will find in the majority of the cases of syphilitic Syphilitic insanity that changes and degeneration have com-insanity. menced in the bones, membranes, or brain, render-

---

* Edinburgh Medical Journal, Feb., 1866.

ing the prognosis extremely unfavorable. Yet patients do recover. I lately saw a woman who had been under the care of a surgeon for syphilitic head symptoms, among others, ptosis of the left eyelid. She became violently maniacal, and was sent to an asylum, where she perfectly recovered in about four or five months. In these cases iodide of potassium is often of as great service as in other forms of syphilitic affection.

If you have reason to suspect that an attack of insanity is connected with rheumatism or gout, and the patient Insanity with has already suffered from either of these maladies, rheumatism. you may direct your treatment with reference to them. There is not, I fear, any method by which we can compel the disorder to leave the brain and invade other organs, but it may be worth while, by counter-irritation, or by poultices and fomentations applied to parts formerly affected, to invite it to the feet, ankles, or knees. And such medicines as potash, iodide of potassium, or even colchicum, may be administered. It is to be noted that the cerebral symptoms may precede the articular inflammation. There may be violent mental disturbance lasting some time, and subsiding quite suddenly, to be followed by swelling and pain in the limbs, varying from a slight affection of the great toe, up to genuine acute articular rheumatism. The transition may take place more than once, the rheumatic symptoms vanishing more or less completely as the cerebral return. The prognosis is, generally speaking, favorable; recovery takes place after a time, but the patient is liable to a recurrence of the attack. Besides the gout there may be other predisposing causes of insanity: one gentleman, whose mania generally terminated in gout, had had one or two epileptic fits. He died, however, of general decay, not insane nor epileptic.

Though insanity is found in connection with acute rheumatism, it is a variety differing from the delirium which I spoke of as making its appearance towards the decline of acute disorders, as fevers, pneumonia, measles, and the like. This insanity, as it appears suddenly without premonitory warning, disappears for the most part as suddenly, one long sleep terminating the attack. Though its unlooked-for advent may cause the utmost consternation amongst the patient's friends, our prognosis need not be unfavorable, for most cases do well, and only require to be carefully watched and guarded during the transient aberration; opium has been found to agree with them, as it does with the asthenic generally, and I have no doubt that chloral also will bring sleep. Indeed, recovery takes place without any special treatment, if only plentiful nourishment is administered, for there can be no question that this condition is brought about by the debilitated state of the patient, and by the tendency to disturbance of the brain circulation, which probably all such persons possess by idiosyncrasy and inheritance. Instead of an acute delirium we sometimes find a melancholy or demented condition coming on as the sequel of one of the acute disorders, more formidable as regards the prognosis, though to the bystanders the symptoms may be less alarming. In the treatment of these forms of insanity, you will proceed on the plan laid down in the lectures on melancholy and acute dementia, remembering the need of food and warmth in both of these varieties, remembering that melancholy is curable, even after a very long period, and that from the most lost and apparently hopeless dementia patients will emerge and recover, if they receive the constant care, watching, and feeding, they so urgently require.

Insanity in acute diseases.

Very violent is the mania which follows an epileptic attack, or series of attacks, in certain cases, yet we may reasonably expect it to subside in a comparatively short time, and measures for the treatment of the patient must be arranged in view of such a result. It sel-

Epileptic insanity.

dom happens that mania follows the first epileptic seizure. According to the frequency of them we may infer that the individual will be a long or a short time free from mental disorder. If the attacks are infrequent, and it is possible to guard him at home during the maniacal period, we may do so, as in a few days he may be in a condition of sanity; but if the epileptic seizures are, or are becoming, frequent, and the maniacal state continues more or less throughout the intermediate time—if in his mania he is violent and dangerous, and his means and surroundings do not admit of safe treatment at home—it will be proper to remove him to an asylum. These persons are often very dangerous, sudden, and furious in their acts, and haunted by voices and other hallucinations. We must try and bring about sleep by chloral or bromide of potassium, and with each sleep the symptoms will be mitigated: occasionally, when we find mere delirium instead of mania with delusions and hallucinations, the whole may subside after one long sleep.

Of mania in conjunction with phthisis little need be said specially. Where the symptoms rise to the height of acute delirious mania, the tubercular complication Phthisical insanity. renders our prognosis unfavorable, and the sufferer will probably sink. Where we find ordinary mania with excitement, and little sleep, but with no very exhausting violence or deep depression, we may entertain great hopes of a recovery, at any rate from the mental disturbance: there may be very little cough, or complaint of chest affection, and our attention may be altogether drawn aside from the latter, if we have no previous history of hæmoptysis or other lung symptoms. Patients may gain flesh while in the insane state. When the latter has passed away, the lung disorder may again become prominent; and some have thought that there is a kind of vicarious action between the two sets of symptoms.

In addition to mania, certain authors describe a form of

insanity which they call monomania, but are not agreed as
to the symptoms which the term denotes. Griesinger, following Esquirol, who first introduced the
word, would confine it to those patients whose mental disorder is displayed in expansive delusions, in over-estimation
of self. Dr. Bucknill says that it is seldom primary, and is,
in the majority of cases, a transformation of melancholia,
i. e., the self-feeling is one of depression, not of exaltation.
Nothing, however, is to be gained by dividing patients into
those affected by mania, in contradistinction to others whose
disorder is monomania. Probably that which is most commonly called monomania is chronic insanity, when the
patient is removed from deep depression on the one hand,
and gay or angry excitement on the other, and when the
bodily health has assumed its ordinary level, and all pathological marks have by time been effaced. The distinction
between mania and monomania is, for the most part, verbal.
Formerly all insanity was called "melancholy;" nowadays
it is often spoken of as mania, and if chronic as monomania.
There is nothing pathological in such a nomenclature, and it
only serves to draw us away from the due consideration of
the pathology of the disease we have to consider and treat.
We may retain such terms as acute delirious mania, acute
melancholia, acute dementia, general paralysis, because they
connote a certain set of pathological symptoms occurring in
individuals of various ages, requiring special treatment, and
capable of receiving a similar prognosis. We may, if we
like, retain, besides, the general terms mania and melancholia; but beyond this we need not go: any further distinc-
tions should be made, not according to mental peculiarities,
but according to the pathological causes or conditions of the
case.

Monomania.

LECTURE XIII.

I HAVE now to lay before you the description of a terrible form of insanity, which is probably the most fatal disease that attacks man, destroying in a short period not only mind, but life itself—so fatal, that a well-authenticated case of recovery is, I believe, unknown—so common, that among 194 patients admitted during the year 1869 into the Devon Asylum, 43 were affected by it. More, I think, has been written concerning this than about all other kinds of insanity; yet about the pathology and nature of the disease, there are still great doubt and controversy. It is best known by the name of General Paralysis of the Insane.

To the French physicians unquestionably belongs the credit of having first recognized and described it as a spe- Discovery of cial form of insanity. The credit, however, must the disease. be divided amongst several. Esquirol recognized the incurability of insanity complicated with paralysis, but he looked upon the latter as a complication, and did not consider the whole a distinct malady. In 1822, Bayle, for the first time, noted that the mental disturbance and paralysis were synchronous, and attributed them to chronic inflammation of the arachnoid. In a complete description of the disease, which he divided into three periods, he calls it *arachnitis chronique*. M. Delaye, in 1824, thought that it was not always accompanied by insanity, and was a softening or atrophy of the brain, with adhesions of the membranes. In 1826, M. Calmeil gave a most complete account of it, and to him frequently is ascribed the merit of having been the discoverer. For many years he has paid great attention to the disease, and in his "Treatise on the Inflammatory Diseases of the Brain," published in 1859, he has given us his latest views of its nature, founded on a valuable series of cases. From that date, 1826, the disorder has been mentioned, at any rate, by all who have written on insanity, and many have devoted much labor to the investigation of the pathology thereof. Among the French, Bayle, Delaye, Calmeil, Georget, Parchappe, Baillarger, J. Falret, Moreau of Tours, Brierre de Boismont; among the Germans, Duchek, Hoffmann, Joffe, L. Meyer, Erlenmeyer, Rokitansky, Wedl, Meschede, Westphal; in England, Austin, Sankey, Lockhart Clarke, Wilks, Bucknill, and others, have contributed the result of their observations of the disease.

There have been many names proposed for it. Some of the best are démence paralytique, folie paralytique, paralysie générale incomplete, paralysie générale progressive; Geisteskrankheit mit Paralyse, allgemeine progressive Gehirnlähmung, paralytischer Blödsinn. In this country it has usually been called general paralysis, or general paralysis of the insane, or paralytic insanity. Lately, some have proposed to call it paresis, instead of paralysis. As by so doing we only substitute for the old name one equally vague and unscientific, it seems scarcely worth while to make the change. Various names have been given, based on the supposed pathology, some calling it a chronic meningitis, others an inflammation of the cortical structure—"périencéphalite chronique diffuse" of Calmeil. It is thoroughly recognized by all alienists under the term general paralysis, and under that I shall speak of it here.

This fatal malady destroys hundreds every year in our

asylums, chiefly men in the prime of life. Its symptoms and progress, and the mode in which you are to recognize it, I shall now endeavor to describe. General paralysis has been said to present three or four stages. Like every- Three stages. thing else, it has a beginning and an end, and there is, of course, an intermediate period of varying duration; but frequently a patient advances with gradual but certain progress from the beginning to the end, without our being able to fix the dates of any stages in the disorder. It may be convenient, however, to describe it at different periods, and for this purpose we may consider three:

1st. The commencement, or period of incubation.

2d. The acute maniacal period.

3d. The period of chronic mania lapsing into dementia, with utter prostration both of mind and body.

In the beginning, those who are familiar with the patient will notice in him an *alteration*. Like other luna- First stage, tics, he will arrest attention by his altered manner Alteration. and habits, before it is plain that he has become insane. I have already described to you the alteration that frequently takes place in a man who is drifting into melancholia or mania. We shall see a change preceding general paralysis similar in some respects, but having its own peculiarities. These are not very easy to describe or detect, and are not present in every case; where we see them, they are valuable aids to diagnosis.

Paralytics, like others, show an *alteration* by extravagant acts, often by an extravagant expenditure of money, by making presents to those they know and those they don't know. Now, in all they do there is a silliness betokening a greater want and defect of mind than is evinced by melancholic or maniacal patients. The same act will be done in two different ways. Maniacal and melancholic patients often show considerable vigor and power of intellect, albeit insane. They will reason and argue sharply, and defend their delusions with much acumen. A general paralytic asserts his delusions, or commits his outrageous acts, but he does not argue keenly in defence of them. He does things which even a patient afflicted with what is termed moral insanity would not do; exposes his person, often apparently half unconscious of what he is about; commits assaults in a foolish manner upon women, without regard to opportunity, place, or consequences. He is extremely restless, regardless of appointments, or the time of meals, bedtime, and the like; he comes and goes, scarcely noticing those about him, gives conflicting and absurd orders to his servants, and rages with passion if they are not executed on the instant. There is a want of plan and method in his madness, which may be contrasted with that of other patients, who in the early stage are far more suspicious and careful, if they are in the state analogous to this. One, and a most important symptom, is early to be observed, that is, forgetfulness. There is a want of memory. A man forgets what he has done, and what he has said, and this explains much that he does not do. He fails to keep appointments and regular hours. For the same reason he cannot sustain an argument. His business and occupation are neglected, and he forgets, too, the consequences of indecent acts, dishonesty, or debauchery.

This loss of memory will be observable in many ways: especially is he likely to forget what he has done a day or two previously; and he will not only be forgetful, he will be careless, apathetic, and indifferent about that which formerly interested him, and when he takes up new schemes and projects, his attention soon flags, and his interest vanishes. We see, in short, in his whole manner of life a weakening of mind, such as may be noticed at the commencement of senile dementia, but which, occurring in a fine and vigorous man of, it may be, thirty-five, too surely indicates the ruin even now commencing.

In this stage patients are rarely seen by an alienist, but

the family adviser will probably be consulted concerning them. In it they may continue for a variable period, a few weeks, perhaps a month or two, never for a very lengthy time. The disease is essentially progressive, and the second stage follows rapidly upon the first in the majority of cases. The patient's mood in this early state is often dull and sulky, less frequently is he actually depressed and melancholic; but, careless of all save the idea of the moment, he wakes into violent rage when remonstrated with or thwarted. In one of these fits of passion his real state is often much more recognizable than when he is quiet and reserved. You will hear that he sleeps badly, that he eats and drinks irregularly, often voraciously, drinking to excess from inattention and forgetfulness of what he has taken. He spills his food on his dress, eating in careless haste, and is neglectful of his person and appearance, often dressing in incongruous garb.

By degrees his dull and morose condition is converted into one of excitement. Something occurs which neces- Second stage, sitates opposition or interference, and the mental Alienation. *alteration* becomes manifest insanity of a kind which requires immediate care and treatment. We now see the patient in a maniacal condition, marked by several peculiarities, to which I must call your earnest attention. Almost all, certainly nineteen out of twenty, paralytic patients are full of ideas of their greatness, importance, and riches. Mental They are self-satisfied in no ordinary degree, and symptoms. think themselves the most wonderful people that ever lived. Here and there we may find one depressed and melancholic, but his melancholia is different from ordinary melancholia, as the man with grandiose notions differs from him who suffers from ordinary mania with delusions of greatness or wealth. There is in the latter a certain probability and reasonableness, even in his wildest fancies; but the ideas of the paralytic are altogether absurd, impossible, and unintelligible, evincing his loss of mind as well as aberration. An ordinary maniac may think himself a duke, or may purchase a carriage and horses which he cannot pay for; but a paralytic will tell us that he is a duke, a marquis, a king, and an emperor all at once, that he is going to marry the Queen and all the princesses, that he has a hundred million of horses, and is going to pull down all London to-day and rebuild it to-morrow.   Ordinary maniacs do not talk in this wild and absurd fashion.   They invent wonderful machines which will make their fortunes, and discover the method of squaring the circle, and so on, but do not ramble on to such a foolish extent.   Another difference is this : patients in ordinary mania generally hold to their delusions, at any rate for a time.   The inventor holds to his machine, the grandee to his title; but the paralytic to-day has forgotten his delusions of yesterday, and in his eager desire to be great, he increases his horses and carriages from thousands to millions, and invents half a dozen fresh fancies to add to what he has already announced.   There is scarcely such a thing as a fixed delusion in this stage.   It is all happiness, grandeur, and wealth in a rapid *crescendo*, and neither argument nor ridicule arrests it in the slightest degree.   Everything around is pressed into the cause, trumpery articles of dress or ornament become robes and orders, a cottage becomes a palace, the housemaid an empress.   Even an asylum, in which the unfortunate man complains that he is confined, is a regal abode, and the other patients courtiers and nobles.   And when strength is failing, and the patient can scarcely stand or lift his hand to his head, he tells us that he can write his name on the ceiling with a 500 lb. weight hung on his little finger.

Here and there we meet with one who, instead of the gayety and excited joyousness which characterize the majority, presents many of the symptoms of melancholia.   Two gentlemen have been under my care whose paralytic insanity was of this kind.   One had many of the commonest delusions of melancholia, thought he was going to be arrested, that people were about to injure him, that they were maligning and going to rob him. Yet he was not melancholic as other men are. He never refused his food, but on the contrary, was very fond of it, and very particular as to what he ate. He had a very good opinion of himself, was very vain of his personal appearance, and, with all his melancholy ideas, was often quite cheerful and chatty. His mind was dull, lethargic, and void of excitement during the whole illness. The other patient was very feeble when first admitted, but he insisted that he could play the violin at a concert, though his left hand was so paralyzed that he could hardly hold a book.

So strong is the feeling of *bien être* in these patients, that they will declare that they never were better and never stronger, when they cannot place their food in their mouths or rise from the chair. They remain to the last, throughout the gradual degeneration of mind down to the lowest depths of fatuity, not only contented, but proud of themselves, their position, health, and strength. Even when they are long past expressing fixed ideas or delusions, we may recognize in vacant dementia their intense happiness.

Along with the notions of greatness, the *délire ambitieux*, as it has been called, which specially marks this disease, we find many of the common delusions of non-paralytic insanity, and we may hence conjecture that the seat and origin are the same in both diseases. Such delusions as these—"Believes himself given over to the devil," "thinks poison is put in his food," "believes he has committed sins too enormous to be forgiven," "thinks he is going to be arrested,"—I heard from four paralytics.

You are, then, to recollect that general paralysis is to be suspected, if we hear a lunatic boasting of his grandeur, riches, or strength, especially if his delusions on this point are altogether wild, and far beyond the bounds of possibility.

To confirm your diagnosis, you will next look for a physical
symptom, which is as nearly constant as the exalted ideas.   If you watch the man closely while
giving utterance to his boastings, and recounting, in high
excitement and exuberant spirits, his good fortune and ex-
ploits, you will notice a defect in his articulation, more or
less marked, a stopping or stutter in the enunciation of a
word or the various syllables of a word, which may recall to
your mind the speech of a man somewhat in liquor, and
from this circumstance such patients, when disorderly in
public places, are frequently thought to be drunk.   This is
not the same as stammering, nor is it the defective articulation of ordinary hemiplegia.   The patient is obliged to
make an effort to get the word out, and possibly is compelled
to shout it aloud, and then succeeds in saying it distinctly.
It may be very slight.   Dr. Conolly says, that at the very
commencement " there is in these patients not a stammer,
no letter or syllable is repeated, but a slight delay, a lingering, a quivering in the formation of the successive words or
syllables, apparently from a want of prompt nervous influence
in the lips and tongue."   Not merely in the sound of the
articulated word will you detect this; the muscular action
of the lips, particularly the upper, will aid the diagnosis.
Dr. Bucknill draws attention to a tremulous motion of the
lips like that seen in persons about to burst into passionate
weeping.   If you closely watch the lips while patients are
speaking, you will note this tremulousness in some, whereas
in others you will observe a stiffness and unnatural immobility of the lips, especially the upper.   You will notice also
a fibrillar tremor of the muscles of the tongue, which is
jerked in or out in a convulsive manner, as if the patient
had not full control over it.   These are the first indications
of paralysis, occurring most frequently at about the time of
the outbreak of decided insanity, sometimes earlier, sometimes later.   For them you will look whenever you meet

with a patient whose insanity is marked by exalted ideas and delusions that he is a very great man. You may not discover the defect of speech on every occasion. Throughout the illness you will find that it varies considerably on different days, but it is apparent in the majority of cases, and, placing our suspicions of the nature of the disorder beyond a doubt, enables us to give a certain, but most unfavorable, prognosis. We may have paralytics without exalted notions, and others in whom we can detect no fault of articulation, and concerning these we may hesitate, and look further for other symptoms; but where we find the stutter and the characteristic delusions, we can have no hesitation.

The defect of speech varies from the slight imperfection I have mentioned, which may be overlooked by all except the practiced eye and ear of one watching keenly, up to a degree which renders the patient absolutely unintelligible; but this occurs later in the progress of the disease.

The patient becomes more and more altered in habits, demeanor, and appearance. A grave parson dresses himself in a white hat and a sporting coat; a decorous father of a family walks about the house half-naked, or takes liberties with the maidservants—absents himself by night and day, buys quantities of useless or absurd articles, or writes letters to all manner of people, signing himself King, Duke, or Commander-in-Chief. Something soon occurs which leaves no doubt in the minds of the friends, and obliges them to interfere, and then the patient bursts out into furious mania when subjected to control.

Now, you are to recollect that these patients are for the most part men in their fullest strength—the finest and most muscular that we can meet with. We have not now to deal with boys or the aged, very rarely with women—never, I may say, with ladies. Such men are reckless in their violence and resistance beyond any other class of patients. As

I have told you, there is an incipient imbecility, which prevents them from reflecting on what they are about. So, in
a blind fury, they will attack all around, exerting their muscular power to the utmost, regardless of all consequences;
and they are not paralyzed in their limbs at this stage to
any extent that will interfere with their violence. Consequently they are not to be managed out of an asylum, and
even in one they cause frequently much anxiety. These
are the patients whose ribs are broken by attendants in
efforts to overpower them, and who in various ways cause so
much confusion in asylum wards.

There are by this time other symptoms which you will
Epileptiform hear of or notice. The patient may have, or have
attacks. had, a "fit." Sometimes this occurs quite early in
the disease, before the mind is much affected, and you are
disposed to think the mental symptoms are due to it. You
may look upon it as an attack of apoplexy, or epilepsy, according to what you see or hear. Such attacks happen more or
less frequently in the course of almost every case of this
malady, which they often divide into stages, the patient never
quite regaining what he lost by one of them. They are
called "congestive," or "paralytic," or "epileptiform," attacks.
They often resemble the *petit mal* of epilepsy; but sometimes
reach the intensity of the *grand mal,* or are of a negative
character, their presence being indicated not by convulsion,
but by sudden collapse and paralysis, slowly passing away
again. Few go from first to last without some of them; but
many, especially the younger patients, do not thus suffer in
the early part of the disorder. There is not the definite fit
of epilepsy; but we may see convulsions lasting for an hour
or two, or, if slight, it may pass off without the patient falling to the ground. It is important to distinguish this from
true epilepsy, as the latter is far more amenable to treatment,
even if complicated with insanity. Patients in the fits of general paralysis seldom bite the tongue, the convulsions are not

so violent, there is not the *aura*, nor the cry, and the mental symptoms will, of course, be quite different.

The attacks resembling *petit mal* will be followed by much graver mental symptoms than those of epilepsy.

You may also notice that the pupils of the eyes are irregular—not always, but very frequently; and when this symptom is present, it is important and pathognomonic. Dr. Nasse, of Siegburg,[1] tells us that of 108 cases of general paralysis examined by him, only in three was no irregularity detected. Austin found only two exceptions in 100 cases of paralysis. You are not to forget, however, that irregularity may exist in non-paralytic insanity as it may in sane persons, or in those suffering from other affections of the brain. Sometimes, instead of irregularity, we find both pupils contracted to pinpoints—a condition which may remain for a considerable period, and then be succeeded by irregularity. Some think it always precedes the latter, but this is doubtful.

It has been said that the gait of these patients is peculiar—that they walk with a slow, cautious step, short and shuffling—that they walk as if about to run, jerking the legs forward. But it is not discoverable at an early stage. I have seen many whose mental condition was unmistakable, who could run, walk, or ride on horseback perfectly well. At an early stage we may be able to detect a difference in the handwriting, and the defect of mind and memory is shown by the frequent omission of words, the repetition of the same sentence, and the incoherent jumble of the whole, which differs altogether from the coherent though insane letter of an ordinary monomaniac. The writings of these, as of others, often afford us most valuable information.

Now, when a patient in this stage is brought to an asylum, what do we see? He is very angry, very violent, and very good-humored by turns, easily pacified and turned aside from

---

[1] Allgemeine Zeitschrift für Psychiatrie, 1868.

his wrath, but dangerous if not judiciously managed. Together with his anger there is great silliness about him, and his countenance betokens vacancy of mind. He often looks stupid and blank while at rest; and when excited, we may notice twitchings and tremors of the various facial muscles, for not only the organs involved in speaking, but all the muscles of the face, tongue, and pharynx may be more or less affected by the incipient paralysis. There is seldom any marked hemiplegic symptom, but occasionally I have seen ptosis of one eyelid. If this be the case, I should expect to hear that there have been epileptiform seizures. Atrophy of the optic papilla may be noticed in some patients if we examine the eyes with the ophthalmoscope. Sometimes with an air of defiance, and sometimes with the greatest delight and self-satisfaction, he relates his accession of rank or fortune. By turns he likes or dislikes those about him, will make sudden attacks on the attendants in charge, and desperate attempts to escape. He may be in a state of what we may call acute mania—noisy, destructive, and dirty, breaking windows, tearing up bedding and clothes, and going about naked. He may sleep little, yet he will not go many days and nights without sleep, so as to cause fatal exhaustion; in fact, it is rare for a paralytic patient to die in this early stage, unless he meets with an accident. The less acutely maniacal patients often sleep well, and almost all eat well— nay, voraciously—bolting their food, swallowing often with some difficulty, for the paralysis which affects the tongue and lips may extend likewise to the pharynx. Frequently they are filthy in their habits, daubing themselves with fæces.

I consider the maniacal period to be the second stage of the disorder in which that of incubation culminates.

Terminations of second stage. After it has lasted for a variable time, from a week to a month, or even longer, it generally yields to treatment, and one of two conditions follows: either the patient gets better, so as to be able to leave the asylum and to pass for a sane man, or the stage of imbecility comes on, and he progresses downwards with more or less rapidity to extinction of mind and body.

I have not always found that patients improve in mind and body *pari passu*. Some of those who had the best right to be called "recovered" in mind, bore traces of bodily weakness or paralysis—a limp, or defect of speech, irregular pupils, or general feebleness, so that they were hardly equal to a walk of a mile. In some, however, I have seen a wonderful disappearance both of bodily and mental symptoms, the improvement lasting for some time. These are the cases which are said to be recoveries from the disease. I have seen some who certainly would not have been pronounced insane by any jury. They had either lost their delusions, or were competent to deny and conceal them. I have received letters from them detailing their travels or amusements, written without a mistake. They have spent their money without extravagance, and lived in their families as decent members of society. But those who had best recovered are long since dead, nor do I know one in whom the disease did not reappear in a longer or shorter time. Moreover—and this is the real test—I never knew one who was capable of work or business. Some lived for a time quietly and rationally in country houses, but the instant they returned to London and attempted to resume their former occupations, they broke down, and were obliged again to be placed in confinement. Yet these men, had they remained in enforced idleness, might have stayed among their friends during the decline of their failing strength. The mental defect is essentially mental weakness. They are incapable of effort or continued application, and deficient in memory, so the attempt causes exhaustion, and lights up again the acute symptoms which had been allayed. Those who knew them intimately in time past see a difference, a slowness or childishness, not apparent to a stranger.

Improvement and apparent recovery.

I mention this, because you may be asked if you consider a patient who has thus apparently recovered from general paralysis, competent to manage his affairs. He may desire to supersede the commission of lunacy which has placed his property in the care of the Court of Chancery, and he may ask you to assist him by your affidavit of recovery. His improvement, however, is but the semblance of recovery—a remission, not the removal, of the disease. It may be quite safe to release him from an asylum, and to allow him a certain voice in the direction of his household; but if his affairs are of such a nature as to have necessitated a commission, they had better remain *in statu quo*.

In many cases the cessation of the acutely maniacal symptoms is not followed by the improvement I have spoken of, but the patient passes along through a period of chronic mania into ever-increasing dementia. Though the excitement and emotional display are less, the delusions remain. He is still a king, a duke, or general; he issues his orders and writes to tradesmen and others, giving commissions to the extent of thousands; and though these are never executed, and he is kept confined within asylum walls, he never recognizes the incongruity. He is always going away "to-morrow," and to-morrow finds him writing the same kind of letters, and doing and saying the same things. The present and the future he gilds with his exalted fancy, and of the past he takes no heed, frequently caring nothing about family or friends. A man in this stage often gets very stout, and remains so for some time. His strength, mental and bodily, varies considerably. Memory is sometimes completely gone, sometimes he remembers a good deal, and the articulation and power of walking fluctuate in the same way. If he suffers from an attack of epileptiform convulsions, he loses much ground, and for some days may be quite lost and paralyzed, often on one side more than the other. This chronic condition often lasts a long time, even years. Such patients are always more feeble in cold weather; in the heat of summer they regain strength, often to a surprising degree; with the first frosts they fall back, and, it may be, sink. Whether at home or in an asylum they are generally happy and easily amused; the annoyance of to-day, if any arise, is forgotten to-morrow, or can be turned aside without difficulty by calling up before them the glories they are expecting in that brilliant future which is forever coming.

We now come to the last stage of all: hopeless dementia, utter fatuity. The patient can just walk round the garden, slowly and shuffling, an attendant holding his arm. His countenance is vacant and puffy, and he takes little notice of what is said, or of the person speaking. He begins to get thin, losing the fat which has accumulated, and if he is confined to bed for a day or two by an attack of convulsions, the skin of his back rapidly gives way, and the bed-sores resulting are difficult to heal. He can with great difficulty hold anything in his hands, which tremble like those of a person palsied by age. A symptom frequently noticed in this stage is loud grinding of the teeth. For hours together a patient will sit and grind his teeth, making a most horrible and discordant noise. The appetite is still good, and he looks forward to and enjoys his meals. The power of deglutition, however, is very feeble, and he will go on filling his mouth without swallowing, till he has it crammed full of food; and the consequence is that he either gets it impacted in the œsophagus so as to compress the larynx, or else it gets into the larynx and trachea. From one or other of these accidents choking is a very frequent mode of death in these cases, and the greatest care ought to be taken that a patient shall never eat alone, or in fact without an attendant at his elbow, for instant suffocation may be caused by a mass of food becoming impacted. The patient now requires to be nursed, like any other far advanced in paralysis. There is complete annihilation both of bodily and mental activity, and

Third stage, progressive paralysis and dementia.

yet by careful nursing even this stage may be prolonged for a very indefinite time. And this brings me to another point—the duration of the disorder—which often is of considerable importance, and on which authorities differ widely. When you pronounce an opinion that the insanity is incurable, nay, that life itself will soon be extinguished, it may be of the utmost consequence to the friends to know the time likely to elapse before the latter must take place. If you turn to one of the chief authorities, M. Calmeil, you read : " Some paralytic patients live eight months, a year, eighteen months; others linger for two or three years, rarely beyond." Dr. E. Salomon says : " The course of the disease may extend from some months to three years; in rarer cases it may reach to five years, but scarcely ever exceeds that time." Griesinger says : " The duration of general paralysis varies from several months to about three years." In my own experience I should say that the average duration was considerably longer. The reason of this is, that my patients have been all of a class able to command the best food and nursing. Griesinger says : "When nursed in their families these patients live longer than in asylums, as they require the same attention in the latter stages as a young child." Life may be prolonged for an indefinite time by dint of unstinted diet and thorough nursing. In the year 1858, a commission of lunacy was held on a baronet of large fortune, who was at that time unquestionably suffering from general paralysis, and who had shown symptoms of brain affection and epileptiform attacks so far back as 1856, he having been married in 1855. This gentleman is still alive. It is, however, the most protracted case I have ever heard of. I should say, that with careful nursing, and with every appliance and means for taking care of a patient, we might put down the duration of life as from three to five years; but in crowded asylums, and with the diet which poorer classes receive, a much shorter period must be assigned.

Who are the subjects of this malady?   We shall find that it is unlike other forms of insanity, for it especially Sex and age of patients. attacks men.   Comparatively few women die of it, and these are almost all of the lower classes : it is the rarest thing to find a lady the subject of general paralysis.   The ratio of liability, according to Dr. Sankey, runs thus: 1. Males of the lower classes; 2. Males of the upper classes; 3. Females of the lower classes ; 4. Females of the upper classes.   Whether the males of the upper or lower classes are more liable, is a moot point not easy to be solved.   The proportion of paralytic patients admitted into a first-class private asylum in twelve years was twenty per cent. of all the males.   M. Calmeil says the males are to the females as 50 to 15.   There are also peculiarities with regard to the age of the persons attacked.   General paralysis does not make its appearance in the very young or the very old, but chiefly attacks those in middle life.   At the age of 20 we should not look for general paralysis; at 25 it is rare, at 60 it is rare, at 70 it is unknown; chiefly at 35 or 40 it commences, and the patients are not only in their greatest vigor, but often fine, handsome, powerful men—men who have enjoyed life and have lived hard.   We do not find it amongst weak, nervous valetudinarians, the subjects of hypochondria and melancholia.   The paralytic patient has rarely had to seek aid from doctors, and in the exuberant feeling of health and gayety he derides the notion of there being anything the matter with him, and refuses to have anything to do with medicine.

Those who consider general paralysis a special form of disease, point to the remarkable fact that it does not attack the chronic inhabitants of asylums, or supervene upon other forms of insanity.   If a young man is insane for a number of years, he does not, after a long period of mania or melancholia, develop symptoms of paralytic insanity.   And if a patient recovers, and recovers perfectly, from an attack of

mania or melancholia, he does not, if he has a second attack
of insanity, show the symptoms of general paralysis. There
may be forms of the latter of which the diagnosis is difficult,
and there may be apparent recoveries which I call remissions; but if the disease is really general paralysis, it would
seem to run a progressive course to dementia and death,
being throughout a malady resembling in many respects
ordinary insanity, yet differing altogether in its fatal character.

LECTURE XIV.

General Paralysis continued—Diagnosis—Illustrative Cases—Diseases
simulating General Paralysis—Prognosis—Treatment—Post-mortem
Appearances—Pathology.

I NOW pass to the diagnosis—a matter of the greatest consequence, seeing that the disease is fatal in such a vast
majority of cases. You will have to distinguish it on Diagnosis.
the one hand from less formidable varieties of insanity; on the
other from certain other affections which, we are told, may be
confounded with it. But these are rare, and the diagnosis is
not difficult. More difficult is it in many cases to say whether
the insanity of a patient in an asylum is general paralysis or
not. We may see some patients presenting the delusions of
general paralysis, whose malady, nevertheless, is ordinary
mania with exaltation; while others may be paralytic, who,
nevertheless, lack the best marked characteristics of the disease. I lately saw a gentleman, aged forty-six, who
had been in an asylum about a week, having been Cases illustrative of
diagnosis.
brought over from Ireland by the medical man who
accompanied me. There was no stutter in his speech, no
tremor or immobility of the lips, no irregularity of pupil, no
contraction nor dilatation. He had apparently full power and
perfect co-ordination of both hands and feet. He played both
billiards and the piano in my presence, and did both well.
He walked with a long swinging stride, but whether this was
habitual to him or not I cannot say. Speaking generally, one
might say that the bodily signs of paralysis were wanting. The
mental symptoms afforded more information, though these
were not very marked. He had no very extravagant delusions, but he thought himself a wonderfully lucky individual,

as he had bought five or six horses for small sums, by which he was to realize some hundreds. He was gay and jocose, on the best of terms with his friend, though he said that it was an infernal shame to have brought him there. He showed loss of memory, for he said that he had left Ireland three weeks, whereas it was only one. Although told that another physician and myself were doctors come to examine him, he never tried to persuade us to let him go, though he said he was quite well and wanted no doctors. This gentleman was pronounced by us to be paralytic: first, on account of the peculiar "larkiness" and hilarity exhibited under the circumstances to two perfect strangers who had come to examine him; secondly, his self-satisfaction and ideas of general good luck and success; thirdly, his indifference with regard to being released; fourthly, the loss of memory;—all of which went to prove that he was suffering, not merely from aberration of intellect, but from incipient paralytic dementia. Another case remained for some time in doubt, and presented in its early stages symptoms by no means characteristic of general paralysis. In February, 1862, a gentleman was brought to an asylum, whose insanity was stated to be of only a few days' duration. He had been riding on the pavement and assaulting the police; he was incoherent and rambling; said the sun was turned into the moon, and such things, but had no grandiose delusions, and was frequently taciturn, not speaking, perhaps, for a whole day. On alternate days his condition varied; on one he was dull and repressed, refused his food, and would not speak; on the other he was gay and excited; but though his conduct was manifestly insane, delusions were not a prominent feature, and he said little, except that he "wanted to go." He was wet and dirty; there was no stutter, and the signs of general paralysis were mostly absent; there was, however, irregularity of the pupils, and when he improved somewhat, and talked more freely, it was evident that there was great defect of memory. He got so much better, however, that in July he went into the country with his wife, and was reported to be quite well. In the following February he was again admitted, and now the symptoms of general paralysis were well marked. His sons were dukes, he was worth millions, and so on. There were great doubts as to the nature of the disorder at the commencement, and only the irregularity of the pupils, the defect of memory, and general absence of mind, made the prognosis unfavorable. This gentleman complained constantly of pain in the head. When said to be recovered he remained in the country idle : the moment he resumed work the symptoms returned, and this time with unmistakable features of the disorder.

Not long ago I saw a gentleman from whose extravagant delusions one might have imagined that he was the subject of general paralysis. He boasted of his extraordinary intellect and strength. He was going into Parliament, and, as a preliminary step, was to assemble 10,000 people in his park, have them photographed, and sell the photographs at five pounds apiece, thus paying off the mortgages on his estate, and making £100,000. He thought that people might live a thousand years if they bathed in beef-tea and beer, wanted to make a tunnel through the earth to the antipodes, and various things of this kind. He was dressed in a most extraordinary costume, and was insane beyond all question. Yet there was no stutter and no loss of memory, and I heard that he had had, and had recovered from, a similar attack in India some years before. This was conclusive to my mind. Had the former attack been general paralysis, he could not have recovered. The mania which had passed away before might pass away again, and so in the sequel it proved.

Another gentleman was pronounced paralytic, and certainly there were many symptoms of this disorder. He had been spending money in a most reckless manner, but he defended all he had done. He thought himself a man of rank, and had a ducal coronet engraved for his paper and envelopes. He was gay and expansive, although he knew he was under legal restraint, quarrelled with his friends, and yet joked with them, and at times there appeared to be a slight hesitation in his speech. I doubt if any one could have pronounced unhesitatingly on one inspection that this was or was not a case of general paralysis. Against it was his age. He was upwards of sixty. He had long suffered from acute bodily disease — disease of bladder and kidneys consequent upon stricture, and in the midst of it mental symptoms showed themselves. But paralysis rarely attacks a man weakened by other disease, while it is common for ordinary mania to commence in such a subject. Time very soon made it plain that it was not paralysis. Though the bodily health got worse, the mind did not. Instead of paralytic delusions appearing and becoming more and more extravagant and absurd, all delusions disappeared, and there remained what we may term moral insanity, a weakness and degeneracy of mind shown in a desire to waste money and buy useless articles, to tell indecent stories, and generally to behave himself in a way the reverse of what he formerly had done. So matters went on till his death, no other symptoms of paralysis ever appearing. I believe the apparent stutter was due to nervous agitation, when obliged to discuss his conduct with strangers in his extreme state of bodily weakness. From the same cause he not unfrequently shed tears. Had this gentleman's bodily ailments been curable, I have no doubt that his mental aberration would have been removed. You will recollect that when a patient is over sixty the symptoms of general paralysis are to be examined with great care, and we are to doubt them unless they be of a most clear and unquestionable character. In this last case there was no irregularity of pupils, no difficulty of walking, no loss of memory; above all, the patient wrote an excellent formal business letter without leaving out a word or making mistakes of any kind. Such letters would by themselves almost decide the point.

The cases of non-paralytic insanity about which there may be doubt, are not chronic cases of mania or dementia. They are recent cases of mania, with exalted delusions, or what is termed moral insanity, with extravagance and indecent conduct. Here you will look for loss of memory, hesitation in speech, defects in letter-writing, especially words left out or repeated, irregularity of pupils, tremor of lips and other facial muscles, and possibly a slow or halting gait. You will consider the sex and age of the patient, the history, the occurrence or non-occurrence of former attacks, or of epileptiform seizures. If the patient some years ago has recovered, and thoroughly recovered, from some similar attack, and has since gone about his work like any one else, the disorder is not paralysis.

There is a malady occasionally seen in asylums which resembles in some respects general paralysis, but is easy to be distinguished. This is a paralysis produced by chronic alcoholism. The two features in which it most resembles the disorder we are discussing are loss of memory, and loss of muscular power and co-ordination. This condition is not uncommon among females, as I have already mentioned : we find it to be the end and result of continued dram-drinking. They do not develop delirium tremens so frequently as men, but this form is not uncommon; but as we find it amongst ladies, so do we not find general paralysis. It is only the rarer forms of the latter malady that resemble chronic alcoholism, those distinguished by a melancholic rather than an expansive state. The muscular weakness does not in alcoholism extend to the organs of articulation. I have known several patients who could hardly stand who spoke quite distinctly. The delusions of such chiefly depend on the entire obliteration of memory. The patients want to see and visit people who have long since died ; and when told of this, when the circumstances are brought back to their recollection, they make the same request five minutes after. Except for the absence of the stutter, the muscular defect may be much the same, but the mental symptoms are rarely alike; and if you make a close investigation of the commencement of the disorder, its history, and supposed cause, you can hardly make a mistake.

We sometimes find acute delirium breaking out in patients Lead paralysis. poisoned by lead, and with it there may be the paralysis produced by that substance. The delirium, however, is usually transient, the palsy does not affect the speech, the history and the blue line on the gums will assist our diagnosis, and the peculiar exalted delusions will be absent.

Senile dementia, which may commence at a comparatively Senile dementia. early age, may be characterized by loss of memory, extravagant and indecent conduct, and delusions. There will, however, be an absence of the specific delusions and the maniacal condition; neither shall we find the inequality of pupils, the stutter, nor stumbling gait. In fact, the failing mind in senile dementia is manifested usually long before any symptoms of bodily paralysis, and you will recollect that general paralysis is rare at the age of sixty, senile dementia seldom beginning so soon.

But we may meet with dementia or mania following apoplexy or hemiplegia, and may notice a stutter in the speech, a defective walk, loss of memory, and dirty habits. The patient, however, presents none of the mental symptoms of general paralysis. If the condition is one of dementia, he will be dull, vacant, torpid, with none of the *bien être* and expansiveness that characterize insane paralytics. If he be maniacal, the special delusions will be wanting, and when the mania passes off, the difference will be clearly seen. Moreover, we shall learn a history which will leave no doubt. The paralytic attack will have preceded the mental symptoms, whether these be maniacal, or only the imbecility of dementia, and the paralysis will be the result of a sudden attack, not of a slowly advancing progressive disease.

Mania and dementia, the result of epilepsy, may be confounded with the state of a paralytic patient who has lately had an epileptiform seizure, which you may be told was an epileptic fit, or series of fits. Here the history of the patient previous to the fit will be our best guide. Were there at that time any of the characteristic delusions of general paralysis? I was called to a gentleman who had had a seizure of this kind. He was lying in bed, not able to stand alone, or to lift his food to his mouth; he kept repeating one word, and was quite childish and lost. But for the previous history, it would have been difficult to say what was the origin of this paralytic dementia. Yet a few questions made it perfectly plain, and it was possible to say that in a few days he would be walking about again, but that he would not live beyond a year or two. He did not live a year. An attack of mania following epilepsy generally subsides in a week or less, and then the patient returns to the state he was in prior to the fit. His mental condition will at no time resemble that of a paralytic patient, though he may be very furious and dangerous. There will be no self-satisfied contentment or exaltation, but rather angry suspicion, rage, or panic, leading him to homicidal or suicidal violence. When this subsides, he may be apparently well and restored to reason, whereas the paralytic will show the effects of the seizure for a long time, and probably will never regain his former mental power.

Locomotor ataxy and other disorders affecting the muscular powers are not likely to be confounded with general paralysis of the insane, inasmuch as mental symptoms are wanting. I shall hereafter have to consider whether the paralytic symptoms of the latter disorder ever precede the mental. On this point there is considerable difference of opinion.

Epileptic paralysis.

In concluding the subject of diagnosis, I would say that cases are occasionally seen which must be looked upon as instances of spurious or *pseudo general paralysis*. The symptoms and course of the disease do not present the usual appearances, and by one observer it may be called general paralysis, while another would deny it the right to this title. Such cases are of great importance in estimating the pathology, and would seem to support the opinion of those who hold that it is not a special variety of insanity, but that it is insanity plus a number of symptoms of paralysis, cerebral and spinal, which, like the mental, may vary indefinitely.

If the diagnosis leads us to the conclusion that the patient is suffering from general paralysis, it follows that the *prognosis* must be extremely unfavorable. Practically, we look upon the disorder as fatal, and probably fatal in three or four years. Indeed, it is a question whether any have ever recovered from it. Patients are dying of it in all our asylums by the hundred, yet our best authorities record no recoveries. Here and there we may see a patient who is said to have recovered; but unless a long period has elapsed, we cannot be sure that the recovery is anything more than a remission.

The consideration of the pathology brings me to another point. Can we in any way account for the disease? what is its cause in any one individual? I have held for some years the opinion, based altogether on my observation of cases, that sexual excess has more to do with the causation of it than anything else. It is difficult to get at the history of this excess. If a man has led a very loose life, we may hear of it; but there may be great excess in married life, and of this we hear little. I have known several cases where the patients were men not very young, who had married young wives, having in former days led very dissipated lives. One man had been a great masturbator, and when married had never had complete intercourse, but had broken down in constant attempts. Some had led lives of great profligacy, which they had carefully concealed from everybody. And when we speak of sexual excess, it is not to be forgotten that what is excess to one man may not be to another. As one drinks with impunity an amount which kills another, so sexual indulgence which is harmless to this man may produce disorder in that. These observations of my own are confirmed both by the opinion of others, and by various circumstances to which I would draw your attention. General paralysis does not attack the young, or the old, and is not in general found amongst the weakly, but rather invades the strong and vigorous, those most likely to be guilty of excess. It rarely attacks women, especially of the higher classes. I myself have no experience of female paralytics; but Dr. Sankey, who was the superintendent of the women's side at Hanwell, and has made this disorder his special study, tell us,[1] "it is remarkable how many of them," that is, the women, "had led irregular lives, and especially had been guilty of sexual impropriety of some sort;" and he gives the particulars of seven cases. He, moreover, tells us, "out of 34 cases, of which the history of the disease is complete, 11 are known to have led an habitually irregular life with respect to sexual indulgence, and of 14 only was the information satisfactory as to the contrary state of things; even of these 14, one had borne an illegitimate child in early life, but since, according to her mother, had lived correctly; and one other was a married woman who had left her husband on the day after her marriage."

Next, I have to speak of the treatment of these patients. Although we do not cure them, although the disorder is still one of the *opprobria medicorum*, we *Treatment.* must never give up the attempt. One cannot understand as yet why this progressive disease should not be arrested,

---

[1] Lectures on Mental Diseases, p. 181.

for clearly the remissions and recoveries are at times so great that very little of the disease can be left, although the tendency to recur may be there, as in other forms of insanity. At any rate, our object in every case is to restore the patient to his friends, and enable him, if their means allow, to pass the close of his life amidst his family. These patients are rarely to be managed out of an asylum in the early stage. If they are wealthy, and a complete establishment can be provided, they may be so surrounded that they are virtually in an asylum for one; otherwise, they are better off in a well-conducted asylum, and quite as happy. At the outset, when first restrained, they are subject to paroxysms of blind, imbecile fury and violence, and are at this time very dangerous, requiring the appliances and skilled officers of an asylum. They also require exercise within secure grounds, and this they can rarely obtain elsewhere. And they are so elated by reason of their malady, that they do not feel restraint like other patients, who are more conscious of their position. They write myriads of letters, ordering horses, carriages, and diamonds, and never wonder why they are not sent, and why they get no answer. When by nature good-humored and pleasant people, no patients so enjoy themselves in an asylum, or are so easily pleased and humored. A promise that what they want shall come some day, turns aside their present ill-temper, and their failing memory has the next moment forgotten the desire. They are childish and childlike in mind, and can be led like children by tact and kindness. They are, at the same time, dangerous and treacherous. Their weak mind regards not consequences, and they will set fire to the house, or secrete a stone, or some such article, to attack the object of a delusion. One can never trust them: many patients we may believe implicitly, these we cannot. Much may be done by medicine in the violent excitement which characterizes the early stages of the disorder; and the drug which above all others seems to act beneficially here is digitalis, which is largely given in our public and private asylums: administered in doses of ℞xv to ℞xxx of the tincture, repeated, if neecessary, every three or four hours, it often produces a wonderful effect, soothing their noisy turbulence, and restoring them to a comparative state of rationality, so that they cease their destructive habits and filthy practices, wear clothes in decent fashion, and take food. Formerly, tartar emetic was given for this purpose; but it cannot be continued like digitalis, and I believe the latter to be now almost universally used. In some cases opium and morphia are serviceable, and frequently we may give them in conjunction with digitalis with greater benefit than alone. In the latter stages of dementia, where we find often great restlessness and want of sleep, along with an advanced stage of paralysis and prostration, opium or morphia may be given without digitalis; and for the mere production of sleep, chloral is as valuable here as in other forms of insanity.

I know no other sedatives that are worth a trial in this disease, unless it be bromide of potassium. This I have not given in large doses to paralytics, as I look upon its effect as decidedly enfeebling. It may be given, however, in doses of 10 or 20 grains with benefit when epileptiform attacks are recurring frequently.

Some years ago it was the fashion to administer to these patients the bichloride of mercury. General paralysis was an inflammation: mercury arrested inflammation, therefore, paralytics took mercury. But I never saw the least good done thereby in the many cases where it was tried. Tonics, on the contrary, are often of the greatest service when the great excitement has passed away; and, as in other head cases, I believe no tonic equals iron and its preparations. Quinine and bark seem of secondary importance; but iron— the tinct. ferri perchloridi especially—often seems to infuse new vigor into the failing limbs of the paralytic.

In the height of the excitement, beware how you give

stimulants, especially brandy. It renders them furious, deprives them of sleep, and undoes the effect of other remedies. As in acute delirium, give at first the more soporific stimulants, stout and ale, if you give any, and reserve your brandy and wine until a later period. When the excitement has passed off and reason is returning, and friends are beginning to think that, in spite of your gloomy predictions, the patient is recovering, he will require a generous diet, with a liberal supply of port wine. And this must be continued during the whole period of his convalescence and subsequent decline into dementia; and the latter will, *cæteris paribus*, be prolonged according to the plenteousness of the food taken. About this time of gradual decay there is little to say here. Such patients must be nursed according to the ordinary rules of nursing. They must not be allowed to lie in bed. They must be taken out of bed, thoroughly washed—for in the advanced stage it is very difficult to keep them dry—and must sit by day in an easy chair, and, so long as they are able, taken for a walk in the garden, or a ride. If allowed to lie in bed, they will very soon contract bed-sores, which, in their condition of depressed vitality, will be most difficult to cure. A strong solution of sulphate of zinc forms a good lotion when the skin is threatening to give way. When it has happened, I know no better application than the oxide of zinc, thickly strewn in powder on the sore, which by repeated dredgings, may be coated over and preserved from the air, and thus will often quickly heal.

Considering the opportunities afforded for post-mortem examination of patients dying of this disease, it may seem strange that doubt should still exist as to its seat, and special Post-mortem pathological character. Every portion of the brain appearances. has been thought to be the part affected. The early discoverers looked upon it as a chronic meningitis, and this view has been reproduced in our own times by L. Meyer. Calmeil, who did so much for its accurate description, thought it an inflammation of the cortical portion; and quite lately Dr. Meschede, in addition to many others, has held the same opinion. The cortical substance by some is supposed to be affected by atrophy, and pigmentary and fatty degeneration of the cells, while by others the morbid change is thought to be an increase of the connective tissue, invading both the gray and white cerebral substance. Changes in the blood-vessels of the cortical substance have been pointed out by various observers in cases of general paralysis, changes in the walls of the vessels, increase of the nuclei, twisting and aneurismal dilatations of the arteries and capillaries, and ob-literation and amyloid degeneration of them. Others point to an atrophy of the nerve-tubes, and to degeneration of the white matter; while Dr. Lockhart Clarke describes holes or vacuoles, seen by him in various portions of the white matter of the brain as well as of the convolutions. These he believes to be perivascular spaces or canals, which originally contained bloodvessels, surrounded by their peculiar sheaths, and which subsequently became empty by the destruction and absorp-tion of those vessels. I have already spoken of these in my fifth lecture.

The majority of observers have described only the morbid appearances found in the brain, which they have considered the seat of the disorder. But others, as Drs. Joffe, Boyd, and Westphal, have called attention to the diseased condition of the spinal cord. The last named has described minutely the morbid processes thereof: he has found inflammatory disease of the spinal dura mater (pachymeningitis), alteration, opacity and thickening of the pia mater, and three different forms of disease of the cord: (1) disease of the posterior columns only throughout their length, from the cervical to the lumbar re-gion, consisting of an atrophy of the nerve-tissues, and a growth of connective tissue which sometimes takes the place of the nerve-tubes, the morbid process being specially devel-oped at the periphery of the posterior columns. In addition to this we find (2) an affection of the posterior section of the lateral columns throughout their whole extent, and (3) a mixed form of affection of the posterior columns and of the posterior portion of the lateral columns.   In the two latter varieties Dr. Westphal looks on the disease as a *chronic myelitis*.   There are present nucleated cells, and a reticulated network of connective tissue surrounding the nerve-tubes; but the large plates of connective tissue are not found as in the first variety.   Dr. Westphal does not connect these appearances pathologically with the diseased conditions found in the brain.   He considers that the disorder does not spread from the brain downwards, or from the cord upwards, for he has not found disease in the mesocephalic parts.   "If we consider all the circumstances, we must for the present regard the cerebral and spinal diseases which simultaneously exist in general paralysis of the insane as, in so far, existing *per se*, and in certain respects independent of each other, as it is impossible for us to define more minutely the nature of the cerebral malady, and to establish a connection between it on the one hand, and the processes of gray degeneration and chronic myelitis of the spinal cord or medulla oblongata on the other."

The history of the investigation of general paralysis is this: observer after observer has found some morbid appearance which he has thought pathognomonic of the disease, but which has been found to exist in the brains of other insane patients, or even in the brains of those not insane.   Although the symptoms during life may make us think that there must be a progressive chronic inflammatory degeneration, leading to a decay of normal structure, and to a development of more lowly organized tissues; yet, so far, although very careful observers have examined the brains of paralytic patients, they have not found the actual pathological condition of this most interesting yet fatal disease.   As I have said, this is partly due to the fact that the sufferers rarely die in the early stage.. Where opportunities occur for examining a brain of a patient dying at a very early period, the actual seat of the mischief, whether cerebral or spinal, may be more certainly defined.

Lastly, we have to consider the nature of this mysterious disease, of which we know no cure, which crushes the strongest in his full prime, terminating both *Pathology.* reason and life. Patients die of it by hundreds in our asylums, yet its pathology is not yet ascertained beyond dispute, and various questions arise on which authorities are not agreed. First, is general paralysis a distinct disease? To this some, chiefly the French, reply in the affirmative, while others, especially the Germans, hold that the paralysis may be a complication of insanity, or the insanity a complication of a general condition of paralysis.

The discrepancies in opinion are in truth caused by our ignorance of the essential pathological condition of insanity: were this ascertained beyond all doubt, we should be able to decide on the identity or difference of the disorder called general paralysis. Looking at the clinical examination of the latter, we may notice, first, that we find the same mental symptoms in paralytic as in non-paralytic insanity, the same delusions, the same joyous excitement, the same depression, the same dementia, gradually, but more rapidly, advancing. Whence we infer that the same portion of the brain is affected in both diseases, and affected in a manner closely alike. Then arises the question, does the one and the other disease commence in the mind-region of the brain, *i. e.,* in the cerebral hemispheres, or can it be that disease of some more distant organs, such as the sensory ganglia, the medulla, spinal cord, or vaso-motor ganglia, produces a disturbance of the mental organ. May we conceive that a disorder arises in the vaso-motor ganglia, which, subsiding in ordinary insanity, allows of recovery; but in the paralytic affection progresses from ganglion to ganglion, thus interfering by degrees with the whole of the nerve-organs, and leading gradually to degeneration and disorganization? The condition of the vaso-motor ganglia in insanity has been scarcely spoken of, yet I may quote the words of Drs. Poincarè and Henry Bonnet, who in the "Annales Médico-Psychologiques," tome xii, 1868, make these observations on them: "In general paralysis the cells of the whole chain of the great sympathetic are covered with brown pigment to a degree much more intense than in other subjects, from whatever affection they may have suffered. In the ganglia of the cervical region, and often in the ganglia of the thoracic, there is evidently a substitution of cellular tissue and of adipose cells for the nerve-cells, which last are comparatively rare. Everything leads us to think that this is the anatomical starting-point of the affection, and that the alterations of the encephalon are the mere consequences of the disorders which this sclerosis, by a paralytic action of the cervical ganglia, produces in the cerebral circulation. There is always a very marked pigmentation of the spinal ganglia and of those which are attached to the cranial nerves. The adipose cells, which are substituted for nerve-cells in the ganglia of the great sympathetic, often exhibit a depth of color which may even be quite black."[1]

These observations may explain differences which exist in the opinions of various writers. There can be no question that coexisting with the mental affection there is a gradually advancing paralysis. Then, we ask, does the disease extend downwards from the brain to the cord, or upwards from the cord to the brain? do we find paralytic symptoms existing before any mental derangement, or do we notice the peculiar mental delusions for some time before there is any defect of speech or gait? or is the one set of symptoms always accompanied by the other? Now, I think it may be stated as

---

[1] Translated in the Journal of Medical Science, July, 1869.

certain, that motor disorder may be noticed before any mental symptoms. A gentleman whom I saw in an asylum had had a paraplegic affection for ten or twelve years. His speech was not impaired, and there was no mental disturbance till ten days before I saw him. He then spent money recklessly, thought he had commands from heaven, and his speech was most inarticulate. The spinal symptoms have been, by Dr. Westphal, divided into *tabic*, when we find gray degeneration of the posterior columns with a loss of nerve-substance and substitution of connective tissue, and *paralytic*, in which the process appears to be a chronic myelitis. In the latter form, the symptoms of motor disorder are more latent, and may be noticed as a weakness or lassitude only. The *tabic* form of gait may exist in patients who have no mental disorder, so that it cannot necessarily depend on the cerebral disease; the *paralytic* form may be hardly noticeable, even if it exists, whereas, at the same time the mental symptoms may be most marked. There is every reason for supposing that the mental and motor disorder depend on pathological states which, though they coexist, are independent one of the other.

The epileptiform or apoplectiform attacks, the convulsive tremors noticeable throughout the disease, the appearance and disappearance of the affection of speech, and other paralytic symptoms, all point, in my opinion, to sudden interference with the circulation, which may depend on disturbance of the vaso-motor system. To the observations already recorded by Drs. Poincarè and Bonnet I may add the opinion of Dr. Westphal: "Considering that we have been studying a series of changes in certain columns of the spinal cord, in the medulla oblongata, pons varolii, and crus cerebri, the supposition is not improbable, that through a temporary excitation (due to the morbid process) of the vaso-motor nerves proceeding from these parts, the anæmias we have mentioned may be produced. Further speculation on this point, however, can lead to nothing until further physiological facts have been obtained."[1]

It is too much to assert that the seat of disease is in these ganglia, nevertheless they demand more investigation than they have as yet received.

---

[1] On General Paralysis of the Insane, by Dr. C. Westphal, translated from Griesinger's Archiv. für Psychiatrie, No. 1, in the "Journal of Mental Science, 1868."

LECTURE XV.

HITHERTO I have spoken of patients whose insanity is plain
and unmistakable. The question for us is, how are we to
cure them. As, with the exception of the paralytic patients,
the insanity is recent and acute, we shall be able to cure a
considerable number. But there are many persons
about whom your opinion will be sought on other Of patients whose
grounds. You will have to say, either to the friends insanity is doubtful.
or in a court of law, whether a patient is or is not
legally of unsound mind—so unsound in mind as to be incapable of taking care of himself and his affairs, and a fit and
proper person to be detained under legal restraint. Most
difficult is it in many cases to come to a decision upon such a
question; still more difficult to give the grounds of our opinion, and to give them publicly in the witness-box. Your
opinion will be required, speaking generally, for one of four
purposes: 1. To place a patient under legal restraint in an
asylum or quasi-asylum for the purpose of treatment; 2. To
deprive a man of the management of his affairs by a commission *de lunatico inquirendo;* 3. To relieve a patient from
the responsibility of some crime committed or contract entered into; 4. To inquire into the state of mind of a testator
at the time he executed his will. The legal portion of the

subject I shall leave till hereafter. I wish now to bring
before you certain classes of patients and certain varieties of
insanity which most frequently give rise to forensic contests.
These are "moral insanity," "emotional," and "impulsive
insanity." Under these names you will find cases quoted in
books, and you may be questioned concerning them by counsel. Such patients may be more accurately described by
other names, and I wish to indicate to you the method of
examining and testing them.

Certain forms are discussed in courts of law, and hotly con-
tested, because they are said by some to lack the symptoms
necessary to be demonstrated before we can pronounce any
one legally insane. Chiefly, the absence or presence of *delu-*
sions is the point at issue. Can a person be found
lunatic who has no delusions? Most lawyers deny
this, even now. Our own profession affirms it, and
points to many persons of undoubtedly unsound mind, in
whom no delusions are to be found.

Insanity
without
delusions.

In reading the history of the great cases of disputed insanity, you may be astonished to find that what is considered
unsoundness of mind in a civil cause is by no means looked
upon as legal insanity in a criminal trial. That which is
deemed proof of a man's being unable to manage his affairs,
does not necessarily absolve him from responsibility if he has
committed murder. When giving evidence upon a commission in lunacy, you are asked, in plain terms, if you think the
patient is fit to take care of himself and manage his affairs—
a question which the facts of the case generally render easy
to answer. But, in a crown case, you are asked if the prisoner
knew what he was doing when he committed the crime, or
if he knew right from wrong, and such questions, which are
totally irrelevant and beside the issue, which is, was he of
unsound mind when he committed it. I shall have to refer
to this again, but I mention it here inasmuch as the proof of
insanity in criminal cases must be stronger than in others,

and this must be borne in mind by all of us who may be called upon to give evidence.

Lawyers and judges vary indefinitely according to their humanity and idiosyncrasy in their opinions as to what constitutes irresponsibility. Some say that a patient is responsible unless he is so insane that he cannot know On legal responsibility. right from wrong, others hold that he is not insane unless he has delusions. This latter theory is constantly propounded in both civil and criminal courts. It was held and believed at one time by both lawyers and doctors. If we look back at the definitions and doctrines of the great medical luminaries of the seventeenth and eighteenth centuries, we shall find that they almost invariably divided insanity into *melancholy* and *mania*, which latter they also called phrensy or fury. *Melancholy* they defined to be " a permanent delirium, without fury or fever, in which the mind is dejected and timorous, and usually employed about one object." "*Mania* is a permanent delirium, with fury and audacity, but without fever."[1]

Now delirium in Arnold's time, 1782, did not mean what it does nowadays. You know very well what the delirium of fever is, or delirium tremens. We should not say that a monomaniac laboring under the delusion that he was the rightful heir to the throne, but in all other respects rational, was suffering from delirium, yet this would have been described as his malady by the writers of the last century. *Delirium sine febre* was our " delusion," *delirium cum febre* was our "delirium." "Phrenitis," says Hoffman, "est insania cum febre, a stasi sanguinis inflammatoria in vasis cerebri orta."

Melancholy by the older writers as far back as the time of Burton, is used to signify monomania or partial insanity, in contradistinction to *mania*, which meant general insanity,

---

[1] *Vide* Arnold on Insanity, vol. i, p. 30.

fury, or phrensy. This distinction between general and partial insanity we hear maintained by lawyers in our own day, and we can trace it back at any rate so far as the seventeenth century, for Lord Hale says[1]—"There is a partial insanity and a total insanity. The former is either in respect to things, *quoad hoc, vel illud insanire.* Some persons that have a competent use of reason in respect of some subjects, are yet under a particular *dementia* in respect of some particular discourses, subjects, or applications, or else it is partial in respect of degrees; and this is the condition of very many, *especially melancholy persons,* who for the most part discover their defect in excessive fears and griefs, and yet are not wholly destitute of the use of reason; and this partial insanity seems not to excuse them in the committing of any offence for its matter capital, for, doubtless, most persons that are felons of themselves and others are under a degree of partial insanity when they commit these offences. It is very difficult to define the invisible line that divides perfect and partial insanity; but it must rest upon circumstances duly to be weighed and considered, both by judge and jury, lest on the one side there be a kind of inhumanity towards the defects of human nature, or on the other side too great an indulgence given to great crimes."

Here Lord Hale lays down the doctrine that partial insanity, melancholy, or monomania, does not absolve from responsibility in criminal cases. Those lawyers who do not go so far as to say this, but would allow that insanity of any kind absolves a man from punishment, nevertheless almost all assert that to prove insanity we must prove delusion. This opinion is maintained both by civil and criminal lawyers, and I have heard it enunciated frequently within the last few years. Two legal opinions I may quote, given by men of great eminence on this side. The first is that of Sir John

---

[1] Pleas of the Crown, 30.

Nicholl, whose judgments are highly esteemed and honored by all lawyers. In a very celebrated judgment pronounced by him in the Court of Probate, in Drew v. Clark, he said—"The true criterion, the true test of the absence or presence of insanity, I take to be the absence or presence of what, used in a certain sense of it, is comprisable in a single term, namely, *delusion*. In short, I look upon delusion, in this sense of it, and insanity, to be almost, if not altogether, convertible terms. On the contrary, in the absence of any such delusion, with whatever extravagances a supposed lunatic may be justly chargeable, and how like soever to a real madman he may think or act on some one or all subjects; still, in the absence, I repeat, of anything in the nature of delusion, so understood as above, the supposed lunatic is in my judgment not properly or essentially insane."

Delusions long considered the test of insanity.

Mr., afterwards Lord, Erskine, at the trial of Hadfield, who shot at the King in Drury Lane Theatre in the year 1800, said—"Delusion, when there is no frenzy or raving madness, is the true character of insanity; and when it cannot be predicated of a man standing for life or death for a crime, he ought not, in my opinion, to be acquitted."

This is the opinion of many, I may say most, lawyers. But lawyers, I need not tell you, have no practical acquaintance with the insane. Their doctrines are based on the traditions and judgments of preceding dignitaries, and in no way depend on the advance of scientific research or more accurate observation of patients. I shall endeavor to show that many patients, undoubtedly of unsound mind, have no delusions, that delusions are not the one "test" of unsoundness of mind, nor even of insanity so called; and, further, that there are many who are beyond all question of unsound mind, who cannot properly be called insane. Counsel will try to trip you on this point, and ask if you consider the patient insane. He may not be insane, strictly speaking, and you may have to admit it; they will then argue that he is not *legally* of unsound mind. But a great lawyer, Lord Coke, in his commentary upon Littleton, forestalled this objection. He, too, uses the expression " unsound of mind." " *Non compos mentis,*" saith he, " explaineth the true sense, and calleth him not *amens, demens, furiosus, lunaticus, fatuus, stultus,* or the like, for *non compos mentis* is most sure and legal." And the Lunacy Act of 1845, 8 and 9 Vict. c. 100, in the interpretation clause, § cxiv, says, " ' Lunatic,' shall mean every insane person, and every person being an idiot, or lunatic, or of unsound mind."

I proceed, therefore, to describe to you various patients who are legally unsound in mind, yet cannot be included in any of the classes already mentioned. And, first, let us take those whose malady is called by some *moral,* by others *emotional* insanity, *affective* insanity, and so forth. I do not myself employ this nomenclature, but it is necessary that you should be familiar with it. The essential feature, whatever name we give it, is, that there are no delusions.

Pinel was, I believe, the first to lay down distinctly the doctrine that insanity may exist without delusion. In 1802, he described this as *manie sans délire,* mania without delusion, and he gives a brief history of three patients thus affected. One of them was liberated by the revolutionary mob which broke open the Bicêtre, but he was soon roused to fury by the excitement around, and was quickly led back to his cell by his new-found friends. After Pinel came Esquirol: to the partial insanity which hitherto had been called *melancholia,* he gave the name of *monomania,* and described two varieties as existing *sans délire,* without delusion, *monomanie instinctive* and *monomanie affective* or *raisonnante.* From his time to our own, all the most illustrious authorities of our profession have recognized this fact, and under one name or other have described patients whose insanity was free from delusions. I may cite, amongst others, the names of Hoffbauer, Georget,

Gall, Marc, Combe, Prichard, Ray, Reil, Rush, Bucknill, D. Tuke, and Maudsley.

Various names have been bestowed on this insanity, various divisions and classifications of it and its varieties have been constructed, according to the theories held as to the mind and its component parts.

The mind is commonly said to be divisible into the intellect, emotions, and will. In accordance with this, Dr. Bucknill speaks of *intellectual, emotional*, and *volitional* insanity, and Dr. Daniel Tuke points out that some such division as this has been adopted by many authors. Reid analyzes the mind, and divides it into the *understanding* and the *will;* Dr. Thomas Brown speaks of the *intellectual states of the mind* and *the emotions;* Morel gives a triple division, *the animal passions, the moral feelings*, and *the intellect;* Bain's division is the *intellect, emotion*, and *volition*, while the emotional or affective part of the mind is by many subdivided into *propensities* and *sentiments*, or *moral sentiments*.

Besides the division of insanity into *intellectual, emotional*, and *volitional*, it has been divided into *intellectual* or ideational, and *emotional* or affective, with a subdivision of the latter into *moral alienation*, or insanity of the moral sentiments, and *insanity affecting the propensities*, or impulsive insanity. Here we come to the *moral insanity*, concerning which so much contention has arisen, and which is so often said to have been invented by doctors as an excuse for crime.

The great teacher of the doctrine of *moral insanity* was Dr. Prichard, who, in his well-known Treatise on In- On so-called sanity, published in 1835, insists strongly on this Moral Insanity. division, and on the fact that "insanity exists sometimes with an apparently unimpaired state of the intellectual faculties." Moral insanity he defines to be "madness consisting in a morbid perversion of the natural feelings, affections, inclinations, temper, habits, moral dispositions, and natural impulses, without any remarkable disorder or defect of the intellect, or knowing and reasoning faculties, and particularly without any insane illusion or hallucination."

Now, I deny that the absence of the moral sense proves or constitutes insanity, any more than its presence proves sanity. It is perfectly true that it is absent in many lunatics, all notions of duty, propriety, and decency being destroyed in the general overthrow of the mind; but it is also true that we can find perfectly sane people who, either from early education and habit—the habit of continual vice—and also hereditary transmission, are devoid of moral sense to an equal or greater degree. Probably greater wickedness is daily perpetrated by sane than ever was committed by insane men and women; so that when immorality makes us question a man's state of mind, it must be remembered that insanity, if it exists, is to be demonstrated by other mental symptoms and concomitant facts and circumstances, and not by the act of wickedness alone. Writers who, like M. Despine, think that the committal of great crimes without concern or remorse, indicates an absence of the " moral sense " amounting to irresponsible defect, overlook the fact that the habit of wrongdoing may be acquired to such an extent that the thing done excites no feeling whatever. An habitual murderer, as a Thug or a brigand, thinks no more of taking life than does a veteran soldier. It is his ἕξις, his everyday habit. As there are, according to Aristotle, spurious forms of courage, one of which is ἐμπειρία, experience, or, in other words, habit; so criminal and bad acts may be so habitual as to be unaccompanied by any feeling of having done wrong. The gradual effacing of the moral sense, and gradual hardening in vice, have been portrayed by many a moralist; but something else is needed to prove the disease or deficiency of mind we look for in the inhabitants of an asylum.

I cannot help thinking that the authors who have most strongly upheld the doctrine of a moral insanity and morbid perversion of the moral sentiments, have often underrated or

neglected the intellectual defect or alteration observable in
the patients. Because no delusion has been found, it has
been assumed that the intellect is not impaired, intellectual
insanity and insanity with delusions being spoken of as
synonymous. But many patients of defective intelligence
have no delusions, as all kinds of idiots and imbeciles. Many
of altered intelligence have not as yet reached the stage of
delusion, and many recover from the latter, or from the stage
at which delusions are present, yet do not recover their full
intellectual powers, but remain semi-cured and semi-insane.
This class is a very large one. Dr. Prichard gives as illustrations of moral insanity seven cases in his own practice,
one communicated by Dr. Symonds, and nine by Dr. Hitch.
These are entitled "Cases of Moral Insanity and Monomania;"
and, as they are quoted frequently in courts of law, I think
it right to say something about them here. They are de-
scriptions, and very valuable ones, of insane patients, not of
varieties of insanity, and there is all the difference between
the two. In strictness, I ought to give these cases in full,
but time prevents. Dr. Prichard's work, however, Dr. Prichard's
is to be found in most medical libraries, and I must cases.
refer you to it. The first patient was a gentleman of high
intellectual attainments, who married a lady no less endowed,
and well known in the literary world. He was greatly attached to her, but extremely fearful lest it should be supposed
that she dictated what he wrote, and he never let her know
what he was thinking or writing about. He then acquired
strange habits, placing everything in a certain order, whether
in his own or other people's rooms. He would run up and
down the garden a certain number of times, rinsing his mouth
with water, and spitting alternately on one side and the other
in regular succession. He employed a good deal of time in
rolling up little pieces of writing-paper, which he used for
cleaning his nose. It did not surprise those who were best
acquainted with his peculiarities to hear that in a short time

he became notoriously insane. He committed several acts of violence, argued vehemently in favor of suicide, and was shortly afterwards found drowned in a canal. Such is the epitome of the history of one who gradually drifted into unmistakable insanity through the stages of alteration and eccentricity. Even if his ideas concerning his wife, and concerning his arrangement of the articles of furniture, could not strictly be called delusions, it is impossible to say that in him was no defect of intellect. He would appear at dinner in his dressing-gown, apologizing for not having had time to dress, when he had been dressing all the morning; and he would go out for a walk in a winter's evening, with a lantern, "because he had not been able to get ready earlier in the day."

The second case is that of a patient who was at first melancholic, timid and irresolute, suspicious of all about him, always changing both his studies and his residence. Soon he fancied himself the object of dislike to all in the house, and when questioned confessed that he heard whispers of malevolence and abhorrence. Here we have another plain case of a patient gradually drifting into delusions and hallucinations.

The third patient, a maiden lady of forty-eight, after an attack of pneumonia, evinced alternations of depression and excitement for eight years, without showing any delusions or marked symptoms of insanity, and then broke down, had many delusions, "saw people looking at her," "thought it was the devil who made her act so." Yet when Dr. Prichard saw her, he could find no insane hallucination. She confessed herself, however, "that she was formerly very different."

The fourth, a farmer, displayed no hallucination or disturbance of the intellectual faculties. Yet we hear that from being a man of sober and domestic habits, frugal and steady in his conduct, he became wild, excitable, thoughtless, full of schemes and absurd projects. He bought cattle and farming stock of which he had no means of disposing; he bought a number of carriages; called on the steward of a gentleman in the middle of the night to survey an estate; and yet we are told that "his intellectual faculties were not disturbed." He was, however, placed in an asylum, and recovered.

The fifth was a gentleman who was for many years in an asylum, but was released by a jury, in opposition to the unanimous opinion of several physicians, who all thought him insane. He scarcely performed any action in the same manner as other men, and some of his habits were filthy and disgusting. If a physician came near him, he recoiled with horror, exclaiming, "If you were to feel my pulse, you would be lord paramount over me for the rest of my life." This individual, however, a chronic monomaniac, "has lived for many years on his estate, where his conduct, though eccentric and not that of a sane man, has been without injury to himself and others."

The sixth was a working tradesman, who, after the death of his wife, denied himself the necessaries of life, and lived in a state of starvation and filth, till removed to an asylum. Here he so far recovered that he was released, and married a servant of the asylum. She soon, however, brought him back to the asylum, where he remained, his derangement being afterwards marked by various delusions.

The seventh, and last, was a gentleman who had had epileptic fits. He became totally changed, remained always in bed, was dirty, irascible, and violent. He was in a state of constant despondency. His friends would not place him in an asylum, and we are told that " the event was calamitous," which, I presume, means that he committed suicide.

To say that " the reasoning faculty remains unaffected" in patients who commit every variety of outrageous and filthy act, and justify it, seems to me to involve a total misapprehension of what the " reasoning faculty" means.

But I will pass on to the cases reported to Dr. Prichard by others. Dr. Symonds's is that of a man who had never fully recovered from an attack of acute mania. He was what is commonly designated flighty or cracked. He advertised for sale property which he knew to be entailed, left his family without reason and without means of subsistence, while his letters were confused and incoherent, the expressions being ridiculously disproportionate to the subjects. He printed a pamphlet concerning his domestic history: "A more insane document than this I scarcely ever perused. The sentences were so involved and undistinguished that, although the ideas were not absolutely incongruous with each other, it was impossible to collect more than the general tenor of a long passage." He was filthy in habits, constantly passing his evacuations in his bed.

Dr. Symonds signed a certificate, though, as he says, " he was unable to trace any positive intellectual error,"—that is, I take it, he could find no delusion.

In all these cases, and in cases 1, 2, 8, and 9, reported by Dr. Hitch, there was plain and palpable intellectual altera- tion and defect, to such an extent as to make it evident that the patients were insane, whether their actions were moral or immoral; and in many of them delusions appeared after a time, though in some instances the patients took a considera- ble period to go through the stages of alteration and aliena- tion, which so many pass through in a few days or weeks.

Dr. Hitch's third is an excellent illustration of intermittent "dipsomania." "At times the gentleman is in habits most abstemious; he never drinks anything stronger than beer, and frequently tastes water only for weeks together. Then comes on a thirst for ardent spirits, and a fondness for low society. He drinks in a pot-house till he can drink no more, or get no more to drink, falls asleep for from twenty to thirty hours, awakes to the horrors of his situation, and is the hum- blest of the meek for several weeks. In about three months the same thing occurs." This form deserves the name of moral insanity, or rather of impulsive insanity, more than any of the foregoing, and must be studied in connection with the propensity to drink.

No. 4. This patient serves as a good example of what may be called moral insanity, if the term is to be used at all. "He had been the inmate of several asylums, but his early history is not given. No delusions were ascertainable; but he enjoyed in a high degree the art of lying and the pleasure of boasting. The former was applied to the production of mischief and disturbance. He was an adept at stealing, and hoarded and secreted in his clothes and bedding articles of all kinds; yet he possessed many good qualities, would be kind and useful in the gallery, and corrected obscene or impious language in others.

"His judgment was quick and correct, he had quick perception, strong memory, and great discretion in matters of business. His madness appeared to me to consist in part *in a morbid love of being noticed.* He is now at large, and has been in the management of his affairs for three years, in which time he has sold an estate advantageously, and conducted his business with profit."

The next patient also deserves to be called morally insane. Always of a bad temper, she gradually gave way to paroxysms of passion, followed by a morose and unyielding sullenness. A change came over her: she neglected her children, and abused her husband; she smashed all the windows in her own house and the workhouse, and then was sent to an asylum, where she would constantly remain in bed if allowed, or suddenly roll on the ground and scream if questioned, or cry and sigh as if in the greatest distress. "As a disagreeable and unmanageable patient, without actual violence, she exceeds most with whom I have met. Her mind appears totally unaffected as to its understanding portion, but in the moral part completely perverted." This case is a very good instance of insanity without delusions, shown, as in the last patient, by outrageous conduct wholly irreconcilable with reason.

The same may be said of No. 6, a man who by many might be called bad rather than mad. "I found him one of the most mischievous of beings; his constant delight was in creating disorder to effect what he called 'fun;' but he had no *motive*, no *impression* on his mind, which induced him to this conduct; he was merely impelled by his immediate feelings. In his state of health I found nothing wrong, except that he did not sleep."

No. 7 is the case of a gentleman who suffered from cerebral symptoms, and eventually died of apoplexy. He entertained deep feelings of hostility to certain persons who had affronted him; but he was never insane, at least according to this report.

No. 8 was a young lady distinguished in the *beau monde*, whose father's embarrassments caused her withdrawal from society. She became coarse and abusive, neglectful of her person, altogether changed in habits and feelings, hated her family, and said "she was dead." After three months in an asylum she was dismissed "much relieved." Intellectual change must have been observable here, as in so many of Dr. Prichard's cases.

Lastly, we have the particulars of a young man whose defect was a morbid want of self-confidence, a fear that he was unequal to his business, and that he should ruin it. He tried to run away, and when stopped, took poison. He was placed in an asylum and recovered, but periodically absented himself from home. In time his affections were altered toward his father and family, and he became suspicious of them all. An elder brother, without any symptoms of madness, had destroyed himself.

Here we have a well-marked instance of intermitting melancholia, with self-depreciation amounting to delusion.

Thus have I briefly commented on all the cases of moral

insanity related by Dr. Prichard. That in some of them insanity existed without insane delusion for some time, I admit; but that it existed without alteration or defect of the intelligence, I deny. Whether we choose to call it emotional insanity or *affective* or *moral*, I hold that the intellect is also involved, that we cannot divorce the emotional and intellectual functions of the mind, *The morally insane show intellectual defect or alteration.* and that this view may be upheld both on *a priori* and *a posteriori* grounds; for *a priori* we should say that the ideational portion of the mind is so intimately joined in operation to the emotional—the stored ideas of the brain are so influenced by the feelings of the moment, whether these arise from within or without—that the two must be sound together, or unsound together; so, *a posteriori*, we see the insanity displayed in absurd and extravagant acts, groundless and foolish likes and dislikes, or reckless squandering of health and property. We say of such a person, either he is mad or he is a fool, thereby attributing to him at once intellectual defect. And we shall see by and by that these acts are often committed by persons notably deficient in intelligence, congenitally or from disease.

It is quite certain that various patients are undoubtedly insane, who present none of the ordinary delusions of insanity. They may not have reached the stage of delusions, and they may go on to recovery without ever reaching it, or they may recover from the stage of delusions, and yet not perfectly recover, remaining in a chronic state of what Dr. Prichard calls moral insanity.

We may find at any age this emotional or moral insanity without delusions. It is the insanity of the young. The second of the cases communicated to Dr. Prichard by Dr. Hitch, is that of a little girl aged seven, who, from being a quick, lively, and affectionate child, became rude, passionate, vulgar, and unmanageable. She was morbid in appetite, and would sleep on the ground rather than in a bed. She was cruel to her sisters, could not apply to anything, and her health was much disordered. She would eat her fæces and drink her urine—in short, was in a complete state of mania, but had no fixed idea or delusion. She recovered in two months.

It occurs in middle age, and, as I have said, a patient sometimes remains in this condition for some months, or even years, before he reaches the stage of delusions, or recovers without ever having reached them.

After an accident, as a blow on the head or an attack of epilepsy, we may perceive a change come over an individual, insidiously gaining ground, till it is plain that he is insane, and his insanity may for a long time be of this description. I have myself seen two gentlemen who might have been called morally insane, whose disorder might be traced to an epileptic attack. I have already mentioned these in the "Journal of Mental Science," April, 1869. One gentleman had originally received a concussion of the brain in a railway accident, and subsequently had an epileptic fit, and after a long interval a second. He was noisy, ostentatious, and boastful, irritable, occasionally low and hysterical. There was an extreme want of consecutiveness in his conversation, and this, with his extravagant notions and bombastic language—all quite foreign to him—plainly revealed his insanity; but he had no positive delusions. He was in an asylum six times, yet he died at home, weak in mind, but sane. Twice he recovered after an attack of gout: although there were no delusions, his conversation on one occasion became perfectly incoherent, and his excitement arose into a state of subacute mania. It was very difficult to sign a certificate in his case—at any rate for one not previously acquainted with him—and yet no one who was with him for twenty-four hours could doubt his insanity.

The other patient's malady also commenced with an epi-

Moral insanity in connection with epilepsy.

leptic fit, from which timè he gradually became an altered man, and had periodical fits of drinking, though he never pushed this to extremes. Three years elapsed before anything occurred which justified the interference of his friends. He then rôde on horseback to the end of Brighton chain-pier, assaulted the police, when bailed did not appear, and was then sent to an asylum. When there, he justified his acts in a manner markedly insane, and wrote hundreds of absurd letters to the same effect. He rambled both in conversation and ideas. Certain officious people, who thought him unjustly detained, sent a solicitor to see him. He betrayed no delusion whatever, but treated the whole matter in so frivolous a way, and wandered away from the point to such a degree that the lawyer pronounced him insane. He was subsequently discharged, and died within a year, I was told, of abscess of the liver.

This form may make its appearance in old age, and constitute what Drs. Prichard and Burrows call "senile insanity." An old gentleman whom I knew well for years as the pattern of strict propriety, honor, and paternal affection, took in his latter days to going with loose women of a low class, on whom he squandered money to a considerable extent. Fortunately for his family his health gave way, and he was obliged to stay at home and be nursed, and his death prevented the necessity of any legal restraint. It would have been impossible, I think, for any medical man to have signed a certificate in this case at the time that he was running after these women, though his friends had no doubt that his mind was deranged. Although he had never shown signs of insanity till his old age, it is worthy of note that two, at least, of his children have evinced symptoms of mental derangement in middle life. In such patients this kind of insanity is the forerunner of senile fatuity and dementia; but some time may elapse before the mind is so decayed as to warrant our giving it this name, and the term senile insanity would appear to be more fitting.

When a man or woman becomes insane, the character of the emotion displayed depends on the general physical condition of the individual, and varies at different times, and the delusions will follow the feeling of the moment. So, when there are no delusions, and the insanity is manifested only in the appearance, habits, and acts, we shall still find that the emotion displayed will vary from the extreme of melancholy to the highest hilarity, according to the general condition of the patient. In melancholia there is almost always a premonitory stage in which no delusion is perceptible, and the depression may, and often does, last for a long time, and then pass off without any definite delusion. I say without any definite delusion; but on close cross-examination we find an all-pervading feeling of gloom, or a feeling that everything is wrong, everything miserable and sad, and life itself a burden; which is, in fact, one great and universal delusion. This is the state of many who commit suicide— a state of perfect insanity, yet with so little derangement of ideas and intelligence that the friends shrink from interfering, and think that cheering up and change of scene are all that is wanted. When you hear that an individual has become low-spirited, even to an apparently slight extent, set it down that he or she is suicidal—even if the friends tell you to the contrary—even if the patient himself expresses a horror of such an act. This he will do, and an hour afterwards will be impelled to throw himself out of the window.

Abnormal irascibility, or abnormal hilarity, may, no less than depression, characterize insanity without delusions. This we see illustrated by various cases narrated by Dr. Prichard and Dr. Hitch. Sullenness, causeless anger, with violent outburst of temper and corresponding acts, accompany the insanity of some, and hold a place midway between the extreme depression called melancholia, and the gayety

The emotional character of the insanity.

and hilarity which others display. In fact, when a man is entirely changed, no matter how, you may reasonably suspect his sanity, having first thoroughly ascertained the truth of this change. By dint of patient and constant examination, you will probably come to the bottom of the whole matter, to the *fons et origo* of the change, and will find that nothing but insanity can account for it. Men do not suddenly change their nature without a cause, and when such a change takes place, the cause must be sought. And if you suspect insanity, you must examine carefully the individual and his history, the history *quoad* insanity of his parents, brothers, and sisters, his history as regards fits, blows on the head, or other exciting or predisposing causes of mental disorder. Then you must well weigh the changes alleged to have taken place in his temper, habits, ideas, and acts, and must hear what he himself has to say about his feelings and doings. You will probably find such an amount of irrationality, incompetence to argue, rambling from the point, or justification of palpably insane acts, as to warrant your deciding that he is of unsound intellect, whether the ordinary delusions of insanity appear or not. And although your opinion may be asked chiefly upon the question of sanity or insanity, yet you are Treatment and not to forget that the question of treatment is in- prognosis. volved therein. Many are curable, especially those whose insanity has not yet reached the stage of delusions, and is of recent origin. Change, rest, and restraint, in or out of an asylum, according to circumstances, may effect a cure, and this you are bound to promote. Insanity following epilepsy or blows on the head cannot be favorably looked at as regards prognosis; but even this may be intermittent, and the remissions may be treated till there is at any rate temporary recovery, and such patients may be restored for a time to their homes or friends. If you meet with this form in patients who have recovered from severe attacks up to a certain point, and there have remained stationary, not being thoroughly restored to their right and sound mind, it may be possible, by judicious care and supervision, to regulate the lives of such in a way which will enable them to live out of an asylum, in the family of a friend or stranger; and you may witness their perfect recovery even after a long period of alienation. These semi-insane people, if free from mischievous or dangerous habits or impulses, have a better chance of improvement out of than in an asylum. Their self-respect is more encouraged; they feel that they have more to live for; and the dread of going back often operates as a wholesome check upon their insane propensities.

The mention of "moral insanity," which some think to be a state of mind in which the moral sense is blunted or

On the so-called legal test of insanity.

lost, leads me to say a few words on what has been called the legal test of insanity. It has been laid down by certain of the judges, that an alleged criminal lunatic is responsible for his acts if he knows the difference between right and wrong; and you will be asked in crown cases whether you think that a prisoner knows right from wrong. No more curious test of insanity was ever invented, none which more plainly shows the absolute ignorance of the subject prevailing amongst those who have no acquaintance with the insane. When Macnaughten was tried in 1843 for the murder of Mr. Drummond, and acquitted on the ground of insanity, the matter was made a subject of debate in the House of Lords, and Lord Chancellor Lyndhurst stated that the law, as laid down by various judges, was, that if a man when he commits an offence is capable of distinguishing right from wrong, and is not under the influence of such a delusion as disables him from distinguishing that he is doing a wrong act, he is answerable to the law. Lord Brougham, with his clear perception, saw the difficulty of this interpretation. "One judge," he said, "lays down the law that a man is responsible if he is 'capable of knowing right from wrong;' another says, 'if he is capable

of distinguishing good from evil;' another, 'capable of knowing what was proper;' another, 'what was wicked.' He was
not sure that the public at large 'knew right from wrong,'
though their Lordships knew that 'distinguishing right from
wrong' meant a knowledge that the act a person was about
to commit was punishable by law." Certain questions were
then put to the bench of judges by the Lords as to the interpretation of the law, and in their answers stress is laid
upon the knowledge of right and wrong, and they talk of a
partial delusion, whatever that may be, which does not absolve a criminal from responsibility.

These answers are supposed, even in our own day, to be
an authoritative exposition of the law as it affects the insane.
So unsatisfactory are they, that one judge abides by them,
while another does not, and nothing definite is settled.
Some lawyers do not scruple to say that a lunatic should be
put to death if he commits a murder, as if he were sane;
while it has been said by a judge "that it was not merely
for the jury to consider whether the prisoner knew right
from wrong, but whether he was at the time he committed
the offence deranged or not." Common sense and common
humanity must coincide in looking upon the latter as the
only view to be taken of the question, and it will The knowl-
be for you to confine yourselves in all such cases to edge of right
and wrong.
the simple exposition of the insanity of the individual, if in your opinion it exists. If you are asked if you
think he knew right from wrong, you may answer, (1.) That
it is not possible so to enter into and examine the internal
consciousness of an insane man at the moment of the commission of a crime, even if we are present, as to be able to
argue as to his knowledge of the wrong he is doing. (2.)
That the defect of mind presumed to be present, whether insanity or imbecility, implies an absence of that perfect working of the intellect and feelings on which knowledge necessarily depends. (3.) If we are told that many of the insane

do know right from wrong, and that they are kept in order
in asylums by this knowledge, by fear of punishment and
hope of reward, we answer that their knowledge of right
and wrong is childlike and imperfect, that the system of rewards and punishments is one adapted to the insane as is
that which we apply to children, and that for violence and
grave offences committed in an asylum no one thinks of holding the patients responsible, or of handing them over to the
law.   Judges have been upheld in their notions of lunatics
knowing right from wrong by the answers of witnesses who
encourage and affirm it as a fact.   But a person of unsound
mind cannot be said by one of us to know right from wrong
in any way which would render him amenable to criminal
punishment.

LECTURE XVI.

THERE is another variety of insanity, or rather another class of insane patients, in whom, as in the last mentioned, no delusions are to be discovered, and whose insanity is manifested rather by what they do than what they say. This is *impulsive* or *instinctive* insanity, the victims of which under an *impulse* or *instinct* do something, commit some crime or act of violence, for which, being insane, they are not to be held responsible, but for which, were they insane, they would be punished. This form of insanity is considered by many to be closely allied to the last, the "moral insanity" of Prichard. By some it is considered as a variety of "emotional insanity." Dr. Maudsley describes it as one division of "affective insanity," "moral insanity" being the other.

Impulsive insanity.

As we saw that a great many patients, in various states and stages of insanity, may be, and have been, grouped together by one feature common to all, viz., the absence of delusions, and are called "morally insane," because, there being no delusions, their intellect is supposed to be sound, so we shall find that a number of different lunatics have been said to be suffering from *impulsive insanity*, having this feature in common, that they committed, tried, or desired to commit, some act of violence, yet appeared to be free from everything like delusion.

Characterized by criminal acts.

The crime itself is held to be evidence of the insanity, and

is accounted for upon the theory that the person is suddenly
and insanely impelled to commit it. We cannot be surprised
that in courts of law "impulsive insanity without delusion"
is regarded with great suspicion, and, together with "moral
insanity," is looked upon by lawyers as a chimera of philan-
thropic doctors, who consider all grave crimes to be acts of
madness. I have no doubt, however, that if we could sufficiently examine all the cases of so-called "impulsive insanity,"
and really ascertain the entire history and phenomena previous and subsequent to the commission of the act, we should
find many other signs and symptoms of insanity, and should
be able to assign to the majority of the patients places in the
ranks of the ordinary varieties and classes of the insane.
And this you must endeavor to do, considering the individual
before you rather than any particular variety or theory of
insanity, and bringing together every fact in his life and history—his bodily ailments, demeanor, words, and acts—which
will prove to your own satisfaction and that of others that
he is unsound of mind.

I believe that the mistake made by those who describe so
many cases as *impulsive insanity* is this: they have not proved
too much, but too little. Instead of saying there is a form
of insanity which impels patients to commit violent acts, they
might have gone much further, and said that all insanity is
All insanity impulsive, all insane patients are liable to commit
impulsive. such acts. A. is an insane patient, therefore it is
likely that he will do such an act. We shall then have to
prove, not that A. is afflicted with a particular kind of insanity, but that being insane in some degree or other, he
committed the act. We have already seen, and laid it down
as a truth, that patients may be insane, and yet have no delusions. If one of these commits a crime, we need go no
further than to say that he, being insane, has committed an
impulsive act of violence, his insanity being manifest from
such and such symptoms. And these symptoms we must

very carefully analyze and set forth, so that they may carry to others the conviction they bring to us. It may be that the act itself is the chief or only symptom. I think close observation will generally disclose others, possibly not always. Yet, as we pronounce patients who have no delusions to be insane because of their outrageous and absurd doings, totally inconsistent with their ordinary character and habits, so we may recognize insanity in an act of violence equally inconsistent with the known character of the individual, or in one which none but a madman would commit. There may be such cases, but I believe them to be few. Where these crimes are committed, I think close and skilled observation will generally link the act with other symptoms or causes of mental aberration, and as science and the study of brain-disorder advance, we shall recognize more and more the alliance of the different neuroses, the affinity—nay, close relationship—of epilepsy and insanity, chorea and insanity, hypochondria and insanity, and even drunkenness and insanity. The extent to which drunkenness can produce irresponsibility is a problem which jurists have never settled, and probably never will settle. Dipsomania may proceed from insanity caused by hereditary taint, or a variety of circumstances; or habitual drinking may itself produce dipsomania, or other forms of unsoundness of mind, to say nothing of *delirium tremens.* But all this is to be observed in view of each particular case. My present purpose is to consider the impulsive acts of the insane, especially of those whose insanity, not being marked by delusions, is chiefly indicated by the act itself. The act, however, is plainly the outcome of some idea present for the moment in the mind, but present, possibly, only for the moment, and then so obliterated that the individual afterwards has lost all trace of it. As Dr. Maudsley says :[1] "It is no longer an idea the relations of

Explanation of the impulse.

---

[1] Op. cit , p. 310.

which the mind can contemplate, but a violent impulse into which the mind is absorbed, and which irresistibly utters itself in action." This being done, the feeling and idea, having expended themselves in action, may cease for a time, till the morbid process is enacted over again in the brain. These speculations tally with what we observe in so many instances. The patient having committed the act he desired to commit, whether one of homicide or merely of violence and mischief, wakes up, so to speak; and whether horrified at what he has done, or satisfied at having given vent in action to the craving experienced, he at any rate feels the latter no longer. This irresistible desire to do something—to commit suicide or homicide, to smash windows, or merely to strike a blow at something or somebody—is quite a different thing from acting under a delusion, under a fear of coming harm, a fancied command from on high, or a causeless enmity. Yet that such feelings are felt is admitted, certainly by all who make insanity their study, and by others also who are most removed from any predilections for the theories of lunacy doctors. A writer in the "Saturday Review"[1] says: "*The law must recognize facts,* and many cases (of homicidal impulse) have occurred which can hardly be described by any other name." And Casper, the great Prussian medico-jurist, whom none will accuse of undue leniency towards alleged lunatics, says: "There are still other cases whose actual existence I am all the less inclined to deny, as I myself have had occasion to make similar observations. These pure cases, that is, those in which, without the individual having labored under any form whatever of insanity, or having been, from any bodily cause, suddenly and transitorily affected by mental disturbance—those cases, therefore, in which there coexisted with otherwise mental integrity, an 'inexplicable something,' an instinctive desire to kill (Esquirol, Marc, Georget,

---

[1] April 25, 1863.

&c.), are extremely rare, or rather there are extremely few
of these cases published; for I am convinced that such pure
cases actually occur far more frequently than their literary
history would seem to show."[1] That such cases exist, and
are not merely invented by doctors to excuse crime, is sufficiently proved, first, by the observation of patients actually
secluded or treated for this one form of insanity; secondly,
by the confession of those who have suffered from an impulse,
and have either controlled it, or have come voluntarily and
begged to be restrained, feeling unable to control themselves
longer. In fact, there can be no doubt about the existence
of insanity marked by such impulses. The disputed question
is, whether the insanity is not always recognizable by symptoms other than the impulsive act.

The impulse and craving may occur in any insane person,
in those whose insanity is patent in many ways, and in those
where it is hid from the eyes of all who have hitherto seen
the individual. Yet I believe we shall generally be able to
find evidence of mental disease if we only have full Rules for
opportunities of observation, and a full history of the diagnosis.
life and antecedents of the man and his ancestors. I say, if
we have full and sufficient opportunity of observation. This
may fail us, as it has failed many. In that case we had
better say so, and decline giving an opinion, as we should do
in any ordinary medical or surgical case where opportunity
of examining the patient thoroughly was denied. The scandal
which has come upon evidence given in doubtful cases of insanity has arisen from medical men giving their opinions
after an amount of knowledge and examination of the patient
which in no degree warranted any opinion at all. Half an
hour's conversation with a patient may tell us very little
about him; it may be necessary to see him again and again;
to see a woman at various periods of the month; above all,

---

[1] Casper's Forensic Medicine, iv, 334, Sydn. Soc. Trans.

to observe a patient without his knowledge—in the night, at meals, in various occupations, and to see what he writes, if he can be got to write. We shall have to consider his motive for the crime—if it be a crime—the method of its performance, and the preparations for it, and his present feelings with regard to it; to ascertain, so far as we can, the presence or absence of hereditary taint, any illnesses or peculiarities observable, his history as regards former attacks of insanity, epilepsy, blows on the head, or drunkenness; to learn, either from personal inspection or reliable evidence, his conduct and demeanor after the committal up to the time of our examination; and to compare all that we see with what we hear.

When patients are in asylums, and there are ample opportunities of watching them, there is seldom any difficulty in recognizing insanity. Dr. Gray, of Utica, gives the particulars of no less than fifty-two homicidal cases.[1] In no one of these was there any doubt about the insanity; and in Bethlehem formerly, and now at Broadmoor, the medical officers can distinguish the insane from those who are sane, though acquitted on the ground of insanity. I am not, however, disposed to think that it is an easy thing to diagnose insanity by merely visiting a prisoner awaiting trial in one of our prisons, and seeing him perhaps on one occasion only. If the examination were conducted with the care and consideration displayed in French cases, there would be less violent writing and dissatisfaction expressed in our journals when a murderer is acquitted on the ground of insanity, or when the sentence of the jury is reversed in the office of the Home Secretary.

I think you will find, if you go to the root of the matter, that the act which is supposed to be committed under the influence of insane impulse is rarely, if ever, the first symp-

---

[1] American Journal of Insanity, October, 1857.

tom of insanity or brain affection shown by the alleged lunatic. You may be told by friends that they have never seen any insanity in him; but some people cannot see it in five out of six of the patients in an asylum. Other symptoms of insanity usually discoverable. If you can get sufficient information, you will probably discover that he has had former attacks, from which he may or may not have been considered as recovered. Some may have thought him well, while others may have always looked upon him as "odd." At any rate, he will have had previous symptoms; or, possibly, he may have been noticed as being changed and peculiar for some time, short or long, prior to the committal of the act. The latter being the outcome and culmination of a morbid process which the mind has undergone, it would be extraordinary if it occurred quite suddenly in a moment of time. It is foreign to what we know of the pathology of disease generally to suppose that such sudden disorder can arise. It is quite possible that symptoms may be disregarded; but careful inquiry will often lead to the discovery of a connected history of premonitory indications, even if the individual has never before been under restraint. It often happens that after a man is condemned to death this kind of inquiry is instituted; a history of insanity is revealed, the sentence is reversed, and scandal caused by the whole proceeding.

If a criminal has had at some time or other an attack, the present act may arise from a recurrence of insanity, or it may have been committed under the influence of a long-hidden delusion, a relic of the former attack, never lost, though kept under and concealed for years. I believe delusion to be common in these cases, more common than is suspected, and that many so-called impulsive acts are really those where delusions have been hidden, whose promptings the patient has obeyed. And no class of patients is so liable to act upon sudden impulse as those who have hallucinations of hearing. A man hears himself called some insulting name, or accused of some filthy act, and he turns round, and, deeming it to come from some person near him, violently assaults the nearest he sees. Here, however, he will justify the act, and we get a clue to the real state of the case; but it may be thus discovered for the first time that he has had such hallucinations for years.

Besides the history we receive of the individual, of the occurrence of former insanity, epilepsy, strangeness, or alteration of character and habits, and what we learn by our own observation and interrogation, we shall have to take into consideration the character of the act, the mode of committal, and the absence or presence of motive. This is a test of a more uncertain character, but one which cannot be entirely overlooked. The act may be so motiveless, that no one can doubt it must have been that of a madman. When a man murders one known to have been most dear to him, we may suspect insanity, and more than suspect it. It is not the amount of wickedness displayed in the act, but the senselessness of it that we are to regard. As I said, speaking of moral insanity, that there was always evidence of intellectual defect and alteration as well as of mere wrong-doing, so in the impulsive acts of the insane there is not only a wickedness, but an eccentricity, a want of motive, or a motive palpably insane, which points to intellectual and ideational defect or alteration, and not merely to crime, such as we recognize in the acts of a Greenacre or Courvoisier.

On examining the recorded examples of homicidal impulse —and these are the cases to which the theory of impulsive insanity is chiefly applied—we shall find that in almost all that are reported in such detail as to be worthy of notice, and many are not, there was, or had been, general mental derangement. Of the fifty-two cases reported by Dr. Gray, there was manifest insanity in all. I quote from Casper:[1]

---

[1] Op. cit., p. 333, note.

"Marc has collected eight cases of so-called homicidal mania. There is, however, not one among them in which general mental disease did not indubitably exist. Cazauvielh[1] has collected as many as four-and-twenty French cases, among which there are several cases of newly-delivered women who felt an impulse to murder their children. This, of course, was no permanent monomania, but rapidly passed off, and only one of these falls to be considered here as coming under this category. All the others, without exception, refer to lunatics." A celebrated case, reported by Dr. Lockhart Robertson in the "Journal of Mental Science,"[2] was that of a man who, when first admitted into an asylum, had been insane nine months, and heard voices. Such a patient I should consider an incurable lunatic, and if afterwards he committed homicidal acts, I should set them down to the voices, or at any rate to his general condition. There would be no need to have recourse to a theory of impulsive insanity. And many cases so called are those of patients suffering from melancholia.

Let us, however, not as witnesses in courts of law, but as physicians, carefully study the impulsive and un-reasoning acts of people of unsound mind. So com-mon are they amongst the insane, that they attract no special attention when they occur in everyday asylum life. We do not call it impulsive insanity when a lunatic all day long tries to smash the windows, or tears his clothes and bedding to shreds, or incessantly endeavors to set himself and the house on fire. Yet, perchance, he can give no reason for any of these things. He has no delusion in connection therewith. He has very few delusions. He is in that state of partial insanity which would be unrecognizable by many; and yet he is in every sense of the word a lunatic, and his impulsive acts are the result of his general condition.

Impulsive acts common amongst all the insane.

---

[1] Annales d'Hygiène Publ., t. xvi, p. 121.   [2] April, 1861.

Were every impulsive act carefully recorded, we should see how numerous they are, and also see that the lunacy of those committing them is plain and undoubted. We should look upon them as peculiarities of lunatics, like dirty habits, shameless masturbation, or hallucinations and delusions.

Besides the various patients who are in one shape or other
Weak-
minded or
imbecile
patients. *insane*, who are changed and altered from their former sane condition, or who commit acts inconsistent with reason and healthy mind, your opinion will be sought in the case of others, who, though not insane in the ordinary sense of the word, are, nevertheless, of unsound mind, and incapable of taking care of themselves and their affairs. When an attempt is made to bring the lunacy laws to bear upon them, a quibble is always raised as to their not being *insane;* but the lunacy laws have for their subject all " persons of unsound mind," whatever the form of unsoundness may be, and this has been decided by the Court of Appeal. I shall mention two varieties of unsoundness, concerning which you may be consulted: one a weakness or imbecility of mind, congenital, or the result of disease in early life, whence the individual is through life deficient, below the standard of other sound people, and incapable of taking care of himself, his condition being a destitution of powers that never were possessed; the other being an enfeeblement and decay of a once healthy mind coming on after insanity, epilepsy, and brain disease of all kinds, or being the dotage and decline of sheer old age. The latter is much easier to recognize and to deal with legally than the former, the subjects of which have given rise to some of our most celebrated forensic contests. They may come under your notice at any period of their lives, but, as a rule, it will be at the time when they are ceasing to be boys and girls, and beginning to be men and women. It is found that though men in years, they are still children in mind; if men, men only in wickedness and vice, children still in intellect and in the

sense of duty and responsibility. These weak-minded youths are not to be called idiots, though they are but one grade higher. They are weak-minded imbeciles, and the imbecility may be congenital, or have been brought about by convulsions and fits in infancy or early life, arresting the due development of the brain. In a humble station, these boys and girls swell the ranks of criminals, and become the constant inmates of a prison, unless they are fortunate enough to be carried off to the more permanent haven of an asylum. In higher society parents are horrified at finding them indulging in vices and propensities tending to the same end, and seek our advice and assistance. But it is not always easy to give them the latter, for it is often very difficult to deal with such patients legally. Testing them for the various symptoms of insanity, we shall find that there is very little to warrant our signing a certificate for their care and detention. Possibly they may be approaching the age of twenty-one, and the question will arise whether they are or are not fit to take care of property? Or they may be uncontrollable by any government, home or tutorial, and even at an early age are addicted to practices which entail the interference and punishment of the law. These children have no delusions; none need be looked for, for none will be found. They are not changed in habits and demeanor. They are now what they always have been—stubborn, eccentric, spiteful, mischievous, often horribly cruel, vain, perfectly devoid of truth, incapable of being taught, but picking up in a desultory way many scraps of information, and holding these with a most tenacious memory; given, perhaps, to some one amusement or hobby, and doing this for a time fairly well, but irregular and restless, fond of change and novelty, and wholly unable to settle down assiduously and constantly to one pursuit. The parents, if gentlefolks, seek the physician's assistance; but, as I have just said, this is often hard to afford. How are we to test these patients? Impressed with the symptoms of dementia, we try their memory, and find it excellent. We watch them at dinner and in society, and we find they conduct themselves with perfect propriety. We examine them as to the value of money, and they evince a keen appreciation of the amount of amusement to be got out of half a crown or half a sovereign. On the common topics of life they will converse readily and accurately, read the miscellaneous news of the journals, and recollect what they have read. And they may excuse their ignorance of other matters on the ground of their education having been neglected, or, if we ask them concerning their property and affairs, may say that these have always been managed for them, and that they have had no occasion to attend to them. In short, a formal examination of such people may tell us nothing. They are on their guard and good behavior, and if we tax them with their sins, they confess them, allow it was wrong, and promise amendment. Only those who live with, and have opportunities of observing them at all times, with and without their knowledge, can give a just and complete account of their mental state. If we ourselves have no such opportunity, we must receive the statement of those who have, and test it, so far as we can, by our own observation. Possibly we may not be able to pronounce an opinion. We must at any rate be careful how we give a negative opinion, based on our imperfect information, in opposition to that of others who have had ampler opportunities of coming to a sound conclusion.

The chief characteristics of these patients are a childish-
Character-   ness in mind, showing itself in an inability to learn,
istics.   think, or reason like others of the same age and
social standing; frequently, but not always, a tendency to low and depraved habits, to vice of a kind not to be looked for at such an age, and an unnatural hatred and malice exhibited to parents, brothers, or sisters. Great stress has been laid on this moral depravity, and theories of moral insanity

have been founded upon it. Without discussing the question of an innate moral sense, I would say that, in conjunction with the depravity, we shall, I feel confident, find in such patients a low and imperfectly-developed intellect, incapable, because of its feebleness and childishness, of finding pleasure in anything but the brutish and sensual enjoyments of the body. It may be able to lay up the facts of every-day life and experience—may know how much pleasure a shilling may buy, but of knowledge to be derived from reasoning, judgment, and reflection, it possesses none. But it is most difficult to say this man is imbecile, and that one is not—to set up a standard, not of insanity, but of sufficiency of mind. It was said by Sir Hugh Cairns in the Windham case that— "In a case of imbecility, where there is either no mind at all, or next to none, the task of coming to a right and just decision is comparatively easy. It is impossible for a man who is said to have only a limited amount of mind, or none at all, to assume at any moment or for any purpose a greater amount of mind than he really possesses. If the mind is not there, or only there in a certain small and limited quantity, no desire on the part of the individual to show a greater amount of mind, or to assume the appearance of a greater amount of mind, can supply him with that which nature has denied him. Hence, when a man is charged with imbecility, if it can be shown that for a considerable time, and in various situations, he has acted like a natural being, any acts of folly which might be alleged against him should be carefully, deliberately, and keenly investigated, because at first sight it is next to impossible that a man can at certain times assume a mind and intelligence which are wholly absent." These remarks show the difficulty we have to pronounce upon the absence of mind—in fact, to prove a negative—and not the entire absence, but the absence of a particular amount and measure of mind. As Sir Hugh Cairns suggested, a man's acts of sanity must be weighed against his acts of folly. In all these cases acts are of far more importance than words; for there being no delusions, and the ideas of these weak and uneducated persons being but scanty, we are not likely to detect much that is erroneous or extraordinary in what they say. By what they do, however, or would like to do, they betray their imbecility and incapacity for taking care of themselves. They are not uncommon, and you will not be long in practice without meeting with some examples. The particulars of one or two I have already recorded in the "Journal of Mental Science,"[1] and will briefly give here. One was a youth, well born, with every advantage of educa-

Cases. tion which wealth could give. When I first knew him he was between fifteen and sixteen years of age. As a child he was looked upon as weak-minded, and though he had been at various schools and tutors, education had stood still, and his handwriting, spelling, and letter-writing, would have been bad for a boy of eight. When I first saw him he was living with a man who was to him virtually an attendant, whom he hated no less than feared. Thence he was sent to a farmer's to learn farming, but one evening he assaulted the maid, took out a horse from the stable, rode off to the nearest town, and took up his quarters at a small public house. Thence, brought back to his first quarters, he escaped to Brighton, pawning all he could carry off. He was placed in lodgings with various attendants, with each of whom he got on very well for a time, during which he was on his good behavior; then he had an outburst of passion because he was not allowed to do as he liked, and would do nothing right till the attendant was changed. His tastes were low, his pleasures either depraved or childish; yet he was not utterly bad: he valued the good opinion of his father and mother and my own, but this he was constantly forfeiting, for which he was sorry, but, as he said, "he could

---

[1] April, 1869.

not help it." Next he went to a medical man's house, and behaved for a month or two so well that the character he took with him was thought to be unjustly exaggerated. But he broke down and behaved outrageously, and then an attempt was made to place him in an asylum. However, the certifying medical gentleman stated nothing in the certificate but acts of depravity, and the Commissioners in Lunacy refused to receive them, so he was released. Since then he twice enlisted in the army, but was bought out again by his friends. On the second occasion, however, he was in the regiment for some months, kept clear of scrapes, and had a good character from his sergeant, but he was looked upon as "not right." He then took to race-courses and set up as a betting man, and after this threatened his father's life, was brought before a magistrate, and locked up. There can be no doubt that this youth will degenerate into one of the regular criminal class, unless he is fortunate enough to get to an asylum. Here he would at times beg to be allowed to go, at others he would defy any one to send him.

Now, of those who by constant intercourse with this youth had the best opportunity of rightly judging of his mental state, no one thought him of sound mind. And yet his unsoundness was not at once manifest, nor was it easy to reduce it to a short verbal description. Probably, on no one given day could any medical man have seen sufficient to enable him to sign a valid certificate, yet he was imbecile and childish. His attainments and mental calibre were those of a child of eight or nine; and although in certain strata of society education marks little, yet in the highest ranks an incapacity to receive even the elements of education is significant. He would repeat the same question over and over again like a demented patient. This, again, though not much in itself, is a common symptom of the loss of memory or attention which characterizes the feeble-minded. He displayed that love of change, that periodicity of outbreak and restlessness, so often met with. He could go on quietly and well for a certain time, but then he found a vent, either in passionate quarrelling, drinking, or riotous behavior of one kind or other. And this I verily believe he could not control or help. He had a good memory and a certain sharpness about details, which are not uncommon, even among idiots. He knew the times of all the omnibuses on the road, and could give the times of trains according to " Bradshaw " by the column. He was sharp enough in calculations of pence and shillings, but he would have been perfectly incapable of taking care of an estate, or any large property. His head was very small, his whole development of brain and mind in defect. He had no powers of reasoning, and he lived, in fact, the life of an animal, only caring to gratify his appetites.

Such another was a youth who was possessed of some few hundred pounds—or would have been in a few months, as he was approaching the age of twenty-one. This his friends wished to protect, and applied to the Lords Justices for an order.[1] He had run the same course as the former, but instead of being sent to learn farming, he had been sent to sea. He knew, however, nothing about a ship, though he had twice sailed to Australia. He had run away while out there, and ran away, in fact, wherever he was. He could tell me nothing about what he had seen, neither could he tell the name of the street in London in which he was living. He was defective both in attention and in judgment. He had no idea of doing anything with his money when he got it, but thought he should set up a dog-cart. He seemed to be entirely ignorant of everything connected with property, securities, and investments. He was plainly unfit to have the care of property, and the Lords Justices made the order accordingly.

---

[1] *Vide* Lect. XIX.

One of these doubtful cases was that of a girl whose father's family was saturated with insanity. She had quarrelled with her sisters, her mother, and innumerable governesses. She had fits of obstinacy, during which she refused to do anything required of her. She was peculiar, would dress fantastically, would cut off the toes of her stockings, and do other odd things which were not mere child's mischief. Vain and conceited, she spoke of her mother and her sisters as poor unenlightened creatures, affected much knowledge, and pretended to read deep books; yet she was intellectually deficient and backward for her age. She spelt badly, and could not be taught. When walking with her mother she would signal to strange men in the street, and talk of her wish to get married. She was such an extraordinary liar that it was a work of time to realize the fact that all her stories were lies. She went to Scotland, and I lost sight of her, but I have no doubt that her unsoundness of mind will become more and more patent.

Your opinion will be asked with regard to the training of these imbecile children, as well as the restraint by legal means. When all tutors and governesses Treatment. have been exhausted, the friends will seek medical aid, finding their own efforts more productive of harm than good. Parents, as a rule, have but little influence, neither are they in general judicious in their conduct towards them. You must recollect that such unsoundness is for the most part inherited, and you will detect peculiarities in the father or mother — great irritability, intemperance, or weakness of character. Fathers are often very harsh and severe to these children; and mothers, on the other hand, screen their faults, and so encourage vicious propensities. Those of you who see them from childhood may do much by counsel and advice to promote their welfare and improvement. You will rescue them from blows, imprisonment, and undue punishment — from the irritation of angry parents, and the indulgence of foolish ones: above all, from being handed over entirely to the mercy of servants and attendants. Sooner or later these boys and girls are found such a pest at home that they are sent away, first of all to school. But few schools can keep them; and then the boys go to a tutor, the girls to a family. Here everything depends on the character of the individual who controls them. It requires a high order of mind, together with unwearied assiduity and vigilance, to train with success these blighted waifs of humanity. Yet it may sometimes be done. The great problem is to find out something, some walk or occupation, for which the child is fitted. Many are capable of doing something. We are dealing with a defective mind, a mind incapable of following the pursuits of those in the same sphere of life — incapable of commanding a regiment or a ship — incapable of studying for a learned profession; but capable, it may be, of executing the mechanical work of doing such things as we see done at Earlswood; or pleased at being occupied about animals— horses, or dogs—and, under judicious and kindly surveillance, capable of a habit of self-control and regularity. Parents may shrink from having their son put to a trade; many would far rather shut up in an asylum sons and daughters who are likely to disgrace the family. But I need not use argument to prove that it is better to bring up boys or girls in a humble occupation, in which they may cultivate self-restraint and self-respect, than to apply restraint by force of law.

I now come to the second class, patients whose minds have
Demented fallen into decay from disease of the brain of some
patients. kind, or from old age. There is little difficulty in recognizing this condition. I only mention it because you are to recollect that they come under the provisions of the Lunacy Acts, just as maniacs or any other insane persons; and if sent away from home, they must be placed under certificates of lunacy, if they cannot be pronounced able to take

care of themselves and their affairs. I have known the mental condition of these individuals disputed in a court of law under such circumstances as I have alluded to; but, as a rule, there is not much contention about it during their lives. Their defect is palpable, irremediable, and ever increases till death; but after that, a contest often arises over their wills, and we hear evidence to prove, on the one hand, that the testator was a drivelling dotard, on the other that he was like other people—so differently do witnesses regard the sayings and doings of other men.

The most constant defect met with among these patients is loss of memory, varying at different times and in degree. Chiefly, the individual forgets recent occur- *Defects to be noticed.* rences, retaining a vivid remembrance of the days of his youth. He may forget the names of those most near to him, the name of the place in which he is residing, and may be unable to give any accurate information respecting his business and affairs. Now, to be of disposing mind—to be capable of making a will—a man must be, as the lawyers say, of "sound mind, memory, and understanding." It is clear that memory is essential to sanity, so clear that I need not dwell upon it. But the degree of failure of memory may vary much. Some people have naturally bad memories; some have great difficulty in recollecting names; others forget dates; and you will have to consider, in view of each individual case, whether the failure of memory is to such an ex tent as to separate the patient from all who can be called sound and sane in mind, and render him palpably unable to take care of himself and his affairs. You will ask, could such a one shift for himself, take a lodging or house, come and go unattended, and pay his accounts? If he could not, he must be allowed to be unsound of mind. It is more difficult, however, to come to a conclusion in respect of a lady. For ladies frequently do not take care of themselves or their affairs at any time of their lives, nor do they pretend or claim to do so. Many could not who are yet of sound mind, and able to make a will. You must take this into account when you are examining ladies with a view to testing their mental strength or weakness. I lately examined a lady who had been in former years an inmate of an asylum, and who since then had lived as a boarder in a family. She met all questions as to her affairs, by saying that she left all that to her man of business, and on common topics she talked well enough. There was no loss of memory, and though I do not suppose she could have lived entirely by herself, yet there was nothing to make me certify that she was legally of unsound mind. It was just a case for the guardianship of trustees, who already existed. Failure of memory you will look for in these cases of dementia, and will estimate it according to its gravity; and you will often find yourself assisted by other symptoms, such as dirty habits and tricks, wetting or fouling clothes and bedding, or conversations devoid of delicacy or decency.

Two gentlemen I saw in this condition, who, up to the time of inquiries made by the Commissioners in Lunacy, had been living under care and guardianship away from their friends, who, nevertheless, did not consider them insane, because they had no delusions.

Cases.

One of them was in an advanced stage of dementia. His memory was gone. He did not know the name of the proprietor of the house, nor that of his daughter, nor, in fact, any name but his own. He did not recollect how long he had been there, whether months or years. By night he had forgotten that he had seen his daughter in the morning, though her visits were of rare occurrence. He kept repeating over and over again the same sentence, without reason and without being addressed. His habits and person were filthy beyond description, as was the miserable room where I found him lying on bedding that was literally a dung-heap, yet in which he remained voluntarily and contentedly. This gentleman's condition was that of dementia following on hemi-plegic attacks. He was not hemiplegic, however, when I saw him, but, with slow and shuffling step, could walk some miles in a day. The state of his person sufficiently indicated that of his mind, which was altogether deficient and gone; yet lawyers were found to argue that, because he had no delu-sions, he was not "insane."

The other had been insane, and frequently an inmate of asylums. His insanity was, as I understood, the result of drink, and it had terminated in dementia. His memory was gone; he did not recollect that he had placed all his affairs in the hands of trustees; but told me that he had a balance at his banker's, and that he drew cheques, which his ser-vant got cashed, when he had done nothing of the kind for years. He, too, would repeat the same sentence and ask the same question over and over again; and was dirty in habits; though not neglected like the former patient.

Now, you will have no difficulty in appreciating the condi-tion of such people. They cannot conceal their defects, especially this great loss of memory; but the opinion you are to give concerning them may have reference to one of several things. You may be consulted as to the power of such a patient to make a will or execute a legal instrument, as the sale of an estate, and you may be requested to act as one of the witnesses in such a matter. You may be asked to sign a certificate of lunacy, or give an affidavit and evidence for a commission in lunacy; or you may have to advise as to the chances of amelioration or recovery. And to take the last of these, we may look as a rule upon chronic dementia as hopeless and incurable. But we must inquire into the his-tory; for it occasionally happens that what at first sight ap-pears very like incurable dementia passes off in course of time. I am not now alluding to what I have already de-scribed as "acute dementia," which is a variety of acute insanity; but we sometimes find that after an apoplectic or epileptic attack, or even after an acute disease such as fever, there is for weeks or months great weakness of intellect, with loss of memory, and complete inability to transact business, and yet the patient may perfectly recover and be himself again. Time, therefore, is our great guide in prognosis here, as in other mental affections; where the dementia is beyond question chronic, it is not likely that the individual will again be able to take care of himself or his affairs. There may be also great improvement in the mental and bodily condition of a demented patient, even when recovery is out of the question. Those who are much neglected, and are to be found occasionally in an abject state of filth and destitution in private houses, are susceptible of much amelioration if properly tended and fed. You will recollect that certificates will be required if they are not under the care of their relations, whether they are in an asylum or in a private house. As regards their competency to make a will or transact business, you will, of course, carefully weigh the extent of the imbecility, and the importance of that which they are about to do. You may allow a patient to sign a receipt for money, whom you might think unequal to transact any involved or lengthy business. Let it be your rule, generally, not to sanction with your presence, or attesting signature, the execution of any document by a person whose mind is in any way affected, for you may find yourselves involved in troublesome legal contests.

LECTURE XVII.

Terminations of Insanity — Liability of Recurrence — Recovery often
Imperfect—How recognizable—Release of Dangerous Patients to be
refused—Concealed Insanity—A Trial to be advised—Recurring In-
sanity — Lucid Intervals — Recoveries numerous — Chance of Life—
Causes of Death—Diagnosis of Bodily Disease—Care of the Chronic
Insane.

I PROPOSE, in the present lecture, to consider briefly the
terminations of an attack of insanity; for you will be called
upon in practice to pronounce an opinion upon various points
in the after-history of one who has at any time so suffered,
whether he has recovered or not. He may recover from an
acute attack, only to continue in a state of chronic insanity.
In this condition is his life likely to be of long or short duration? If he recover altogether, is he liable to a recurrence,
and what is his chance in a second or third attack? If he
were to insure his life after having recovered from one attack,
what is the value of his life? To answer these questions is
no easy matter. We must have recourse to those asylums
whose numbers are large, otherwise our deductions must be
formed upon very insufficient data; but it is very difficult to
follow the fortunes of all those who are discharged from a
large asylum, and to speak with accuracy of the subsequent
history of their life and death. Dr. Thurnam, however, while
at the York Retreat—the asylum belonging to the Society of
Friends—had singular facilities for tracing the subsequent
history of the patients discharged thence; and, among many
most interesting tables of statistics, he gives one, which I
will quote:

"Table showing the history of two hundred and forty-four persons who died at, or after discharge from, the York Retreat, from 1796 to 1840, with the number who died during, and after recovery from, the first or subsequent attack of mental disorder."

Cases followed through life.	Died Insane during the First Attack.	Recovered from the First Attack.					
		Total.	Recovery Permanent. Died Sane.	Had subsequent Attacks.			
				Died Sane.	Died Insane.	Total.	
Males, 113	55	58	21	6	31	37
Females, 131	58	73	24	14	35	49
Total, 244	113	131	45	20	66	86

Now although, as Dr. Thurnam says, certain deductions must be made from the picture which this table exhibits, it must still be allowed to be a melancholy one. 244 persons of the middle ranks of life, not poor and destitute, but well-to-do people, as the Friends generally are, become insane, and of these only 131, or 53.6 per cent., recover from the first attack; the rest never recover, and die insane. But looking at the after-history of the 131, we find that only 45, or 18.4 per cent. of the whole remain permanently sane. The rest are again insane, once or oftener, and of these only 20 die sane. "In round numbers, then, of ten persons attacked by insanity, five recover and five die, sooner or later, during the attack. Of the five who recover, not more than two remain well during the rest of their lives, the other three sustain subsequent attacks during which at least two of them die. But although the picture is thus an unfavorable one, it is very far from justifying the popular prejudice that insanity is virtually an incurable disease; and the view which it presents is much modified by the long intervals which often occur between the attacks, during which intervals of mental health (in

Liability to subsequent attacks.

many cases of from ten to twenty years' duration) the individual has lived in all the enjoyments of social life."

Although the statistics derived from my own experience would be too scanty to be worth anything, they would, I believe, fully bear out the assertion of Dr. Thurnam. If we could carefully watch every case of insanity from its commencement, I fear we should see that a less number than 53 per cent. recover from the first attack, so great is the proportion of those who are incurable from the first, or who, from the prejudices of friends, are not subjected to treatment till the chance of cure is gone; and if by dint of proper treatment the above percentage recover, they only recover again to become insane in a large proportion. Although it would not only be uncharitable, but unscientific and at variance with facts, to look on all who have once been insane as lunatics for the rest of their lives, it must yet be confessed that popular prejudice receives considerable support from these statistics, and men may look with reasonable suspicion on former inmates of an asylum, when they hear that of those said to have recovered only two out of five remain permanently well. We may fairly say, that when a man or a woman has once been insane, no one can tell when he or she may not again become so. The changes and chances of life are not to be guarded against. With the utmost caution a former patient may be suddenly exposed to the shock of some horrible sight or accident, to the loss of one most dear, or to reverses of fortune. And, therefore, if you are consulted about the propriety of such a person contracting marriage, or entering into a partnership or any engagement whatever, recollect that he is exposed to extra risk on account of what he has already gone through, and that his previous recovery does not insure his subsequent immunity or subsequent recovery from future attacks. I have said already that a woman who has at any time been insane ought to be preserved from the peril of childbirth for her own sake, to say nothing of the danger incurred by her children.   A man is, of course, exposed to less personal risk by marriage : probably to him the married state is rather an advantage than otherwise.   He is thereby induced to lead a regular life, and has at hand a constant companion and nurse, who is aware if his nights are sleepless, or if he has peculiar habits or ideas, such as often escape for a length of time the observation of friends or more distant relatives. But we are not to forget that the man may become insane again, nay, will most likely be so, that his wife will have all the anxiety, and be exposed to the dangers consequent upon such an event, and that children may inherit allied maladies, or the disorder itself in its many forms.

When we closely examine the state of those said to have

Recovery frequently imperfect.

recovered, we may find that the recovery is suffi- cient perhaps to warrant their being discharged from the asylum, and to be called cured by their friends, but that ever afterwards they are odd and eccentric, or easily upset by the merest trifles, or they periodically break out into violence or an acute state, which ought rather to be called an exacerbation of their habitual condition than a fresh attack of insanity.   I had formerly under my care on various occasions an old farmer whose first attack was, I believe, at the age of seventeen, his last was when he was upwards of eighty, and in the interval he had been in an asylum nearly thirty times.   He used to stay some months, his excitement then passed away, and he returned home to be his own master.   He was discharged in the books as "re- covered," but he had not really regained sound mind—he had only recovered from an acute attack of excitement; he did not even lose his delusions, for he had, if I am not mis- taken, a persistent delusion throughout his whole life that he was married to a noble lady.   Dr. Sankey, in his Lec- tures, lays great stress on these half-recovered cases.   He believes that recovery from the first attack is not so common as might be thought from statistics; "that, therefore, what appears to be, and is usually called, a second attack, is no such thing. I believe that there is a remnant of the old disease, a smouldering of the morbid processes still left in these cases, though often very difficult of detection. . . . This under-current of disease is, as I have said, more marked or less marked. In those cases in which it is obvious, and constantly so, the patient would be simply called a chronic lunatic, or he would have perhaps that form of chronic insanity to which the title *folie circulaire* has been given; but in the class in which the mental symptoms are exaggerated at distant periods, and a great degree of intellectual integrity remains in the interval, the disease would be called by a host of names, according to the different views of different authors. For my own part, I would include all these cases under the one term of *recurrent mania,* or *recurrent insanity.*"[1]

Dr. Sankey goes on further to say, that he has examined the reports of a great many persons accused of acts of violence, and he found in every case that the violent deed was not the *first insane act* of the lunatic. When we hear of cases of impulsive insanity, and it is stated that no insane symptoms had ever been observed before the commission of the act, he is of opinion that such statements emanate from those who are not capable of making a correct diagnosis, or who ignore the fact that there has been a former attack of insanity, or suppose perfect recovery to have taken place, and the subsequent attack to be altogether a fresh and distinct event.

How are you to know when a patient is recovered? We have the same difficulty in deciding this as is so often experienced in determining in the first instance, whether a man is, or is not, insane.

How is recovery to be recognized?

---

[1] Lectures on Mental Diseases, p. 94.

We find patient's friends, lawyers, and others not versed in the study of mental diseases, contending that a man is cured when the chief symptoms of acute insanity have abated, and he can talk rationally on some points—when, in short, they are unable to see insanity plainly depicted in his words and actions.   And then in this semi-recovered condition they demand his release.   He may have only got rid of half his delusions, or may have learned to conceal them, or may have lost them, and yet be in a weak and unstable nervous state, requiring repose and a considerable period of convalescence; yet the demand for his release may be loud and persistent, and in withstanding it, you will meet with many difficulties. More especially will this be the case with private patients. The friends of paupers care less for their release.   In public asylums they are carefully kept at the expense of the county, but the friends of private patients, thinking that those who have charge of them have an interest in their detention, set up their own opinion concerning the question of recovery in opposition to the interested, as they suppose, advice of the medical attendant.   If patients are ever discharged too early from public asylums, it is probably due to the overcrowded state.   There can be no question that they are frequently released too soon from private establishments on account of the importunities of friends, and the unwillingness of proprietors to submit to the insinuations and misrepresentations of the latter.   When there is brought against a medical man the accusation that he is detaining a sane man for the pecuniary advantage to be gained thereby, it requires considerable moral courage to withstand such pressure.   Yet in many cases it is our duty to do so, and by dint of temperate arguments, and the assistance of collateral friends and advisers, to prevent the disastrous result which may follow the release of a half-cured patient.

Such a state of things is contemplated by the legislature,

and provided for. If a lunatic's friends determine to release him from an asylum, the medical attendant may, if he considers him dangerous, refuse to liberate him. In the Lunacy Act, 1845, 8 & 9 Vict. c. 100, § 75, we read : " Be it enacted, that no patient shall Release of dangerous patients may be refused.
be removed, under any of the powers hereinbefore contained, from any licensed house or any hospital, if the physician, surgeon, or apothecary, by whom the same shall be kept, or shall be the regular medical attendant thereof, shall by writing under his hand certify that in his opinion such patient is dangerous and unfit to be at large, together with the grounds on which such opinion is founded, unless the commissioners visiting such house, or the visitors of such house, shall, after such certificate shall have been produced to them, give their consent in writing that such patient shall be discharged or removed; provided that nothing herein contained shall prevent any patient from being transferred from any licensed house, or any hospital, to any other licensed house or any other hospital, or to any asylum; but in such case every such patient shall be placed under the control of an attendant belonging to the licensed house, hospital, or asylum to or from which he shall be about to be removed for the purpose of such removal, and shall remain under such control until such time as such removal shall be duly effected."

Here, then, you see that power is given to prevent the release of dangerous patients. We cannot, however, prevent their being transferred to another asylum; but when the friends apply to the commissioners for an "order of transfer," the latter always write to the medical attendant, and require from him a certificate that the patient is capable of being removed with safety; and without such certificate no "order of transfer" is granted. It often happens that removal to another asylum is of great service to a patient whom we cannot release: great soreness may have arisen between him and those who have had the control of him, and removal and change of scene and attendants may effect a cure which would not otherwise have come to pass.

But, to revert to our question, how are you to know when a patient is recovered, and may fitly be trusted with the management of himself and his affairs?   As an alteration in the general bearing, demeanor, and habits of a man is the surest sign of mental disorder, so an alteration from the state in which we receive him as a patient, is an indication of amelioration or recovery.   But our difficulty in pronouncing an opinion as to perfect recovery is often great when we have never known the patient in his previous sane condition. You, who will become not asylum doctors, but family advisers, will first see a man sane, then insane; and if, at the termination of an attack of insanity, you are called to examine him, you may be able to say at once that he is, or is not, himself, and may give most valuable assistance to the asylum doctor, who may erroneously suppose that he is not, or is, cured.   Friends are so apt to be biassed, and near relatives are so often themselves crotchety and peculiar, that we hail with satisfaction the information to be gained from others. Friends are frequently over-eager to release the lunatic because of his displeasure, or over-fearful of setting him at liberty lest he relapse.   Alteration in character and manner will be a test of recovery when the patient is greatly improved, and has got rid of delusions, when, in fact, it might be very difficult to sign a certificate for him.   With all this amendment, his manner may not be natural.   He may be unduly depressed, excitable, or irritable.   His friends will ascribe this to the detention, if they wish his release, and will tell you they are quite sure that it is thus produced, and that it will pass away when the cause is removed.   But it is a fact within my experience, that we do not see this depression or excitement in those who are perfectly cured, and know that their stay in the asylum is only a question of weeks or days.   Friends imagine that a patient cannot be

aware that he is in an asylum without its having a prejudicial effect; but this is not so, for he will go on to perfect
recovery in it in spite of their fears and remonstrances.
Sometimes it happens that, when a patient is progressing
favorably to recovery, and is not half but wholly cured, his
friends are much more anxious for his release than he is himself, and in this case his wishes and opinion ought to be consulted rather than theirs.

We shall have to base our diagnosis of recovery upon what
we hear from the patient himself concerning his illness, its
cause, and symptoms, such as acts, delusions, or hallucinations; upon what we see of him, his forsaking or continuing
eccentric habits, peculiarities of dress or demeanor; on what
we hear of him from attendants and others, when he is out
of our observation; and on what we are told by relatives,
friends, or medical attendants. And then we shall have to
decide whether a condition of apparent recovery is a genuine
and perfect recovery, or merely an interval between attacks
of recurrent insanity.

It is a bad sign when a patient will not allow that anything has been the matter with him, or insists that his condition has been caused by his friends shutting him up, ignor-
ing all that occurred before he was shut up, and attributing
evil motives to all concerned. A patient may assert wrongly
that he has recovered, or that he never was ill at all; that
his delusions, so called, were not delusions; and that his acts
were justifiable. Of course, if his delusions are absurdities,
and he holds them now, his state is not a matter of doubt;
but a man who has recovered from delusions may be unwill-
ing to allow that he has held any, and may explain them
away, singling out the grain of truth that may be at the
foundation of them, and justifying the whole by this. Now,
it may be thought that a patient cannot be recovered who
justifies previous delusions, even if he does not hold them;
but much allowance must be made for individual tempera-

ment and character. Some men and women cannot bear to think that they have been insane, or have entertained insane fancies, or done insane acts, and they satisfy their consciences and salve their wounded pride by explaining away as much as they can. This we must often overlook, and must not too rigidly compel confession from patients, or too closely cross-examine them as to all the details of the past. As I have told you, delusions spring to such an extent out of the feeling of the moment, that a patient a month or two afterwards, in an altered physical condition, cannot go back to the ideas he held in his former state, and may deny that he held them, or may justify them, because he is unable now to enter into a contemplation of another state of things. You must consider the whole manner in which he speaks of the past: if he is ashamed of himself, and would rather let the subject alone, and talks rather of the future, and of returning to work or home, and if all his talk of the present and future is healthy and hopeful, we must not be too particular in judging of the manner in which he speaks of the past. But if he is perpetually harping on the past, reviewing and discussing every detail, always complaining and threatening retaliation, lawsuits, and the like—if he craves for liberty in order to set about such proceedings rather than to return to his usual avocations—we must look with suspicion on his condition, and advise further detention and surveillance, though possibly in a modified form. In coming to a decision on such cases there is no general rule to be laid down or observed. Experience, and the intuitive appreciation of insanity which experience gives, are the only guides to a right judgment.

Another patient may not deny that he has had delusions, Insanity may and may not seek to explain away or justify them, be concealed. but he will assure us that he holds them no longer. There may have been much discussion as to some one or two special delusions which remain after all acute symptoms have subsided, and our patient, grown cunning by experience, and gathering that so long as he holds these opinions he will be restrained and looked on as insane, suddenly gives them up, professes that he holds them no longer, and perhaps expresses an unnecessary degree of astonishment at his ever having held them at all. Yet he may hold them all the time, only denying them to regain his liberty. Here you must take into consideration the whole history of the case. A patient who, during a somewhat acute state of insanity, entertains various delusions, will probably lose them as he passes into a quiet convalescent state. There will be marked improvement in his whole condition; sleep will return, regular habits of eating, attention to cleanliness. fondness for ordinary occupations and amusements; and, in accordance with all this, we should expect also that the delusions and fancies of the insane mind will pass away. But if a man tells you that he has lost his delusions, and yet you observe no change for the better in his habits and appearance—if he still dresses in an extraordinary way, and behaves outrageously—we cannot believe his assertions to be true. With the inconsistency of a lunatic, he may act a delusion at the very time that he denies that he entertains it. We must endeavor to discover whether he has really lost them, or whether he is merely making the assertion to deceive us. Possibly we may find that although he denies them to us, he will confess them to his relations and friends, to other patients, or the attendants. He may betray them in his letters. He will deny that he hears voices, yet we may overhear him talking when alone to imaginary people, and answering imaginary questions. We may notice ornaments about him illustrating delusions concerning imaginary rank and titles, or unfounded hostility towards wife or friends shows that he still entertains the former delusions concerning them.

Where a patient's insanity is displayed not so much in delusions as in acts, and partakes more of the nature of so-called moral insanity, it is not easy to say whether he is or is not recovered. For he is restrained and kept from acts of extravagance or vice, and we cannot, therefore, be sure whether he would return to these or not. But from his general behavior, and by comparing his present with what we hear of his former mode of life—by observing whether there is anything absurd or bizarre in his ways or acts—we may arrive at a tolerably accurate diagnosis. We shall also take into consideration the way in which he justifies his former acts, for this he may do in a manner highly indicative of insanity. I had rather hear a patient deny than justify a very insane act. In the confusion of his brain he may have almost forgotten it; or he may prefer to deny it altogether; pleading "not guilty;" but I have known a lunatic justify acts that none but a lunatic would have perpetrated, and none but a lunatic would defend.

We may have our doubts as to a patient's recovery, may disbelieve his statements, and think his friends too sanguine, but may hesitate about detaining him longer in an asylum. There comes a period in the history of almost every convalescing patient at which change is necessary, when, if he be further restrained in the same place and in the same fashion, he is likely to go back rather than forwards. Although we do not consider him fit to be restored at once to full and unrestricted control over himself and his affairs, we A trial to be recommended. wish to test his recovery, to put him on his trial, and to give him change. The law provides for this emergency. The Commissioners in Lunacy, upon the receipt of a certificate of the patient's fitness, will grant "leave of absence" from the asylum, hospital, or house, for any reasonable length of time, provided the patient is removed "under proper control" to a place specified. The control may be that of relatives or friends, or an attendant, or medical man. This plan I advise you to adopt in every case in which you are not quite certain how the patient will go on when the restraint is first removed. It is often an advantage that the individual should know that he is only away on trial and probation, and that he can be brought back at a moment's notice.   It enables us to judge whether he is cured or not: many improve in a remarkable manner when thus sent away, and our forebodings are not realized; others show that their seeming recovery was not real, and may be brought back without trouble and delay, and their friends, seeing that the trial has been a failure, are more satisfied than they would have been had it not been granted.   In many cases we can never, so long as a patient is subjected to the restraint of an asylum, ascertain his actual mental condition in the way that it is revealed by his being left comparatively to his own devices for two or three months.

In speaking of the pathology of insanity, I mentioned a class of cases where, the insanity is remittent or recurring, a period intervening in which the patient appears either quite or nearly recovered, or at any rate, altogether different from what he is during the time of the attack.   This recurring insanity is not uncommon, but is very unfavorable as regards prognosis, and very difficult to deal with when the periods of apparent sanity are of any duration; for the patient then demands his release, and may threaten us with the consequences of his detention.   As I said in the former lecture, we may see a man apparently recover from an acute attack, and just as we think him well and able to go out into the world, without any reason or warning he breaks down, and the whole of the symptoms recur, and this may happen again and again during many years.   I do not know that we have anything to warn us that a patient's insanity will be recurring, except that the recovery is usually very rapid.   Rapid recoveries must always be looked on with suspicion.   The slowest recoveries that I have ever seen in patients suffering from acute mania have been in those who have remained well ever since.   If a

Recurring insanity.

patient recovers very rapidly, probably he will not remain well long; but we may not be able to detain him, and he will go out, break down, and be again admitted. Some are never well long enough to gain their release. They alternate, month about, between comparative sanity and most evident insanity, mania or melancholia; and as time goes on their sanity will be less apparent, and the violent stage will alternate with a state of quiet and harmless imbecility, the mind wearing out, but the recurring disease being as potent as ever.

Now, it is important that we should endeavor to break through the habit of periodical attacks, to destroy the periodicity of disease. We cannot do it by medicine; but it may be done sometimes by change of scene. In most cases change of scene and surroundings will have some effect, will lengthen the period of sanity, or render less severe the attack; but instances have come under my notice where, by a judicious change or series of changes, the periodical attack was finally averted and the patient cured. This should always be tried where means are forthcoming, and where the attack is of a nature to allow of its being treated out of an asylum under proper control. It sometimes happens that patients will brook no control, and will have their entire liberty or nothing. If they are subject to paroxysms of sudden homicidal mania, it may be impossible to allow of their leaving an asylum; but in many of these recurring cases of mania or melancholia it is quite possible to try the effect of change of scene; and I hold that no patient has been fairly tested till some such plan has been tried.

A person who suffers from recurrent insanity is, above all others, such as is described by Lord Coke as "a *lunatic* that hath sometimes his understanding and sometimes not, *aliquando gaudet lucidis intervallis*, and therefore he is called *non compos mentis*, so long as he hath not understanding."

The older lawyers contemplated the existence of what they called lucid intervals in all lunatics, who, during Lucid intervals. such lucid intervals, were held to be capable of entering into marriage, or contracts, or of making a will. There was no legal difference between one lunatic or another as regarded the probability of a lucid interval occurring: in fact, all that was known in those days concerning lunacy was derived from the lawyers, the medical profession being very little consulted in the matter. In the present day the doctrine of lucid intervals and of partial insanity has been much upset by decisions, at any rate in civil courts. The existence of insanity, however slight, has been held to invalidate any civil act, and the existence of a recurrent insanity, if thoroughly proved, would, in my opinion, vitiate anything done in the lucid interval. At the same time, it is to be remembered that lunatics have been admitted as competent witnesses in courts of law, and many lawyers would sanction the signature of a lunatic to a deed, if it could be proved that he was at the time in a lucid interval, and understood the nature of what he was doing. Signatures are constantly obtained, and the validity of them must depend upon the circumstances of the case—not upon any general principle—for unless a man is pronounced insane by a commission *de lunatico inquirendo*, he is, *primâ facie*, supposed to be sane. On this point a circular was issued, in 1864, by the Commissioners in Lunacy, which I subjoin:

19 WHITEHALL PLACE, S. W., July, 1864.

SIR: The Commissioners in Lunacy have, from time to time, and more especially in a recent case, had occasion to consider the question of the signature of documents or papers affecting property by patients detained under medical certificates as insane. It is no part of the duty of the Board to determine the general question of the validity of such transactions, which is one for the decision of courts of law or equity in each particular case.

The Commissioners, however, are decidedly of opinion that, as a general rule, proprietors and superintendents, having charge of persons as of unsound mind, ought not, in any circumstances, to sanction, or knowingly afford facilities for, the signature by such persons of deeds or documents, cheques or other papers disposing of, or otherwise affecting, their property or income. Any transaction relative to the property of lunatics, or alleged lunatics, should be conducted under the authority of the Lord Chancellor, and the provisions of the Lunacy Regulation Acts, the Trustees' Relief Act, or other statutes applicable to the circumstances. Any persons taking upon themselves to act without such authority incur grave responsibility, and the Commissioners will in future expect from you a strict compliance with the rule they have here laid down.

I am, Sir, your obedient servant,

W. C. SPRING RICE, Secretary.

Although I have spoken in a gloomy strain of the subsequent history and fortunes of recovered lunatics, it is not the less certain that recoveries do take place in great numbers, and that modern science tends to increase the number. If we take the records of an asylum, as Dr. Thurnam did, examining all the cases admitted, curable and incurable, the percentage of cures will probably be about that which he gives. But if we take curable cases only, it will be much higher—nay, I venture to say that if we were to examine curable cases only, and of these, such as were submitted to skilled treatment so soon as symptoms of mental derangement were discovered, we should find that three-fourths, or even more, had recovered. Numbers of such patients never go into an asylum: their malady is slight, and passes off, or a cure is effected without the necessity of removal from home, and so they do not swell the statistics of recorded recoveries. It stands to reason that the worst cases are sent to asylums. It is a fact of experience, that many are not sent till they have reached the stage of incurability. And when we consider how many are sent thither afflicted with general paralysis, epilepsy, or congenital defect of mind, it is clear that any percentage of cures must be greatly affected thereby.

Recoveries numerous.

You must labor, then, in your position as medical advisers, to bring under treatment at as early a period as possible all who show any symptoms of mental disorder. Where you know of, or have reason to suspect, the presence of hereditary taint, it behooves you to watch narrowly for the earliest indications of evil, to ward them off by judicious treatment, medical and moral, and if this cannot be carried out without legal interference, to insist on its being at once had recourse to. The arrest of insanity in its very beginning is that which, above everything, should be studied by all medical men. The abolition of the restraint of chronic lunatics has brought undying fame to the name of Conolly, but asylums full of chronic lunatics are an *opprobrium medicorum*. Those who pass their lives in the management of them, in the invention of amusements, the planting of fields and gardens, and the feeding, tending, and cleansing of the patients, are apt to look upon all this as the end of their labors, and a favorable report from the visiting commissioners concerning the state of the house as the summit of their ambition. But he who could advance the cure of lunatics in an equal degree to that in which Conolly promoted their comfort and happiness, would win fame no less brilliant, and the gratitude of mankind throughout the ages.

Even now, in spite of relapses, recoveries are sufficiently numerous to repay us richly, and to form a satisfactory basis for scientific observation : and if a patient breaks down a second time, we may hope again to cure him. The old farmer of whom I spoke, after having been in an asylum some thirty times, died at last in his own house, among his own people ; and on all these various occasions he had gone away so much better that he was called "recovered," though his mind was not in all respects sane and sound. And others I have known, who came again and again, though not so often, and finally died at home of general decay or ordinary disease. The ultimate fate of any one who has ever once been insane, is very grave, from one point of view—so grave as to make us dissuade others from intermarriage and such contracts; yet as regards the individual himself there is enough of hope to allow of our cheering him at the termination of an attack, and trusting to cure him should he have _{Chances of} another. If, however, you are consulted as to his ^{life.} chance of life, you will undoubtedly give, as your opinion, that it is inferior to that of a sane person. A man, we will suppose, has recovered from an attack of insanity— his first attack. He is liable to a second—liable, therefore, to the various accidents which so often befall lunatics before they are placed under proper care and control. And the second attack, or the third, may be of a very acute nature, in which he may die. Then, being subject to attacks of insanity, he may squander his property, lose his business, and come to the condition of a pauper; and if recovery again takes place, he may recover only to undergo great privations, which may materially shorten life. If you are asked as to the probable duration of life of a chronic lunatic confined in an asylum, you may speak with greater certainty in view of the particular case. Such patients are under constant medical care: if they have everything that money can bring, they have all that medical skill can do to promote health and ward off evil. Their diet and drink are regulated, as are the hours of sleep and exercise. If they are in good health, and the malady does not tend to wear them out by great excitement or depression, their lives may be in no way inferior to those of persons exposed to the accidents of every-day life. But each case must be judged apart. One could not say that the lives of all chronic cases were good. But in every asylum you will be shown some octogenarian inmates, who by their long sojourn prove that insanity of itself does not shorten life.

What is the mode and immediate cause of the death of the

insane? Many die in the acute stage, and we often feel a difficulty in stating in our certificate the exact cause, Causes of whether after a post-mortem examination or not. death amongst the We see a patient in an attack of acute mania which insane. runs a rapid course. Sleep is absent, and in ten days or a fortnight he dies. He gets weaker and weaker, and at last collapse sets in, and the heart fails; profuse perspiration breaks out, and he gradually sinks from exhaustion of the heart's energy. On performing a post-mortem examination we find merely signs of great hyperæmia of the brain, or of increased action, but do not perceive any actual lesion, or any trace of that which has caused the stoppage of the heart. The patient's strength and nerve-force have in fact been exhausted, and have never had the chance of being renewed. If we examine another case, of much longer duration, the same appearances may meet us. That which happens to one in a fortnight, may, in another, come about in two or three months. Sleep is not so completely wanting, the violence is not so great or so incessant, yet the waste is greater than the repair, and death follows; and on examination we are equally at a loss to give a definite reason for the termination of life. I have seen medical men who were unaccustomed to make post-mortem examinations of such patients greatly surprised at finding so little after such severe disorder and rapid death; but the process by which that metamorphosis which goes on in our daily lives is arrested or terminated, sometimes leaves no marked signs for us to scrutinize after death. Acute mania, like the poison of the serpent or prussic acid, may kill and leave no trace. We know, by watching the patient's strength slowly ebb and fade, that exhaustion is the mode of death; but it is the disease which kills, as do typhus and cholera, and therefore it is vain to talk about there being no such disorder as acute mania, or to say that lesions or marks of inflammation are always to be found, whether by the microscope or naked eye. Two patients are attacked with acute mania; in ten days one is well, the other is dead. The same thing may happen in less time in the case of two suffering from delirium tremens. Is it likely that anything like an appreciable organic lesion has existed in either of these cases which can have been perfectly removed by one long sleep? That there have been disturbances in the molecular constitution of the nerve-centres, we know; but we do not believe that these would be discernible, even if we could apply the microscope during life.

It may often be, then, that we shall have to describe patients as dying of acute mania or acute melancholia producing fatal exhaustion; and to this we may have to add that such exhaustion was accelerated by the impossibility of giving sufficient food. Many are brought to us who have been allowed to go so long without being fed, that all hope of sustaining life is past.

When, however, we survey the non-acute forms of insanity, or the patients who live for years in a chronic state, it appears that many, I might say most of them, die not of the insanity, but of diseases to which sane people are liable. According to the insanity, however, and the condition to which they are reduced by it, they are more or less liable to the attacks of other diseases. Patients suffering from chronic mania or monomania, who have a considerable amount of nervous energy and of intellect, albeit deranged, will live much longer, and withstand disease much better, than demented persons whose vital powers are at the lowest point. The demented are very prone to get fat; taking but little exercise, their whole system is feeble, and the heart and muscular tissue undergo retrograde metamorphosis. In this state their great foe is acute bronchitis; and this, in my experience, carries off the majority of them, and, indeed, of all chronic lunatics. These very fat patients seem especially its victims: the circulation becomes impeded, the heart cannot force the blood onwards, they are choked with mucus, and die rapidly. I warn you to watch very closely the approach of this malady, if such patients are under your charge. The ordinary cough medicines are of little use; but I have found the greatest benefit from the use of a steam-kettle in the room: it should be kept boiling night and day, and a good large jet of steam should constantly moisten the air. In the case of these patients, as with young children, and, in fact, in bronchitis generally, I believe this remedy to be of incalculable value. In my own experience—which has been only of the upper classes—I have not found phthisis at all prevalent amongst chronic lunatics. One gentleman died of acute mania after an attack of hæmoptysis, and in the lungs of two who died of general paralysis, tubercles existed; but amongst 73 deaths in the last few years, only one was returned as caused by phthisis. In the public asylums the proportion of those who die of this disorder is large.

If you ever see much of the insane, you may have to form a diagnosis of bodily disorders occurring in patients suffering from a recent or chronic form of mental affection. Most difficult is it at times to ascertain if anything be the matter with such people, and, if anything, what the seat and nature of the ailment are. One class will simulate every kind of disorder, will complain of agonies, of obstruction in the bowels or urethra, inability to swallow, headache, or sickness—to say nothing of matters more palpably fanciful, as eruptions, broken bones, or paralyzed limbs. Another class will tell us nothing — nay, will strenuously deny serious illness—partly from a fear of medical interference and physic, partly because they are too demented or deluded to realize their true state, which possibly they attribute to supernatural or inevitable causes. In dealing with these we have need of an accurate knowledge of disease, and of patient and painstaking investigation of every fact and every organ. We are prone to think that an individual, melancholic and hypochondriacal, may be narrating to us

Diagnosis of bodily disease.

sufferings existing only in his or her hypochondriac fancy, as a reason for refusing food, and avoiding all exertion or occupation. But they may be real, and we should commit a grave error if we ignored their existence. Then a chronic case, a demented man, who tells us nothing, suddenly appears out of sorts, does not eat as he is wont, sits listless and dejected. We can extract no information, no complaint. Like an animal or child, he attracts attention only by his appearance and the alteration observable. We examine him, his pulse and tongue, the state of the urine, if it is possible to obtain some, the motions and temperature. If he is ordinarily a hearty feeder, we inquire as to his eating: has he lost appetite? If not, we do not think him very ill. There is no better test. But if he will, contrary to his usual custom, take no food; if he appears thirsty and will drink copiously, or if he rejects both food and drink, we try to discover what is amiss. Is he sick, has he diarrhœa or constipation, has he lung mischief? Very insidious is the latter. Great ravages may have been made in the lung without any cough or other symptom to draw attention to the uncomplaining sufferer. Loss of appetite in old-standing cases is perhaps the most valuable warning; but in those more recent, refusal of food is so common, that very close inquiry is necessary, and we may have to insist on its being taken in spite of the alleged indisposition. But here the latter will be not concealed, but put forward and dwelt upon, and it will generally be represented as most serious, causing great suffering and sense of illness. If we find that the tongue is perfectly clean, the temperature normal, the pulse quiet, and urine healthy, we shall with reason doubt the statement, and look upon it as having a purpose. Nevertheless, cases will often puzzle and cause us to hesitate, and we must never be content with anything short of a thorough examination of the patient. If there is frequent sickness, we must be sure there is no hernia. If there be little water passed, or a constant dribbling, we may find a distended bladder. And whenever we hear of an unexpected and unaccountable death, nothing but a post-mortem examination should satisfy us as to the cause thereof.

It may often fall to your lot to have to treat chronic cases of mania or dementia, patients who are in a state of unsoundness of mind, but are harmless, not re- quiring the restraint of an asylum; they demand, nevertheless, careful watching and nursing, being frequently in a state of second childhood, like children or even infants in uncleanliness, and utterly unfit to take care of themselves. Such patients are often found by the Commissioners in private houses in a state of great neglect. They are perfectly man-ageable without the appliances of an asylum, but require con-stant and watchful care. One difficulty you will have to encounter is the keeping them clean. Their tendency is to sink into an apathetic state, in which they discharge their evacuations regardless of place or time, like wild animals or very young infants. In or out of an asylum they may cause trouble in this respect; but in or out of an asylum dirty habits may be much eradicated by careful attendants. Some attendants, who have had no experience of such cases, are altogether amazed when told that they are to blame for wet or dirty beds or clothes. They think that it is a concomitant of the imbecile state, no more to be altered than the failing memory or the shuffling and feeble walk. You will find, however, that a patient must be very far gone indeed who cannot be taught the habit of relieving himself at regular intervals, and in a proper receptacle. Even when a patient is unconscious, and sunk in the last stage of paralytic de-mentia, accidents, though they cannot be altogether avoided, may be made the exception instead of the rule. And I be-lieve that any chronic demented patient, whose mind remains the same from year's end to year's end, may be taught to be cleanly. Some, who have a good deal of mind, whether re-cent or chronic cases, will be dirty wilfully, to give trouble or

The treatment of the chronic insane.

annoyance. They must be dealt with very firmly, and forced to go to the closet or to get out of bed. Imbecile patients, who are dirty from sheer want of attention, are at least as capable of being taught to be clean as a child of a twelve-month, or a dog or cat. In short, patients dirty by night or day imply careless or inefficient attendants. Do not listen to the excuse that it cannot be helped: change the attendant, or threaten to do so, and you will probably find that the habit is eradicated. Another circumstance, which is equally a test of the care of the attendant, is the presence or absence of bed-sores. No chronic lunatic should be kept in bed by day and night simply for infirmity, unless he is actually ill. He should be washed and dressed, and seated in an easy-chair, even if he is unable to walk about. By this method, by thorough cleansing, and by thickly powdering with oxide of zinc powder any part of the back which is likely to give way, bed-sores may be avoided in patients who linger on in an extreme stage of paralysis even for years. In such cases a wet bed cannot always be avoided ; but proper precautions, and the establishment of systematic and regular times for micturition and defecation, will reduce " accidents " to a minimum. More is to be done by these measures than by the use of urinals or other apparatus. Many will not suffer them to remain properly adjusted, or cannot bear the pressure occasioned. Such appliances are costly, often out of order, and soon become very offensive.

LECTURE XVIII.

General Remarks on Treatment—Importance of Early Treatment to be urged by Family Practitioner—Restraint to be advised when necessary—Objections of Friends to be met—Use of an Asylum—Attendants—Delusions, how to be met—Asylums not necessary for all the Insane—On the Choice of an Asylum—Feigned Insanity—Hints for Detection—The Odor of the Insane.

I HAVE a few remarks to make upon the general treatment and management of insane persons, which will occupy the present lecture. In all probability but few of you will have to treat insanity as a specialty: the majority will meet and have to deal with it as it occurs in the course of the practice of a physician, surgeon, or general practitioner, and in this way you will see patients and their friends at an earlier period than those who practice more specially as lunacy doctors. The friends shrink from calling for the latter's advice or assistance till every other means has been tried; upon you will devolve the responsibility of taking the earliest, often the most important, steps for the security and cure of the individual. And I assure Importance of early treatment. you the friends will prove to you as great a source of difficulty as the patient himself. They will refuse to believe that his mind is affected, and shut their ears and eyes to all they hear or see, insomuch that they will say that the disorder commenced quite suddenly, without any warning, on a particular day, when every one else has noticed its approach for months. Now, in the earliest stages, insanity is a very curable disorder; but through the obstinacy of friends it happens over and over again that the curable stage is past and gone long before any remedial measures have been taken, and the patient is brought to us a confirmed and hopeless lunatic, requiring care not cure, to be shut up in restraint for the term of his natural life. And often a patient in this stage is put in an asylum for the sake of avoiding trouble and expense, who might very well live outside, mixing under some sort of surveillance with a family, and with the world at large. During the time that an asylum might effect a cure, the friends would not hear of sending him thither; but when all hope of cure is over, he is placed there because it is cheap and saves trouble.

Now, I hold that at the present day our method of dealing with the insane should be this: First, we should endeavor to ward off an attack of impending insanity, and this, I believe, may be done very frequently. If it is not done, if the storm breaks, and breaks with violence, so that the patient, together with those about him, is in danger, to an asylum he ought to be sent, where everything surrounding him is specially adapted to his wants. If he does not recover, but quiets down into a " partially insane " man, tranquil and orderly, yet requiring supervision, and unfit to be in his own home, he ought not to remain in an asylum, if he is capable of enjoying himself in a greater degree beyond its walls.

Duty of the family practitioner.

At the very commencement of symptoms threatening mental disorder, you will have the least difficulty in getting your advice followed. At this stage you may be able to advise and consult with the patient and with his friends at the same time, and you may, in forcible terms, lay down the necessity of change of scene, cessation of work, and attention to diet and medicines. At this time you have not to inculcate the necessity of resorting to legal measures. Either in his own house, or in a friend's, or on a tour with some member of his family, with or without an attendant, the patient may pass a period of rest and treatment, and you may reasonably hope that your advice as to all this will be followed, and if followed strictly, will be attended by recovery.

But if the patient gets worse instead of better—if he will take no advice, and submit to no treatment except on compulsion—if delusions show themselves, and become more and more formidable, it will be your duty to represent, not to the patient—for this is useless—but to his friends, the urgent necessity for legal restraint; that he may, in the first place, be kept in safety; in the second, be subjected to treatment with a view to cure. Here you will be met with every conceivable objection. Wives are afraid to take any step of the kind without the co-operation of the husband's relatives—husbands without those of the wife. They are afraid that the patient, even if he recovers, will never forgive the step you are urging. They would sooner wait a little longer, till something occurs that more loudly calls for legal interference. They are sure that if he is placed in an asylum it will drive him "quite mad," when he knows where he is, and sees the other patients. Now, you may assure such people that it is absolutely requisite that the individual shall be placed somewhere under legal restraint; and that if he is insane enough to require this, he himself will care little whether the place of restraint is an asylum or a private house. If he is indignant at being restrained, and clamorous for liberty, he will clamor as loudly in a private house as in an asylum, and probably make more determined attempts to get out, owing to facilities for escape being more numerous. If he is wildly maniacal, he will care little where he is; if profoundly melancholic, all places will be to him alike. And as regards the other patients, we find that each one is so wrapped in himself, in his own delusions and projects, in his own misery or his own greatness, that he little heeds the rest; and in the acute state, at any rate, their presence does him no harm, often the contrary. Later, perhaps, he may shrink from

Restraint to be urged when necessary.

Objections to be met.

them, when mental health is returning, and then it may be advisable that he should be removed from such a scene, and placed among sane people. It may be worth while to consider for a moment the advantages gained by a patient who is placed in an asylum, and the mode in which a cure is there effected. There can be no question that the perfection of treatment would be to place a patient in an asylum where the other inmates were not insane, but sane people. We should then have all the advantages we have at present without any of the drawbacks. The patient would be surrounded by a fresh scene and fresh faces. New subjects would be presented to his mind by way of occupation and amusement, to take the place of his morbid ideas; but this proceeding cannot be carried out; we therefore fall back on asylums as they are. Here the patient finds, above every-

The use of an asylum.

thing, rest and safety. He is kept from accident and suicide. He is cut off from his friends and all with whom his delusions are so often connected. And here I would urge you to impress upon the friends the necessity of leaving a patient alone and unvisited when he is first placed in an asylum. To sever home-ties and ideas is one of the main objects you have in placing him there; and if friends, in mistaken kindness, visit him from day to day, he might as well be at home. All letters must, in the majority of cases, be interdicted, at any rate at first, and the patient must be told plainly and openly that he is not well enough to carry on a correspondence, and that his letters, if written, will not be sent. Nothing irritates a man more than to be told that his letters are sent, while he finds, by the absence of all replies, that they are not; or concludes that if sent, they are disregarded by those to whom they are addressed. Patients are not to be treated entirely as children, nor can they be satisfied with trifling excuses and evasions, though they resemble children in that we are obliged to act for them, and cannot consult with them. In quiet, then, and forced inactivity, many a man recovers in an asylum by rest alone without any very special treatment, so far as medicine is concerned. His health may be tolerably good; possibly he refuses to take medicine, and may not be in a condition in which we care to force him to swallow it. The struggle and ill-feeling thence arising would more than counterbalance the probable good to be gained from the physic, yet he may recover, and that in no long time. He recovers simply because he has been kept in an asylum, or, as some would say, because he has been subjected to moral treatment. Doubtless, you have all heard of the moral treatment of insanity. But shutting a man up in an asylum can hardly be called moral treatment. It is simply restraint, which may be highly beneficial, and even remedial, as it is a means whereby the patient obtains rest and seclusion from all that is harassing and vexing, but it is not what I understand by moral treatment. For in old days men were placed in asylums, and then and there confined in a restraint-chair or strait-waistcoat, by leg-locks and handcuffs, and fed, washed, and dressed; and this, together with some purging and blistering, constituted the treatment. But we should hardly call this moral treatment. By the latter, I mean that personal contact and influence of man over man, which the sane can exercise over the insane, and which we see so largely and beneficially exercised by those having the gift, whether superintendents, matrons, or attendants. There can be no proper treatment of an insane person without it, and, beyond all question, the recovery of many has been delayed or prevented by its absence. There are patients, however, who are not within its reach. A man or woman in a state of acute delirious mania is beyond moral treatment, and needs only that which is physical or medicinal. That is why it is of little importance whether we treat such in or out of an asylum, provided we can place them in a suitable apartment. But we may see another who will never get well out of an asylum. What do we notice here? A morbid and intense *philautia,* an extreme concentration of the whole thoughts and ideas on self and all that concerns self: whether the individual's feelings are those of self-satisfaction and elation or of depression, whether he thinks himself the greatest man in the world or the most miserable, he is constantly absorbed in the contemplation of self, and thinks the whole world has its attention directed to him. Now, when such a being is at home, he generally contrives to make himself the centre and focus of every one's regard; and if away from home, in a lodging or family, he may be able to do the same thing—nay, in the majority of cases, this cannot fail to be the case, for the arrangements of the household must more or less depend on the presence of such an inmate; but place him in an asylum of fifty patients, and he occupies at once merely the fiftieth part of the attention of those about him. He is given to understand that the establishment goes on just the same whether he is there or not, but that being there, he must conform to the rules, his going away depending to a considerable extent on his own efforts, and his observance of the precepts and advice which he receives. He is encouraged to follow the latter by the approval of those about him, whose approval he ought to value: he is dissuaded or even prevented from doing that which he ought not. He is indulged with a certain amount of liberty, according as he shows that he is fitted to enjoy it, with liberty to go beyond the premises, to visit places of amusement, to have money at his command, to choose his own recreation and occupation; and this liberty he forfeits if he abuses it, and strict surveillance and watching are exercised until he shows that he can control himself.

Now, in all this it is necessary that we have the co-operation of attendants. In an asylum such as I have mentioned Attendants. attendants must be numerous, and for the purposes of judicious treatment an asylum should not be too small. A patient may keep one containing only half a dozen inmates in a continual turmoil, and his self-importance is only increased thereby; but merged among forty or fifty, he becomes at once a much smaller fraction of the whole. On the other hand, no asylum should be so large as to preclude that personal attention which constitutes real moral treatment. The day may come when ladies will devote themselves to the nursing of lunatics, as they now labor in general hospitals. But as matters stand at present, we have to control insane ladies and gentlemen by means of servants, and great difficulties thus arise. A good attendant is a treasure beyond price, but it is not in the power of every one, whatever the desire, to be a good attendant; *nascitur, non fit.* It requires a combination of patience, tact, and judgment, of boldness, firmness, and unvarying good temper, possessed by the few rather than the many. Yet we cannot cure patients without attendants. Male patients cannot, for obvious reasons, be attended in all cases by females, whether servants or ladies; and gentlemen cannot be procured to act the part of attendants, nor would they on many occasions be more fitting. It is incumbent on us, therefore, to select with the utmost care those to whose charge we are forced to commit the insane, to watch them with unceasing vigilance, to remove those who, by constitution and infirmity of temper, or weakness of health, are unfit for the arduous task, and to retain by ample pay and reward, by relaxation and indulgence, those we feel to be faithful servants. Were I writing a book about asylums, I might say more, but other topics demand attention.

By the moral control exercised personally by man over man, the patient's thoughts and feelings are to be directed from his morbid self-contemplation to that care and concern for others which is his normal state. Those about him will endeavor to supplant by other ideas, subjects, and occupations, his delusions and insane thoughts. As the former gain a foothold and predominance, the latter fade and

Moral treatment.

disappear. Direct controversy on the truth or falsehood of delusions does little. Towards the close of an attack of insanity, in the period of convalescence, a patient may now and then be convinced of the falsehood of one of his fancies by direct demonstration; but at the height of the disorder this cannot be done, and it is often unwise to attempt it. Controversy perpetually renewed only tends to fix and confirm the fancy, which often departs quickly if never alluded to.

Under the head of moral treatment must be considered the question of occupation, exercise, and amusement; for nothing is of greater importance, not only to the welfare of the chronic, but to the cure of recent cases. All three are in turn requisite and indispensable, though not all are equally required by the same individual. To one bodily exercise is a necessity. In subacute, restless, sleepless mania, protracted muscular work will bring sleep, and act as a sedative more efficacious than drugs. Hard exercise will distract another whose thoughts are fixed unceasingly on melancholy subjects. I have known a man dig all day in the garden—dig a pit and fill it up again if other occupation for his spade was not to be had—and profit thereby. In public asylums there are far more opportunities for giving the inmates hard bodily work than exist among private patients. It is very difficult to subject the latter, particularly ladies, to sufficient exercise. Many a lady would be the better, could she be made to do the hard day's work done by many in our public asylums; but beyond walking, it is next to impossible to provide any exercise for her. Gentlemen fare somewhat better: they can ride, play cricket, billiards, skittles, football; but play is not the same thing as regular work, and regular work and long-continued exercise are of more value than the short but severer labor of games. So with regard to mental exercise and occupation. There are many brains which require to lie fallow and do nothing; if they must be amused, we recommend a course of Pickwick, or such like fare, or backgammon, or bagatelle; but some patients require harder mental work. To distract their thoughts they need to fix their minds on a subject deep enough to engross attention, and employ them day after day, and week after week. Such are generally intellectual people, and their occupation must be intellectual. For them I have found no work so suitable as the study of new languages; it is intellectual without being emotional, and does not require a great number of books or much assistance. I have known ladies study Greek and Hebrew, to say nothing of German, Italian, and Spanish. There is no end to this occupation, and to a busy mind it is often very fascinating. But people differ: another may prefer some new fashion of embroidery or lace-work; and drawing and water-color painting should be encouraged in all who have the very slightest artistic leaning.

You will see recorded in books how, by various devices, delusions have been dispelled. A woman thought that frogs were in her inside. Her physician intro-duced some frogs into the nightstool: she believed that she had passed them, and was cured of her delusion. But by such a scheme you admit the truth of the delusion, and, by inference, of all other extraordinary fancies which may be alleged. A patient may say, " True, I have got rid of six frogs, but others are still left behind." You cannot then say the whole thing is an impossibility and an insane delusion. A patient of mine who hears voices and noises, once heard at night a knocking or ringing at the front door. Her nurse treated this at first as one of her delusions, but on its repeti-tion discovered that a policeman had rung, owing to a win-dow having been left open. The patient has ever since triumphantly quoted this as a proof that her so-called delu-sions are realities. Never be tempted by any present chance of success into admitting the truth of a delusion, or doing anything which by inference admits the same. Sooner or later, in the present or in some subsequent attack of insanity, the patient will turn round and place you in a position of difficulty owing to your having made such a concession. And be not too anxious to prove the falsity of a delusion. Frequently the patient starts from some premises which cannot be absolutely disproved, and in logical argument may seem to have the best of it. Rather try to oust the idea by the substitution of others. It is astonishing how patients ignore proof and demonstration. The people they say are dead stand before them alive and well, yet they declare it is some one else. The partaking of food does not make them think the less that their throat is closed, or their inside completely gone.

The more acute the insanity, and the more variable and numerous the delusions, the more favorable is the prognosis. When there is considerable disorder of the bodily health, sleeplessness, disinclination to eat, emaciation, or constipation, we may hope that delusions will vanish as the health improves. If it improves, and there is not *pari passu* a corresponding improvement in the mental symptoms, the prognosis is unfavorable. If the health is completely restored, if the patient sleeps well, eats and drinks well, regains flesh and looks, and still delusions remain, our augury as to the final result will not be encouraging. Perhaps this is why patients get well after many years of melancholia. During all the time they remain in a depressed state, both of body and mind, and generally look thin and miserable, refusing food as much as possible, and being altogether out of health. The chronic cases in asylums who best preserve their health, and look fat and ruddy, and live the longest, are those whose delusions are not of deep depression, but of what we term mania or monomania.

I have already said, that at a time when an asylum is necessary and offers the only chance of cure, the friends of a patient will often do anything rather

Asylums not necessary for all the insane.

than send him there, will go to any expense to avoid the stigma of the asylum, and run great risk of violating the law. But when the case has become chronic, and the patient is a harmless monomaniac or dement, they cast about to discover how he may most cheaply be kept for his natural life. An asylum offers great advantages in this respect—for there are asylums of all grades—and to an asylum he goes. The question of restraining chronic lunatics, whether private or pauper, in asylums, is one which is attracting, and will attract, attention more and more. The notion that all insane persons must dwell in them has arisen from various causes. For generations such people were looked upon, not as sick, but as a class apart from all others. They were handed over to be kept in houses, the proprietors of which were not medical men, but laymen, ignorant and uneducated. No one in those days thought the insane capable of mixing with sane members of society. In asylums they dwelt from year to year, a few walking beyond the premises, but none sleeping beyond, or going to any place of amusement like ordinary men. Now, from all asylums patients are sent to the seaside, to the theatre, the picture galleries; each proprietor vies with his fellows in providing recreation and entertainment for his patients — in proving, in fact, how little they need the restraint of an asylum. There will always be a certain number who cannot be allowed so much liberty, who cannot be taken to the seaside, who cannot even walk beyond the bounds of the asylum grounds, whose life is one incessant struggle to escape by fraud or force, or execute, perchance, some insane project fraught with danger to themselves or others. Some there will be whose limited means procure for them greater luxury and enjoyment amongst the numerous boarders of an asylum than could be afforded were they placed alone in a private family. But there are many with ample means, patients who make the fortunes of asylum proprietors, whose lives would be infinitely happier did they live beyond asylum walls. I would refer you to what Dr. Maudsley has eloquently written on this subject. After mentioning various objections urged against their release by the advocates of the present state of things, he says: " Another objection to the liberation will be that the insane in private houses will not be so well cared for as they are, nor have any more comfort than they now have in well-conducted asylums. The quarter from which this objection is urged taints it with suspicion : I never heard it put forward but by those who are interested in the continuance of the present state of things. Those who make it appear to fail entirely to appreciate the strength of the passion for liberty which there is in the human breast; and as I feel most earnestly that I should infinitely prefer a garret or a cellar for lodgings, with bread and water only for food, than to be clothed in purple and fine linen, and to fare sumptuously every day as a prisoner, I can well believe that all the comforts which an insane person has in his captivity are but a miserable compensation for his entire loss of liberty—that they are petty things which weigh not at all against the mighty suffering of a life-long imprisonment."

How are you to know if a patient is capable of living beyond the walls of an asylum? The answer is simple; give him a trial : many unpromising cases I have known to benefit so much by the change that they would scarcely have been recognized. Few chronic lunatics are dangerous to others: these are easily known, and we should be slow to place in a private family any one who has ever committed a homicidal act, unless he is fully and perfectly recovered; suicidal patients require the protection of an asylum so long as any insanity remains, but there are scores of eccentric monomaniacs who are perfectly harmless, who only require surveillance and a limit to their supply of money, and can enjoy life thoroughly amidst the amusements of town or sports of the country, their eccentricities being greatly smoothed away by the constant society of educated ladies and gentlemen. As the last generation did away with the fetters and mechanical restraint used in asylums, so let the present release from the restraint of an asylum all those capable of enjoying a larger amount of liberty and a freer atmosphere than that in which they now fret and chafe.

If an asylum is inevitable, and thither the patient must go, the question will arise, how is a choice to be made. Various points must here be considered. Is the case likely to be of some duration? or is it acute and urgent, requiring immediate restraint? Is transit to an asylum likely to be difficult? Is the patient, when placed there, likely to be able to go beyond the premises? Is it desirable that he should be near, or at a distance from, his home and relatives? Are there circumstances about the case, such as sexual excitement, which make it essential that he or she should not come into contact with patients of the other sex? All these matters will guide us in the choice of an asylum. It may be important to have recourse to the nearest and most easy of access—to one within a cab or carriage drive. In many acute cases, especially of females, it may be most prejudicial to place the patient in contact with others of the opposite sex. In some cases a very small asylum, where the routine is domestic and home-like, is advantageous, but other patients may cause too much commotion in such a one, and may do better when merged in the community of a more populous institution. Much will, of course, turn upon the question of expense. As a rule, the cheaper the terms the larger is the asylum; but for some, a large and cheap asylum may act more beneficially, so far as cure is concerned, than a small one, where the individual may be the object of even too much solicitude. Where there is no hope of cure and the case is chronic, the patient should be placed where he can have the greatest amount of occupation, amusement, and liberty, compatible with his safe-keeping on the one hand, and his peculiar tastes and idiosyncrasies on the other.   It is too much the fashion to think that all asylums must be in the country.   Green fields, though charming at first to denizens of a town, are extremely monotonous, and many a patient would gladly exchange his country walks and muddy lanes for the shops of Regent Street or for Rotten Row.

Next, I must say a few words upon feigned insanity.   A Feigned insanity. disordered mind has been simulated from the earliest ages—witness the dementia which David successfully feigned, and the imbecility which saved the life of Lucius Junius Brutus—and it will be assumed perpetually by those who have a motive for shifting from their shoulders the responsibility of their acts.   Fortunately few know how to feign insanity.   It is only a Shakspeare who can depict the assuming of a Hamlet or an Edgar.   The majority of simulators are clumsy performers, whom you will detect without difficulty; but here and there you may chance to see a case which is not so easy to decide, and which, though eventually you may be satisfied as to its character, cannot be recognized at a moment's notice.   Doubtless they who have the insane ever before their eyes will most readily detect the sham disorder, yet there are certain points which will enable you to come to a conclusion respecting the greater number of cases. If we except the instances of hysteria, catalepsy, pretended fasting, and the like, which can hardly be called feigned insanity, we shall find that most persons who simulate the malady have an obvious motive for so doing.   Therefore we do not meet with it frequently in ordinary private practice ; but if any of you become surgeon to a jail or to the army, you will not seldom be called on to see malingerers who adopt this as a means of getting to comfortable asylum-quarters, or obtaining a discharge from duty.   As, however, men do really become insane under the same circumstances, you will have carefully to discriminate between the real and affected symptoms.

Uneducated as the mass of such persons is, the attempt will be clumsy and generally easy to detect: but here and there an educated man, who brings himself within reach of the law, may with greater success carry on the cheat.

The first remark to be made is, that the insanity simulated may be transitory or persistent. The individual may pretend that he was in a delirious or unconscious state at the time the criminal act was committed, or he may be apparently insane at the time we see him. Secondly, he may be in an acute and active state of feigned excited mania or melancholia, or may pretend to be in a quiet and apparently chronic condition of monomania or dementia. Thirdly, he may put on this appearance soon after the commission of his wrong act, to make it appear that it was committed by him while insane; or he may feign insanity while in prison, to get away to the better fare and idle life of an asylum.

If you are told by a prisoner that at the time he committed the act he did not know what he was about, or that he has no recollection of it, he virtually simulates the form of transitory mania which is seen occasionally in conjunction with epilepsy, or taking the place of the latter. You will recollect, however, that such attacks are extremely rare, that they are not usually so transient as to be unnoticed by others, or so severe as to take away all recollection of what was done in them. Here you will inquire into the previous history of the individual as regards former attacks of insanity, epilepsy, blows, or cerebral affections. *Insanity pleaded to excuse a former act.*

He may tell us that he suffered from an irresistible impulse to commit the act, from some sudden and overwhelming idea: he may simulate the so-called *impulsive* insanity. Applying what I have said already concerning this, you will look for other symptoms, for a history of previous attacks or previous head-affections: you will not consult the individual about these, for you may easily put such into his mouth, but to the best of your ability arrive at an account of his past life: and you must consider the character of the deed not only as regards its enormity, but also its senselessness, want of motive, or eccentricity. Such acts, if really committed under the influence of either of these forms of temporary insanity, are usually violence against self or others. If this plea is put forward as an excuse for small and petty thefts or forgery, acts of indecency or exposure of person, we may reasonably suspect it. The latter are committed by madmen, but not by those whose insanity passes off so soon as the act is over.

More commonly, however, we are called on to see a person who is apparently insane at the time of our inspection. Comparing a true with a feigned case, I may say, generally, that a real lunatic, when approached by a stranger, appears at first rather better than worse, and more on his guard; he tries to bring his wits together and understand what is going on. But a sham lunatic, when we go to him, redoubles his efforts to seem insane: he is more energetically noisy, idiotic, and maniacal. A sham lunatic, recollect, always wishes to be thought a lunatic. If we ask him whether he is out of his mind, he tells us at once that he is. In fact, he dare not say the opposite; whereas a real patient rarely confesses it, unless he be in the depth of melancholia.

Insanity assumed at the time of inspection.

Feigned insanity is almost always overdone. As there is no subject on which such erroneous notions prevail among people in general, so the imitation is, with rare exceptions, a bungle. If noisy and violent mania is the form assumed, detection is easy. The malingerer, unlike the true maniac, will tire himself out and go to sleep. No sane person can maintain the incessant action, singing, and shouting of a genuine maniac for any but the shortest time. No genuine maniac would, in the middle of all this, at an early stage of the attack, go to sleep, and sleep many hours. Watch such people without their knowledge, and you will have little doubt as to the case.

If a less excited mania is feigned, and the feigner will talk and answer questions, he generally overdoes his part by pretending to have lost all reason and memory. He will not give one correct answer to the simplest question; he will not know his own name; but will display an ingenuity in evading answers and in talking nonsense entirely at variance with the loss of mind he pretends to have suffered. Or he will answer questions correctly about everything that does not concern himself, but so soon as we question him as to his crime or history, he becomes suddenly demented and entirely deprived of memory and intelligence. Loss of memory is not common amongst the insane, except in cases of dementia, primary or secondary. It may be feigned, but will rarely be a clever simulation. Here we must look for an absence of mind; and if we see a presence of mind, and a sharpness and quickness displayed in many ways, the notion of dementia is incompatible. Dirty habits may be adopted to further the deceit, and malingerers will daub themselves with, or even eat, their fæces; but in conversation we may generally discover that they are not so lost as they seem. Frequently something casually mentioned in their presence is done in consequence of the hint, showing that their attention has been fixed on all that has been said.

A man may feign melancholy, or sit silent and desponding, and say nothing. Here some knowledge of the insane may be requisite to guide us to an opinion. He may refuse his food, and say that poison is put in it. We must watch him, and look for physical symptoms. Is his tongue clean, his skin cool, and pulse normal? Does he sleep well at night? Does he alter his conduct according to that which is said in his presence? Does he dress and undress himself? Melancholia, or *melancholia cum stupore,* is a form distinct from others, from mania especially, and this distinction is not likely to be carefully preserved by a malingerer. Neither mania, melancholia, nor primary dementia comes on in patients, full blown, in an hour. The history of the previous days is almost conclusive in the majority of cases, especially if there is a knowledge of the sleep the pretended lunatic has enjoyed.

The detection of feigned insanity is, and ever will be, Hints for detection. difficult, when we have to examine men and women in whom madness and badness are so intermingled that observers cannot determine which it is that regulates their conduct. Amidst our criminal population are hundreds who can hardly be said to be sane and responsible, but who, in the lower ranks of life, commit a succession of crimes, perhaps of no great magnitude, which render them the almost perpetual inhabitants of jails. Some of them are so violent, outrageous, and destructive, so silly in their motiveless fury, and childish in mind, that we may call them imbeciles or insane, and have good grounds for our opinion. Such there will ever be on the border-land of insanity. But each of these must be judged by himself. My purpose here is not to speak of doubtful, but of feigned, insanity—insanity feigned by those of whose sanity at other times we have no doubt.

We cannot depend on any physical signs for the certain detection of simulation. We find among the insane the pulse neither slow nor quick, a cool head, and normal urine; and he will be bold who shall affirm that he can detect insanity or its absence by the sense of smell, though such men are to be found. Nevertheless, there is almost invariably such a disturbance of the health in a person whose insanity is just commencing, that our suspicions should be aroused if this be wanting. Want of sleep, a coated tongue, constipation—all, or some of them, are nearly always to be found; so that if a man suddenly feigns insanity, we look for these and for the symptoms of recent and acute mental disorder. If the insanity simulated is that of quiet and apparently chronic monomania or dementia, we shall know that these forms do not come on suddenly, and that there must have been a previous stage.

Various plans have been advocated for the purpose of making the simulator confess the imposture, and give up his acting. Speaking in his presence of remedies which will probably have to be used, such as the actual cautery, and the sight of its preparation, may frighten some pretenders. The sight of the stomach-pump may make a man take his food; but then a lunatic will take it for the same reason. In accordance with the truth, *in vino veritas*, feigned insanity has, it is said, been detected by the opening influence of an intoxicating amount of wine; this, however, is hardly applicable to the inmates of jails. Little is to be gained from drugs, unless it be from a good dose of tartar emetic, which may make a man confess rather than have another. This, of course, is to be given only when our mind is made up concerning the case, and when we want to put an end to the play. A cold shower bath may cure another, but probably nothing is so efficacious as the application of a galvanic battery. In a very interesting paper, Dr. David Nicolson, one of the medical officers at Portland, has related the valuable aid derived from this instrument. His remarks on feigned insanity among prisoners are well worth perusal.[1] When you are convinced that a person is shamming, you will probably effect a rapid cure by a few turns of the machine, or a repetition of it twice a day for a few days.

There are cases on record where skilful cheats have deceived for a long period even alienist physicians, but such are rare. Consider if there is a strong motive for feigning insanity: if there has never been anything of the kind prior to the motive arising, and if the insanity is violent and acute

---

[1] Journal of Mental Science, January, 1870.

in character, we may reasonably suspect it, and close observation will generally leave no doubt of the deception.

I alluded a minute ago to a belief not altogether uncom-
The odor of   mon, that the insane possess a peculiar odor, and
the insane.   that insanity may be detected by the nose. I will
not relate to you the various opinions and modifications of
opinion on the subject. It is one of those matters which
can hardly be brought to a definite test, for the sense of
smell is altogether subjective, and a preconceived notion may
go far to help a person to discover an odor. Doubtless many
lunatics smell offensively. I have already told you that in
acute mania there is often an intolerable effluvium, especially
from women. Many patients can with difficulty, even in a
chronic state, be kept sweet, and, if very stout, their odor
may be perceptible enough. Many of the poorer classes wear
their clothes a long time, and thus acquire a stale and disagreeable smell. But that there is a smell peculiar to the
insane, which emanates from every insane person, I myself
have failed to discover. It may be that my sense of smell
is not so acute as that of others, though of this I am unaware ;
but certainly I believe that I have seen insane ladies and gentlemen who, washing and dressing like other people, were as
free from smell as the sane who sat with them at table unconscious of their presence. Unfortunately, we are not likely
to advance beyond mere theories and opinions on the subject,
and my own opinion is all that I will advance at the present
time.

LECTURE XIX.

The Law of Lunacy—Private Patients—Order and Certificates—Single
Patients—Notice of Discharge or Death—Leave of Absence—Order
of Transfer—Pauper Patients—The Property of Patients—Commission of Lunacy.

IT now becomes my duty to tell you something about the
legal methods of dealing with persons of unsound mind.
Legislation has again and again, during five hundred years,
regulated the manner in which the persons and property of
such people are to be cared for; and although the statutes
relating to the subject are not less than forty in number, I
hope to be able to put before you in brief that which it is
essential for you to remember while practicing your profession. And I may as well say at the outset that I am not lec-
turing for those who have, or are to have, the care and charge
of an asylum. Any of you who undertake this duty will
learn the details, legal and medical, by special study. My
present object is to teach to those who are not specially concerned with this branch of practice that which they require
for the purpose of sending a patient to an asylum, attending
one who does not require the restraint of an asylum, and
giving evidence before a commission in lunacy, or on other
occasions when a man's sanity is called in question.

The subject naturally divides itself into two parts, one
which relates to the person, the other to the property of a
lunatic; and the former may be subdivided into one portion
relating to the person of private lunatics, and that which is

concerned only with the custody of paupers. I therefore shall speak of it under these heads.

I. { 1. The care and custody of private lunatics.
{ 2. The care and custody of pauper lunatics.

II. The care of the property of lunatics.

Here I would remark that a man does not necessarily come under the cognizance of the lunacy laws because he The lunacy laws do not affect all lunatics. happens to be a lunatic. He may be a lunatic for years, and may be tended and restrained in his own house, or in that of a relative or friend, provided that his own friends or relations take care of him, and take care of him properly. It is the common law of the land that a man's friends may restrain him from harm, or protect him, if he is unable to protect himself. But if the lunatic is not taken care of by his own friends, or if they neglect him, and he is found to be wandering at large or improperly confined or maintained, then the Lunacy Acts reach him, the Lord Chancellor or Home Secretary may order him to be visited in the friends' or his own house, and necessary steps to be taken for his amelioration.

The Lunacy Acts define with tolerable accuracy the persons who may take care of lunatics without legal supervision. They must be persons "who derive no profit from the charge." Any one deriving profit, whether as proprietor of the house or lodging, or as companion, nurse, or attendant, must comply with the statutes I am about to describe.

There is, however, one exception to this. The committee of a person found lunatic by inquisition may take charge of such person, or may commit him to the charge of another, without medical certificates, upon his own order, having annexed to it an office-copy of his appointment.

With these exceptions—viz., the care of a patient by his Documents necessary for restraining a lunatic. own relatives or friends, or his own committee or committee's agent—all private lunatics are to be restrained and kept only after the due execution of three legal documents, which are called the "Order and Medical Certificates." Although you, as medical men, are chiefly concerned with the latter, it is right that you should also be familiar with the "order," that you may be able to instruct the friends of a patient.

Here is the order in the statutory form. Generally speaking, we fill up printed forms, but the whole may be in writing if no printed form is at hand. The "order."

ORDER FOR THE RECEPTION OF A PRIVATE PATIENT.

I, the undersigned, hereby request you to receive *John Jones*, whom I last saw at 20 *Smith Street, Paddington*, on the *twenty-first March*, 187Q,(a) a (b) *person of unsound mind,* as a patient into your house.

(a) Within one month previous to the date of the order.

Subjoined is a statement respecting the said *John Jones.*

       Signed,   Name, *Mary Jones.*
     Occupation (if any),
        Place of abode, 20 *Smith Street, Paddington.*

(b) Lunatic, or an idiot, or a person of unsound mind.

Degree of Relationship (if any), ⎫
   or other circumstances of con- ⎬ *Wife.*
   nection with the Patient, ⎭

Dated this *twenty-first* day of *March*, one thousand eight hundred and *seventy.*

     To *Robert Brown, Esq.*,(c)
          Proprietor,(d) *Bath House Asylum.*

(c) Proprietor or superintendent of.
(d) Describing the house or hospital by situation and name.

I have here filled up the order with the name of an imaginary patient, *John Jones*, the other names being, of course, equally fictitious. Now, observe that the person signing the order must have seen the patient within a calendar month. This is a recent and most proper regulation. Formerly, a person might sign an order for the reception of one whom he had never seen in his life; but now he must have seen him within a month, must state where he saw him last, and affirm that he is of unsound mind. In the marginal notes you will see that the patient may be described as *a lunatic, idiot*, or *person of unsound mind*. One of these he must be called, and it is usual to adopt the last as the least painful to friends, and, at the same time, most comprehensive. "Subjoined is a statement." This must accompany the order, and to it I shall come immediately. Who may sign the order, and who may not? I suppose, in my imaginary case, that the wife signs it. It should, in my opinion, be signed by the nearest relative; but frequently there is a great objection to so doing on the part of relatives, and the statute allows any one to sign who can show any sort of reason for interfering, as a friend, a magistrate, or the minister of the parish. He or she must, however, have seen the patient within the month, and this the date at the bottom will indicate. But certain people may not sign the order. First, no person may sign who receives any percentage on, or is otherwise interested in, the payments to be made by, or on account of, any patient received into an asylum or other house. Secondly, no one can sign the order who is the medical attendant, or the proprietor, of the asylum into which the patient is to go. Thirdly, no one can sign who is the father, brother, son, partner, or assistant, of either of the medical men who sign the certificates, or who himself has signed one of the certificates. The order must be directed to the person under whose care the patient is to be placed, whether it be the owner of a private house or lodging, or the owner or superintendent of a private lunatic asylum or hospital.

Who may or may not sign the "order."

This order, you are to recollect, will authorize the reception of a patient during one calendar month from its date, and no longer. If a month has expired, a fresh order will be necessary.[1]

Duration of the "order."

Underneath the order on the printed form is placed the "Statement," which I will fill up with supposed particulars.

The "statement."

---

[1] 25 and 26 Vict. cap. 3, sec. 23.

STATEMENT.

If any particulars in this statement be not known, the fact to be so stated.

Name of patient, with christian name at length, ... } *John Jones.*

Sex and age, ... *Male,* 35.

Married, single, or widowed, . . . *Married.*

Condition of life and previous occupation (if any), ... } *Clerk.*

Religious persuasion, so far as known, . *Church of England.*

Previous place of abode, ... 20 *Smith Street, Paddington.*

Whether first attack, ... *Second.*

Age (if known) on first attack, . . *Thirty.*

When and where previously under care and treatment, ... } *Bath House Asylum, in* 1865.

Duration of existing attack, . . . *Three weeks.*

Supposed cause, ... *Unknown.*

Whether subject to epilepsy, . . . *No.*

Whether suicidal, ... *Yes.*

Whether dangerous to others, . . . *No.*

Whether found lunatic by inquisition, and date of commission or order for inquisition, ... } *No.*

Special circumstances (if any) preventing the patient being examined before admission, separately by two medical practitioners, ... } *None.*

Name and address of relative to whom notice of death to be sent, . . . } *Mary Jones,* 20 *Smith Street, Paddington, W.*

Signed, Name,(e) *Mary Jones.*

Occupation (if any),

Place of Abode,

Degree of Relationship (if any), or other circumstances of connection with the Patient. }

(e) Where the person who signs the statement is not the person who signs the order, the following particulars concerning the person signing the statement are to be added.

This statement, which is the appendix, as it were, to the order, needs little explanation. It is a statement of the facts of the case for the guidance of the proprietor of the asylum, and for the information of the Commissioners in Lunacy. As in the order, the name of the patient must be

stated in full, christian and surname, and every other detail
must be filled up in some way. No space must be left blank.
There are certain points on which friends are very reluctant
to give accurate information, and yet it is important that we
should have it. They are very apt to give the duration of
the existing attack as being very short, when it may turn
out on inquiry that the patient has been insane for a long
period, though possibly only dangerous or excited during a
few weeks or days. Then we rarely get the true cause assigned. Frequently this is hereditary transmission—a fact
which friends are most loath to mention. And they do not
like to describe a patient as suicidal or dangerous, and yet it
is of great importance to those who are to have the charge
that this should be stated, and if there be any doubt, it is
better to state the suspicion than to give a direct negative to
the question. With regard to the last question but one,
"special circumstances, &c.," I must say a word. Inasmuch
as it is often very difficult for a medical man to gain access
to a patient, and it may be of the utmost consequence that
such a patient should be at once deprived of the power of
doing harm to himself or others, there is a clause in the Act
—16 and 17 Vict., c. 96, sec. 5—which provides that "any
person (not a pauper) may, under special circumstances preventing the examination of such person by two medical practitioners, be received as a lunatic into any house or hospital,
upon such 'order' as aforesaid, and with the certificate of
one physician, surgeon, or apothecary alone, provided that
the statement accompanying such order set forth the special
circumstances which prevent the examination of such person
by two medical practitioners; but in every case two other
such certificates shall, within three clear days after his reception into such house or hospital, be signed by two other
persons, each of whom shall be a physician, surgeon, or
apothecary, not in partnership with or an assistant to the
other, or the physician, surgeon, or apothecary, who signed

the certificate on which the patient was received, and not connected with such house or hospital, and shall within such time and separately from the other of them have personally examined the person so received as a lunatic."

Such is the meaning of the question commencing with the words "special circumstances."

The statement is commonly, but not necessarily, signed by the person who signs the order. It may be signed by any one having the knowledge requisite, and he must state his relationship or connection after the signature.

We now pass to that which more immediately concerns ourselves, viz., the medical certificates.

And first, who may and who may not sign these? Any physician, surgeon, or apothecary may sign a certificate, if he be a person registered under the Medical Act passed in the session 21 and 22 Victoria, cap. 90. Not only must he be legally qualified, he must also be registered. This is not generally known; but the reception of a certificate from a non-registered practitioner would, in my opinion, lay the proprietor of an asylum open to the charge of illegally receiving. *The two medical certificates.*

Certain medical men, however, are precluded from signing the certificates.

1. The two medical men must not be professionally connected, must not be in partnership, nor may one be the assistant of the other. *Who may or may not sign them.*

2. Neither of them must be the proprietor of the house or asylum into which the patient is to be received, nor must he receive any percentage on the payments to be made for the patient, nor must he be the medical attendant after reception of such patient, whether in a private house or an asylum.

3. No medical man who, or whose father, brother, son, partner, or assistant, is wholly or partly the proprietor of, or the regular professional attendant in, a licensed asylum or

hospital, shall sign a certificate for the reception of a patient into such house or hospital.

4. No medical man who, or whose father, brother, son, partner, or assistant, shall sign the "order" already spoken of, shall sign any certificate for the reception of the same patient.

Thus, you observe the various persons—the person signing the order, and those signing the certificates—are to be entirely independent one of another, and all three are to be independent and unconnected with the proprietor of the asylum, or the medical attendant of the patient, if he is not in an asylum. So the co-operation of four independent persons, of whom three must be medical men, is requisite for the restraining of any one under the Lunacy Acts, and each of the two medical men who are to sign the certificates must examine the patient separately. This you must recollect, because in all probability it will happen that you will be called to meet another practitioner to consult with him as to the propriety of placing some one under legal restraint. Although you together make an examination for the purpose of consultation, you must again visit and question the individual separately, and, repeating the examination, you must elicit that which you are about to write down in your certificate. Otherwise, if at any future time the alleged lunatic were to bring an action against the proprietor of the asylum for false imprisonment, the certificates would be invalidated by neglect of this rule.

I now pass to the consideration of the form of the medical certificates, one of which I will fill up, as I filled up the order, with imaginary details.

MEDICAL CERTIFICATE.

I, the undersigned, being a (a) *Fellow of the Royal College of Surgeons of England*, and being in actual practice as a (b) *Surgeon*, hereby certify that I, on the *twentieth* day of March, 1870, at (c) 20 *Smith Street, Paddington*, in the county of *Middlesex*, separately from any other medical practitioner, personally examined *John Jones*, of (d) 20 *Smith Street, Paddington, clerk*, and that the said *John Jones* is a (e) *person of unsound mind*, and a proper person to be taken charge of and detained under care and treatment, and that I have formed this opinion upon the following grounds, viz. :

1. Facts indicating insanity observed by myself. (f) *He is under a delusion that he has committed some unpardonable sin, that he is Antichrist, and that his name is mentioned in all the newspapers. His appearance denotes great agitation and depression.*

2. Other facts (if any) indicating insanity communicated to me by others. (g) *I am informed by his brother, Robert Jones, that he has attempted to jump into the river, and out of window.*

Signed, Name, *William Green.*

Place of Abode, 10 *Richmond Street, Paddington.*

Dated this *twenty-first* day of *March*, one thousand eight hundred and *seventy*.

(a) Set forth the qualification entitling the person certifying to practice as a physician, surgeon, or apothecary, *ex. gra.*:—Fellow of the Royal College of Physicians in London, Licentiate of the Apothecaries' Company, or as the case may be.

(b) Physician, surgeon, or apothecary, as the case may be.

(c) Here insert the street and number of the house (if any), or other like particulars.

(d) Insert residence and profession or occupation (if any), of the patient.

(e) Lunatic, or an idiot, or a person of unsound mind.

(f) Here state the facts.

(g) Here state the information, and from whom.

Now, if you consider this form of medical certificate, you will notice that, according to the directions appended in the margin, you are first of all to state your legal qualification. Not merely are you to say that you are a physician or surgeon; you are to give the name of the diploma you hold. In addition to this, you must assert that you are in actual practice; a retired practitioner, or a medical man who has given up the profession and is otherwise occupied, cannot sign either of the certificates. Then comes the date, and this is important. The dates of the certificates are quite different from those of the order. The order may be signed and dated by any one who has seen the patient within a month, and it is valid for a month from the signing thereof. But the medical

certificate is only valid for seven days, not from the signing,
but from the examination of the patient. The date
of the examination, the first date in the certificate, is
the important part: within seven days from this the
reception of the patient must take place, or the certificate
expires. It may be signed and dated at any time between
the examination and the reception. The date of the day of
the month and the year must be given, and also the place of
examination. And you are to specify the street and number
of the house, if it has one, as well as the county. Also your
examination of the patient must take place without any
medical man being present, as I have already explained to
you. Other people may be present, but they must not be
medical men practicing. The names, christian and surname, of the patient must be written at length, together
with his residence, profession, or occupation. You then
affirm that the said patient is one of three things—a lunatic, idiot, or person of unsound mind; and, as I said in the
case of the order, it is better to use the last expression,
which comprises every variety. You also affirm—and this,
too, is important—not only that the individual is of unsound mind, but that he is " a proper person to be taken
charge of and detained under care and treatment;" in other
words, to be taken care of as a lunatic under certificates of
lunacy. There may be many patients afflicted with unsoundness of mind, temporary or other, for whom we might
hesitate or refuse to sign certificates of lunacy. Formerly
the medical man merely stated his opinion that the patient
was of unsound mind, without giving reasons, and upon
such a certificate the patient was received. The same practice still continues in Ireland; but in England and Scotland
you are obliged to state your reasons for coming to such a
conclusion; and the Commissioners will reject the certificate and release the patient if they do not consider the reasons strong enough. Now, the reasons are divided in the

Duration of medical certificates.

form into two parts—the facts observed by yourselves, and
those communicated by others; and I need not tell   The facts
you that those observed by yourselves are the most   indicating
important, the others being necessarily hearsay re- insanity.
ports, which frequently you may have reason to disbelieve.
Now, these facts are supposed to be observed by you on the
day of examination, the day mentioned as the date, and
when they consist of the result of conversation carried on upon
that day, there can be no doubt about the matter.   When,
however, your opinion is based not upon a particular delusion, but upon the general conduct of an individual, there
is often great difficulty in getting enough on one particular
day to warrant your signing a certificate.   And the Commissioners in Lunacy insist on this being done.   In their
Fifteenth Report (1861) they say: " It would, of course, be
impossible that any examining medical man should exclude
from his consideration facts known to him of the antecedents
of the patient, immediate or remote; these are entitled to
their full influence ; but the legislature has been careful to
guard against such facts exercising undue influence in the
certificate he is called on to give, by requiring that this certificate shall be directly deducible from examination on a particular day and at a specified place ; and that the opinion expressed therein as having been formed on such particular day
shall be set forth as the result of his having observed at that
time in the person under examination some specific fact indicating insanity."
    You will, therefore, have to connect that which you may
have observed previously with what you observe on the particular day.   If a patient justifies his past conduct, and de-
fends it in an insane manner, you may elicit sufficient for
your purpose ; or, without asserting delusions, he may admit
that he has entertained them previously, or otherwise indicate that he has not given them up.   Frequently, when you
anticipate that you will have to examine a patient for a certificate, and have reason to think that he will deny his be-

liefs, it is as well not to subject him to any cross-examination upon them till the actual day arrives. But I shall have something to say concerning the examination of patients subsequently: here I am only speaking of the requisite formalities.

It is not necessary that any facts communicated by others should be inserted. Where those observed by your-

Facts communicated by others. selves are plain and unmistakable, it rather weakens than strengthens a certificate to supplement them with others received on hearsay. But frequently that which you observe is explained and illustrated by what the patient has said to others; and acts committed by him, acts of attempted homicide, suicide, or other violence, may not have been witnessed by you, yet may be valuable indications of insanity.

Two certificates complete the formalities requisite for placing a patient under restraint. Each must be the independent opinion of a registered practitioner, who, in signing this legal document, does so under grave responsibilities. If he does it negligently or fraudulently, he is liable to an action at law, and to be mulcted in heavy damages. Upon such order and medical certificates, a proprietor or superintendent of an asylum may receive a person as a lunatic,

Copies of order and certificates to be sent to Commissioners. pleading them in justification; but he must send a copy of them to the Commissioners in Lunacy within twenty-four hours; and then, after the expiration of two clear days, and before the expiration of seven days, he also transmits to the Commissioners a

Also a statement of health. "statement," containing his own observations upon the mental and bodily state of the patient. The same thing is done by the proprietor, if the patient is removed, not to an asylum, but to the house of a private individual, becoming what is called a "single patient."

You will have noticed in the newspapers reports of prose-

"Single patients." cutions, instituted by the Commissioners in Lunacy, against various persons, for wrongfully receiving and taking care of people of unsound mind; and, from the phraseology adopted, you may think, as many do, that they were prosecuted for receiving these patients *without a license.* But this is not so. No license is required for the reception of one patient. When two are received, then a license becomes necessary. What is requisite is that these single patients should be received upon an "order" and two certificates, just as if they went to an asylum, and that copies should be sent to the Commissioners, thus registering the patient on their records.

As you may have occasion to send patients to reside in this way with a family, and may wish to attend them while there, I will briefly describe the regulations to be observed. You wish to send one to the house of some private individual, male or female. The order and certificates are procured in the usual way, and copies of them are to be sent by the proprietor of the house to the Commissioners in Lunacy within twenty-four hours of the admission of the patient, together with a notice of the admission signed by the said proprietor. *If you are to be the medical attendant, you must not sign either of the certificates.* After two clear days, and before the expiration of seven days, you will send to the Commissioners a "statement" of the mental and bodily condition of the patient. Then once a fortnight at least you will enter in a book, to be kept at the house for the inspection of the Commissioners, an account of the patient under the following heads:

Date.	Mental State and Progress.	Bodily Health and Condition.	Restraint or Seclusion since last Entry. When and how long. By what means and for what reason.	Visits of Friends.	State of House, Bed, and Bedding, &c.

This is called the "Medical Visitation Book," which will

be inspected and signed by the Commissioners when they visit the patient. When the patient leaves, a " Notice of Notice of Discharge" must be sent to the Commissioners by discharge. the proprietor in the following form :

FORM OF NOTICE OF DISCHARGE.

I hereby give you notice, that   a single patient, received into this (a)   on the   day of   18   , was discharged therefrom (b)   by the authority of day of   18   .

Signed, _____

(c)_____

_____

Dated this   day of   one thousand eight hundred and seventy
      To the _____

(a) House.
(b) Recovered, or relieved, or not improved.
(c) Superintendent or proprietor of —— house or hospital at ——.

If he dies, a "Notice of Death," signed by the medical at-Notice of tendant, must be sent to the Commissioners and also death. to the Coroner of the district, who may hold an inquest if he thinks fit. There is a special form for the notice of death.

NOTICE OF DEATH.

I hereby give you notice, that   a single patient, received into this (a)   on the   day of   18 , died therein on the   day of   18   ; and I further certify, that
was present at the death of the said
and that the apparent cause of death of the said   (b) was

Signed, _____

(c)_____

_____

Dated this   day of   one thousand eight hundred and seventy
     To the Commissioners in Lunacy.

(a) House or hospital.
(b) As ascertained by post-mortem examination, if so.
(c) Medical attendant of ——

I give you the forms of this and of the notice of discharge.

Blank forms like the above may be purchased, but it is not absolutely necessary that the order and other documents should be on a printed form. The whole may be in manuscript if a printed form is not procurable, provided that the wording is the same.

If it is thought advisable to send the patient for change of air to the seaside or elsewhere, or to allow him to go "Leave of home upon trial, "Leave of Absence" may be ob- Absence." tained from the Commissioners.

OFFICE OF COMMISSIONERS IN LUNACY,

19 Whitehall Place, S. W.,

18 .

By virtue of the power vested in us by the 86th section of the Act 8 and 9 Vict. c. 100, we hereby signify our consent to the removal under proper control, of   a certified patient in   House, to for the period of   calendar month   from

} Commissioners
   in Lunacy.

To

NOTE.—In forwarding "the approval in writing" required by the above section, it should be stated, whether it is "of the person who signed the order," or "of the person who made the last payment."

If it is necessary to remove him from one place of residence to another, or from one asylum to another, this may be done by obtaining an "Order of Transfer" from the Com- "Order of missioners, in which case fresh certificates will not Transfer." be required.

TRANSFER OF PRIVATE PATIENT.

CONSENT.

We, the undersigned, Commissioners in Lunacy, hereby consent to the removal, on or before the   day of   18   , of   a private patient in   House

Given under our hands this   day of in the year of our Lord, one thousand eight hundred and

} Commissioners
   in Lunacy.

ORDER.

I*   the undersigned, having authority to discharge   a private
patient in   House,   hereby order and direct that the said
be removed therefrom to   House
     Given under my hand this*   day of   in the year of our
     Lord one thousand eight hundred and
               Signed,
               Place of abode,

NOTE.—This order must be signed and dated subsequently to the consent of the Commissioners:
and it must be signed by—

Generally
1. The person who signed the order for the patient's admission:
2. If such person be incapable (by reason of insanity, or absence from England, or
   otherwise), or if he be dead, then by the husband or wife of the patient:
3. If there be no husband or wife, then by the patient's father:
4. If there be no father, then by the patient's mother:
5. If there be no father or mother, then by any one of the patient's nearest of kin:
   or by the person who made the last payment on the patient's account.
In cases of Chancery patients—The Committee of the person.

If the patient escapes, he may be recaptured within four-
Escape and   teen days upon the original order and certificates:
recovery.   if fourteen days have elapsed, a fresh order and certificates must be obtained. Notice of the escape and recap-
ture must be sent to the Commissioners. If not recaptured,
notice of the escape must be sent within two clear days.

All these enactments apply equally to private patients in
asylums, and to single patients.

I will now say a few words as to the method of proceeding
Pauper   when we desire to place a pauper in an asylum. Of
patients.   the management of public asylums I say nothing, but
it may fall to your lot to have to send thither poor people
who have been under your care.

The law enacts that the medical officer of a poor-law
district, on becoming aware of a lunatic, shall give notice
thereof to the relieving officer, or, if there be not one, to the
overseer. In the same way any person may give notice of
the same to the relieving officer or overseer. The latter is
in turn to give notice to a justice of the peace of the county
or borough, who within three days shall cause the lunatic to
be brought before him, or shall visit him at his house, and
shall examine him, with the aid of a medical man. If the

latter gives a medical certificate, and the justice is satisfied that the pauper is a lunatic, and a proper person to be taken charge of and detained under care and treatment, he shall make an order for his reception into an asylum. If two medical certificates are given, one by the medical officer and a second by any other medical man, the justice *must* make the order without any option.

If the pauper cannot be taken before a justice or be visited by him, he may be visited by an officiating clergyman, together with the relieving officer (or overseer), and their joint order may be given for his removal, after the medical certificate or certificates are signed. The medical certificate is in precisely the same form as that I have already given. It must not be signed, however, by any medical man who is the medical officer of the asylum, nor by any one whose father, brother, son, partner, or assistant shall sign the order.

If the relieving officer cannot at once take the lunatic to the asylum, he may take him to the workhouse, and in point of fact a great number of patients are taken there first: but it is enacted that "No person shall be detained in any workhouse, being a lunatic, or alleged lunatic, beyond the period of fourteen days, unless in the opinion, given in writing, of the medical officer of the union or parish to which the workhouse belongs, such person is a proper person to be kept in a workhouse, nor unless the accommodation in the workhouse is sufficient for his reception : and any person detained in a workhouse in contravention of this section shall be deemed to be a proper person to be sent to an asylum within the meaning of section sixty-seven of the Lunacy Act, chapter 97 ; and in the event of any person being detained in a workhouse in contravention of this section, the medical officer shall, for all the purposes of the Lunacy Act, cap. 97, be deemed to have knowledge that a pauper resident within his district is a lunatic and a proper person to be sent to an asylum ; and it shall be his duty to act accordingly, and further to sign such certificate with a view to more certainly securing the reception into an asylum of such pauper lunatic as aforesaid."—(25 & 26 Vict. c. 3, sec. 20.)

This section enacts that any medical officer having knowledge of a lunatic being in his district, being a proper person to be sent to an asylum, shall give notice of it in writing to the relieving officer or overseer.—(*Vide ante*, p. 395.)

The foregoing remarks apply to pauper patients resident Wandering in a parish or district. But patients are often found lunatics. at large—wandering lunatics, as they are called—and the law deals with them in this capacity. It is enacted (16 & 17 Vict. c. 97, sec. 68), that every constable, relieving officer, or overseer, who shall have knowledge that any person wandering at large within the parish is deemed to be a lunatic, shall immediately apprehend and take such person before a justice. The justice, calling to his aid a medical man and obtaining from him a medical certificate, may make an order for the lunatic's reception into an asylum or hospital. Or the justice may act on his own knowledge, and may examine the lunatic at his own abode or elsewhere.

This is to be done whether the patient is a pauper or not. Patients may be found wandering at large and be taken care of in this way till their friends can be communicated with, or they may be taken to an asylum, if paupers, and thence transferred to the asylum of their own parish. But in this manner they are to be dealt with according to the law.

There are other patients for whose amelioration the law Lunatics makes provision. These are people not wandering improperly at large, but ill treated or neglected by their rela- treated by friends. tions or friends. Not unfrequently do we read in the newspapers of lunatics found caged in cellars, attics, or outhouses, and more or less neglected or cruelly treated. Or, short of this, a lunatic may be allowed by his relatives to remain in his own house in a state in which he is dangerous to himself or others. Here the enactment is in some respects similar to the last mentioned. The constable, relieving officer, or overseer of any parish, having knowledge of there being such a lunatic not under proper care and control, or being cruelly treated or neglected by any relative or other person having the care or charge of him, shall give information on oath within three days to a justice of the peace, who shall visit and examine such person, or direct some medical man to visit and examine him; and shall then require any constable or relieving officer to bring the lunatic before any two justices of the county or borough, and they shall call upon a medical man to examine him, and, with his certificate, send him to an asylum. They may, however, suspend the removal for a period not exceeding fourteen days; and they may hand the patient over to his friends, if satisfied by them that he will be properly taken care of.

You are not to forget, however, that it is lawful for any one to restrain a lunatic who is dangerous to himself or others, by virtue of the common law, apart from the lunacy statutes. This has been decided more than once. In Scott v. Wakem, an action of trespass was brought against a medical man for placing the plaintiff under restraint while in a state of delirium tremens; and Baron Bramwell ruled that a medical man may justify measures necessary to restrain a dangerous lunatic. The same opinion was held by Chief Justice Cockburn, in Symm v. Fraser and another, in 1863. Here Mrs. Symm, a widow, had been restrained while in a state of delirium tremens. It is done, in fact, constantly: certificates of lunacy are not signed for patients whose malady only lasts for a few days. We use the measures necessary for their safe custody, as we should for those delirious from fever or other diseases. And in the case of dangerous lunatics, you will recollect that you are justified in restraining them by force from doing mischief, till the order and certificates necessary for placing them in

Dangerous lunatics may be restrained under the common law.

an asylum are signed.   Do not be timid in taking such steps.
Do not, as is so often the case, let the patient go on till something dreadful occurs.   The bench of judges will take care
that you are held blameless in such a case, whatever prejudiced juries may think.   The Chief Justice, in the latter of
the actions I have named, desired the jury "to consider the
case not only with reference to the interests of the individuals committed to the care of medical men, but also with a
view to their interests in another sense—taking care not to
impair or neutralize the energy and usefulness of medical
assistance, by exposing medical men unjustly to vexatious
and harassing actions."

There is one other legal procedure on which I must say
something.   Hitherto I have been speaking of the
legal methods of restraining the person of a lunatic,
private or pauper.   But the law, by another process, makes provision for the proper protection of the property of a patient.

*Of the prop-
erty of
patients.*

In old times the King was held to be the natural guardian
of idiots and lunatics, and committed the care of them to
whom he chose; but now the Lord Chancellor is directed by
the Crown to perform this office, and such people become
wards of the Court of Chancery.   There is a numerous array
of statutes relating to " Chancery lunatics," as they are called
—statutes which have grown up alongside of those I have
already mentioned, and which in some respects clash with
them.   There is a separate Board of Commissioners to look
after such patients, and the consequence is that in many
details confusion exists.

For, although a patient may have been for twenty years
a certified patient in an asylum, visited regularly by the
Board of Commissioners in Lunacy, at the head of which
Board is, nominally, the Lord Chancellor, yet so far as his
property is concerned, the said patient is considered of sound

mind; and to deal with it on his behalf a commission must be issued by the Lord Chancellor to try whether Commission he be of unsound mind—a fact which may have of lunacy. been known to one Board of Commissioners for a long period.

Not to go into details which do not concern you, I may say, that the present practice is for some one or more persons interested in the patient to petition the Lords Justices to direct that an inquisition shall be held as to the state of mind of the said patient. This petition must be accompanied by affidavits of the mental condition, and you may be called upon to give such an affidavit. The patient must have notice given him of the presentation of the petition, and, if he chooses, he may, within seven days of such notice, demand a jury. If the Lords Justices direct an inquiry, it is held, generally speaking, by one of the Masters in Lunacy. But if the Lord Chancellor think fit, he may direct the issue to be tried in one of the Superior Courts of common law. When the property of the alleged lunatic does not exceed in value the sum of one thousand pounds, a commission of lunacy may be avoided. By the Act 25 and 26 Vict. c. 86, sec. 12, in order that the property of insane persons, when of small amount, may be applied for their benefit in a summary and inexpensive manner, it is enacted as follows: " Where, by the report of one of the Masters in Lunacy or of the Commissioners in Lunacy, or by affidavit or otherwise, it is established to the satisfaction of the Lord Chancellor that any person is of unsound mind and incapable of managing his affairs, and that his property does not exceed one thousand pounds in value, or that the income thereof does not exceed fifty pounds per annum, the Lord Chancellor may, without directing any inquiry under a commission of lunacy, make such order as he may consider expedient for the purpose of rendering the property of such person, or the income thereof, available for his maintenance or benefit, or for carrying on his trade or business : provided, nevertheless, that the alleged insane person shall have such personal notice of the application for such order as aforesaid as the Lord Chancellor shall by general order direct."

The alleged lunatic may demand a jury, and the demand must be complied with, unless the Lord Chancellor is satisfied by personal examination that the individual is incompetent to express or form a wish on the subject. Practically, we find that many patients are in this condition: no jury is demanded, and then the issue is tried by one of the Masters with a jury.

Whether there is a jury or not, you may have to be examined on oath as a witness, and, it may be, cross-examined, and it behooves you to form a very clear and accurate conception of the opinion you are going to give, and the grounds on which you will uphold it. Counsel will try to entrap you in every way, and ask you to define insanity, or unsoundness of mind. Do not, however, be tempted into discussing any abstract questions; confine yourself to the case before you, the state of mind of the alleged lunatic, and that which he has said or done. You will be assailed with questions as to whether you think this or that act indicative of insanity. Such an act may possibly be done by a sane person, but a number of such acts may be conclusive as to the insanity of any one, or one act may at once stamp the particular individual as insane.

Your opinion may be asked as to the advisability of holding a commission of lunacy, for it is not expedient to take this costly step if the patient is likely to recover soon, or to die. Solicitors often fancy that a commission of lunacy is to be taken out as soon as a patient is put under legal restraint, but this is not so. Unless his affairs urgently demand it, such a step should be deferred until it can be seen whether he is likely to recover in a reasonable time or not. I have known a patient nearly well before the commission was held: and if he is likely to recover within a few months, it is most unfair to subject him to the expense and stigma of a commission, and throw upon him the trouble and cost of superseding it. Your prognosis will be based upon the principles enunciated throughout these lectures, which I need not repeat here. Time is in this your great auxiliary: though patients do recover after years of insanity, they do so but seldom. If a patient has been under care and treatment for a twelvemonth, and does not show manifest signs of real improvement, his case is sufficiently unfavorable to warrant at all events an inquisition. For, as I have said, this may be superseded on recovery. The patient will petition the Lord Chancellor or Lords Justices to supersede the petition and set free himself and his property, and he must support his petition by medical affidavits. Here the questions of recovery, or partial recovery, or apparent recovery, will arise, and you will recollect what I said on these heads in a former lecture.

LECTURE XX.

THERE remains one subject on which I must say something. I have spoken of the legal formalities necessary to be observed when a man or woman is placed in confinement, and have mentioned that you will be called upon to sign medical certificates and affidavits of the unsoundness of mind of a patient. I propose to say a few words concerning the way in which you are to examine such people with a view of testing their mental condition. Very general must my observations be, for it is not possible to lay down rules for the performance of such a task with anything like strictness. Yet some hints may be useful to those who are quite without experience in the matter. You have two things to decide before you sign a certificate : first, whether the individual is or is not of unsound mind ; secondly, whether he is a fit and proper person to be detained under care and treatment. These are distinct questions, and it is clear that the legislature, by thus distinguishing them, allows to medical men a certain judgment in deciding whether or not a person who may be of unsound mind is a proper person to be detained under care and treatment as a lunatic protected or restrained by certificates of lunacy. Many patients during acute illnesses may be for a time of unsound mind, yet can in no sense be called proper persons to be de-

Two points to be kept in view.

tained as lunatics under care and treatment; and there may be some of feeble mind, yet gentle, harmless, and docile, who do not require the protection of the lunacy laws, and are not proper persons to be detained. As I have said elsewhere, it is not always easy to sign a certificate for a patient concerning whom we may make a general declaration in an affidavit, for the Commissioners in Lunacy insist that all that is alleged of the patient shall have been observed on a given day. It must not be the outcome of an acquaintance extending over some years, and although you have a general opinion that the individual is weak-minded or insane, it may be based rather on what you have heard than on what you see.

Concerning the cases of acute disease in which the mind is temporarily disordered, little is to be said. You will not think of signing certificates here. And in acute insanity, where medical assistance is urgently needed, there will be little difficulty in appreciating the state of mind, and signing a certificate. In these cases the real difficulty experienced is more frequently in gaining access to the patient, and in engaging him in conversation. This done, his malady is revealed, and our end is accomplished. In gaining admittance to a patient, our difficulties may come from the patient himself, or from ill-judging or ill-meaning friends, who, because they think

The insanity may be undoubted, but access difficult.

that all doctors are leagued together to shut every one up in a madhouse, or because they have an interest in keeping the patient where he is, frustrate the endeavors which perhaps his nearest of kin are making for his safety or cure. Such persons resist the inspection of the patient, on the plea that he is not insane, but only a little excited, and requires rest and quiet. They will insist that he is not dangerous, and to the best of their ability they will keep him from doing anything very outrageous. I suppose that scarcely one lunatic has ever been placed in an asylum without some of his friends or acquaintances denouncing the sinfulness of the proceeding. There is, however, little danger, though there may be some difficulty, in visiting such a patient. There is more to be apprehended from one who himself dreads and avoids you, and who, from a fear that you are coming to do him some harm, may resist to the uttermost, using murderous weapons. In such a case, it is not possible to lay down rules which are universally applicable. You have to converse with the patient, to assure yourself of his insanity, to sign a certificate. Here, if at all, it may be justifiable and necessary for you to resort to stratagem, to invent an excuse for an interview, to feign to be other than a doctor. Such measures are to be avoided when it is possible, and they often can be avoided, by tact or by open and straightforward plain speaking. They often lead to great difficulties, cause the patient to distrust all about him, and give him occasion to make great complaint. But I am not prepared to say they can always be dispensed with. If a madman has armed himselt with a revolver, and vows that he will not be shut up, and if he has, by previous experience, found out that doctors are a necessary item in the process, he will be a bold man who will go in a strictly professional capacity to sign a certificate. One thing is certain, that stratagems are better left alone in many cases where friends urge their adoption, especially the devices invented by friends, which frequently are so clumsy that you may by them be absolutely debarred from having the requisite conversation with the alleged lunatic. I have, on arriving at a house, been shown suddenly into a patient's room, and introduced to him as some person of whose name, occupation, or relationship I was utterly ignorant. If you are introduced, not as a doctor, but as a lawyer, man of business, or the like, you cannot discuss the patient's health, mental or bodily; and questions which you may wish to put will sound impertinent or absurd, or will make him suspect you to be a doctor in disguise, and he may then refuse to

Stratagem not often, though sometimes, necessary.

hold any conversation with you.   In most cases go as a doctor, and as nothing else.   You have then a reason, whether he admits it or not, for cross-examining him closely as to his bodily and mental health.   If stratagem is absolutely necessary, consider it well beforehand, its probable direction and consequences, and be sure that those in league with you play their parts faithfully.   I am assuming now that the insanity of the patient is not doubted, but that conversation with him is difficult.   The peculiar features of the insanity will furnish suggestions for your plan of proceeding.   One man has invented a marvellous scheme for enriching himself and all belonging to him.   You are come to treat with him for the purchase of his patent, or a partnership in his business. Another is going to buy houses and lands.   You have houses and lands to sell.   There is little difficulty in dealing with such, or in gaining access to them.   But if a man is suspicious, fears a conspiracy, and shuts himself up against police, bailiffs, or the like, he may resist strenuously all efforts to observe him.   Such a patient is, however, by the nature of his case, fearful; and if, accompanied by sufficient assistants, you boldly confront him, he will probably not be able to escape entering into conversation with you.   If access is denied to you, not by the patient, but by others, you must consider how the law stands.   A man's own house in this country is his castle, and, sane or insane, he cannot be removed thence except for some good reason, and after lawful proceedings.   The law allows a man's relatives or friends to remove him from home for treatment and cure upon a legal order and certificate; but if a husband chooses to keep his insane wife in his own house, or a wife her in- *Access may be denied, not by patient, but by friends.* sane husband, no one can order his or her removal unless it can be shown that he or she is improperly treated or neglected.   Cases of this kind often arise, and the lunacy authorities are appealed to and requested to give an order for the patient's removal; but they have not the power, and the only method of effecting it is to lay information before a justice or justices, as I have mentioned in my last lecture.[1] If a patient is properly treated in a relative's house or his own, and has medical advice and care, no magistrate would feel called on to order his removal, even if other relatives desired it. But if a person who is no relation takes charge of and detains a patient against the wishes of all the family in his own or the patient's house, it is probable that a magistrate's order might be obtained, and access demanded. The Commissioners in Lunacy have little power over patients until they are brought under their jurisdiction. When they prosecute persons for illegally receiving and detaining patients, they do so only when they can prove that the patient is taken into the house, or taken charge of, "for profit," and taken charge of "as a lunatic," that is, by one who must have known him to be a lunatic. A friend taking charge of a lunatic without profit, for friendship's sake alone, would not be reached by this portion of the Act, and the Commissioners could not order the removal, which is only to be effected through the intervention of a magistrate.

Passing from cases where our difficulty lies in gaining access to the patient, I come to those where opportunities of observation and conversation are afforded,
The insanity may be doubtful.
but where the insanity of the individual is doubtful or difficult to detect, or is denied by himself or certain of his friends or relations. The difficulty may lie in the slightness of the insanity, or in the ingenuity with which the patient baffles our endeavors to detect it.

If the alleged lunatic has been previously under our care, and is known to us, we shall need little information from others; but we are often consulted, as medical men, by the friends of patients with whom we are previously unacquainted, and of whose sane condition we are entirely ignorant. We

---

[1] *Vide* p. 410.

are consulted by friends who wish us either to say that the patient is insane or sane, according as they themselves think, and they wish, of course, to enlist our assistance and evidence to support their own view of the question. Now, do not be led away by the *ex parte* statement which you will receive about a doubtful or disputed case of insanity from those who first consult you. Do not be induced to be an *ex parte* witness, retained like a barrister on one side or the other. Receive all you hear as matter requiring proof, and recollect there are two sides to all such questions.

Information of others not to be received without caution.

Before you go into the presence of a patient, find out as much as you can concerning him from people who differ in the opinion they hold, if it be possible, from as many persons of all ranks as you can, relations, acquaintances, servants, and consider whether their accounts agree or not. And if they disagree, and one side represents him to be sane, and the other insane, consider which is likely to be the better informed, the least prejudiced, the least interested, and the more reliable. One party, who does not wish the patient removed or interfered with, or taken out of its hands, will say that he is not violent or dangerous, but only a little "excited;" that all his so-called delusions are not delusions, for they are all based on facts. Others will justify what he has done, or say that he was provoked to do it. "Excited," "excitable," "excitement," are words which are bandied about in an extraordinary manner. One person is said not to be insane, but only "excited," while "excitement" in another case is alleged as the chief evidence of insanity. It is a vague word meaning nothing, and I advise you not to employ it in writing certificates, or giving evidence concerning insane patients. If friends use it, request them to explain what they mean, whether excitement of speech, excited acts and gestures, or what? As for delusions not being delusions because they are based on something true, we know that the greater part of delusions, like dreams, arise

out of some fact, or combination of facts, and have these as
their groundwork; but they are none the less delusions.
And if, on the other hand, friends allege that the patient is
under delusions, when he holds certain opinions, or asserts
certain facts, which, though improbable, are possible, you
will have to consider whether these may be true, even if the
friends would wish to persuade you that they are all phantoms, or whether a man may not hold extraordinary, or even
extravagant opinions, without their proceeding from insanity.
All the information that can be got you will receive and
weigh, and will then test it by personal conversation and
examination of the patient.

I now suppose that you are brought face to face with the
alleged lunatic. If you are shown into a room
where he is with other people, you may not be able
to say at a glance which is the individual, and may not be at
liberty to ask. It is something more than awkward to commence a conversation with the wrong person, so that I
strongly advise you to make sure before you enter the room
that you will have no difficulty in fixing on the right one.
You can ask such questions concerning the number of people
there, the appearance of the individual, or the distinguishing
marks of his dress, as to render any mistake impossible.
This may seem a piece of trifling advice, but I have known
the difficulty occur. If you can, get a friend to introduce you,
and open the conversation, and there can be no better way
of doing this than by inquiring after the patient's health.
Frequently you can be introduced by his ordinary medical
adviser, or you may tell him that you have come as
his substitute. There will be little difficulty in discovering
the insanity of the melancholic. Though he thinks he is
past all human aid, he will freely tell you his woes and
fancied misfortunes. The gay, exalted, and hilarious paralytic and maniac will disclose his malady readily enough.
But when you have to deal with the suspicious monomaniac,

On visiting a patient.

the man of concealed hallucinations and delusions, with patients who have been shut up already, or with people who
are merely weak-minded, or whose insanity is displayed in
acts rather than in words and delusions, you may converse
for a very long time without being able to detect the hidden
disorder, or to satisfy yourself that what you have heard is
true, and that what has been done has been done from insanity, and not from depravity or wanton mischief. Subjects of
There is no better way of commencing the con- conversation.
versation than by inquiring after the patient's health, because
it is a conversation on a point in which he is concerned.
You may talk to a man forever on points which do not concern him, on the weather or the crops, on politics and the
topics of the day, and he may converse freely, rationally, and
like an ordinary being, if he has no delusions concerning
such matters. You must bring round your conversation to
himself, for this is the point on which he will display his
insanity. He is the subject of whom all his delusions are
predicated. You may talk over an enormous range of ground
and an infinity of topics, you may even talk of matters concerning which he has delusions, but if you do not connect
him with them, your labor may be in vain. And now you
see the advantage of appearing in your own character of
doctor. You assume the right of questioning the patient
about everything which directly or indirectly affects his
health, such as occupation, residence, mental work or worry,
habits—in fact, his daily existence. He may assert that you
are not his medical adviser, that you have no business to
question him, and that he wants none of your advice; but
you will assure him that you have been requested by his
family or his own medical man to see him, and will tell him
that they have been alarmed at his symptoms, at what he
has said, or done, or threatened to do, and this he must explain away or deny. And in his justification, explanation
or denial of insane sayings and doings, he will generally open

up the real state of his mind. If you gain his confidence, and he enters into conversation, it is as a rule not difficult to detect the insanity. But he may refuse to talk, and, without keeping absolute silence as a melancholic or demented patient, may yet tell you nothing whatever. Such answers as he does give are pertinent and correct, but he will not converse concerning himself or any one else. When this is the case, you cannot sign a certificate, and there is nothing to be gained by pressing a patient beyond a certain point; it is better to take your leave and see him again on a subsequent day.

I warned you that in many cases it is time lost to talk on indifferent topics which do not concern the patient: for the same reason there is nothing to be gained by going into the presence of the patient, ostensibly to talk to some one who is in the room with him. You cannot turn from such a person, and suddenly commence to question the patient; and if he, upon your entry and assumed business with another, gets up and leaves the room, you have no excuse for detaining him. Your visit must be to him and to no one else. I mention this because it is a plan often proposed by friends, which as often fails, and the failure of your first attempt often involves the second in greater difficulties.

You may possibly observe something in the patient's appearance, dress, or occupation, which may form a topic of conversation and afford a clue to his mental peculiarities. It may be so extraordinary as at once to indicate insanity, or it may suggest delusions which you may by its aid extract. Nor will you forget during the interview to survey the apartment, supposing it to be the patient's own, and notice anything that is *bizarre* or startling.

Patient's appearance to be noted.

Much has been written concerning the physiognomy of the insane. It is supposed that insanity stamps itself in the countenance of a man, and is recognizable there. In many cases it is, but it is recognizable in some only by those persons who knew the patient in his sane state. Nevertheless, when we approach a patient for the first time, we shall generally find that his emotional state shows some peculiarity. He is not perfectly easy, unconstrained, and void of all undue emotion. Either he is a little too gay, or a little too dull. On entering into conversation we may find him in high spirits, jocund, hilarious, and boisterous towards a stranger; or dull, suspicious, and snappish; or decidedly depressed and melancholy. And these various moods may of themselves, without further information, aid us in discovering the corresponding delusions. The gay and hilarious man will have exalted ideas concerning himself, his personal strength, beauty, and prowess, his wealth, rank, and prospects; the depressed man will have all the delusions of melancholia, will think his soul is lost, his fortune and business ruined, or his body a prey to all manner of disease: while the irritable and suspicious man will think that there is a conspiracy to ruin him, or that people are accusing him of unnatural crimes, that every one looks at him in the streets, and that the newspapers refer to him in all they report. From noting the general manner and demeanor I have often discovered delusions which have been unknown to the friends, and hitherto carefully concealed.

It is always satisfactory to discover delusions. Although insanity may and does exist without them, yet there can be no doubt of its presence when we discover them. But you must make perfectly sure that what you think or are told is a delusion, and one beyond all reasonable question. Certain statements admit of no doubt. A patient told me that he had the devil in his inside, who had converted everything there into cinders, and he produced, in support of this, some black powder, which he said was his fæces thus converted. But many assertions we only know to be delusions from information derived from others—information not always forthcoming, and not always

Alleged delusions to be verified.

credible. A very common delusion is that which a man entertains concerning his wife's infidelity. But if this is all you can discover, and you have no informant but the man on the one side and the wife on the other, are you necessarily to believe her statement that it is a delusion? You will consider the man's general state, his mode of asserting the fact, and the grounds he gives for his belief, and you may very likely, without further testimony, convince yourself from his whole story that he is insane. You will in a certificate state the delusion, your belief that it is a delusion, and your grounds for the belief. Always say that such and such a fancy is a delusion, if it is a thing possible to happen or to have happened; or that you believe it to be a delusion, and your grounds for such belief. Thus, " The patient tells me that he is ruined, which I am assured by his wife, or son, or lawyer, is an entire delusion ; " or, " The patient asserts that his wife is unfaithful, but he cannot tell me the name of any man, or give any grounds whatever for his belief, which I look upon as altogether a delusion."

Friends may have an interest not only in shutting up an individual, but in making it appear that statements made by one who is undoubtedly insane are all of them delusions. Madmen have an unpleasant way of revealing family secrets, and it is convenient to call all such revelations delusions. Here you must, if possible, derive information from others who are not primarily concerned — old servants, medical men, acquaintances, and the like. But for them I should certainly have been disposed to accept as delusions some of the facts that have been told me by patients, and even now I am in doubt about some, never having been able to arrive at the truth. You must well consider who the person is who makes a statement to you concerning a patient and his delusions. Is he or she the person who wishes to place the patient under restraint? Has he or she any interest in so doing beyond the welfare of the alleged lunatic? Fathers and mothers do not often wish to confine their sons and daughters as lunatics, unless they really are such, but it sometimes happens that fathers would like to shut up as mad an unruly son who is vicious and bad. I receive with the greatest caution that which I hear from husbands concerning wives, and *vice versa*. Then, beside the interest which one person may have in confining another, we must make all due allowance for the possibility of our informant being frightened, prejudiced, or ignorant. We must also admit of the patient's being an ignorant person, or one holding very extraordinary opinions on certain points, as religion or politics. Others who differ with him may look on such ideas as quite sufficient to warrant their assertion that the man is mad. We must also make due allowance for the class of life of the alleged patient, especially if we have to base our opinion upon violence of conduct and language. If a gentleman or lady of exalted station and refined manners uses blasphemous and obscene language and vile epithets, we may reasonably question their sanity; but if one of the *plebs* calls his wife filthy names, and threatens to beat her, it does not follow that he is under a delusion as to her fidelity, or that he is insanely dangerous or homicidal. All due allowance must be made for the rank, station, and previous habits of the individual. Counsel may ask us whether we consider swearing, indecent, or profane language, proof of insanity? Of course it is not, looked at *per se;* but when uttered by this or that person, it might be as direct evidence of the state of mind as anything could be. A lady once told me that she knew her husband must be mad when he met her at the station in a white hat. Wearing a white hat is not usually considered evidence of insanity, but such an act on the part of this gentleman—a grave clergyman—convinced his wife that something was very much amiss. So, when you hear people talk of a patient's having delusions, you must request them to state exactly what these are, and it may be that you will have to cross-examine them pretty closely before you examine the patient. You will then examine him upon them, either bringing round the conversation to such points, or telling him that you have heard such things alleged of him. You need not be supposed to believe them, but you can inform him that such things are said of him, and beg for, or at any rate hear, his explanation. And if he denies the whole that you say you have heard, confront him, if possible, with those who have told you. I say, if possible, for friends are very reluctant to assist in such matters, and wish that the lunatic should not know whence we get our information. We are constantly requested not to mention the name of this or that informant. Do not be hampered by any promises whatever. If a matter is to be mentioned, it must have come to us from some one, and patients of the partially insane class can see through the shallow subterfuges so often invented by friends, and their distrust and dislike are only increased and strengthened thereby.

Still greater will be the difficulties which you will have to encounter in signing certificates for patients who have no delusions. You may be called on to do this in the case of a man who is said to be " morally insane," who is altogether altered in character and habits, and who in various ways behaves absurdly or out-rageously. Everything here will depend on the opportunities you may or may not have of recognizing the change in the individual. If I can say of my own knowledge that a patient is totally altered, it is perhaps the strongest assertion that I can make in support of the opinion that he is insane; but if I am called in to see for the first time one who is said to be thus changed, I cannot compare his present with his former state. I can only compare the present with what I hear of the past. Now, these patients have generally sense enough to behave themselves decently while in the presence of a stranger, especially if they know him to be a doctor.

Examination of patients who have no delusions.

We do not see their eccentric or insane acts, and they may absolutely deny them. They will justify or explain away a thousand little sayings and doings which, though they may sufficiently illustrate the change which has come over them, may, nevertheless, when taken singly, sound trivial, and are not enough to constitute insane acts. It is not likely that you will be able to sign a certificate in any such case after one single interview : probably you will have to visit and examine such a patient several times, and a comparison of what has passed on the several occasions will greatly aid you in coming to a conclusion. If the disorder is acute and rapidly advancing, you may discover delusions in a patient in whom a week previously there were none : in others delusions may have existed and have passed away, yet the man has not yet recovered, but remains changed, eccentric, restless, excitable, insane, obviously unfit to take charge of himself or his affairs. In many of these, though we can discover no delusion, there is obvious intellectual defect. The patient rambles from subject to subject, and do what we will we cannot keep him to the point. Ask him half a dozen simple questions, and you will not get a plain and direct answer to one of them. He will display not an incoherence of words, such as we find in the babble of delirium or acute mania, but an incoherence and inconsequence of thought, which is quite unnatural to him and incompatible with the proper conduct and occupation of men in general. Then if we question him closely as to the extravagance or absurdity of his acts, his attempts to justify them are ofttimes ridiculous and childish. Before we come into the presence of one of these patients we may obtain all the information we can upon the following points from as many friends as possible : Is there anything which they consider to be the unmistakable origin of the disorder? Has he had any epileptic, or epileptiform, or apoplectiform attack, or anything at all of the nature of a fit? Has he ever had a blow or fall on the head, or any bodily

disorder which at the time affected the head ?   Has he undergone any serious loss, worry, anxiety, overwork, or loss of
rest ?   If they tell you that he is altered, make them state
distinctly in what respect he is altered.   Are his altered acts
those of commission or omission ?   Does he neglect his business, forget his appointments, forget the dinner hour?   Or
does he buy useless things, or articles at a price beyond his
means ?   Does he keep loose company, ill-treat and abuse
those nearest to him, profess dislike or indifference to those
he has hitherto most dearly loved ?   Has he become bold,
noisy and talkative, instead of being shy and reserved ?   Has
he made any extraordinary changes in his personal appearance, his dress, hair, or beard ?   Does he now take more
drink than he ought, having previously been sober ?   Is he
excessively restless, never settling to anything, but constantly
coming and going ?   From the answers we receive to these
questions we may, if our informants are credible, satisfy ourselves of the patient's insanity before we enter his presence.
It is probable that such questions will in the main be answered
truly.   We may then ask one more, which is as likely to be
answered untruly.   Has any relative of the patient's ever
been insane ?   In our examination of the individual we shall
bear in mind all that we have heard, and shall consider the
mode in which he gives his answers, their coherence, his justification or denial of his acts, and the reasons for his treatment of or estrangement from his family and friends, if such
exist.   And herein, as I have before reminded you, our
questions must be applicable to the condition, education, and
station of the individual, be he gentle or simple.   We must
avoid the discussion of abstract right or wrong, and the question of whether such acts as his are right or wrong.
We have only to consider whether they were done
by him because he was insane, and would not have
been done by him in his sane mind.   We are concerned not with things wrong or right, moral or immoral,

Insanity, not
enormity of
acts, to be
regarded.

but with things irrational. As men have held the most extravagant opinions, so have they committed the most diabolical crimes, while sane. But the manner and method of their deeds and opinions we have to criticize. The arguments used to uphold them may bring to light an insanity not visible in the acts, and may indicate the disorder of the mind from whence they sprang. There is a strong love of argument and controversy in many such patients, and they often defend themselves in an exceedingly ingenious, yet no less insane fashion.

You may have to examine, for the purpose of signing a certificate, one who is not and never has been insane, in the ordinary sense of the word, but whose unsoundness of mind is of the nature of weak-mindedness or imbecility, defective rather than insane mind. You have here no former condition of healthy mind with which to compare the present. You must compare it with an assumed standard of average humanity, and the question will be, at what point will you decide that soundness ends, and unsoundness of this description begins? In conversing with such a person you will find no delusions, no loss of memory; there will be no definite commencement of the defective state, nor any assignable cause. All that you have to guide you is of a negative character. It is the absence or negation of mind, rather than the positive presence of symptoms of insanity. There may be positive vice, vicious habits and propensities, fondness for low company, thieving, lying, and the like; but your difficulty will be, first, to recognize this for yourselves, for such offences will not be committed in your presence; and, secondly, to decide whether they proceed from depravity and badness, or from imbecility, which renders the individual irresponsible. There are many of our criminals who, were they higher in society, would be considered irresponsible, and placed in asylums; being what they are, they fill our jails. But I have already spoken of

The examination of imbeciles.

these patients; I here merely wish to make a few suggestions for your guidance in dealing with this most difficult class. Unless the individual has been under your observation for a long time, you will scarcely be able at once to give a decided opinion in a doubtful case. The friends will come to you strongly biassed. Either they wish to shut up the alleged lunatic because he disgraces his family by his vice and iniquities, or they wish to prevent him from squandering his property; or, on the other hand, they wish to make out that there is nothing the matter with him, if, perchance, the Commissioners in Lunacy consider that he ought to be protected by certificates. You will not, therefore, be able to receive that which you hear from friends without considerable caution and discrimination. You are brought face to face with a youth of this class, and proceed to question him. If you tax him with his vices, he either denies them, or, admitting them, confesses and acknowledges that they are wrong; but probably he can mention many others who do the same things. You proceed to test his knowledge; and this, in my opinion, is the only test, especially when vice is absent. Is he teachable, capable of receiving instruction and profiting by it? The chances are that, being hard to teach, dull and disinclined to learn, his education has been neglected, and he has been placed with tutors to be kept rather than taught; or put to learn farming, or sent to sea, or to some other calling for which he is equally unfitted. So that his ignorance on special subjects may be due to his preceptors rather than to himself. But a gentleman's son ought to have learned by the time he is twenty-one to read, write, and spell; and if at this age his spelling and letter-writing are those of a child of eight, we may reasonably think that deficiency may be the cause, if he has had fair opportunities. The ignorance and inability to learn may be a good ground for making an affidavit for a commission in lunacy that a patient is incapable of managing his affairs; but in the matter of signing a certificate, I think it also ought to be shown, and you ought to be able to say, that in your opinion the individual is a proper person to be detained under care and treatment as a lunatic, because he is not fit to be at large unless closely watched. Many of these people will run away from any place in which they are living in a vague and purposeless way. They cannot be trusted alone, for they would get into mischief, and they cannot be allowed to have the control even of a small sum of money. Indoors they may destroy furniture or their clothes, wantonly set things on fire, or practice horrible cruelty to children, dogs, or cats. Where we find this to be the case, we may reasonably think and say that such a one is a proper person to be detained under care and treatment, if it appears from the mental deficiency that his whole condition is that of an imbecile or idiot.

Far more easy is it to sign certificates for those who, from old age or brain disease, are fatuous and demented. The examination of the demented. You will here have signs and symptoms of a more certain weight and significance than are to be found in the last-mentioned class. You can compare the present condition with the past. Whereas a man was once vigorous in intellect, clear in conception, and of good memory, we now have but the wreck of mind remaining. Chief of all we find a failing memory. There is no recollection of what happened yesterday or the day before—no recollection of your last visit, possibly not even of your name. If a patient drifts into dementia from a state of mania or melancholia, we may find still some of his old delusions or the traces of them. But in many who are demented from paralysis or epilepsy, there may be no delusions, but an absence of mind and intellect—a repetition of the same question, or the same story, or the same sentence, with entire forgetfulness of having asked such a thing before, and an equal forgetfulness of the answer received. You will be asked to sign certificates concerning such patients to legalize their residence in an asylum or family, or to deprive them of their rights by a commission of lunacy, and you will, as I have said, have little difficulty in coming to a decision. Loss of memory is a morbid state far more perceptible and appreciable than the defective intelligence of the weak-minded youths I have last spoken of, and such patients demand care and personal attention in a way that many of the others do not. Of course, it will be for you to consider the extent and the constancy of this impairment of memory, and how far it would necessarily render a man incapable of managing his affairs. As, on the one hand, no person's memory is perfect, as we all at times forget a name or date, so, on the other, every man whose mind is not completely obliterated, or who is not unconscious, can recollect by the eye, or in some way, something of past events, or those persons nearest and dearest to him. Therefore, when you meet with imperfect memory the result of disease, and no other symptom, you will have to decide whether the imperfection is sufficient to render the patient unsound of mind in the eye of the law. "Sound mind, memory, and understanding," is the phrase lawyers use to` indicate capacity. Does the patient before you possess all of these? Clearly a man cannot manage his property who cannot recollect its nature or amount. If he cannot recollect whether he has a wife, or the number of his children, he cannot be considered competent to make a will. If he has so forgotten places that he does not know whether the house he is in is his own or another's, nor the name or situation of it, he cannot be said to be dwelling there of his own free choice, or to be able to arrange such matters for himself. The facts in these cases speak for themselves. An old man may dwell in his own house, may sign his name to a piece of paper as he is directed, may hand to any one a sum of money previously prepared and put into his hand, and so may be said to manage his own affairs; but you may find that to-day he has totally forgotten every occurrence of yesterday, that he knows nothing about his property, thinks people are alive who are long since dead, and that all his management consists in signing everything that is placed before him. Patients of this feeble mind are, by reason of their feebleness, contented and happy. They put up with any treatment, however bad. They do not run away, and are said to remain voluntarily, wherever they may be. But their volition is as feeble as the rest of their minds, and their submission and surrender of all independence speak for themselves. And they are hopelessly incurable. They have to be taken care of for their natural lives, whereas the weak-minded youths may, in many instances, be improved. Hopes may be entertained of them, but of the demented there is no hope. They have possessed a mind, but have lost it past recall. Therefore certificates may be signed with much less hesitation than in the last-mentioned cases.

Most unquestionably your aid and advice will be asked for the purpose of placing under legal restraint the inveterate drunkards so often called *dipsomaniacs*. The examination of so-called "dipsomaniacs." The question of restraining them by special legislation, and in special inebriate asylums, is attracting much attention in the present day; but so far nothing has been done in this country, and I have only to speak to you of the existing law, which is the law of lunacy. It is not easy to advise legislation on the subject. We have at present a machinery consisting of Lunacy Acts, asylums, and Commissioners in Lunacy, by which any one can be put under restraint who is of unsound mind. What further addition can be made? Inebriate asylums may be instituted, in which people may voluntarily place themselves for the cure and eradication of the habit; but it is not to be supposed that legislation will go so far as to sanction the forcible incarceration of every person who may be called by his friends an habitual drinker. For those who are really of unsound mind, the present means are sufficient; and in the examination of one alleged to be a dipsomaniac, you will have to ascertain not only that he is a fit person to be taken care of and detained, but also that he is of unsound mind. Although I cannot hope to give you any very definite or precise rules for your guidance in coming to a decision on this most difficult point, yet some few hints may be of service.

I abolish dipsomania from the varieties of moral insanity, together with such monomanias as erotomania, pyromania, and kleptomania. The unsoundness of mind which exists in connection with habitual drinking must be estimated like unsoundness in any other individual. Not every drunkard is insane, nor can he be confined because he ruins his health and property, any more than a confirmed gambler or opium-eater. There is an insanity, the marked feature of which is a craving for drink, but it is not the condition of a man who, after his work is over, goes to the public house and gets drunk, whether he does so nightly or occasionally. He may squander his money and wreck his constitution, but during his working hours he is a sane and intelligent man. It is not the condition of a man who periodically drinks himself into delirium tremens. During the delirium we may, of course, sign certificates of insanity, if it is absolutely necessary for his protection to do so; but when he has recovered, he cannot be detained because at some future time he will most probably drink himself into another attack. In the interval he may be a perfectly sane man.

We shall have no difficulty in signing a certificate when unmistakable insanity has been produced by drink, whether it present the symptoms of mania, melancholia, or dementia. Such will be recognized and dealt with as any other case of insanity.

There are, however, certain persons who seem impelled to drink, as others are impelled to murder or suicide. And this impulse is so strong, that they are rendered entirely unfit to take care of themselves or their affairs. If left to themselves, they would drink continuously till they reached the stage of delirium tremens or alcoholic paralysis. Closely examining them, we find them to be people who, from congenital or acquired weakness of mind, are unable to exercise any self-control, and are practically of unsound mind. They may have suffered from blows on the head, fits, previous attacks of insanity, or they may have by inheritance an insane neurosis. They probably desire to place themselves under control, and will voluntarily enter an asylum if it be possible. Here the drinking is most frequently the result of the insanity, which is, however, aggravated by the perpetual alcoholization.

Except in view of a particular case, one is obliged to speak in very general terms of such patients; but, as I have said concerning other doubtful forms of insanity, there is generally to be discovered some mental defect or peculiarity other than the act or habit of drinking, if we look for it carefully and have sufficient opportunity for its discovery. It is for the most part quite impossible to sign a certificate upon a single examination of one of these, but a longer acquaintance may remove our doubts, and enable us to say that he is not of sound mind, memory, and understanding. It is of course essential that we see him free from the influence of recent drink : always inquire into that which an alleged lunatic has had to drink since his last sleep: serious consequences might ensue were we to sign a certificate for a man who was only drunk.

This drinking insanity may be periodical or permanent. In the former case the patient must be liberated, as any other who has recovered from his insanity. He may be liberated upon trial, and if his recovery is only apparent, he may be readmitted. Very frequently it is permanent, and, in fact, is only the commencement of a more marked degeneration of mind.

Lastly, in your examination of a patient be careful, above
everything, that he has fair play. You are about to
do that which will deprive him of that we all hold

Conclusion.

most dear, and he is in some respects in the position of an
accused person. You are examining him to satisfy yourself
of the real state of his mind, not to trip him up and extract
that which will sound well in a certificate. If he is a person inferior to you in intellect, you may puzzle him by cross-
examination, so that he may seem really wrong in his head ;
but you know that a man in the witness-box may in the same
way "lose his head," and, without the slightest intention of
doing wrong, swear black is white. If the case is not urgent,
and admits of doubt, always see a patient twice before you
sign. Some vary considerably, especially women, at different
times, and if possible you should see them at their best and
at their worst.

You are not to omit the inspection of a patient's letters
and writings. Many, who are very shy and reticent when
brought face to face with a medical man, will in that which
they write, reveal the delusions and fancies under which
they are acting. The whole style of a patient's letter, the
signature and direction, may show the idea predominating
in the mind ; and defect of intelligence, the imbecile and
childlike weakness, the failure of mental power, and forgetfulness of dementia, may be all displayed in written characters. Letters will assist you in finding out concealed ideas,
or may illustrate points on which you have only been able
to gain imperfect information from the patient or his friends.
Once more I must warn you, that you undertake a serious
responsibility when you sign a certificate of lunacy. You are
performing an act which deprives another of his liberty and
rights, and are signing a legal document which you may have
to defend in a court of law. Never put anything in a certificate which you cannot justify in the witness-box. You will
not be absolved from responsibility because your certificate

has been received by the Commissioners in Lunacy. A man may even be insane, and yet if your certificate be not true, and if all the requirements of the law be not carried out, you will be held responsible. Let that which you say in it be as short as possible, if only it be strong. And do not add to the facts which really indicate insanity others which do not indicate it at all. Be accurate in the filling up of the whole certificate. Scarcely a single certificate is ever sent in from a medical man that has not to go back to him for the correction of some error or the insertion of something omitted.

In your statement of facts, see that you state fully what you observe and what you mean. Do not write down a series of single words, such as "great excitement, delusions, refusal of food," but say, "I found the patient looking so and so, doing this or that, and he said that," &c. And if what he said was not unquestionably a delusion, you must add that it is a delusion, as you believe or are informed. And when you speak of refusal of food, or excessive drinking, or the like, take care that you speak of what you have yourself observed, or else that you state that such a fact has been communicated to you by others. I often find that the two sets of facts are intermingled by medical men. Do not use vague terms, as incoherence, excitement, fatuity; but reduce your statements, as far as possible, to the enunciation of concrete facts.

Here, gentlemen, I bring these lectures to a close. They are but brief sketches of some among the many topics which I might discuss. Of their imperfection no one is so aware as myself; nevertheless, they may serve as suggestions for further reading and observation; and I venture to hope that you will find, that from them you have derived some hints, when at a future time you have to treat insanity, or take the necessary steps for placing under legal restraint an insane patient.

APPENDIX.

SYNOPSIS OF THE LAWS OF THE SEVERAL STATES OF THE UNION

RESPECTING THE CONFINEMENT OF THE INSANE.

LEGISLATION in this country respecting the confinement of the insane in hospitals, asylums, or other places of detention, is of comparatively recent origin. It was supposed that they would be cared for and watched over by their friends with as much fidelity and tenderness as if their disease were of the body rather than of the mind, and accordingly they were left to perform this duty in the way and manner which seemed most likely to keep the patient from harm and accomplish his recovery. Even after the establishment of hospitals supported by the state, no express legislation was supposed to be necessary to authorize the managers to hold their patients in custody. Various subordinate incidents of the measure were prescribed by law, while the measure it-self—the essential thing—was left to the discretion of the friends. As a matter of police, the law always provided for the care of that homeless, friendless class, who roamed about endangering the lives and property of their fellow-men. Of late years, this general confidence in the motives and intentions of men has been somewhat weakened by apprehensions that the unqualified privilege allowed to the friends of the insane to deprive them of their liberty, has been abused. Suspicions have been raised that sane persons have been thus imprisoned in order that some dishonest relative might be the better able to promote some scheme of iniquity. The consequences of this feeling may be seen in much trouble-some litigation, and a prevalent distrust and alarm among all who are obliged, either by the claims of their profession or of their relation-ship, to assume control over the insane. Under this state of feeling, it seemed highly necessary, in order to avoid public scandal and furnish protection to those who are engaged in the offices of humanity, that this privilege of depriving the insane of their liberty should be authorized by the legislature, and its conditions so managed as to afford the least possible chance for its abuse. For several years this subject engaged the attention of the "Association of the Medical Superintendents of Hospitals for the Insane, in North America," which finally prepared and unanimously adopted the project of a law consisting of such provisions as seemed best calculated to accomplish the object in question, and recommended that they should be incorporated into the law of every state. In the states of Pennsylvania and Connecticut, this has been already done (with some slight modifications) so far as the confinement of the insane is concerned. It will serve our present purpose to present entire, in its place, the Pennsylvania act.

In most of the states, the laws respecting the insane have reference, in a great degree, to the state hospital, prescribing the conditions on which patients can be received. They regulate the confinement of the insane in a particular establishment, but are silent respecting this measure considered generally. In some, especially the newer states, interference with the liberty of the insane is legalized only as a measure of police, and in the care of their property they are treated like minors.

In the following account of the laws of the several states, I have endeavored to give only the essential points, as briefly and comprehensively as possible. It is possible that very recent legislation may have made some changes, but with that exception, it may be received as quite correct. The reader will bear in mind, however, that, in many of our states, legislation on the subject of insanity is still in a very rudimentary condition, which will explain some of the apparent deficiencies revealed in this sketch.

MAINE.

Insane minors may be sent to the hospital by parents or guardians, within thirty days after attack.

In all other cases commitment to the hospital can be made only by the municipal authorities of the town or city in which the patient resides. These, on application of friends or of a justice, inquire into the mental condition of the patient; and if they think him insane, and that the comfort and safety of himself or others will be promoted by confinement in the hospital, they order his committal. He is to be detained till restored, or discharged by legal process.

Appeal may be made from the action of municipal authorities, each party naming a justice of the peace. These make inquiry and have power to reverse or confirm the decision of the authorities.

Patients in hospital, not committed by the Supreme Judicial Court, and not afflicted with homicidal insanity, may be removed by order of the municipal authorities, at the end of six months and no sooner, at the request of the persons liable for their support. Should these authorities decline to order a discharge, like application and inquiry may be repeated at intervals of six months.

Persons committed to the hospital under the above provisions may be placed under guardianship, on application of the municipal officers to the judge of Probate. These certify "that it is for the patient's interest and to prevent a waste of property," whereupon the judge appoints a guardian without notice to patient.

Persons on trial for crime, pleading present insanity, are committed to hospital, by order of the court, for the purpose of observation. The court may take the same step previous to trial, if satisfied that such plea will be made.

Persons acquitted of crime on the ground of insanity are to be sent by the court to the hospital, to be there detained till cured, or discharged by due process of law. The same course is taken even if the grand jury fail to indict, because satisfied of insanity. The discharge of any such patient from a hospital may be ordered by any judge of the Supreme Judicial Court. Also by two justices of the peace, respectively named by friends of the patient and trustees of the hospital—" on satisfactory proof being given that if enlarged he would not be dangerous to' the peace and safety of the community." Still further, the discharge may be ordered by the judge of Probate upon sufficient recognizance for safe-keeping.

Any convict in the penitentiary, supposed to be insane, is to be examined by a committee of two or more physicians appointed by the governor. If found insane he is to be placed in the hospital.

NEW HAMPSHIRE.

" The parents, guardians, or friends, of any insane person, may cause him to be sent to the asylum." The certificate of one physician to the fact of insanity is required by the rules of the asylum.

A judge of Probate may order the confinement of a lunatic who is dangerous to be at large; notice being first given to the selectmen of the town to which said lunatic belongs, or to his guardian, " or to any other person, as the judge may order."

Pauper lunatics may be placed in the asylum by the overseers of the poor of the towns to which they belong. If the overseers fail to do so, the Court of Common Pleas may order the committal.

A lunatic confined in any jail may be sent to the asylum by the Court of Common Pleas.

Lunatics confined in the state's prison may be placed in the asylum by order of the governor and council.

Patients committed by judges or courts are to be detained till discharged by "due process of law," or, "till the insanity is removed."

"Any person committed to the asylum, may be discharged by any three of the trustees, or by any justice of the Superior Court, whenever the cause of the commitment ceases, or a further residence at the asylum is, in their opinion, not necessary."

Application for guardianship of an alleged lunatic is to be made to the judge of Probate, who directs the selectmen of the town to which the said person belongs to make inquisition and examination into the case. If after personal examination they report him to be insane, the judge appoints a guardian; first, however, serving a notice upon the patient and citing him to appear and show cause why the application should not be granted.

VERMONT.

Private patients are admitted to the insane asylum upon application of relatives or friends, with a certificate of insanity from a respectable physician.

When it is desired to place an insane person under guardianship, application is made to the Probate Court, by relatives, friends, or overseers of poor. This court thereupon commissions two justices of the peace to inquire into the facts. These personally examine the patient, giving him notice in advance. Upon their report the court appoints or refuses to appoint.

When a person tried for crime is acquitted on the ground of insanity, the jury shall state the fact in their verdict. If in the opinion of the court it would be dangerous to the peace and safety of the community to allow the person to go at large, the court shall order his confinement in the hospital or elsewhere. If the offence committed have been murder or manslaughter, he may be placed either in the hospital or the state prison at discretion of the court; if some other crime, in the hospital, or the county jail, or other suitable place. The expense shall be borne by the party, if he have property; otherwise by the state.

If in the case of any person held in prison on charge of committing some crime or misdemeanor, the grand jury fail to indict, through a belief in his insanity, they shall certify this fact to the court. If in the judgment of the court his enlargement would be dangerous, confinement may be ordered, in jail, hospital, or other place, at discretion of the court; and the expenses met as in the preceding case.

When a convict confined in state prison for life, or for a specified term, shall have exhibited indubitable symptoms of insanity for at least thirty days, the directors of the prison may, at their discretion, cause his removal to the hospital, there to remain until recovery or expiration of sentence. If recovery occur before expiration of term, he shall be returned to the prison, and there serve out the remainder of his time. Any prisoner recovered from insanity, but not yet returned to prison from the hospital, who may abscond from the hospital or from his keeper, shall suffer the penalties attached to escaping from state prison.

Any insane convict not recovered at the end of his sentence, may be placed in, or continued in, the state hospital, at the expense of the state or other parties who may be found responsible.

MASSACHUSETTS.

The certificates of two physicians, given within one week after inquiry and personal interview, are necessary to secure the admission of a patient into any hospital for the insane. One of these is to be, if possible, the patient's family physician. If the hospital be a state institution, notice of the application must be given to the mayor or selectmen of the patient's place of residence. In either case, full written statements of the history and character of the patient's disease must be sent to the hospital, and there preserved.

Any judge of Supreme; Judicial, Superior, Probate, Boston Police— and in certain cases Municipal—Courts, may commit to a state lunatic hospital any insane person whom he may deem fit. Certificates of two physicians are still essential.

The judge may appoint place of hearing complaint at his discretion; and .may either require or dispense with the presence of the alleged lunatic. He may also in his discretion summon a jury of six to hear and determine as to the insanity of the party complained of.

Insane paupers may be committed by the overseers of the poor.

Patients in insane hospitals may be discharged by the trustees of hospital, by judges of Probate, Supreme, Judicial, and Superior Courts.

When a person accused of crime is acquitted by reason of insanity, or fails to be indicted for the same cause, the court may order his confinement in one of the state lunatic hospitals.

Convicts in state prison alleged to be insane are examined by a commission, consisting of the prison physician and four superintendents of Massachusetts insane hospitals. This reports to a judge of the Superior Court, who if satisfied of the existence of insanity, orders removal of convict to a state hospital, there to be treated until sufficiently restored to be properly returned to prison. Persons confined in other places may be placed in hospital upon representation of facts by the attending physician to a judge of Superior or Probate Court.

Upon petition under oath, setting forth belief that a certain person is unjustly confined as a lunatic, made to a judge of the Supreme Judicial Court, the judge may at discretion appoint a commission of three to make inquiry. This body shall be sworn, and shall give notice to petitioner and to the authorities of the hospital, shall summon and swear witnesses, hear evidence, and make personal examination. No notice is to be served on patient, nor is he to have counsel, or be present at inquiry. He is not to be examined by petitioner or counsel, unless by permission of his physician, or by special order of the judge. The commission are to visit the patient at the hospital, and not remove him. Report of commission being made, the judge takes such action as he deems proper.

Guardians are appointed by the Probate Court on the petition of relatives, friends, or town authorities. The court must give the alleged insane person fourteen days' notice of the time and place fixed upon for the hearing. If after a full hearing the court is satisfied of the person's incapacity, it appoints a guardian of his person and estate.

RHODE ISLAND.

Insane persons may be placed in the hospital by their legal guardians if any; otherwise by their relatives or friends; or, if paupers, by the authorities of their respective towns or cities. A certificate of insanity signed by one physician is always essential.

Any justice of the peace, upon complaint of any respectable person that another is furiously mad and dangerous to be at large, may commit the alleged lunatic to the hospital.

Upon written statement, made by any respectable person, to any judge of the Supreme Court, that another is insane, and that his own or others' welfare requires his restraint, the judge shall at once appoint a commission of three persons, who shall take evidence, receive the statements of the alleged lunatic or his counsel, and make full inquiry into the facts. Reasonable notice must be given to the party complained of, who may be arrested if he fail to appear; and who, at the discretion of the judge, may be confined while the inquisition is pending. If this commission report that confinement is advisable, the judge shall make an order to that effect.

Upon written statement, similarly made, that a certain person is unjustly confined as insane, a commission is appointed as above, to hear evidence and examine the patient. If they report the patient not insane, the judge shall order his release.

If a person charged with crime be acquitted on the ground of insanity, the·jury shall state that fact. If the judge consider the accused unsafe to be at large, he shall thus certify to the governor, who is thereby authorized to provide for the maintenance of the prisoner and cause him "to be removed to any insane hospital, either within or without this state, during the continuance of such insanity."

Removal of patients from hospital may be effected, generally, by the parties who placed them there.

Application for placing under guardianship a person alleged to be insane may be made to the Court of Probate, by relatives, friends, or municipal authorities. Notice is issued to the patient of the hearing. If, however, representation is made to the court by the physician in charge of the patient, that knowledge of, or presence at, the hearing, would be seriously injurious to his health, these are dispensed with, and the order of guardianship given or refused at the discretion of the court.

CONNECTICUT.

Patients are placed in the insane hospital by "legal guardians, or relatives, or friends in case of no guardian;" but in no case without the sworn certificate of at least one physician, given within one week after personal examination. Such patients are removable by the parties committing them to the asylum.

Any justice of the peace, complaint being made, may investigate the state of an alleged lunatic, and if he find him dangerous to himself or others, or requiring hospital care and treatment—he being at large—he shall order him to be confined in some suitable hospital or other suitable place of detention. This, however, shall be done only upon a medical certificate as before described.

On application of any respectable person, any judge of the Superior Court shall appoint a commission of three or four—at least one to be a physician, and one a lawyer, or judge, or justice—whose duty it shall be to inquire into the alleged insanity of the person complained of. They shall hear such evidence as may be offered, and the statement of the party complained of, and his counsel. Upon these they shall report as to the fact of insanity and the advisability of confinement. Due notice must be given to the alleged lunatic of the proceedings ordered by the judge. The judge is authorized to place the party in confinement while the case is pending.

Upon complaint of any respectable person that another is unjustly confined as insane, the judge of the Superior Court may, at his discretion, appoint a commission, as before described, to investigate the facts. These shall hear evidence, and shall have one or more personal interviews with the patient, " so arranged, if possible, that such person shall not know or suspect the object or purpose of such interview." If this commission shall report the patient sane, the judge shall order his discharge.

A like commission shall be appointed with like duties whenever the officers or managers of an asylum, hospital, or other place of detention, may request it.

Commissions at the request of outside parties shall not be appointed during the first six months of detention, when this is by order of a judge of a Superior Court. Nor shall such inquiry be repeated, in any one case, at a less interval than six months.

Upon receiving satisfactory evidence that a person is insane, and suffering for want of proper care or treatment, a judge of the Superior Court may order him to be placed in a hospital, or other suitable place, at the expense of those who are legally responsible.

Patients in hospital under any of the above provisions may be discharged by the hospital authorities in accordance with their rules.

Persons acquitted of crime on account of insanity, shall be sent to jail by the court. By entering suitable recognizance, any other persons may remove them and confine them as the court may direct or approve.

Application for discharge of such persons may be made to the County Court, which may dispose of them as it deems proper.

Applications for guardianship of lunatics are made to the Probate Court by some relative, or by selectmen of the town to which the party belongs. The court, if satisfied, appoints a " conservator." The patient is summoned to appear, by a copy of the writ being left at his usual place of abode. No legal provision is made for the restraint of his person; but this would be permitted.

NEW YORK.

Persons complained of as furiously mad are confined by order of two justices of the peace, with the provision that within ten days they shall be placed in a hospital for the insane.

If any person becoming furiously mad has property of his own, or has relatives or guardians liable for his support, it shall be their duty to send him to a hospital. Failing this, the overseers of the poor make complaint as above, and cause his removal to a hospital, recovering expenses by suit.

No alleged lunatic shall by any process be confined without the sworn certificate of two reputable physicians; a brief report of the evidence to be filed in the office of the county clerk.

Any alleged lunatics adjudged insane and ordered to be confined by justices of peace as above, have, or their friends for them, power of appeal to a county judge. He shall stay removal of any such lunatic, and forthwith call a jury to investigate the case. The jury, aided by the testimony of two reputable physicians, finding him sane, the judge shall at once discharge the prisoner; otherwise he confirms the order for immediate removal to an asylum. The parties making complaint against an alleged lunatic, may, if the justices refuse to order confinement, likewise appeal to a county judge. He may summarily determine, or call a jury, as he thinks fit.

The discharge of patients from the state hospital is wholly in the hands of its managers—excepting persons confined on criminal charges —who, however, are to be guided by the certificate of the superintendent, as to recovery, safety, incurability, or insusceptibility to further benefit from treatment. Patients of the criminal class may be discharged by order of a justice of the Supreme Court, if on investigation it seem safe, legal, and right so to do.

When a person is acquitted, or escapes indictment by reason of insanity, the jury shall certify that fact to the court, which shall inquire into his present condition, and if he be found insane shall order him to be sent to the asylum.

If any person in confinement under indictment, or under sentence of imprisonment, or under a criminal charge, or held for want of bail, or as witness, or to keep the peace, &c., shall appear to be insane, the county judge shall investigate his state, calling upon two respectable physicians and other witnesses, and, if he deem it best, call a jury to decide as to his sanity. If satisfied of his insanity, the judge may order his removal to the asylum, to be there confined till recovered.

When the physician of either state prison shall certify that any convict in his charge is insane, the inspector or board of inspectors shall examine said convict, and if satisfied of his insanity shall order his removal to the asylum for insane convicts. If he continue insane after term of sentence expires, he may be sent to his county almshouse, or given into the custody of his friends, upon proper sureties; or, upon medical and other evidence, the county judge may order his continued confinement, in said asylum, beyond term of sentence. If a convict recover sanity before expiration of sentence, he is removed to the Auburn State Prison for the remainder of his time.

Applications for the appointment of "committees" (guardians) for alleged lunatics, are made to the Supreme Court, the County Courts, the Court of Common Pleas in New York County, and the Superior Court of the City of Buffalo. Petition, with reasons, is addressed to the proper court, which, if it see fit, appoints a commission to examine and inquire into the case. The lunatic is entitled to due notice—though dangerous madness, or peculiar circumstances, may excuse this notice. The commissioners summon a jury and witnesses. The alleged lunatic is entitled to be present, and may have counsel. He may be inspected and examined. If the jury find him insane, and the commission so report, the court appoints the "committee" at its discretion, in the interest of the lunatic. Often there is one committee for estate and another for person; the latter generally some of the nearest of kin. The Supreme Court has the general care and control of the person and property of the insane. Upon recovery of an insane person, application is made to this court for removal of committee and restraint.

NEW JERSEY.

Friends may place a patient in the state asylum, by signing a written request, and presenting a certificate of insanity signed by one physician.

Paupers may be committed by any judge of the County Court, on application of the overseers of the poor, in case said judge shall be satisfied by respectable medical testimony that the pauper is curably insane.

Persons insane and indigent, but not paupers, may be committed to the asylum by two judges of the County Court, if satisfied by medical testimony that the cases are curable.

Persons who have escaped indictment, or been acquitted of a criminal charge, on the ground of insanity, shall be committed to the asylum, if the court be satisfied that the insanity still continues.

If any person shall become insane while in confinement under indictment, or on civil process, the court, after ascertaining the facts by careful inquiry, may order removal to asylum.

Application for the appointment of a guardian may be made to the Court of Chancery, which thereupon appoints a commission of inquiry. If this commission find the party incapable, their finding is returned to the Orphans' Court of the proper county, which appoints a guardian.

PENNSYLVANIA.

The following is the text of the act of April 20th, 1869, now in force in Pennsylvania:

"SECTION 1. *Be it enacted by the Senate and House of Representatives of the Commonwealth of Pennsylvania in General Assembly met, and it is hereby enacted by the authority of the same,* That insane persons may be placed in a hospital for the insane by their legal guardians, or by their relatives or friends in case they have no guardians, but never without the certificate of two or more reputable physicians, after a personal examination, made within one week of the date thereof, and this certificate to be duly acknowledged and sworn to or affirmed before some magistrate or judicial officer, who shall certify to the genuineness of the signature and to the respectability of the signers.

"SECTION 2. That it shall be unlawful, and be deemed a misdemeanor in law, punishable by a fine of not exceeding one hundred dollars, for any superintendent, officer, physician, or other employee of any insane asylum to intercept, delay, or interfere with, in any manner whatsoever, the transmission of any letter or other written communication addressed by an inmate of any insane asylum to his or her counsel, residing in the county in which the home of the patient is, or in the city or county in which the asylum is located.

"SECTION 3. On a written statement, properly sworn to or affirmed, being addressed by some respectable person to any law judge, that a certain person then confined in a hospital for the insane is not insane, and is thus unjustly deprived of his liberty, the judge shall issue a writ of *habeas corpus*, commanding that the said alleged lunatic be brought before him for a public hearing, where the question of his or her alleged lunacy may be determined, and where the onus of proving the said alleged lunatic to be insane shall rest upon such persons as are restraining him or her of his or her liberty.

"SECTION 4. Whenever any person is acquitted on a criminal suit on the ground of insanity, the jury shall declare this fact in their verdict, and the court shall order the prisoner to be committed to some place of confinement for safe keeping or treatment, there to be retained until he may be discharged in the manner provided in the next section.

"SECTION 5. If, after a confinement of three months' duration, any law judge shall be satisfied by the evidence presented to him that the prisoner has recovered, and that the paroxysm of insanity in which the criminal act was committed was the first and only one he had ever experienced, he may order his unconditional discharge; if, however, it shall appear that such paroxysm of insanity was preceded by at least one other, then the court may, in its discretion, appoint a guardian of his person, and to him commit the care of the prisoner, said guardian giving bonds for any damage his ward may commit: *Provided always*, That in case of homicide or attempted homicide the prisoner shall not be discharged unless in the unanimous opinion of the superintendent and the managers of the hospital, and the court before which he or she was tried, he or she has recovered and is safe to be at large.

"SECTION 6. Insane persons may be placed in a hospital by order of any court or law judge, after the following course of proceedings, namely: On statement, in writing, of any respectable person, that a certain person is insane, and that the welfare of himself or of others requires his restraint, it shall be the duty of the judge to appoint, immediately, a commission, who shall inquire into and report upon the facts of the case. This commission shall be composed of three persons, one of whom at least shall be a physician and another a lawyer; in their inquisition they shall hear such evidence as may be offered touching the merits of the case, as well as the statements of the party complained of or of his counsel; if, in their opinion, it is a suitable case for confinement, the judge shall issue his warrant for such disposition of the insane person as will secure the object of the measure.

"SECTION 7. On statement, in writing, to any law judge, by some friend of the party, that a certain person placed in a hospital under the fifth section is losing his bodily health, and that consequently his welfare would be promoted by his discharge, or that his mental disorder has so far changed its character as to render his further confinement unnecessary, the judge shall make suitable inquisition into the merits of the case, and, according to its result, may or may not order the discharge of the person.

"SECTION 8. Persons placed in any hospital for the insane may be removed therefrom by parties who have become responsible for the payment of their expenses: *Provided*, that such obligation was the result of their own free act and accord, and not of the operation of law, and that its terms require the removal of the patient in order to avoid further responsibility.

"SECTION 9. If it shall be made to appear to any law judge that a certain insane person is manifestly suffering from the want of proper care or treatment, he shall order such person to be placed in some hospital for the insane, at the expense of those who are legally bound to maintain such insane person; but no such order shall be made without due notice of the application therefor shall have been served upon the persons to be affected thereby and hearing had thereon.

"SECTION 10. If the superintendent or officers of any hospital for the insane shall receive any person into the hospital after full compliance with the provisions of this act, no responsibility shall be incurred by them for any detention in the hospital.

"SECTION 11. That nothing in this act shall be construed so as to deprive any alleged lunatic or habitual drunkard of the benefit of the writ of *habeas corpus* or trial by jury, or any other remedy guaranteed to alleged lunatics or habitual drunkards by any existing laws or statutes of the Commonwealth of Pennsylvania."

Any court of Common Pleas may issue a commission of one or more persons, in the nature of a commission *de lunatico inquirendo*, which shall summon a jury of not less than six nor more than twelve men, to try a question of lunacy. Application for such commission is to be made by a relative, by blood or marriage ; or one interested in the estate. The inquisition may be traversed by any one who is aggrieved. Upon a finding of insanity, the court appoints a committee of person and estate.

DELAWARE.

The trustees of the poor in the several counties are required, on recommendation of the chancellor and the resident associate judge of either county, to place in some hospital for the insane the insane poor of their county. The Levy Court has power to remove an insane person from jail or prison to an almshouse. The Court of Chancery, after ascertaining insanity by means of a jury, appoints " trustees " for the person and property of lunatics not indigent.

MARYLAND.

On application being made, the Circuit Court of the county, or the Criminal Court of Baltimore, will cause a jury of twelve men to investigate the mental condition of an alleged lunatic. If he be found to be insane, and also a pauper, the court at discretion send him to almshouse, hospital, or other place of confinement.

If an alleged lunatic be complained of as dangerous, or for breach of peace, a similar course is pursued, though he be not a pauper.

A person tried for crime, if acquitted on the ground of insanity at time of crime, and found to be insane at time of trial, shall be sent by the court to the almshouse, hospital, or other confinement at its discretion, there to be held till " he shall have recovered his reason, and be discharged by due course of law." The same course is to be pursued with a person charged with improper conduct, or any crime, but not indicted; jury, as before, inquiring whether he was, and still is, insane.

If any of the above persons possess property, the court appoints a trustee.

The general care and custody of persons *non compos mentis* lies with the Court of Chancery, both as to person and estate. The trustee appointed by this court may commit the patient to a hospital only at the direction of the court.

DISTRICT OF COLUMBIA.

Private patients may be committed to the Government Hospital for the Insane upon the certificate of two respectable physicians of the District.

Whenever any judge of the Circuit or Criminal Court, or justice of the peace, reports to the Secretary of the Interior that two respectable physicians have certified to him, under oath, that they know the party alleged to be insane, and believe him a fit subject for hospital treatment, the secretary shall make an order for his admission to the hospital.

Persons charged with crime and found insane, and also convicts becoming insane in the penitentiary, are sent to the hospital by order of the secretary.

OHIO.

Complaint of lunacy is made under oath to any judge of Probate. He summons the accused, together with witnesses, including one physician. Satisfied of insanity, he may order commitment to the insane asylum or to other place of confinement. He has power also to appoint guardians of person and estate.

All persons confined as insane are entitled to the benefit of the writ of habeas corpus. This may be indefinitely repeated, upon alleged recovery.

Any person accused of crime or misdemeanor, alleged insane at time of offence, is brought before an examining court. If found insane, he may be committed to confinement as a lunatic.

Persons acquitted on ground of insanity may be ordered to be confined, if the judge deem them unsafe to be at large. Persons becoming insane while in confinement, after sentence of death or imprisonment, may be pardoned, or have sentence commuted or suspended, at discretion of the governor. Persons otherwise confined may be transferred to hospital or almshouse by a judge of Probate, if he be satisfied of their insanity.

INDIANA.

Complaint of lunacy may be made to any justice of the peace. He summons a jury of six, sworn to be unprejudiced, unrelated, and uninterested. If they find a verdict of sanity, or not dangerous to be at large, costs fall on the complainant. Otherwise, the judge appoints a temporary custodian, and within ten days reports the case to the Court of Common Pleas. This re-tries the case with a jury of twelve men. If he be found insane, the appointment of a custodian is confirmed; and if there be property, a guardian is appointed. If on the original examination the justice and jury of six find him not insane or dangerous, complainant may appeal to the Court of Common Pleas. If he fail to obtain a verdict of insanity, complainant forfeits one hundred dollars.

Application for guardianship is made to the Probate Court. A jury is summoned to investigate the facts. The judge may dispense with the personal appearance of the party, if satisfied it would be detrimental to his health. If found to be insane, a guardian is appointed by the judge.

ILLINOIS.

No person can be held in confinement as insane, unless by order of a court and in accordance with the verdict of a jury.

Commitment of a patient to confinement as a lunatic is effected as follows: Any respectable person makes a written statement to any circuit or county judge that A. B. is insane and requires confinement. With this application is inclosed a certificate of insanity signed by two physicians. Upon receiving these, the judge causes the party to appear before him and convenes a jury to try the question of insanity. If a verdict of insanity be given, the judge makes an order for commitment to the state hospital. If the lunatic have property, a " committee " is appointed by the court.

MICHIGAN.

The indigent insane are admitted to the hospital by order of a Probate judge. The facts of insanity and indigence are testified to by two respectable physicians, and other witnesses called by the judge. If satisfied of the truth of the allegations, the judge orders patient to be

APPENDIX.

supported at the hospital by the county for two years, unless sooner restored.

No insane person shall be confined in the same room with a criminal; nor in any jail longer than ten days.

Upon application for guardianship, made by relatives or friends of any insane person, to the Probate Court, the judge shall give fourteen days' notice to the party concerned, naming time and place of hearing. Upon full examination and hearing, the judge appoints, or declines to appoint, a guardian of person and estate.

A person in confinement, waiting trial, or in various other circumstances, may, after careful medical examination by order of certain courts, be transferred from jail to the insane hospital, to remain till cured. If a grand jury decline to indict an offender, on account of insanity, the judge may discharge, or order continuance in prison.

If a jury shall acquit on the ground of insanity, the court will discharge, or commit to prison, according as the prisoner's enlargement seems safe or dangerous.

Convicts becoming insane, may, by order of the Circuit Court of the county where imprisoned, be given into the custody of the superintendents of the poor in said county.

WISCONSIN.

Patients are admitted to the insane hospital upon the certificate of insanity of two skilful physicians, resident in the same county as patient. The fact of medical examination and genuineness of signatures is certified by the local municipal authorities.

Alleged improper confinement in hospital is to be inquired into by the trustees of that institution, aided by two or more "skilful and experienced physicians" whom they shall elect for the purpose. All patients are entitled to the benefits of habeas corpus. This writ may be repeated in the same case, if it be alleged that recovery has occurred since the first issue.

When a jury acquits on the ground of insanity, they state that ground. The judge, at his discretion, discharges, or, if safety require, commits to prison, or delivers to friends, on proper surety for safe-keeping. He may also place such criminals, or those becoming insane after conviction, in the insane hospital, but must remove them on certificate from the superintendent that their presence is detrimental to the safety and welfare of other patients.

Convicts in state prison, becoming insane, are examined by three

physicians appointed by the governor. On their affidavit of the existence of lunacy, he may cause removal to some safe and convenient
insane hospital, for treatment, till cured or till expiration of sentence.
Guardianship is obtained upon a sworn statement made to any judge
of the County Court. Upon receiving such petition and statement, the
judge gives the person concerned fourteen days' notice. The party is
to personally appear at the hearing, "if able to attend." If satisfied
of the propriety of the step, the judge appoints a guardian of person
and estate.

MINNESOTA.

Private patients are admitted to the hospital for the insane upon
request of relatives, and approbation of the superintendent, without
medical certificate.

Complaint against a person as insane, is made before a judge of Probate or a county commissioner. A commissioner, or justice of the
peace, of the same county, or any relative by blood or marriage, may
apply to a judge of Probate for guardianship. This judge names time
and place for hearing, cites accused to appear; gives him and some
near relative not applying for guardianship, six days' notice of proceedings. The judge summons a jury of six; counsel is allowed, and witnesses, including one physician, called. If the jury find the party to be
insane, the judge appoints from one to three guardians. Guardianship
may be terminated by the same judge without a jury.

Upon complaint of insanity being proved, the judge has power to
commit to hospital only when destitution is also proved.

When a jury state that they acquit an accused on the ground of
insanity, the court shall discharge, if it deem him safe to be at large.
Otherwise shall order confinement in prison; or deliver, under security
for safe-keeping, to friends.

IOWA.

In this state the care of the insane is wholly vested in a standing
commission of three, appointed in each county by the Circuit Court.
This commission consists of one lawyer, one physician, and the clerk
of the Circuit and District Courts for that county. It is the duty of this
commission to receive complaints, and investigate all cases of alleged
insanity. No person can be admitted to the hospital for the insane, except by their order. On receiving a complaint that any resident of the

county is insane, they instruct some respectable physician to examine the party, and report to them immediately. This examining physician may be the medical member of the commission, or the family physician, or any other. In their discretion they may forthwith act upon his report, and send or decline to send the patient to the hospital; or they may have the patient before them for further examination before final decision. The jurisdiction of this commission is complete in its county, extending alike to private and pauper patients, rich and poor, quiet and dangerous.

Complaints of illegal confinement in the insane hospital may, however, be made to, and investigated by a court.

Probate judges have power at their discretion, on proper application being made, to appoint guardians, when satisfied of the necessity. The wife of an insane man shall, if competent, be one of his guardians.

KANSAS.

When any person shall become furiously mad, or so as to endanger his person or the persons or property of others, it is the duty of his guardian, relatives, "or other person under whose care he may be, and who is bound for his support," to restrain and confine him temporarily. Failing friends, the same duty devolves on any judge of a court of record or any two justices of peace who may be cognizant of the facts. Complaint must be at once made by friends or others to the Probate judge of the county. If he believe the complaint to be well founded, he summons a jury to make inquisition. He may set aside the verdict of one jury, but cannot disregard two concurrent verdicts.

Upon verdict of insanity being rendered, the judge appoints a guardian of person and estate.

NEVADA.

Upon sworn complaint, representing any person as dangerous to be at large, any district judge may summon the party before him. He also calls two or more witnesses who have been with and near the party since he became insane, to testify to words, conduct, and manners. Two physicians also are summoned to be present, hearing witnesses and examining accused. If these physicians certify to recent and curable insanity, or to suicidal, homicidal, or otherwise dangerous madness, and if the judge be satisfied of the truth of the allegation of insanity as specified, he shall direct the person to be delivered into the charge of the Secretary of State. He shall also determine as to whether patient, friends or state are responsible for expenses. Shall appoint a guardian if the patient have property. The Secretary of State shall take measures to place his insane wards in the insane asylum, at Stockton, Ca.

CALIFORNIA.

Upon a complaint under oath, made to any county judge, that a certain person is dangerous to be at large, or is "suffering from mental derangement," the judge summons the accused to appear before him. He at the same time and place secures the attendance of two respectable physicians. If satisfied from examination and evidence that the party is unsafe to be at large, he orders his commitment to the insane asylum.

Guardians are appointed by the Probate courts. Upon receiving a sworn petition, representing insanity and incapacity, the Probate judge gives the party five days' notice of the fact. "If able to attend," the person is brought before the judge. The truth of the petition being established to his satisfaction, he appoints a guardian.

The courts have power to commit to the insane asylum any person charged with an offence punishable with death or imprisonment who shall have been found to be insane at time of offence, and who continues so.

VIRGINIA.

Upon suspicion of insanity, any justice may summon the party to appear before him. Calling to his aid two other justices, he examines, and hears evidence from physicians and others. If satisfactory proof of insanity is adduced, the patient may, at discretion of the justice, be committed to the state asylum for the insane, or delivered to the friends, under security for safe-keeping and proper care, till cause of confinement cease.

Persons charged with crime, or convicted, may be confined in the asylum by order of the court.

When a person is decided to be insane by the examining justices, or by a court before which he is charged with offence, the court of his county or corporation shall appoint a "committee," which shall have the charge of his person and his estate.

Patients are admitted into the hospital by a unanimous vote of its examining board.

WEST VIRGINIA.

"On an application on behalf of a person for his admission into the hospital [for the insane], the examining board may receive him as a patient therein . . ." This board consists of the superintendent of the hospital, and one or more of its directors. The board examines and inquires into the mental condition of the offered patient, as well as into the expediency and the terms of his admission.

"Any justice who shall suspect any person in his county to be a lunatic, shall issue his warrant, ordering such person to be brought before him. He shall inquire whether such person be a lunatic, and, for that purpose, summon a physician and any other witnesses." If he find the person to be a lunatic and to require confinement, he shall order his removal to the hospital for the insane,—provided the person be a citizen of West Virginia. The justice may, however, in his discretion, deliver him into the custody of relatives or friends upon satisfactory security for his safe and proper keeping, until well, or till returned to the sheriff to be disposed of according to law.

Persons adjudged lunatic, and ordered to the hospital, who cannot be received there, shall be confined in jail till a vacancy occurs in the hospital, or till legally discharged.

KENTUCKY.

The several Circuit and Chancery Courts have power and jurisdiction over the insane resident in their respective counties. They have the power to appoint "committees" for the persons and estates of those adjudged insane. Inquisitions of lunacy may be made by these and by some other judicial functionaries. The subject of inquisition must be in court, and the issue tried by a jury. If the judge be dissatisfied with the verdict, he may set it aside and order a new inquest.

TENNESSEE.

A certificate from one or more reputable physicians, is the only legal form necessary in placing a private patient in the state hospital.

Persons chargeable upon the county or the state are committed to the hospital by any justice of the peace. Any respectable citizen makes a written statement of belief that the person in question is insane, that

APPENDIX. 461

the disease is of less than two years' duration, or that he is unsafe to be at large, and that he is indigent; and that certain witnesses named in the statement will testify to its truth. One of these witnesses must be a respectable physician. The justice summons and examines these witnesses, and such others as he deems fit. If satisfied of the existence of insanity as alleged, he requires the physician to certify to the fact. Then the justice himself writes a certificate setting forth his belief that the party is insane, and " his being at large is injurious to himself, and disadvantageous, if not dangerous to the community," and that he is properly chargeable for support in the hospital upon the county or the state. These two certificates justify the commitment of a patient to the hospital.

The discharge of all patients upon recovery is within the province of the superintendent of the hospital in which they were placed. This officer has power to discharge immediately any person whom he believes not to be insane, or to be otherwise an unfit inmate. He is bound by oath not to enter into any combination to oppress or deprive any person of his or her civil rights.

The County Courts, on information of lunacy and incapacity, call a jury of twelve to inquire as to mental condition and as to property. If the jury decide against the sanity of the party, the court appoints a guardian or guardians.

NORTH CAROLINA.

Complaint to a justice, and examination before three, and the subsequent proceedings, are the same here as in Virginia. Express provision is made, however, for the calling of at least one medical witness.

If the superintendent doubts the fitness of a certain case for hospital treatment, he convenes the board of supervisors to decide the point.

The guardian of any person found insane by a jury, may be compelled to place him in the asylum if he be proved mischievous.

When a person accused of crime is found by a jury to have been insane at time of offence, he may be placed in the asylum by the permission of a judge of the Superior Court.

Application for appointment of guardian is made to the County Court,—a jury being summoned to decide as to sanity of the party.

SOUTH CAROLINA.

Persons complained of as lunatic are brought before a justice of the quorum, who calls to his aid two physicians of the state. A party being found lunatic is ordered to the hospital, unless deemed incurable and harmless. Persons found insane by inquisition from the Court of Chancery, or on trial in a court of common law, or on request of husband or wife, or next of kin, may be admitted to the insane hospital.

Judges of the Court of Sessions may send to the asylum persons charged with crime, if found to be insane.

GEORGIA.

Complaint of lunacy is made to the justices of the inferior courts in their respective counties. A jury of seven, including one physician, is summoned. These hear evidence, examine accused, and determine as to mental condition. Friends or relatives are to receive ten days' notice of hearing. The justice may commit to the state insane asylum, and may fix the expenses of maintenance upon patient, or his relatives, or the county. He has also full power to appoint guardians of person and estate. The wife of an insane man shall be appointed as one of his guardians if she comply with the legal requirements. Another guardian is appointed to act with her.

Recommitment to the asylum, after three months' absence, requires a repetition of the original forms.

ALABAMA.

A person in indigent circumstances may be placed in the insane hospital at the expense of his county. Application is made to a judge of Probate, who calls witnesses, one to be a respectable physician, and investigates the mental condition of the person and his financial resources. He may at discretion call a jury to his aid. If satisfied that the party is insane and poor, he shall order his commitment to the hospital as above.

When a pauper becomes insane, the fact must be reported to a judge of Probate, who investigates the case, calling medical testimony, and if he deem the case likely to be benefited by hospital treatment, he orders his commitment to the hospital at the county charge.

When a person has been acquitted of crime or misdemeanor, or has escaped indictment, on the ground of insanity, the fact shall be certified to the court, who thereupon shall carefully inquire whether the insanity still continues. If it do, the court shall order his confinement in the hospital.

Any person in confinement, under indictment, or for want of bail for good behavior, or for keeping the peace, or appearing as a witness, &c. &c., who shall appear to be insane, shall be the subject of careful investigation by the circuit judge of the county where confined. This judge shall call medical and other testimony, and at his discretion, a jury. Satisfied of his insanity, the judge may discharge him from imprisonment and place him in the hospital, there to remain till cured. Then, if the judge shall have so directed, the superintendent shall inform said judge and the sheriff of the patient's recovery, whereupon he shall be remanded to prison to await the proceedings proper in the case.

When a jury shall find a person insane the Court of Probate shall appoint a guardian of his person and estate. Whenever recovery shall be alleged, supported by certificates of two physicians, a hearing shall be had before the judge of Probate. The guardians shall be cited to appear; and if he resist removal, a day shall be appointed for a jury-trial, as on the original inquiry. If the jury find the party sane, the guardian is liable at the discretion of the judge to be taxed with the costs; otherwise the petitioner shall bear costs.

MISSISSIPPI.

Any persons whom the trustees and superintendent may consider fit subjects for treatment shall be received as pay patients in the state hospital, upon the certificate of insanity signed by a respectable physician.

Upon complaint of any citizen of the same county that a certain lunatic is allowed to go at large in said county, it is the duty of the Court of Probate to summon a jury of twelve to make inquisition. If a majority of this jury declare the person to be insane, the court orders his commitment to the asylum.

Whether placed in the asylum in the manner just mentioned, or by the voluntary act of his friends, the estate of the lunatic is chargeable with the expenses of his commitment and support.

Persons acquitted of crimes or misdemeanors may be committed to the asylum on a certificate from the Circuit Court judge that they were acquitted on the ground of insanity. The same course seems to be allowed in cases of persons accused, not brought to trial. These last, on recovery, are returned to the place whence they came, to answer the charges against them,—if this was required by the judge committing. Those persons, tried and acquitted, who are sent to the asylum are to be held "until restored to right mind." Expenses are chargeable to the patient's estate, or to the state.

Inspectors of the penitentiary, on recommendation of the physician, may place any insane convict under their charge in the asylum to remain till restored to sanity, "or discharged by the expiration of his sentence." If cured before expiration of sentence he is to be returned to the penitentiary.

The superintendent shall discharge patients—not criminal—when satisfied of recovery; or satisfied that they are unfit subjects; or on application of relatives or friends, if these give proper evidence of ability to provide for them. This officer is bound by oath to enter into no "combination to oppress or deprive any person of his or her liberty or civil rights."

Upon request of relatives, friends, or overseer of the poor, the Orphans' Court summons a jury of twelve men to inquire into the capacity of an alleged lunatic. If the jury find him insane, the court appoints one or more guardians of his person and estate,—to be under its supervision.

MISSOURI.

As in Arkansas and Kansas, it is the duty of friends, and failing these, of certain officers, to make complaint against persons furiously mad, or so disordered as to be dangerous to persons or property, and to confine them till they can be brought before the court. The complaint is addressed to the County Court. The court summons a jury, to decide as to sanity, and if the jury deem the party insane, the judge appoints a guardian of person and estate.

Patients are admitted to the insane hospital upon order of court, or upon application of friends with certificate of two physicians.

The state executive has power to transfer criminals from the penitentiary to the hospital for the insane.

ARKANSAS.

The provisions for complaint, temporary confinement, and trial of lunacy in this state are almost precisely the same as in Kansas, except that the summoning of a jury is not obligatory upon the judge of Probate. If the judge, with or without a jury, decide that the party is insane, he appoints a guardian of person and estate. The judge may order confinement, and has the general supervision of guardian and ward. Petitions for the removal of guardianship are decided upon in the same way as the original application.

If in the course of any legal procedure the question of lunacy be raised, a jury shall be summoned forthwith to decide that question. The same course is pursued with criminals under death-sentence, at the petition of the sheriff. In case the jury give a verdict of insanity, the governor suspends sentence till recovery.

LOUISIANA.

No person subject to habitual madness, even with lucid intervals, shall be allowed charge of his property or person. A petition for interdiction may be signed by blood relatives, by husband or wife, or by a stranger; or the courts may request interdiction, after hearing counsel for accused—chosen by himself or by the judge. The interdiction is granted by the judge of the parish where the party resides. The judge hears or reads evidence, examines patient either personally or by proxy, and may require examination and affidavit from physician as to mental condition. If found insane, a curator is appointed by the judge to care for person and estate. Another person is appointed as superintendent of the person interdicted, having access to him at all times, and reporting health and welfare to the judge once in three months.

TEXAS.

Complaint of lunacy may be made to any chief justice of a county, setting forth that A. B. is lunatic, and that the welfare of himself or others requires his restraint. The justice then summons a jury of twelve men to make return of " sound mind or not," having the accused in court. When the jury render a verdict of unsound mind, and that restraint is desirable, the justice may commit to the insane asylum, or, upon satisfactory security for proper care and safe-keeping, deliver the accused into the custody of his friends, to be restrained " until cause of confinement ceases." He also determines the responsibility for expenses.

Patients may be placed in the hospital on a written request of guardian, near relative, or friend, or of persons or counties liable for their support. Such request must be sworn to as to truth of representations made, and accompanied by a sworn certificate of insanity from a physician, dated within two months.

Criminals or persons charged with crime, found to be insane, may be committed to the insane asylum by the courts, there to be confined till released by the same authority.

Guardianship is effected precisely as restraint is procured, as stated in the first paragraph, by a county justice and jury, the party being present.

The reader will have observed that, in placing a person in a hospital for the insane, in England, every step in the process is regulated by some form prescribed by law. In this country, even in those states whose law requires a certificate of insanity and the application of a friend, no form is prescribed. That is left to the parties who offer them. Most of the hospitals have certain printed forms which they require to be used for this purpose. The following are the forms used by the Pennsylvania Hospital for the Insane:

CERTIFICATE OF PHYSICIANS.

We certify that, after a personal examination of   made within one week of the date of this certificate, we find   to be insane, and a proper subject for hospital treatment.

_____1870.   _____ M.D.

_____1870.   _____M.D.

CERTIFICATE OF MAGISTRATE OR JUDICIAL OFFICER.

I certify that the foregoing certificate was duly acknowledged and   to before me, this   of   1870, that the signatures thereto are genuine, and that the signers are physicians of respectability.

_____

APPLICATION.

I request that the above-named   may be admitted as a patient into the Pennsylvania Hospital for the Insane.

_____1870.   _____ }

(To be signed by a guardian, relative, or friend.)

The following are required by the McLean Asylum, at Somerville, Mass., and the Butler Hospital, at Providence, R. I., the certificate for the McLean being signed by two physicians:

CERTIFICATE.

I hereby certify that   of   is insane.

_____1871.   _____M.D.

APPLICATION.

I hereby request that the above-named insane person be admitted into the

_____

(To be signed by a relative or some responsible person.)

INDEX.

Classics in Psychiatry

An Arno Press Collection

American Psychiatrists Abroad. 1975

Arnold, Thomas. Observations On The Nature, Kinds, Causes, And Prevention Of Insanity. 1806. Two volumes in one

Austin, Thomas J. A Practical Account Of General Paralysis, Its Mental And Physical Symptoms, Statistics, Causes, Seat, And Treatment. 1859

Bayle, A[ntoine] L[aurent] J[esse]. Traité Des Maladies Du Cerveau Et De Ses Membranes. 1826

Binz, Carl. Doctor Johann Weyer. 1896

Blandford, G. Fielding. Insanity And Its Treatment. 1871

Bleuler, Eugen. Textbook Of Psychiatry. 1924

Braid, James. Neurypnology. 1843

Brierre de Boismont, A[lexandre-Jacques-François]. Hallucinations. 1853

Brown, Mabel Webster, compiler. Neuropsychiatry And The War: A Bibliography With Abstracts and Supplement I, October 1918. Two volumes in one

Browne, W. A. F. What Asylums Were, Are, And Ought To Be. 1837

Burrows, George Man. Commentaries On The Causes, Forms, Symptoms And Treatment, Moral And Medical, Of Insanity. 1828

Calmeil, L[ouis]-F[lorentin]. De La Folie: Considérée Sous Le Point De Vue Pathologique, Philosophique, Historique Et Judiciaire, Depuis La Renaissance Des Sciences En Europe Jusqu'au Dix-Neuvième Siècle. 1845. Two volumes in one

Calmeil, L[ouis] F[lorentin]. De La Paralysie Considérée Chez Les Aliénés. 1826

Dejerine, J[oseph Jules] and E. Gauckler. The Psychoneuroses And Their Treatment By Psychotherapy. [1913]

Dunbar, [Helen] Flanders. Emotions And Bodily Changes. 1954

Ellis, W[illiam] C[harles]. A Treatise On The Nature, Symptoms, Causes And Treatment Of Insanity. 1838

Emminghaus, H[ermann]. Die Psychischen Störungen Des Kindesalters. 1887

Esdaile, James. Mesmerism In India, And Its Practical Application In Surgery And Medicine. 1846

Esquirol, E[tienne]. Des Maladies Mentales. 1838. Three volumes in two

Feuchtersleben, Ernst [Freiherr] von. **The Principles Of Medical Psychology.** 1847

Georget, [Etienne-Jean]. **De La Folie:** Considérations Sur Cette Maladie. 1820

Haslam, John. **Observations On Madness And Melancholy.** 1809

Hill, Robert Gardiner. **Total Abolition Of Personal Restraint In The Treatment Of The Insane.** 1839

Janet, Pierre [Marie-Felix] and F. Raymond. **Les Obsessions Et La Psychasthénie.** 1903. Two volumes

Janet, Pierre [Marie-Felix]. **Psychological Healing.** 1925. Two volumes

Kempf, Edward J. **Psychopathology.** 1920

Kraepelin, Emil. **Manic-Depressive Insanity And Paranoia.** 1921

Kraepelin, Emil. **Psychiatrie:** Ein Lehrbuch Für Studirende Und Aerzte. 1896

Laycock, Thomas. **Mind And Brain.** 1860. Two volumes in one

Liébeault, A[mbroise]-A[uguste]. **Le Sommeil Provoqué Et Les États Analogues.** 1889

Mandeville, B[ernard] De. **A Treatise Of The Hypochondriack And Hysterick Passions.** 1711

Morel, B[enedict] A[ugustin]. **Traité Des Degénérescences Physiques, Intellectuelles Et Morales De L'Espèce Humaine.** 1857. Two volumes in one

Morison, Alexander. **The Physiognomy Of Mental Diseases.** 1843

Myerson, Abraham. **The Inheritance Of Mental Diseases.** 1925

Perfect, William. **Annals Of Insanity.** [1808]

Pinel, Ph[ilippe]. **Traité Médico-Philosophique Sur L'Aliénation Mentale.** 1809

Prince, Morton, et al. **Psychotherapeutics.** 1910

Psychiatry In Russia And Spain. 1975

Ray, I[saac]. **A Treatise On The Medical Jurisprudence Of Insanity.** 1871

Semelaigne, René. **Philippe Pinel Et Son Oeuvre Au Point De Vue De La Médecine Mentale.** 1888

Thurnam, John. **Observations And Essays On The Statistics Of Insanity.** 1845

Trotter, Thomas. **A View Of The Nervous Temperament.** 1807

Tuke, D[aniel] Hack, editor. **A Dictionary Of Psychological Medicine.** 1892. Two volumes

Wier, Jean. **Histoires, Disputes Et Discours Des Illusions Et Impostures Des Diables, Des Magiciens Infames, Sorcieres Et Empoisonneurs.** 1885. Two volumes

Winslow, Forbes. **On Obscure Diseases Of The Brain And Disorders Of The Mind.** 1860

Burdett, Henry C. **Hospitals And Asylums Of The World.** 1891-93. Five volumes. 2,740 pages on NMA standard 24x-98 page microfiche only